LIVING LANGUAGE®
ULTIMATE
FRENCH
ADVANCED

ULTIMATE

FRENCH

ADVANCED

WRITTEN BY

ANNIE HEMINWAY,

ALLIANCE FRANÇAISE, NEW YORK

EDITED BY

ANA SUFFREDINI AND

HELGA SCHIER, PH.D.

LIVING LANGUAGE®
A Random House Company

Published by Living Language, A Random House Company,
201 East 50th Street, New York, New York 10022.

Living Language® publications are available at special discounts
for bulk purchases for sales promotions or premiums, as well as for
fund-raising or educational use. Special editions can be created in
large quantities for special needs. For more information, write to
Special Sales Manager, Living Language, 201 East 50th Street,
New York NY 10022.

Random House, Inc. New York, Toronto, London, Sydney, Auckland
www.livinglanguage.com

Living Language is a registered trademark of
Random House, Inc.

Printed in the United States of America

Library of Congress Cataloging-in-Publication Data is available upon request.

95-2700

ISBN 0-609-80251-8

10   9   8   7   6   5   4   3

Pour mes étudiants . . .

ACKNOWLEDGMENTS

Thanks to Crown Publishers' Living Language™ staff: Kathryn Mintz, Jessica Frankel, Christopher Warnasch, Julie Lewis, Camille Smith, Lois Berkowitz, John Sharp, Lenny Henderson, Susan Husserl-Kapit, Liliane Lazar, and Michel Sitruk. Special thanks to Diane Rafferty, *Connoisseur* magazine, *France* magazine, *Champs-Élysées,* the Québec Government Office, and the U.S. Chamber of Commerce for providing essential materials. Special thanks to Jeffrey Shenk, Suzanne Nairne, Soisick Gaonac'h, Catherine Lauliac, Dewey Markham, Brigitte Huard, Renata Luisi, Ruth Lubic, Armande Gandon, Julia Farrell, Patricia Allen, Virginia Carry, Karen Holland, Ruth Furth, and Peter Gruenthal.

CONTENTS

LIVING LANGUAGE®

ULTIMATE

FRENCH

ADVANCED

INTRODUCTION

Living Language™ *Ultimate French Advanced* is a continuation of the beginner–intermediate *Ultimate French* program. If you have already mastered the basics of French in school, while traveling abroad, or with other *Living Language*™ courses, then *Ultimate French Advanced* is right for you.

The complete course includes this text together with eight hours of recordings. However, if you are confident of your pronunciation, you can also use this manual on its own.

With *Ultimate French Advanced* you'll continue to learn how to speak, understand, read, and write idiomatic French. The program will also introduce you to some of the more interesting aspects of French culture and business. You'll be able to participate in engaging conversations about a variety of topics, as well as recognize and respond to several styles of formal and informal speech.

The course will take you everywhere, from vineyards to perfume factories to fashion shows, while teaching useful vocabulary and expressions. You'll practice deciphering newspaper articles and economic reports. You'll also learn about subtle cultural distinctions in personal interaction, such as the French style of giving or receiving compliments, that will help smooth your way abroad.

COURSE MATERIALS

THE MANUAL

Living Language™ *Ultimate French Advanced* consists of twenty lessons, four reading passages, and two review sections. The reading passages appear after every five lessons. There are review sections after Lesson 10 and Lesson 20. It's best to read and study each lesson in the manual before listening to it on the recordings.

Dialogue: Each lesson begins with a dialogue in standard, idiomatic French, presenting realistic situations—a job interview, a report on the news, a meeting with a health care professional—set in various French locales. All dialogues are translated into colloquial English.

En Bref (In Brief): The notes in this section refer to specific expressions and phrases in the dialogue. They'll introduce you to the cultural and historical background relevant to a particular expression and allow you to see grammar rules and vocabulary "in action."

Grammaire et usage (Grammar and Usage): After a brief review of basic French grammar, you'll concentrate on the more advanced grammatical forms and their usage. You'll learn how to express yourself more accurately and appropriately by using idiomatic French. The heading of each topic is listed in the table of contents.

Jeu de mots (Word Play): This section focuses on a single expression, phrase, or word from various angles. For instance, you'll discuss the different French translations of "tired" and learn some of the more colorful French idioms and maxims. This in-depth vocabulary study will improve your idiomatic usage of French and help you avoid common linguistic pitfalls.

Le coin des affaires (Business Corner): In this section you'll explore different areas of the French economy, as well as cultural and historical information relevant to business etiquette and procedures. Discussing topics such as dress codes, import and export, the French government and its involvement in the economy, this section will enable you to conduct business in France with confidence.

Exercices (Exercises): This section allows you to review the grammar and vocabulary covered in the lessons. You can check your answers in the *Corrigé des exercices* (Answer Key) appearing after *Leçon* 20.

Lecture (Reading): The four reading passages—appearing after *Leçons* 5, 10, 15, and 20—are not translated. The material covered in the preceding lessons and vocabulary notes on the more difficult words and phrases will enable you to determine the meaning, just as you would when reading a newspaper article or business report abroad.

Révision (Review): The two review sections appear after *Leçons* 10 and 20. Similar in structure to the *Exercices,* these sections will allow you to integrate and test your mastery of the material covered in the preceding lessons.

Appendixes: There are nine appendixes—a guide to pronunciation, the days, months, and seasons, impersonal expressions that require the subjunctive, adverbs with spelling irregularities, a list of subjective pronominal verbs, a letter-writing section, a dictionary of grammatical terms, a summary of French grammar, and verb charts.

Glossary: The extensive two-way glossary will prove an invaluable reference as you work through this program and then apply your knowledge through contact with the French and traveling abroad.

Index: The manual ends with an index of the major grammar points covered in the lessons.

The appendixes, glossary, and index make this manual an excellent resource for future reference and study.

RECORDINGS (SETS A AND B)

This program provides you with eight hours of audio instruction and practice. There are two sets of complementary recordings: the first is designed for use with the manual, while the second may be used independently. By listening to and imitating the native speakers, you'll improve your pronunciation and comprehension while learning to use new phrases and structures.

RECORDINGS FOR USE WITH THE MANUAL (SET A)

This set of recordings gives you four hours of audio practice in French only. It features the complete dialogues of all twenty lessons. The recorded material appears in **boldface** in your manual. You'll first hear native French speakers read the complete dialogue without interruption at normal conversational speed. Then you'll have a chance to listen to the dialogue a second time and repeat each phrase in the pauses provided.

If you wish to practice your comprehension, first listen to the recordings of the dialogue without consulting the translations in the manual. Write down a summary of what you think the dialogue was about, then listen to the recordings a second time, checking how much you understood against the translations in the manual.

After you study each lesson and practice with the recordings, go on to Set B, which can be used on the go—while driving, jogging, traveling, or doing housework.

RECORDINGS FOR USE ON THE GO (SET B)

Set B recordings give you four hours of audio instruction and practice in French and English. Because they are bilingual, these recordings may be used without the manual, wherever it's convenient to learn.

The twenty lessons on Set B correspond to those in the manual. A bilingual narrator leads you through the four sections in each lesson.

The first section presents the most important phrases from the original dialogue. You will first hear the abridged dialogue without interruption at normal conversational speed. You'll then hear it again, phrase by phrase, with English translations and pauses for you to repeat after the native French speakers.

The second section reviews and expands upon the most important vocabulary introduced in the lesson. You will practice words and phrases collected from the *Dialogue, En bref* (In Brief), *Jeu de mots* (Word Play), and *Le coin des affaires* (Business Corner) sections. Additional expressions show how the words may be used in other contexts. Again, you are given time to repeat the French phrases after the native speakers.

In the third section you will explore the lesson's most important grammatical structures. After a quick review of the rules, you can practice with illustrative phrases and sentences.

The conversational exercises in the last section integrate what you've learned and help you generate sentences in French on your own. You'll take part in brief conversations, ask and respond to questions, transform sentences, and occasionally translate from English into French. After you respond, you'll hear the correct answer from a French native speaker.

The interactive approach on this set of recordings focuses on the idiomatic spoken word and will teach you to speak, understand, and *think* in French.

Now let's begin.

LEÇON 1

A. DIALOGUE

L'ARRIVÉE.

Au beau[1] milieu de l'Atlantique, une hôtesse[2] annonce un léger changement de parcours alors que M. Rutledge dort à poings fermés.[3]

VOIX AU MICRO: **Vu la fermeture[4] des aéroports de Paris, nous avons le regret de vous annoncer que nous serons dans l'obligation d'atterrir à Bruxelles.**

Une heure plus tard . . .

M. RUTLEDGE: **Pardon, Mademoiselle,[5] pensez-vous que nous allons rattraper[6] le retard du départ?**

MLLE FONTENELLE: **Nous sommes censés[7] arriver à Bruxelles à neuf heures quarante-cinq.[8]**

M. RUTLEDGE: **À Bruxelles!**

MLLE FONTENELLE: **En raison d'une grève-surprise[9] des bagagistes des aéroports de Paris, nous devons atterrir à Bruxelles.**

M. RUTLEDGE: **Mais j'ai une réunion à Paris à quinze heures trente!**

MLLE FONTENELLE: **Un car[10] d'Air France sera à votre disposition pour vous conduire à la gare de Bruxelles ou vous emmener à Paris.**

M. RUTLEDGE: **Ah! C'est bien ma veine![11]**

Le voisin de M. Rutledge, amusé par la situation, entame[12] une conversation avec lui.

M. DUVERNOIS: **Permettez-moi de me présenter, je m'appelle Pierre Duvernois. Vous dormiez lorsque l'hôtesse a annoncé le changement de programme et je n'ai pas osé[13] vous réveiller.**

M. RUTLEDGE: **C'est très gentil de votre part. Ralph Rutledge, enchanté de faire votre connaissance.**

M. DUVERNOIS: **Moi de même.[14] Vous êtes en vacances?**

M. RUTLEDGE: **Non, en voyage d'affaires.**

M. DUVERNOIS: **Est-ce que cela va perturber votre programme?**

M. RUTLEDGE: **Un confrère m'attend à Charles de Gaulle[15] à huit heures quinze, ce qui n'est pas très grave.[16] Mais j'ai une réunion importante dans l'après-midi.**

M. DUVERNOIS: L'essentiel, c'est d'être en super forme. Vous avez de la chance[17] de pouvoir dormir car moi je ne peux jamais fermer l'œil en vol et le décalage horaire[18] me tue!

M. RUTLEDGE: La journée s'annonce difficile; je vais essayer de dormir quelques heures avant d'arriver en Belgique.

M. DUVERNOIS: Bonne nuit!

L'avion atterrit à Bruxelles. Après avoir trouvé un chariot, M. Rutledge passe la douane. Encombré de valises bourrées d'échantillons,[19] il se dirige vers l'agence de location[20] de voitures.

M. RUTLEDGE: Je voudrais louer une voiture pour la journée que je laisserai à Paris.

L'EMPLOYÉ: Quel modèle désirez-vous? Une Renault 5, une Peugeot 205, une Ford Escort?

M. RUTLEDGE: Combien coûte la location d'une Renault à transmission automatique, quatre portières[21] avec climatisation?

L'EMPLOYÉ: Quatre cent cinquante francs par jour et cent francs de surcharge, kilométrage illimité et assurance tous risques compris.

M. RUTLEDGE: C'est parfait. Pourriez-vous me donner les directions pour Paris?

L'EMPLOYÉ: Oh! Je suis désolé, j'ai un plan de Bruxelles mais je n'ai plus de cartes routières.[22] Adressez-vous aux renseignements à la porte douze. Les hôtesses d'accueil se feront un plaisir de vous aider. Voici votre contrat et la clé. Signez en bas à droite. Bon voyage!

Au comptoir des renseignements.

L'HÔTESSE: Monsieur?

M. RUTLEDGE: Ne me dites surtout pas que vous faites la grève le mardi ou que vous êtes à court de[23] cartes routières car je dois absolument me rendre[24] à Paris!

L'HÔTESSE: Voici une carte, monsieur. Prenez la première à gauche en quittant l'aéroport, allez tout droit[25] jusqu'aux feux puis suivez la direction de l'Autoroute du Sud.

M. RUTLEDGE: Combien de temps faut-il compter pour aller à Paris?

L'HÔTESSE: Environ trois heures s'il n'y a pas d'embouteillage.[26]

M. DUVERNOIS: Monsieur Rutledge!

M. RUTLEDGE: Vous êtes toujours[27] là!

M. DUVERNOIS: **Ne m'en parlez pas! Il m'a fallu un temps fou pour dédouaner mes achats!**

M. RUTLEDGE: **Vous devez être exténué! Je viens à l'instant de louer une voiture. Je serais ravi de vous emmener à Paris.**

M. DUVERNOIS: **Oh, non! Je ne voudrais pas vous déranger.**

M. RUTLEDGE: **Pas du tout! J'ai horreur de voyager seul. Allez, venez, la voiture est par ici.**

M. DUVERNOIS: **J'accepte à une seule condition: je vous offre un petit déjeuner bruxellois avant de mettre le cap sur Paris.**

M. RUTLEDGE: **Comment refuser une telle invitation? Mais nous ne pouvons pas trop nous attarder.**

M. DUVERNOIS: **Ne vous inquiétez pas. Nous ne sommes qu'à un quart d'heure du centre-ville. En voyant les pâtisseries, vous remercierez les grévistes de vous avoir fait faire ce détour.**

Arrival.

Right in the middle of the Atlantic, a flight attendant announces a slight change of course, while Mr. Rutledge sleeps soundly.

VOICE OVER THE LOUDSPEAKER: Due to the closing of the Paris airports, we regret to inform you that we will have to land in Brussels.

One hour later . . .

MR. RUTLEDGE: Excuse me, Miss, do you think we will make up for our late departure?

MISS FONTENELLE: We are supposed to arrive in Brussels at seven forty-five A.M.

MR. RUTLEDGE: Brussels!

MISS FONTENELLE: Due to an unexpected strike by the baggage handlers at the Paris airports, we have to land in Brussels.

MR. RUTLEDGE: But I have a meeting in Paris at three-thirty P.M.!

MISS FONTENELLE: An Air France bus will be available to take you to the Brussels train station or directly to Paris.

MR. RUTLEDGE: Just my luck!

Mr. Rutledge's neighbor, amused by the situation, strikes up a conversation with him.

MR. DUVERNOIS: Allow me to introduce myself. My name is Pierre Duvernois. You were sleeping when the flight attendant announced the change of course, and I didn't dare wake you.

MR. RUTLEDGE: That's very kind of you. Ralph Rutledge, pleased to meet you.

MR. DUVERNOIS: So am I. Are you on vacation?

MR. RUTLEDGE: No, on a business trip.

MR. DUVERNOIS: Is this going to upset your schedule?

MR. RUTLEDGE: A colleague will be waiting for me at Charles de Gaulle at eight-fifteen A.M., which is not too serious. But I have an important meeting in the afternoon.

MR. DUVERNOIS: The main thing is to be in good shape. You're lucky to be able to sleep. I can never sleep in flight, and the jet lag kills me.

MR. RUTLEDGE: This is going to be a hard day; I'm going to try to sleep for a few hours before we arrive in Belgium.

MR. DUVERNOIS: Sleep well.

The plane lands in Brussels. After finding a luggage cart, Mr. Rutledge goes through Customs. Loaded down with suitcases full of samples, he heads for the car rental desk.

MR. RUTLEDGE: I would like to rent a car for the day and drop it off in Paris.

EMPLOYEE: What model would you like? A Renault 5, a Peugeot 205, a Ford Escort?

MR. RUTLEDGE: How much does it cost to rent a four-door Renault with automatic transmission and air-conditioning?

EMPLOYEE: Four hundred and fifty francs a day, one hundred francs drop-off charge, unlimited mileage, and all risk insurance included.

MR. RUTLEDGE: Perfect. Could you give me directions for getting to Paris?

EMPLOYEE: Oh! I'm sorry. I have a map of Brussels, but I'm out of road maps. Go to the information desk at gate twelve. The ground staff will be happy to help you. Here's your contract and the keys. Sign on the bottom right. Have a good trip!

At the information desk.

ATTENDANT: Sir?

MR. RUTLEDGE: Please, don't tell me that you strike on Tuesdays or that you are running out of road maps because I absolutely have to get to Paris!

ATTENDANT: Here's a map, sir. Take the first left when leaving the airport, go straight until you reach the lights, then follow the signs to the *Autoroute du Sud.*

MR. RUTLEDGE: How much time will it take to get to Paris?

ATTENDANT: About three hours if there are no traffic jams.

MR. DUVERNOIS: Mr. Rutledge!

MR. RUTLEDGE: You're still here!

MR. DUVERNOIS: You're telling me! It took me ages to clear customs with everything I bought.

MR. RUTLEDGE: You must be exhausted! I just rented a car. I'd be delighted to take you to Paris.

MR. DUVERNOIS: Oh, no! I wouldn't want to bother you.

MR. RUTLEDGE: Not at all! I hate traveling alone. Come on, the car is over here.

MR. DUVERNOIS: I accept on one condition: I am treating you to a typical "Bruxellois" breakfast before we head to Paris.

MR. RUTLEDGE: How can I refuse such an offer? But we can't stop for too long.

MR. DUVERNOIS: Don't worry. We're only fifteen minutes from downtown. When you see the pastries, you'll thank the strikers for forcing you to take this detour.

B. EN BREF (In Brief)

1. *Beau* is often used to stress or exaggerate something: *une belle somme* (a tidy sum of money), *un beau menteur* (an awful liar).

2. *L'hôtesse de l'air* (feminine)/*le steward* (masculine): flight attendant; *l'équipage:* the crew.

3. If you are in a very deep sleep, *vous dormez à poings fermés,* and you need not worry about spending a sleepless night, *passer une nuit blanche.*

4. This is a very common formula in French: *vu la situation* (given the situation), *vu les circonstances* (given the circumstances). Note that *vu* does not agree in gender or number with the following noun.

5. *Mademoiselle* (Miss) is used when referring to a young woman. A mature *mademoiselle* tends to be called *Madame,* regardless of marital status. However, some feminists *d'un certain âge* (middle aged) may insist on *mademoiselle* if they are not married. There is no equivalent for Ms. in French.

6. *Rattraper* can be used both literally and figuratively: *rattraper une erreur* (to make up for a mistake), *rattraper un objet qui tombe* (to catch a falling object), *rattraper son sommeil* (to catch up on sleep).

7. *Être censé* (to be supposed to) is interchangeable with *devoir. Nous sommes censés être à l'aéroport à midi./Nous devons être à l'aéroport à midi.* (We are supposed to be at the airport at noon.) Remember that *être censé* is never followed by a preposition and always agrees with the subject.

8. The 24-hour clock is used for all official schedules, such as transportation and theater, and for all official appointments, such as business meetings and doctor's visits. The 12-hour clock is used in an informal setting and in casual conversation.

9. Strikes are a common occurrence in France. Different types of strikes include: *une grève sauvage* (a wildcat strike), *une grève perlée* (a slow-down strike), *une grève sur le tas* (a sit-down strike), and *une grève de solidarité* (a sympathy strike).

10. *Un car,* short for *autocar,* is an inter-city bus or a coach, while *un autobus* is an intra-city bus.

11. Used in colloquial speech only; *chance* is the more proper term for "luck." *Il a décroché ce poste grâce à un coup de chance.* (He got that job thanks to a stroke of luck.) Another colloquialism for "luck" is *pot. Tu n'as vraiment pas de pot!* (You're really out of luck!)

12. *Entamer* appears in many useful expressions: *entamer un gâteau* (to slice into a cake), *entamer son capital* (to dip into one's fortune), *entamer des pourparlers de paix* (to open peace talks).

13. Note that *oser* is never followed by a preposition.

14. *Moi de même* (so do I) is a more formal way of saying *moi aussi* (me too).

15. Paris has two international airports: *Charles de Gaulle* and *Orly.*

16. *Ce n'est pas grave = cela ne fait rien = cela importe peu.*

17. Be careful with auxilliary verbs. In English, you <u>are</u> lucky, while in French, you <u>have</u> luck. Similar usages include: *avoir faim* (to be hungry), *avoir tort* (to be wrong), *avoir chaud* (to be warm).

18. Jet lag is *le décalage horaire;* there is no adjective corresponding to the noun. Therefore, if you are jet-lagged, *vous souffrez du décalage horaire* or *vous êtes fatigué à cause du décalage horaire.*

19. In quantity expressions, *de* does not agree with the following noun but remains singular: *plein de documents* (full of documents), *rempli d'erreurs* (full of mistakes).

20. Beware of *faux-amis,* words that look similar but have different meanings in French and English. *La location* means "rental," not "location."

21. *La portière* refers to car and train doors or to curtains; a door in your house or apartment is simply *une porte.*

22. *Un plan* is a city map whereas *une carte routière* is a road map.

23. *À court de* (to be short of, to run out of) can refer to both concrete and abstract nouns: *Il est à court d'argent.* (He is short of money.) *Nous sommes à court d'imagination.* (We are running out of imagination.)

24. *Se rendre* is a bit more formal and precise than *aller.* It implies going somewhere with a purpose. *L'ambassadeur va se rendre au Vietnam pour signer un accord.* (The ambassador will go to Vietnam to sign an agreement.) Do not confuse *se rendre* with "to surrender."

25. If you go straight, *vous allez tout droit* (silent *t*), but if you turn right, *vous tournez à droite* (pronounced *t*).

26. A more colloquial word for "traffic jam" is *bouchon* (literally, "cork"). *Nous sommes pris dans un bouchon.* (We're caught in a traffic jam.)

27. *Toujours* can mean both "always" and "still."

C. GRAMMAIRE ET USAGE (Grammar and Usage)

1. *LE PRÉSENT* (THE PRESENT TENSE)

French verbs are classified according to their infinitive endings: *-er, -ir,* and *-re.* To form the present indicative of regular verbs,[1] simply drop the infinitive ending *(regarder → regard-; choisir → chois-; partir → part-; répondre → répond-),* and replace it with the appropriate present indicative ending. Note that there are two different models for conjugating *-ir* verbs (one with an extra *-iss-* syllable and one without) and that there is no way to determine which is appropriate simply by looking at the infinitive. Instead, the correct conjugation pattern must be learned on a case by case basis. Following are four model regular verbs.

[1] For the complete conjugations of irregular verbs—those that do not follow the regular pattern of their verb group—please consult the verb charts in Appendix I (page 347).

	REGARDER	CHOSIR	PARTIR	RÉPONDRE
je	regarde	choisis	pars	réponds
tu	regardes	choisis	pars	réponds
il/elle/on	regarde	choisit	part	répond
nous	regardons	choisissons	partons	répondons
vous	regardez	choisissez	partez	répondez
ils/elles	regardent	choisissent	partent	répondent

The present indicative is used to make a general statement and to describe ongoing actions in the present. It can be translated in three ways into English.

M. Duvernois parle à une hôtesse.
Mr. Duvernois is talking (talks, does talk) to the flight attendant.

Ils partent en vacances en mai.
They are leaving (leave, do leave) on vacation in May.

In addition, the French present tense can be used:

a. to describe a past action closely connected to the present.

M. Duvernois revient de vacances et les ennuis recommencent!
Mr. Duvernois came back from vacation, and the problems began!

b. to express a historical fact or information that is considered common knowledge.

Zola publie Nana *et le scandale éclate.*
Zola published *Nana,* and the scandal broke out.

c. to describe past events more dramatically.

Il s'avance vers le roi et se présente.
He moved toward the king and introduced himself.

Il dormait à poings fermés; soudain, une hôtesse prend le micro et annonce un changement de parcours.
He was in a deep sleep; suddenly, a flight attendant took the microphone and announced a change of course.

d. with *depuis* and *il y a que,* to express an action that began in the past and continues in the present.[2]

Elle travaille à Bruxelles depuis cinq ans.
She has been working in Brussels for five years.

Il y a trois mois qu'il habite à Paris.
He has been living in Paris for three months.

e. in maxims and proverbs.

Rien ne sert de courir, il faut partir à point. (La Fontaine)
Nothing is gained by running; you must leave on time.

2. *QUESTIONS SIMPLES* (SIMPLE QUESTIONS)

There are several ways to ask a simple yes/no question in French. The one most commonly heard in daily, informal conversation is a simple rise in voice at the end of a statement.

Vous venez avec nous?
You're coming with us?

Another common formula used in conversation is placing *est-ce que* at the beginning of a sentence.

Est-ce que vous voulez vous joindre à nous?
Do you want to join us?

In a more formal setting and in proper written French, inversion of the subject and the verb is preferable.

Savez-vous à quelle heure commence la réunion?
Do you know at what time the meeting starts?

However, inversion cannot be used with the *je* form unless the verb ends in *-e* (there are a few exceptions such as *puis-je* and *vais-je*). When using inversion, don't forget to add a *-t-* between verbs ending in *-e* and the subjects *il, elle,* and *on.*

Aime-t-il voyager seul?
Does he like to travel on his own?

---

[2] "Since," "for," and "ago" will be covered in depth in *Leçon* 7.

When inversion is applied to sentences whose subject is a noun (*not* a pronoun), the noun appears at the head of the sentence and the corresponding pronoun follows the verb.

Le vol 506, est-il arrivé?
　Has flight 506 landed?

There are two ways to answer a simple yes/no question affirmatively. If the question was affirmative, use *oui.*

Vous habitez à Toulouse?—Oui, j'habite à Toulouse.
　Do you live in Toulouse?—Yes, I live in Toulouse.

If the question was negative, use *si,* meaning "on the contrary, yes."

Vous ne parlez pas espagnol?—Si, je parle espagnol.
　You don't speak Spanish?—Yes, I do speak Spanish.

D. JEU DE MOTS (Word Play)

There are many ways of expressing how tired you are in French.

Vous êtes fatigué?
　Are you tired?

Je suis mort de fatigue!
　I'm dead tired!

Après la randonnée de seize kilomètres, je suis éreinté/exténué/sur les genoux!
　After the ten-mile hike, I'm worn out!

Je suis épuisé[3] après un si long voyage.
　I'm exhausted after such a long trip.

Je suis surmené—j'ai besoin de vacances.
　I'm overworked—I need a vacation.

Je suis crevé. (colloquial)
　I'm pooped!

Je suis lessivé. (colloquial)
　I'm wiped out.

Je suis claqué. (colloquial)
　I'm beat.

Cette excursion m'a harassé.[4] (not very common)
　This excursion exhausted me.

---

[3] *Épuisé* has another very common usage: *Ce roman est épuisé.* (This novel is out of print.)
[4] Be careful not to confuse *harasser* with the English verb "to harass," which is expressed in French with *harceler. Son patron la harcelait sexuellement.* (Her boss sexually harassed her.)

14

E. LE COIN DES AFFAIRES
(Business Corner)

VOYAGER EN FRANCE (TRAVELING IN FRANCE)

The French transportation system is very sophisticated. France's primary international gateway for air service is Paris, which has two international airports: *Charles de Gaulle* and *Orly,* both easily accessible from Paris. Extensive bus, rail, and air service connects Paris to the rest of France. In addition, helicopter flights link *Charles de Gaulle* airport with *la Défense* (Paris's major, modern business complex, located on the western edge of the capital), making it a very popular location for international office tenants such as IBM, Apple Computer, and Olivetti. In Paris, local transportation is inexpensive and easy to use. Many companies subsidize their employees' *Carte orange,* a monthly pass for the bus and subway system.

Although there are some regularly scheduled international flights to other major French cities, such as Lyon, Nice, and Marseille, it may prove more convenient, depending on your ultimate destination, to fly to a nearby location outside of France instead. Luxembourg, for example, is ideal for destinations in northeastern France. Air France is the primary carrier for both domestic and international travel, while Air Inter offers more than thirty flights daily between all major French cities. Domestic flights fall into one of three categories: *vol bleu, blanc,* or *rouge.* The *vols rouges* are designed only for commuters paying the full fare, while the *vols blancs* and *vols bleus* are open to anyone, and fares depend on the time of travel and the passenger's age, family status, etc.

The French *SNCF (Société Nationale des Chemins de Fer)* operates the fifth largest railway network in the world, with 21,875 miles of railroad track. The system is very efficient and reliable, and much business travel is done by train. The *TGV, Train à Grande Vitesse,* connects major cities in record time, often making it faster to travel by train than to fly. It is advisable to make a reservation *(faire une réservation)* by phone or through Minitel for all rail travel. Advance reservations are required for the *TGV,* but it is often possible, if space is available, to make one a few minutes before departure on computers located at the station. If you travel at night, you may reserve *une couchette* (a bunk), or a room in a *wagon-lit* (sleeping car). The food on trains is acceptable, though not exceptional, but the station restaurants and *brasseries* are often quite good. As with air travel, a wide range of fares is available, depending on your age, family status, and the duration of travel. Before boarding a train, you must *composter* (punch) your ticket in one of the machines located at the entrance to the platform, or you risk paying a heavy fine if the *contrôleur* (conductor) discovers your unstamped ticket.

France maintains more than 4,000 miles of *autoroute* (highway) and an enormous network of *routes nationales* (national roads) and *routes départementales* (secondary roads). The tolls on *autoroutes* are high, and you may consider taking the well-maintained *routes nationales* instead, though these are often much slower due to heavy traffic. Keep in mind, too, that gasoline in France is about four times as expensive as in the United States, and for this reason many companies use diesel fuel. Americans can drive in France with their U.S. driver's license for a period of up to three months. If you plan to stay longer, you'll need *un permis de conduire international* (an international driver's license), which can be obtained at the *préfecture*.

When driving in France, make sure you have your *permis de conduire* (driver's license), *carte grise* (registration), and *police d'assurance* (insurance policy) with you. You should strictly adhere to the *Code de la route* (traffic laws), as the highways are actively patrolled. Be sure to familiarize yourself with European road signs *(les panneaux de signalisation)*, which in some cases differ significantly from those found in the United States. Avoid driving during peak periods, especially at the end of July and the beginning of August, when roads leading to the south of France are jammed with traffic and the number of serious accidents on the roads is very high. Driving in Paris can be quite a challenge even for the most experienced driver, and you may want to consider avoiding it altogether.

There is no nationwide roadway assistance program in France. Instead, there are toll-free emergency telephones every 1.25 miles on the *autoroutes*. On other roads, it is best to call a local garage (listed in the yellow pages) or to call the police by dialing 17. If you are involved in an accident, be sure to fill out *un constat à l'amiable* with your version of what occurred. If you are not comfortable with your knowledge of French, you may want to request a bailiff to issue a report: *un constat d'huissier*.

Given the size of the railroad network in France, there is no wide-range bus system connecting major French cities. However, you will find *autocars* (inter-city buses) connecting smaller cities and rural towns that are no longer serviced by trains. In general, bus travel is not recommended for business purposes.

EXERCICES

A. *Conjuguer les verbes entre parenthèses au présent de l'indicatif.* (Conjugate the verbs in parentheses in the present tense.)

1. *Vous (répondre) au téléphone.*
2. *Est-ce qu'il (pleuvoir) à Paris en ce moment?*
3. *Nous ne (finir) jamais avant 19 heures.*
4. *Ils (écouter) attentivement le conférencier.*
5. *Tu (savoir) à quelle heure M Duvernois doit arriver?*
6. *Je (sortir) un plan de mon sac de voyage.*
7. *Je (prendre) le train à la Gare du Nord.*
8. *Elle (choisir) un cadeau pour sa collègue.*
9. *Qu'est-ce que vous (faire) ce soir?*
10. *Nous ne (être) pas disponibles avant 18 heures.*

B. *Mettre les phrases à la forme interrogative en utilisant l'inversion.* (Put the sentences in the interrogative form using inversion.)

1. *Vous comprenez l'explication.*
2. *Ils veulent signer le contrat.*
3. *Elle emmène ses enfants en Europe.*
4. *Je choisis une bonne bouteille de vin pour notre table.*
5. *Vous êtes à court d'idées.*
6. *Nous arrivons à midi.*
7. *Il va prendre une importante décision.*
8. *Elles risquent d'obtenir l'autorisation à la dernière minute.*
9. *Il y a toujours des embouteillages dans ce quartier.*
10. *Vous faites un voyage en Europe chaque année.*

C. *Traduire.* (Translate.)

1. He never sleeps on a plane.
2. A colleague is waiting for me at the airport.
3. How much does this road map cost?
4. Bring me tea with lemon, please.
5. They always finish before us.
6. Are you (polite) coming with us?
7. We accept your invitation.
8. I can't give you (polite) an answer.
9. They rent a car at the airport.
10. We are very lucky!

LEÇON 2

A. DIALOGUE

À L'HÔTEL.

M. Chabert et sa nièce Karen font des réservations pour une célébration très spéciale dans un hôtel de Fontainebleau.[1]

KAREN: **Mais Jacques, tu as oublié tante Margaret!**

M. CHABERT: **Mon Dieu! Tante Margaret! Elle m'en voudrait[2] à mort si elle savait que je ne l'avais pas inscrite sur la liste des invités!**

MME LOISEAU: **Il vous faut donc une chambre de plus; ne vous inquiétez pas, cela ne pose aucun problème.**

M. CHABERT: **Vous savez, ce n'est pas facile d'organiser une fête lorsqu'un tiers[3] des parents vient des USA[4] et le reste de Reims[5] et de Fontainebleau!**

MME LOISEAU: **Vous célébrez un anniversaire,[6] si je me souviens bien.**

M. CHABERT: **Oui, une de mes sœurs qui habite aux États-Unis a décidé de[7] faire une surprise à son mari pour son cinquantième anniversaire. Et bien sûr, c'est Karen qui fait un stage[8] en France et moi-même qui devons tout mettre sur pied.**

MME LOISEAU: **C'est très gentil de votre part. Nous disons donc quinze chambres du cinq au huit juin.[9]**

KAREN: **C'est ça, quinze chambres. Avez-vous des chambres non-fumeur?**

M. CHABERT: **Des chambres non-fumeur, tu rêves!**

KAREN: **Tu sais bien que tante Margaret est le fer de lance d'une association de lutte antitabac[10] à Boston.**

MME LOISEAU: **Mais si, nous avons une dizaine[11] de chambres non-fumeur au troisième étage.[12] Et vous voulez des chambres avec salle de bain privée?**

KAREN: **Salle de bain privée et calme absolu.**

MME LOISEAU: **Vous aurez l'impression d'être à la campagne car la plupart de nos chambres donnent[13] sur la cour intérieure.**

M. CHABERT: **Voyons . . . je devrais bien jeter un coup d'œil à la liste que ma sœur m'a envoyée. . . . Euh . . . coffre-fort, nettoyage à sec, repassage, garderie.[14]**

MME LOISEAU: Oui, bien sûr, tous ces services sont à votre disposition.

KAREN: Et la soirée?

MME LOISEAU: Je vous ai réservé le salon Richelieu qui est plus intime que la grande salle à manger. Vous prendrez l'apéritif dans le jardin à dix-huit heures si le temps le permet. Le dîner sera servi à dix-neuf heures trente dans le salon qui sera à votre disposition pour le reste de la soirée.

M. CHABERT: Tout ça semble épatant.

KAREN: Au fait, est-ce que tu t'es occupé de Jennifer Clark?

M. CHABERT: Oh! Jennifer! Nous avons une invitée un peu exigeante. C'est une femme d'affaires très occupée. Elle est toujours pendue au téléphone et elle envoie une centaine de télécopies par jour.

MME LOISEAU: Nous avons plusieurs chambres équipées de deux lignes téléphoniques directes, un téléviseur, un magnétoscope[15] ainsi qu'un télécopieur. Une salle[16] est également à la disposition des clients pour les séminaires et conférences.

KAREN: Elle sera aux anges![17]

M. CHABERT: Bon, je crois que l'on n'a rien oublié. Maintenant, passons aux choses sérieuses: les finances!

MME LOISEAU: Comme je vous l'ai indiqué, le tarif des chambres est de cinq cent francs par nuit. Je vous compterai le même prix pour les chambres de luxe. Pour garantir votre réservation, je vous propose de verser des arrhes[18] représentant le montant de la première nuit.

M. CHABERT: C'est parfait.

MME LOISEAU: Désirez-vous une note[19] séparée pour chaque chambre?

M. CHABERT: Non, vous me ferez[20] une note détaillée à la fin et on s'arrangera en famille.

KAREN: Entre le mini-bar et les notes de téléphone, on risque de s'amuser!

M. CHABERT: Ne sois pas si cynique, Karen, je suis sûr que tout se passera à merveille!

MME LOISEAU: Vous pouvez compter sur moi! Et, Mademoiselle, mon chef-pâtissier fera un gâteau pour l'anniversaire de votre père dont vous me direz des nouvelles!

AT THE HOTEL.

Mr. Chabert and his niece Karen are making reservations for a very special celebration in a Fontainebleau hotel.

KAREN: But Jacques, you forgot Aunt Margaret!

MR. CHABERT: My God! Aunt Margaret! She would hold it against me till the day she died if she knew that I hadn't included her on the guest list!

MRS. LOISEAU: You need another room then. Don't worry, that won't be a problem.

MR. CHABERT: You know, it's not easy to organize a party when a third of the relatives are coming from the U.S.A. and the rest from Reims and Fontainebleau.

MRS. LOISEAU: You're celebrating a birthday, if I remember correctly.

MR. CHABERT: One of my sisters who lives in the United States decided to throw a surprise party for her husband's fiftieth birthday. And, of course, it's Karen, who is doing an internship in France, and I who have to arrange everything.

MRS. LOISEAU: That's very kind of you. So let's say fifteen rooms from the fifth to the eighth of June.

KAREN: That's it, fifteen rooms. Do you have any non-smoking rooms?

MR. CHABERT: Non-smoking rooms. You're dreaming!

KAREN: You know very well that Aunt Margaret is the spearhead of an anti-smoking association in Boston.

MRS. LOISEAU: But, yes, we do! We have about ten non-smoking rooms on the fourth floor. And do you want rooms with a private bath?

KAREN: Private bath and absolute calm.

MRS. LOISEAU: You'll feel as if you're in the country because most of our rooms face the inner courtyard.

MR. CHABERT: Let's see . . . I'd like to take a look at the list my sister sent me. . . . Safe, dry cleaning, pressing, nursery.

MRS. LOISEAU: Yes, of course, all these services are available.

KAREN: And the party?

MRS. LOISEAU: I reserved for you the Richelieu room, which is more intimate than the large dining room. You'll have cocktails in the garden at six P.M., weather permitting. Dinner will be served at seven-thirty P.M. in your private room, which will be all yours for the rest of the evening.

MR. CHABERT: That sounds great!

KAREN: By the way, did you take care of Jennifer Clark?

MR. CHABERT: Oh! Jennifer! We have a guest who is a bit demanding. She's a very busy businesswoman. She's always on the phone and sends about a hundred faxes a day.

MRS. LOISEAU: We have several rooms equipped with two direct telephone lines, a television and VCR, as well as a fax machine. A room is also at the guests' disposal for seminars and conferences.

KAREN: She'll be in heaven!

MR. CHABERT: Good, I think we haven't forgotten anything. Now, let's move on to a serious matter: money!

MRS. LOISEAU: As I mentioned to you, the price of the room is five hundred francs a night. I'll charge you the same price for the deluxe rooms. In order to ensure your reservation, I suggest that you put down a deposit that would cover the first night.

MR. CHABERT: Perfect.

MRS. LOISEAU: Do you want a separate bill for each room?

MR. CHABERT: No, I'd appreciate it if you'd prepare an itemized bill at the end, and we'll settle it among ourselves.

KAREN: Between the mini-bar and the telephone bills, it's going to be fun!

MR. CHABERT: Don't be so cynical, Karen. I'm sure everything will go smoothly!

MRS. LOISEAU: You can count on me! And, Mademoiselle, my pastry chef will make your father a birthday cake that you're sure to rave about.

B. EN BREF

1. Fontainebleau, located 70 miles southeast of Paris, is famous for its castle and for its *galerie et escalier François 1er* (gallery and staircase dating to François I). Its 7,000-acre forest is very popular with hikers.

2. *En vouloir à quelqu'un* appears in many useful French expressions: *Ne m'en veuillez pas, je ne l'ai pas fait exprès.* (Don't be mad at me; I didn't do it on purpose.) *Je leur en veux de nous avoir menti.* (I hold a grudge against them for lying to us.) *Vous ne m'en voulez pas?* (No hard feelings?) *Il s'en voulait d'avoir fait une telle gaffe.* (He could have kicked himself for making such a blunder.)

3. Other quantity expressions include: *un quart* (a quarter), *un cinquième* (a fifth), *une moitié* (half of a whole), *un demi* (half of a measurable quantity). *Un demi* must be followed by a noun. For example: *Donnez-m'en la moitié.* (Give me half.) *Nous partons dans une demi-heure.* (We're leaving in half an hour.)

4. *De* + a definite article is used with masculine or plural names of countries and continents; *de* alone precedes feminine singular ones. *Il rentre de France.* (He just came back from France.) *Il vient d'Italie mais elle vient du Brésil.* (He's from Italy, but she's from Brazil.)

5. Reims, best known for its Gothic cathedral where Charles VII was crowned in 1429, is the capital of the Champagne region.

6. *Un anniversaire:* a birthday. *Un anniversaire de mariage:* a wedding anniversary. *L'anniversaire de la mort de Debussy:* the anniversary of Debussy's death.

7. *Décider de:* to make a decision. *Se décider à:* to reach a decision that requires careful consideration. *J'ai décidé de prendre des vacances.* (I decided to take a vacation.) *Après avoir hésité pendant des années, ils se sont décidés à adopter un enfant.* (After years of hesitation, they finally decided to adopt a child.)

8. Here's another *faux-ami. Stage* looks like the English "stage," but it means "internship." To indicate a stage in a theater use *une scène,* and for a phase, use *une étape. Il fait un stage à la Banque de France.* (He has an internship at the *Banque de France.*) *Nous avons fait le voyage en trois étapes.* (We made the trip in three stages.) *Stage* is also easily confused with its French look-alike *étage,* which means "floor." *Son bureau est au dixième étage.* (Her office is on the eleventh floor.)

9. When dates are introduced by a preposition, the definite article should also be used *(à + le = au; de + le = du): Je voudrais une chambre du premier au sept juin.* (I'd like a room from the first to the seventh of June.) When both the day of the week and the date are specified, the preposition-plus-article combination precedes the day. *Il sera à Paris du lundi 18 au vendredi 22 septembre.* (He'll be in Paris from Monday the 18th to Friday the 22nd of September.) If only the day is specified, the definite article should not be used. *Il sera à Paris de mardi à jeudi.* (He'll be in Paris from Tuesday to Thursday.)

10. The French are very fond of the prefix *anti-.* Feel free to use it often. *Une campagne antipollution:* an anti-pollution campaign. *Des mesures antidémocratiques:* undemocratic measures. *Un abri antiatomique:* a fallout shelter.

11. The suffix *-aine* signifies an approximate amount: *une dizaine de livres* means "about ten books." *Une cinquantaine de personnes:* about fifty people. *Une centaine de pages:* about a hundred pages. *Douzaine* can mean "exactly one dozen" or "a dozen or so," depending on the context. *Il a acheté une douzaine d'œufs.* (He bought a dozen eggs.) *J'ai invité une douzaine de personnes.* (I invited about a dozen people.)

12. Remember that in France, *le rez-de-chaussée* is the main floor. *Le premier étage* is the second floor, *le deuxième étage* is the third floor, and so on.

13. *Leur villa donne sur la mer.* (Their villa faces the ocean.) *Ma fenêtre donne sur le parc.* (My window overlooks the park.) *Cette porte donne sur le jardin.* (This door leads to the garden.)

14. With enumerations or lists of any kind, definite articles can be dropped.

15. *Un magnétophone* (a tape recorder), *un magnétoscope* (a video recorder), *un lecteur de disques compacts* (a CD player), *un baladeur* (a Walkman).

16. In French, there are several ways to refer to a room. *La salle* is used for meeting rooms or classrooms. *La chambre* is where you sleep, unless it is *la Chambre,* the house in the *Parlement. La pièce* is a generic term used for any kind of room.

17. Angels appear often in French idioms: *Un ange passe.* (There was a pregnant pause.) *Sois un ange et rends-moi ce service.* (Be an angel, and do me this favor.) *Mon ange.* (My darling.) *C'est son ange gardien.* (It's his/her guardian angel.) *Elle est sage comme un ange.* (She is as good as gold.)

18. A deposit for a rental (a car, a hotel room, an apartment) is called *des arrhes.* A bottle deposit is *la consigne,* and the deposit you make in a bank is *un versement.*

19. You pay *l'addition* in a restaurant, *la note* or *le compte* in a hotel, and *la facture* to the electric company or the doctor.

20. Note that the future tense is used to make a polite request. For more on the uses of the future, refer to *Leçon 8.*

C. GRAMMAIRE ET USAGE

1. *LES VERBES PRONOMINAUX* (PRONOMINAL VERBS)

In the infinitive, pronominal verbs can be recognized by the pronoun *se* preceding the verb form. They are conjugated just like their non-pronominal counterparts, but they are always accompanied by the appropriate personal pronoun: *me, te, se, nous, vous,* or *se.*

Il se souvient toujours de mon anniversaire.
He always remembers my birthday.

Te souviens-tu s'il y a un coffre-fort dans l'hôtel?
Do you remember if there's a safe in the hotel?

Les enfants s'amusent dans le jardin.
The children are enjoying themselves in the garden.

There are four types of pronominal verbs.

a. Les verbes réfléchis.

In a reflexive construction, the subject and the object are the same; i.e., the subject acts upon itself. While some verbs are reflexive in both French and English, many are reflexive only in French, and some only in English.

Elle s'habille pour aller à une soirée.
She is getting dressed (dressing herself) to go to a party.

Il se regarde dans le miroir.
He is looking at himself in the mirror.

In negative constructions, the reflexive pronoun is placed between the negative particle *ne* and the verb.

Nous ne nous reposons jamais assez en vacances.
We never rest enough when we are on vacation.

Ne t'inquiète pas, tout s'arrangera!
Don't worry, everything will work out.

With inversion, the reflexive pronoun immediately precedes the verb–subject combination.

Se lave-t-il les cheveux tous les jours?
Does he wash his hair every day?

Ne vous occupez-vous pas de cette affaire?
Aren't you in charge of this business?

b. Les verbes réciproques.

Reciprocal verbs indicate that the subjects (always plural) act upon each other.

Ils se disent bonne nuit, ils s'embrassent et ils vont se coucher.
They say good night to each other, they kiss each other, and they go to bed.

Ces jumelles ne se ressemblent pas du tout.
These twins don't resemble each other at all.

25

Elles se disputent sans cesse.
They keep fighting with one another.

c. Les verbes pronominaux subjectifs.
A lot of verbs are technically neither reflexive nor reciprocal—they just happen to take a pronominal form.[1] Always learn them with their *se* pronoun.

Il s'aperçoit toujours de ses erreurs à temps.
He always catches his mistakes in time.

Ils ne se plaignent jamais.
They never complain.

Si vous n'ouvrez pas la fenêtre, nous allons nous évanouir.
If you don't open the window, we're going to faint.

Ils se sont enfuis à l'arrivée de la police.
They fled when the police arrived.

d. Les verbes pronominaux passifs.
With these pronominal verbs, the subject is not a person and does not perform the action of the verb but merely experiences or is subjected to it. (Hence, the name "passive.")

Les toiles de cet artiste hollandais se vendent bien.
This Dutch artist's paintings sell well.

Le vin blanc se boit frais.
White wine is drunk chilled.

Les asperges se mangent avec les doigts.
Asparagus is eaten with your fingers.

Comment ça se traduit?
How is this translated?

Ça ne se fait pas.
It is not done.

2. *LES EXPRESSIONS DE TEMPS I* (EXPRESSIONS OF TIME I)

a. To express the time from the hour to half past the hour, use the current hour plus the number of minutes elapsed: *six heures* + *dix*.

Il est six heures dix.
It's ten past six.

---

[1] For a list of the more common subjective pronominal verbs, please refer to Appendix E (page 321).

To express the time from half past the hour to the full hour, use the formula above, or use the coming hour minus *(moins)* the number of minutes left: *huit heures — vingt.*

Il est sept heures quarante.
It is seven forty.

Il est huit heures moins vingt.
It's twenty to eight.

As in English, there are also some useful, special time expressions:

Il est dix heures moins le quart.
It's a quarter to ten.

Il est cinq heures et demie.
It's half past five.

Il est midi.
It's noon.

Il est minuit.
It's midnight.

Remember that the 24-hour clock is used in all official schedules and for all formal appointments.

L'avion arrive à dix-huit heures vingt-cinq.
The plane arrives at six twenty-five (P.M.).

Votre rendez-vous chez le dentiste est à quatorze heures?
Your dentist appointment is at two (P.M.)?

   b. In Europe, the date is given with the day first, followed by the month, and then the year. Note that the days of the week and the months of the year[2] are not capitalized.

Nous sommes mercredi, le 20 mars 1997.
Today is Wednesday, March 20, 1997.

The French refer to a full week using *huit jours* (eight days), and to a fortnight using *quinze jours* (fifteen days):

Paul prend toujours huit jours de vacances en avril.
Paul always takes a week's vacation in April.

Quinze jours ne suffisent pas pour négocier cette affaire.
Two weeks are not enough to negotiate this deal.

---

[2] For a list of the days of the week and months and seasons of the year, please refer to Appendix B (page 318).

Appelez-moi mardi en huit.
Call me a week from Tuesday.

c. Note the difference between *jour, matin, soir* and *journée, matinée, soirée.* The latter are used to stress that an action lasted the entire day, morning, or evening.

Elle passe cinq jours à Bruxelles.
She is spending five days in Brussels.

Nous lisons tous les soirs.
We read every evening.

but:

Elle a travaillé toute la journée.
She worked all day.

Nous avons bavardé toute la soirée.
We chatted all evening.

3. *L'USAGE DE "DONC"* (USAGE OF *DONC*)

Donc can be used in several different ways:

a. to indicate the consequences of an action.

Vous avez accepté l'invitation, donc vous devez y aller.
You accepted the invitation, so you have to go.

Je pense donc je suis.
I think; therefore I am.

b. to show surprise.

C'était donc son demi-frère qui a gagné à la loterie?
So it was his half-brother who won the lottery?

Ce n'était donc pas vrai?
So it wasn't true?

c. to add stress in interrogative and exclamatory sentences.

Allons donc!
Come on!

Pourquoi donc es-tu encore en retard?
Why in the world are you late again?

Demande-leur donc!
    Go on, then, ask them!

Écoute donc!
    Just listen!

D. JEU DE MOTS

While doing business in France, you're likely to run into the word *affaire* on more than one occasion.

Que penses-tu de l'affaire Dupuy?
    What do you think of the Dupuy case?

Je crois que le PDG essaie d'étouffer l'affaire.
    I think the CEO is trying to hush up the matter.

Paul se rend-il compte que ce contrat est une affaire en or?
    Does Paul realize that this contract is a gold mine?

Tu sais, on ne peut pas monter une affaire sans un centime!
    You know, one can't start a company without a penny!

Mais on m'a dit que l'affaire était dans le sac!
    But I've heard that the deal is in the bag!

Ce n'est pas mon affaire.
    It's none of my business.

J'espère vraiment qu'il va se tirer d'affaire.
    I do hope he'll be able to manage.

Tu ferais mieux de t'occuper de tes affaires!
    You'd better mind your own business!

E. LE COIN DES AFFAIRES

L'EXPÉDITION (SHIPPING)

France has one of the world's most sophisticated transportation infrastructures, making business transactions and shipments very smooth and timely. Air transportation to France is offered by most major U.S. airlines, as well as by Air France and many other international airlines. Paris and Lyon are the two major French entry ports for air transport *(le transport aérien).* For sea transport *(le transport maritime),* there are twelve major seaports, including Bordeaux, Le Havre, and Marseille, many of which are equipped to process container ships. French roadways are one of the most important links in Europe's transportation network and are undergoing continual expansion and improvement. Finally, the French rail system is world renowned and ever-improving. By the year 2015, *TGV* lines will cover approximately 6,000 miles. The French government hopes to cover the entire country and to connect France with newly emerging European economic centers by combining new and conventional lines.

To ship *(expédier)* goods to France and other countries in the European Union, the following documents are generally required: a commercial invoice *(une facture)*, a bill of lading or airway bill *(un connaissement)*, and a certificate of origin *(un certificat d'origine)*. Agricultural products, plants, and animals require additional documents, and it is best to consult the importer before shipping. The Foreign Agricultural Service of the U.S. Department of Agriculture also provides specific information on these requirements.

The commercial invoice serves as the basis for levying customs charges *(les frais de douane)* and must therefore provide a detailed description of the contents of the shipment (type, quality, etc.), especially noting factors that affect the value of the goods. The invoice should indicate the time and place it was issued and provide basic information about the seller and the buyer (their names and addresses) and about the nature of the transaction, including the method of shipment; the terms of delivery and payment; the number, type, and outside markings of all packages in numerical order; and the quantity and price (unit and total cost, plus any surcharges) of the goods. A signature from the exporting firm would be helpful on all invoices.

French must be used in addition to English in all documents involved in business transactions as well as on all labels, packages, and merchandise, unless the merchandise is intended for re-export from France or consists of typical foreign products, products with a name that is also used in France, or products with brand names.

The bill of lading (issued for land or sea freight) or air waybill (issued for air freight) is the agreement between the goods' owner and carrier. It requires no consular approval and may be either straight or negotiable.

A certificate of origin identifying the country in which a product originated or was manufactured is required only for certain goods (such as fertilizers, household appliances, and electronic medical equipment), but it is *strongly recommended* for all shipments, as goods may be detained by Customs without one. The certificates can be obtained from the U.S. Chamber of Commerce and need not be certified by either French or U.S. Customs officers. The information in the certificate of origin, however, must agree with that provided in all other shipping documents.

To ensure the proper handling *(la manutention)* of your shipment, you may want to use one of the following indications: *fragile* (fragile), *haut* (this side up), *denrées périssables* (perishables), *urgent* (rush). For further information on shipping procedures to France, contact your local U.S. Chamber of Commerce.

Following are some common shipping-related terms and acronyms in English and French:

Franc à bord	FOB (free on board)
Franc de toute avarie	FAA (free of all average)
Franc à quai	FAQ (free alongside quai)
CAF (Coût, assurance, fret)	CIF (cost, insurance, freight)
Fret payable à destination	FPAD (freight payable at destination)
Règlement à la livraison	COD (cash on delivery)
Règlement à la commande	CWO (cash with order)
Paiement d'avance	CIA (cash in advance)
Aux risques et périls du propriétaire	at the owner's risk
Rendu droits acquittés	DDP (delivered duty paid)

VOCABULAIRE

la cargaison	cargo
le carton ondulé	corrugated cardboard
une boîte	box
une caisse	crate
une balle	bale
une palette	pallet
conditionner des marchandises	to package goods
emballer des marchandises	to pack goods
déballer	unpack
un emballage	packaging
un emballage sous vide	vacuum pack
un emballage hermétique	airtight package
les marchandises destinées à l'exportation	goods for export
le camionnage	trucking
à l'épreuve des chocs	crushproof
l'expéditeur	sender
le destinataire	consignee
les frais de transport	freight charge
le certificat de douane	clearance certificate
la garantie	warrant
en port payé	prepaid port

EXERCICES

A. *Conjuguer les verbes entre parenthèses au présent de l'indicatif.*

1. *Pourquoi (se plaindre) ils sans cesse?*
2. *Nous (se dire) bonne nuit avant de nous coucher.*
3. *Elle ne (s'apercevoir) jamais de ses erreurs.*
4. *Les deux fils de M. Chabert (se disputer) constamment.*
5. *La cuisine japonaise (se manger) avec des baguettes.*

B. *Compléter les phrases suivantes en utilisant les verbes "se souvenir, s'amuser, s'inquiéter, s'occuper, se promener" au présent de l'indicatif.* (Complete the following sentences using the verbs *se souvenir, s'amuser, s'inquieter, s'occuper,* and *se promener* in the present indicative.)

1. *Tante Margaret _____ de plusieurs causes humanitaires.*
2. *_____ vous de votre premier séjour à Paris?*
3. *Pierre _____ toujours quand il va à une soirée.*
4. *Nous _____ dans la forêt de Fontainebleau.*
5. *La sœur de M. Chabert _____ tout le temps.*

C. *Traduire.*

1. They are resting in the garden.
2. Don't worry, Jennifer will like her room. *(tu)*
3. The French always kiss each other to say hello.
4. Patrick washes his hands before eating the cake.
5. Do you remember if there's a VCR in the room? *(vous)*

D. *Transposer les heures en utilisant l'heure officielle.* (Rewrite the time using the 24-hour clock.)

1. *5:25 P.M.*
2. *10:45 P.M.*
3. *2:20 P.M.*
4. *7:35 P.M.*
5. *8:10 P.M.*

LEÇON 3

A. DIALOGUE

AU TÉLÉPHONE.

Julia vient d'arriver à Paris où elle souhaite trouver un emploi. Elle s'arme de courage et appelle[1] quelques numéros qui figurent dans son carnet d'adresses.[2] Julia feuillette son carnet.

JULIA *(à elle-même):* **Par qui est-ce que je vais bien pouvoir commencer? Mark? Ah non, c'est vrai, il est en déplacement en Suisse en ce moment. Oh! Sylvain! Voyons ce qu'il devient.**

Elle compose le numéro.

JULIA: **Bonjour, est-ce que je pourrais parler à Sylvain?**

LUC: **Mon frère est pas là.**

JULIA: **Ah! C'est Luc? C'est Julia à l'appareil. Tu peux dire à Sylvain que je l'ai appelé, s'il te plaît.**

LUC: **Euh ouais . . .[3]**

JULIA: **Et dis-lui que je le rappellerai plus tard.**

LUC: **O.K.[3]**

JULIA: **Au revoir et merci.**

LUC: **Ciao![3]**

Julia raccroche[4] le téléphone, pensive.

JULIA *(à elle-même):* **Luc est toujours dans les nuages. Sylvain recevra-t-il jamais mon message? On verra . . .**

Julia attend la tonalité et compose un autre numéro.

LA CORRESPONDANTE: **Allô!**

JULIA: **Madame Balavoine?**

LA CORRESPONDANTE: **Ah non, vous vous trompez de numéro.**

JULIA: **Oh . . . excusez-moi.**

Julia raccroche. Elle a oublié de composer l'indicatif numérique car la mère d'Hervé, son coiffeur à Chicago, habite en banlieue.[5]

MME BALAVOINE: **Allô!**

JULIA: **Madame Balavoine?**

MME BALAVOINE: **Oui . . .**

JULIA: **Bonjour Madame. Je suis Julia, une amie de votre fils Hervé.**

MME BALAVOINE: **Ah . . . Hervé m'a beaucoup parlé de vous . . .**

JULIA: **J'ai un petit paquet pour vous qu'il m'a chargée[6] de vous remettre.**

MME BALAVOINE: **Comme c'est gentil . . . Je serais ravie de faire votre connaissance. D'ailleurs,[7] j'ai promis à Hervé de vous emmener[8] dans mon salon de thé préféré. Êtes-vous libre jeudi ou vendredi après-midi?**

JULIA: **Vendredi après-midi me convient très bien.**

MME BALAVOINE: **Eh bien, je vous donne rendez-vous chez Dalloyau,[9] quatre-vingt dix-neuf rue du Faubourg Saint-Honoré, à quinze heures trente.**

JULIA: **Comment est-ce que je vais vous reconnaître?**

MME BALAVOINE: **J'ai une bonne cinquantaine[10] d'années, les cheveux blond cendré.[11] Vous verrez, Hervé tient de sa mère.[12]**

JULIA: **Bon, très bien, à vendredi!**

MME BALAVOINE: **Très bien. Au revoir.**

JULIA *(à elle-même):* **Le thé, les sorties, c'est bien beau . . . mais il ne faut pas oublier le travail. Et si je téléphonais à M. Sabatier . . .**

Le téléphone sonne plusieurs fois et quelqu'un décroche.

LE STANDARDISTE: **Société Duvallois, bonjour!**

JULIA: **Bonjour monsieur, je voudrais parler à M. Sabatier, poste 248.**

LE STANDARDISTE: **C'est de la part de qui?**

JULIA: **Julia McKinley.**

LE STANDARDISTE: **C'est à quel sujet?**

JULIA: **C'est personnel.**

LE STANDARDISTE: **Ne quittez pas . . . M. Sabatier est toujours en ligne. Ah! voilà. Je vais vous le passer dans quelques instants.**

JULIA: **Merci beaucoup.**

M. SABATIER: **Hello, Julia! Comment allez-vous?**

JULIA: **Très bien merci.**

M. SABATIER: **Votre tante m'a prévenu de votre arrivée.**

JULIA: **Je suis désolée de vous déranger mais j'ai besoin de quelques conseils pour dénicher un emploi à Paris.**

M. SABATIER: **Vous ne me dérangez pas du tout. Croyez-moi, le bouche à oreille, il n'y a que ça de vrai! Vous savez, votre tante m'a rendu service bien des fois[13] lorsque je vivais à Chicago. Cela me ferait très plaisir de lui rendre la pareille en vous donnant quelques tuyaux.[14]**

JULIA: **Oh merci beaucoup.**

M. SABATIER: **Venez à mon bureau avant la fin de la semaine car je pars pour Tokyo vendredi. Je vous passe ma secrétaire avec qui vous pouvez prendre rendez-vous.**

JULIA: **D'accord. À bientôt.**

Quelqu'un frappe à la porte. Pascal entre.

PASCAL: **Bonjour!**

JULIA: **Pascal! Tu tombes bien!**

PASCAL: **Ah bon?**

JULIA: **J'ai l'estomac dans les talons! Je n'ai pas eu le temps de déjeuner.**

PASCAL: **On appelle Didier?**

JULIA: **Excellente idée.**

PASCAL: **Je te parie qu'on va tomber sur son répondeur.**

Pascal compose le numéro puis ils écoutent le message enregistré de Didier.

LE RÉPONDEUR: **Vous êtes bien chez Didier Blondel. Je ne suis pas disponible pour le moment. Laissez votre message après la tonalité. Je vous rappellerai dès que possible.**

PASCAL: **Je te l'avais bien dit! Jamais chez lui celui-là! Allez,[15] viens, on[16] va déjeuner.**

ON THE PHONE.

Julia has just arrived in Paris, where she wants to find a job. She gets up her courage and calls a few numbers from her address book. Julia leafs through her book.

JULIA (to herself): Where should I start? Mark? Oh, no, that's right . . . he's on a business trip in Switzerland right now. Sylvain! Let's see what he's up to.

She dials the number.

JULIA: Good morning, could I speak to Sylvain?

LUC: My brother's not in.

JULIA: Oh! Is this Luc? It's Julia. Could you please tell Sylvain I called?

LUC: Yeah . . .

JULIA: And tell him I'll call him back later.

LUC: Okay.

JULIA: Bye, and thanks.

LUC: Ciao!

Julia hangs up, still thinking.

JULIA (to herself): Luc's head is always in the clouds. Will Sylvain ever get my message? We'll see.

Julia waits for the tone and dials another number.

PERSON AT THE OTHER END: Hello!

JULIA: Madame Balavoine?

PERSON AT THE OTHER END: No, you've got the wrong number.

JULIA: Oh . . . excuse me.

Julia hangs up. She forgot she had to dial the area code because the mother of Hervé, her hairdresser in Chicago, lives in the suburbs.

MRS. BALAVOINE: Hello!

JULIA: Madame Balavoine?

MRS. BALAVOINE: Yes . . .

JULIA: Good morning. This is Julia, a friend of your son, Hervé.

MRS. BALAVOINE: Oh . . . Hervé has told me a lot about you.

JULIA: I have a small package he asked me to give you.

MRS. BALAVOINE: How nice! I'd love to meet you. Besides, I promised Hervé I'd take you to my favorite tearoom. Are you free Thursday or Friday afternoon?

JULIA: Friday afternoon would be perfect.

MRS. BALAVOINE: Well, meet me at Dalloyau, ninety-nine *rue du Faubourg Saint-Honoré*, at three-thirty P.M.

JULIA: How will I recognize you?

MRS. BALAVOINE: I'm well into my fifties, and my hair is ash-blond. You'll see, Hervé takes after his mother.

JULIA: Great! See you on Friday!

JULIA (to herself): Tea, entertainment, that's all well and good, but I shouldn't forget about work. How about calling Mr. Sabatier . . .

The phone rings several times and someone answers.

OPERATOR: *Société Duvallois,* good morning!

JULIA: Good morning, I'd like to speak to Mr. Sabatier, extension two-four-eight.

OPERATOR: Who should I say is calling?

JULIA: Julia McKinley.

OPERATOR: What is this in regard to?

JULIA: It's personal.

OPERATOR: Hold on . . . M. Sabatier is still on the other line. Oh, here we go. I'll put you through in a second.

JULIA: Thanks a lot.

MR. SABATIER: Hi, Julia! How are you?

JULIA: Very well, thank you.

MR. SABATIER: Your aunt told me you were coming.

JULIA: I'm sorry to bother you, but I need some advice about getting a job in Paris.

MR. SABATIER: You're not bothering me at all. Believe me, word of mouth is the only way. You know, your aunt did me a lot of favors when I lived in Chicago. I'd be very happy to pay her back by giving you a few tips.

JULIA: Oh, thank you.

MR. SABATIER: Stop by my office before the end of the week because I'm going to Tokyo on Friday. I'll put you through to my secretary to make an appointment.

JULIA: All right. See you soon.

There's a knock at the door. Pascal walks in.

PASCAL: Hi!

JULIA: Pascal! Good timing!

PASCAL: Why?

JULIA: I'm starving! I didn't have time to eat lunch.

PASCAL: Should we call Didier?

JULIA: Great idea!

PASCAL: I'll bet you anything we'll get his answering machine.

Pascal dials the number; they listen to Didier's recorded message.

ANSWERING MACHINE: You've reached Didier Blondel. I am not available at the moment. Leave your message after the tone. I'll call you as soon as possible.

PASCAL: I told you! That one is never home! Come on, let's go to lunch!

B. EN BREF

1. To call someone, you can: *téléphoner à, appeler,* or *donner/passer un coup de fil à* (colloquial).

2. *Carnet* has many different uses: *un carnet de timbres* (a book of stamps), *un carnet de rendez-vous* (an agenda), *un carnet de chèques* (a checkbook), *un carnet de tickets de métro* (a book of subway tickets), *un carnet de commandes* (an order book), *un carnet de notes* (a report card).

3. In slang, *oui* becomes *ouais,* much as *yes* becomes *yeah* in American English. Likewise, *salut* or the Italian *ciao* are often used instead of *au revoir,* and the English *okay* is as common as *d'accord.*

4. *Je raccroche le téléphone* (I'm hanging up the phone). *J'accroche mon manteau* (I'm hanging up my coat). *Je décroche le téléphone* (I'm picking up the phone).

5. To say "in" a certain place, use *en* if the place is unmodified, and *dans* if it is modified. Compare: *Il vit en France.* (He lives in France.) *Il vivait dans la France de Louis XIV.* (He lived in Louis XIV's France.) *Elle habite en banlieue.* (She lives in the suburbs.) *Elle habite dans la banlieue nord de Lille.* (She lives in the northern suburb of Lille.)

6. Here the past participle *chargée* agrees with the direct object *me* (referring to Julia).

7. Note the various usages of *ailleurs: ailleurs* (elsewhere), *d'ailleurs* (besides, moreover), and *par ailleurs* (otherwise, in other respects).

8. In French, different verbs are used to signify "to bring" or "to take," depending on whether you are referring to a person or a thing. *Apportez-moi des fleurs.* (Bring me some flowers.) *Amenez votre frère à la soirée.* (Bring your brother to the party.) *Elle emporte trois valises en vacances.* (She is taking three suitcases on her vacation.)

9. Dalloyau, founded in 1801, has five stores in Paris and also five in Japan. It is famous for its catering and its tearoom ambience.

10. *Il a une quarantaine d'années.* (He is in his forties.) *Elle frise la soixantaine.* (She is pushing sixty.) *Il a la cinquantaine bien tassée.* (He is well into his fifties.) But: *Elle est née dans les années soixante.* (She was born in the sixties.) *Ah! Paris dans les années vingt!* (Ah! Paris in the twenties!)

11. Compound adjectives do not agree in gender and number with the nouns to which they refer. Compare: *Elle a les cheveux blonds.* (She has blond hair.) *Elle a les cheveux blond cendré.* (She has ash-blond hair.)

12. Prepositions often change the meaning of a verb. Compare: *Il tient à sa mère.* (He is attached to his mother.) *Il tient de sa mère.* (He takes after his mother.)

13. While most adverbs of quantity are followed by *de* without the article (*Elle a trop de travail pour vous passer un coup de fil.* She has too much work to call you.), *bien* and *la plupart* are followed by *des,* and *encore* can be followed by *du, de la,* or *des. Je lui ai dit bien des fois.* (I told him many times.) *La plupart des coups de fil sont pour elle.* (Most of the phone calls are for her.)

14. *Tuyau* literally means "pipe, tube."

15. *Allez* (or *allez, allez*) is an informal expression used to encourage, to console ("there, there"), or to urge people to hurry up. Note that the *vous* form is used even for people you normally address with *tu.*

16. In familiar speech, *on* replaces *nous. On va au cinéma ce soir.* (We are going to the movies tonight.) *On n'a rien compris à ce qu'il disait.* (We didn't understand anything he said.)

C. GRAMMAIRE ET USAGE

1. *LES PRONOMS OBJETS DIRECTS ET INDIRECTS* (DIRECT AND INDIRECT OBJECT PRONOUNS)

Direct object pronouns *(me, te, le, la, nous, vous, les)* replace direct object nouns and precede the verb.

J'emmène Cristel dans un salon de thé.
  I'm taking Cristel to a tearoom.

Je l'emmène dans un salon de thé.
  I'm taking her to a tearoom.

Vous écoutez les messages.
You listen to the messages.

Vous les écoutez.
You listen to them.

Indirect object pronouns *(me, te, lui, nous, vous, leur)* replace indirect object nouns and generally precede the verb.

Vous téléphonez à Mme Balavoine.
You're calling Mrs. Balavoine.

Vous lui téléphonez.
You're calling her.

Je laisse un message à mes amis.
I'm leaving a message for my friends.

Je leur laisse un message.
I'm leaving a message for them.

When a direct and indirect object pronoun appear together in a sentence, the indirect object pronoun comes first, unless the direct and indirect object pronouns are in the third person, in which case the direct object pronoun comes first.

Tu me donnes son numéro de téléphone.
You give me his/her phone number.

Tu me le donnes.
You give it to me.

Elle vous montre les statistiques.
She's showing you the statistics.

Elle vous les montre.
She's showing them to you.

J'envoie le document aux avocats.
I send the document to the lawyers.

Je le leur envoie.
I send it to them.

Nous demandons le dossier au secrétaire.
We ask the secretary for the file.

Nous le lui demandons.
We ask him for it.

In the imperative, both pronouns follow the verb, with the direct object pronoun preceding the indirect object pronoun, except in negative imperatives, where the word order is the same as in affirmative sentences. The only exception is *en,* which always follows the indirect object pronoun.

Envoyez-moi le contrat.
Envoyez-le-moi.
Ne me l'envoyez pas.

Apportez-leur les livres qu'il a demandés.
Apportez-les-leur.
Ne les leur apportez pas.

Donnez-nous des renseignements.
Donnez-nous-en.
Ne nous en donnez pas.

Object pronouns can refer to more than just concrete nouns. The object pronoun *le* is often used to announce or to refer to a previously introduced phrase or concept.

Comme je vous l'ai dit, il faut prendre une décision dès que possible.
As I told you, we have to make a decision as soon as possible.

Accepteront-ils notre proposition? Je ne le crois pas.
Will they accept our offer? I don't think so.

Passez nous voir chaque fois que vous le pourrez.
Come visit us whenever you can.

In some idiomatic expressions, *le, la,* or *les* is used without an antecedent.

Je vous le donne en mille!
You'll never guess!

Nous l'avons échappé belle.
It was a narrow escape.

Il se la coule douce.
He is taking it very easy.

They can also refer to phrases: notice that *le* can refer to a plural noun.

Je les traite de meurtriers car ils le sont.
I call them murders because that's what they are.

Bien des délits ont cessé de l'être.
Many crimes are no longer considered as such.

2. *FUTUR ET PASSÉ IMMÉDIAT*
(THE IMMEDIATE FUTURE AND PAST)

a. The immediate future (formed with *aller* in the present indicative followed by a verb in the infinitive) indicates the proximity or imminence of an action and often replaces the real future in everyday conversation.

Je vais vous passer M. Sabatier dans un instant.
I'll put you through to M. Sabatier in a second.

La secrétaire va vous fournir ses coordonnées.[1]
The secretary will provide you with information on how to reach him.

b. The immediate past is formed with *venir* in the present tense + *de* + a verb in the infinitive. It refers to an action that has just taken place.

Ils viennent d'approuver le projet.
They have just approved the project.

Nous venons de les appeler.
We just called them.

Venir de can also be used in the imperfect to indicate an event that took place immediately prior to another event in the past.

Tu venais de partir quand le téléphone a sonné.
You had just left when the phone rang.

Vous veniez de signer le contrat lorsque la Bourse s'est écroulée.
You had just signed the contract when the Stock Exchange crashed.

Julia venait d'arriver à Paris quand elle a rencontré Jean-Luc.
Julia had just arrived in Paris when she met Jean-Luc.

Be careful with word order in these two tenses when two pronouns are involved:

Elle va vous passer M. Sabatier.
She's going to pass you Mr. Sabatier.

Elle va vous le passer.
She's going to pass him to you.

Je venais d'envoyer le document à Frédéric quand il m'a téléphoné.
I had just sent Frederic the document when he called me.

Je venais de le lui envoyer quand il m'a téléphoné.
I had just sent it to him when he called me.

---

[1] *Coordonnées* is a collective term referring to someone's complete business address including telephone, fax, pager number, etc.

3. NÉGATION AVEC "NE" ET "PAS"
(NEGATION WITH *NE* AND *PAS*)

The simple negation *ne . . . pas* (not) is probably one of the first things you learned in French. But did you know that its individual components, *ne* and *pas*, can also be used alone in a sentence?

Ne is used without *pas* in many proverbial and idiomatic expressions.

Il n'est pire eau que l'eau qui dort.
Still waters run deep.

Qu'à cela ne tienne.
That's no problem.

Ne can also be used without *pas* with *cesser, pouvoir,* and *oser,* especially in simple tenses or when followed by an infinitive. This form tends to be a little more formal or literary.

Il n'ose contredire sa patronne.
He doesn't dare contradict his boss.

Je ne peux vous répondre.
I cannot give you an answer.

Elle ne cesse de se plaindre.
She never ceases to complain.

Pas is used alone in familiar spoken language, although it is not grammatically correct.

J'entends pas ce qu'il dit.
I can't hear what he is saying.

Tu parles pas assez fort.
You don't speak loud enough.

D. JEU DE MOTS

The verb *tomber* is used in many idiomatic expressions which may come in handy.

Vous tombez mal, je suis si occupée!
Bad timing! I'm so busy!

Luc tombe de sommeil, il devrait aller se coucher.
Luc is falling asleep on his feet; he should go to bed.

Nous sommes tombés en panne.
We broke down.

Elle n'est pas tombée de la dernière pluie.
   She wasn't born yesterday.

Les bras m'en sont tombés quand j'ai appris la nouvelle.
   I was flabbergasted when I heard the news.

Je suis sûr qu'il tombera dans l'oubli.
   I'm sure he'll fall into oblivion.

Leurs projets sont tombés à l'eau.
   Their plans fell through.

Le Nouvel An tombe un jeudi cette année.
   New Year's falls on a Thursday this year.

Ce n'est pas tombé dans l'oreille d'un sourd.
   It didn't fall on deaf ears.

Cela tombe sous le sens.
   It's obvious.

Je suis tombé des nues.
   I was completely taken aback.

Il est tombé sur la tête!
   He's got a screw loose!

Il est tombé amoureux.
   He fell in love.

Laisse tombé!
   Drop it!

E. LE COIN DES AFFAIRES

LA TÉLÉCOMMUNICATION (TELECOMMUNICATION)

In France, telephone, telegram, and postal services are all provided under the auspices of the government-run *PT (Poste et Télécommunications)*. Virtually all telephone services are controlled by the *DGT (Direction Générale des Télécommunications)*, though the move toward deregulation is in progress. The telecommunication industry is one of France's most successful sectors, with most of its circuits digitized. A direct-dial telephone system links France to the United States and the rest of the world. You are highly unlikely to run into any problems with the phone system in France. Calls to the United States may be charged to international telephone cards such as AT&T, MCI, and Sprint. Most public phones are operated by *télécartes* (phone cards) that can be purchased in post offices and subway and railway stations, as well as many newspaper stands and tobacco shops.

When dealing with clients over the phone, remember that French society tends to be more formal than ours. When calling a place of business, ask for your party by saying *Est-ce que je pourrais parler à . . . ?* (May I speak to . . . ?), or if you know your party's extension, be sure to specify it: *Passez-moi le poste . . .* (Give me extension . . .). If you reach someone's assistant or secretary, you will probably be asked, *C'est de la part de qui?* (May I ask who's calling?) and *C'est à quel sujet?* (You are calling in reference to?) If you're lucky, the next thing you'll hear after you respond is *Je vous le/la passe.* (I'm transferring your call to him/her.) Otherwise, you are likely to hear one of the following: *Il est en conférence.* (He's in a meeting.); *Elle est sortie.* (She stepped out.); *Il n'est pas disponible.* (He's not available at the moment.); or *Elle sera de retour dans une heure.* (She'll be back in an hour.). You can then respond with *Est-ce que je pourrais laisser un message?* (Can I leave a message?) or *Je rappellerai dans l'après-midi.* (I'll call back in the afternoon.). The secretary may then say, *Je lui transmettrai votre message* (I'll give him/her your message) or *Je lui dirai que vous avez appelé* (I'll tell her/him you called). If you are unsuccessful after several attempts and feel that you are being put off, be sure to remain very polite, as aggressiveness will probably prove counterproductive. Simply reiterate that your call is important.

In the early 1980s, *France Telecom,* operating under the *Ministère des Postes et Télécommunications,* launched an electronic telephone directory service to replace printed telephone books. A computer terminal called a *Minitel* was given to users free of charge to access the electronic database and conduct a search. Almost immediately, a plethora of additional services developed on the *Minitel,* including access to the stock exchange and international news services, as well as to French banking services, listings of French cultural events, weather and travel information, French magazines, home shopping services, and games. The French use Minitel to buy theater tickets, make reservations at their favorite restaurant, and book flights and trains. One of the most popular applications is on-line communication, much like Internet and E-mail. Minitel can also be accessed from the United States with a modem-equipped computer by contacting the Minitel Services Company at (212) 399-0080. Users in the United States are able to communicate with family and friends in France, learn French with "electronic" pen pals, and access most of the aforementioned services.

The French postal system handles many transactions other than delivering mail. You can wire money, open a savings account, and buy government bonds or life insurance, all at the post office. Naturally, you can also send regular letters, registered letters *(lettres recommandées),* and, in Paris, express messages that travel by compressed air under the streets *(pneumatiques).* Despite the advanced state of telecommunications in France, telegrams are still used to acknowledge major events, such as weddings *(Tous mes vœux de bonheur.),* funerals *(Mes sincères condoléances.),* and promotions *(Toutes mes félicitations.)* and can be sent from the post office. Most French post offices are open Monday through Friday from 9 A.M. to 7 P.M. and on Saturdays until noon. The main post office in Paris, located at *rue du Louvre,* is open twenty-four hours a day for select services.

France uses a five-digit zip code; the first digits designate the *département,* telling you where the letter you received comes from, and the others refer to the section of town or the *arrondissement.* For example, if you live in the *onzième arrondissement* in Paris, your postal code will be 75011. This information may prove useful, as address listings in the phone book or Minitel for Paris usually include only the *arrondissement,* not the entire postal code.

EXERCICES

A. *Remplacer les objets soulignés par un pronom objet direct ou indirect.*
(Replace the underlined objects with a direct or indirect object pronoun.)

1. *Julia téléphone à Luc d'une cabine.*
2. *Elle m'envoie le double du contrat.*
3. *Ils n'acceptent pas notre proposition.*
4. *Vous donnez des renseignements à Mme Balavoine.*
5. *Elle feuillette son carnet d'adresse.*
6. *Caroline donne le paquet à la cousine d'Hervé.*
7. *Nous avons oublié son numéro de téléphone.*
8. *Je ne vais pas reconnaître mon ancienne amie.*

B. *Remplacer les objets soulignés par un pronom objet direct et indirect.*

1. *Nous demandons l'indicatif numérique à la standardiste.*
2. *Mathilde a-t-elle envoyé son C.V. à M. Sabatier?*
3. *Sert-elle le meilleur champagne à l'amie de son fils?*
4. *Mathilde envoie la plus belle carte postale à Didier.*
5. *Mme Sabatier a donné le meilleur tuyau à Julia.*
6. *Nous annonçons la bonne nouvelle à nos clients.*
7. *Je donne l'adresse du salon de thé à ma belle-sœur.*
8. *Tu expliques les raisons de ton retard à tes collègues.*

C. *Mettre les phrases suivantes au futur immédiat.* (Put the following sentences in the future tense.)

1. *Julia fait la connaissance de Mme Balavoine vendredi.*
2. *Hervé téléphone à sa mère ce soir.*
3. *Nous déjeunons dans un salon de thé.*
4. *Sylvain reçoit beaucoup de messages.*
5. *Je lui offre un téléphone cellulaire.*

D. *Mettre au passé immédiat.*

1. *Je (raccrocher) quand il a frappé à la porte.*
2. *Il (acheter) un téléphone sans fil.*
3. *Elles (entrer) dans la chambre quand le téléphone a sonné.*
4. *Julia (arriver) à l'aéroport d'Orly.*
5. *Elle (partir) quand il a appelé.*

LEÇON 4

A. DIALOGUE

QU'EST-CE QU'ON PASSE[1] À LA TÉLÉ CE SOIR?

Sabine et Lodge passent la soirée à regarder la télévision.

SCARLETT: **Mais je sais que je t'aime.**

RHETT: **C'est bien là ton malheur.**

SCARLETT: **Oh! Rhett! Rhett! Si tu t'en vas, que vais-je devenir, où vais-je aller?**

RHETT: **Franchement ma chère, je m'en fiche complètement!**

LODGE: **Je rêve ou quoi?**

SABINE: **Mais non, c'est bien *Autant en emporte le Vent!***

LODGE: **Je n'ai pas fait cinq mille kilomètres pour entendre Clark Gable doublé!**

SABINE: **Voyons ce qu'il y a sur France Deux[2] . . . Ah! *Bouillon de Culture!*[3]**

LODGE: ***Bouillon de Culture!* Quel drôle[4] de nom!**

SABINE: **C'est une émission hebdomadaire[5] dont l'objectif est de promouvoir les livres et la culture au sens large du terme.**

LODGE: **"Des têtes parlantes" à la télé, c'est plus efficace qu'un somnifère! Il n'y a que les Français pour aimer ça!**

SABINE: **Tu te trompes! Ces débats passionnants suscitent souvent des discussions enflammées sur le plateau!**

LODGE: **Enflammées!!!**

SABINE: **Puisque tout est trop américain ou trop français . . . prends la télécommande et débrouille-toi!**

LODGE: **Ah! De la pub! La publicité française, ça j'adore—une véritable énigme!**

SABINE: **Une énigme?**

LODGE: **Absolument! Il faut toujours deviner de quel produit il s'agit. Une femme tient en laisse une panthère; elle embrasse un homme dans le Parc Monceau,[6] et surprise . . . c'est une pub pour la dernière Citroën!**

SABINE: **Au moins, c'est bon pour ta matière grise, ça fait marcher ton imagination. À propos d'imagination et de créativité . . . mets donc Canal Plus.[2]**

LODGE: Canal Plus?

SABINE: Oui, c'est une chaîne payante très branchée[7] qui diffuse des films récents, les meilleurs documentaires et même des actualités américaines sous-titrées!

LODGE: C'est cette chaîne?

SABINE: Non, c'est la suivante.

LODGE: Mon Dieu! *Les Golden Girls*!

SABINE: Ah! oui, *Les Craquantes*. Allez, zappe[8] et tais-toi!

LODGE: Ce qui m'étonne le plus, c'est que vous, les Français, vous ne cessez de vous plaindre de l'invasion américaine dans votre culture, mais chaque fois qu'on change de chaîne, on tombe sur une émission étrangère et moi je sais très bien ce que tu regardes!

SABINE: À vrai dire, je n'ai guère le temps de regarder la télé.

LODGE: Ça, c'est la meilleure! L'année dernière, tu m'appelais régulièrement à Washington pour savoir le dénouement de ton feuilleton favori.

SABINE: Tiens, regarde, ça c'est un film bien français qui jouit[9] d'un grand succès: un film policier avec beaucoup de suspens!

LODGE: Tu es sûre que c'est un film français? J'ai l'impression . . .

SABINE: Méfie-toi de tes impressions! Là, c'est vous, les Américains qui avez fait un remake de *La femme Nikita* avec Bridget Fonda.[10]

LODGE: Tu sais, j'aimerais bien regarder un peu de sport . . .

SABINE: Du sport! Ce que tu vas trouver à cette heure-ci, c'est sans doute[11] un match de catch.[12]

LODGE: De quoi?

SABINE: De catch! Et peut-être même de catch féminin.

LODGE: Ah non! Tout mais pas ça! Je sais qu'il est tard, mais si on allait prendre un verre à la brasserie du coin?

WHAT'S ON TELEVISION TONIGHT?

Sabine and Lodge spend the evening watching television.

SCARLETT: But I know I love you.

RHETT: That's your misfortune.

SCARLETT: Oh! Rhett! Rhett! If you go, what shall I do, where will I go?

RHETT: Frankly my dear, I don't give a damn!

LODGE: Am I dreaming or what?

SABINE: No, it's *Gone With the Wind*!

LODGE: I didn't travel three thousand miles to hear Clark Gable dubbed!

SABINE: Let's see what's on France Two . . . Oh! *Bouillon de Culture*!

LODGE: *Bouillon de Culture*! What a strange name!

SABINE: It's a weekly show whose goal is to promote books and culture in the broad sense of the term.

LODGE: "Talking heads" on television are more efficient than a sleeping pill! Only the French would like that!

SABINE: You're wrong! These fascinating debates often generate heated discussions on the set.

LODGE: Heated!!!

SABINE: Since everything is either too American or too French, take the remote control, and do it yourself.

LODGE: Oh! Commercials! I love French advertising—a real enigma!

SABINE: An enigma?

LODGE: Absolutely! You always have to guess what product they're selling. A woman holds a panther on a leash, she kisses a man in the *Parc Monceau,* and surprise . . . it's an ad for the latest Citroën!

SABINE: At least it's good for your gray matter and stimulates your imagination. Speaking of imagination and creativity . . . turn to *Canal Plus.*

LODGE: *Canal Plus?*

SABINE: Yes. It's a very trendy pay channel that broadcasts recent films, the best documentaries, and even American news with subtitles!

LODGE: Is it this channel?

SABINE: No, the next one.

LODGE: My God! *The Golden Girls*!

SABINE: Oh, yes! *Les Craquantes*! Come on, change the channel and keep quiet!

LODGE: What is amazing is that you, the French, never stop complaining about the American invasion of your culture, but every time you change the channel, you come across a foreign show, and I know very well what you watch!

SABINE: Actually, I don't have much time to watch television.

LODGE: Listen to this one! Last year, you called me regularly in Washington to find out the ending of your favorite show!

SABINE: Look! This is a typically French film that's enjoying great success: a detective story with a lot of suspense.

LODGE: Are you sure it's a French film? I have a feeling . . .

SABINE: Don't trust your feelings! In this case, it is you, the Americans, who did a remake of *La Femme Nikita* with Bridget Fonda.

LODGE: You know, I'd like to watch a little bit of sports.

SABINE: Sports! What you'll find at this hour is probably a wrestling match!

LODGE: What?

SABINE: Wrestling! And maybe even women's wrestling.

LODGE: Oh! No! Anything but that! I know it's late but . . . what about going for a drink at the brasserie on the corner?

B. EN BREF

1. The verb *passer* can take on different meanings, depending on how it's used. *On passe un film à la télé.* (They're showing a film on television.) *Sabine passera un examen jeudi.* (Sabine will take an exam on Thursday.) *Nous passerons nos vacances en Grèce.* (We'll spend our vacation in Greece.) *Que se passe-t-il?* (What's happening?)

2. *France 2* and *France 3* are public channels. Private channels include *TF1, Arte* (coproduction with Germany), and *M6. Canal Plus* is the main cable station, which broadcasts documentaries, recent feature films, and educational programs. *Eurovision* is a new pay channel.

3. *Bouillon de Culture* (literally: "culture bubble") is a weekly TV show on which writers and artists of all kinds discuss their work.

4. When *drôle* follows a noun, it means "funny, amusing," but when *drôle de* precedes a noun, it means "strange, weird, phoney." Compare *une histoire drôle* (a funny story) and *une situation drôle* (an amusing situation) with *un drôle de type* (a strange guy) and *une drôle d'idée* (a strange idea). *La drôle de guerre* ("the phony war") is commonly used to refer to the period between September 1939 and May 1940 when World War II had officially begun, but the Germans had not yet invaded France.

5. *Quotidien* (daily), *hebdomadaire* (weekly), *mensuel* (monthly), *annuel* (yearly).

6. The *Parc Monceau*, located in a fashionable area of Paris, northeast of the *Champs-Élysées,* is the home of the *Cernuschi* and *Nissim de Camondo* museums. The design of the park began in 1778 for Philippe d'Orléans. The objective was to create a land of illusion with many exotic buildings, such as pyramids and pagodas. The park is famous for its wrought-iron entrance gates, numerous statues, and magnificent old trees.

7. You are *à la mode* (fashionable, trendy) if you are *branché* (literally, "plugged in"), *câblé* (literally, "cabled in"), or *en vogue* (literally, "with the flow").

8. *Zapper* is a colloquial term for *changer de chaîne* (to change channels).

9. *Jouir de* is another versatile verb: *Ils jouissent de toutes leurs facultés.* (They are in full possession of all their faculties.) *Il jouit d'une santé solide.* (He enjoys good health.) *Elle jouit d'une grande fortune.* (She is very wealthy.) Note that this verb may take on sexual connotations (when used by itself) and should be used with extra care.

10. The French film *La femme Nikita* was adapted by the American film industry and called *Point of No Return.* Other popular American films that were based on French originals include *Three Men and a Baby (Trois hommes et un couffin), Cousins (Cousin, cousine), A Man and a Woman (Un homme et une femme),* and *Sommersby (Le retour de Martin Guerre).*

11. *Sans doute:* probably; *sans aucun doute:* without a doubt.

12. Be sure not to confuse *le catch* with *la lutte.* The former refers to staged wrestling matches (similar to "Wrestlemania" in the United States), while the latter refers to the sport of wrestling. Also, *la boxe* is boxing. French philosopher and semiologist Roland Barthes offers an interesting interpretation of wrestling and other modern myths in his book *Mythologies.*

C. GRAMMAIRE ET USAGE

1. *LA COMPARAISON* (COMPARISON)

a. Le comparatif.
The comparatives of superiority and inferiority are formed by placing *plus . . . que* (more . . . than) or *moins . . . que* (less . . . than) around the point of comparison.

Cet acteur est plus populaire à l'étranger que dans son pays.
This actor is more popular abroad than in his own country.

Cette émission est moins appréciée par les adultes que par les adolescents.
This program is less appreciated by adults than by teenagers.

Likewise, equality (as . . . as) is expressed by *aussi . . . que* with adjectives and adverbs and by *autant . . . que* with verbs.

Cette méthode est aussi efficace qu'une autre.
This method is as efficient as another one.

Les présentateurs de cette chaîne sont aussi ennuyeux les uns que les autres.
One anchor on this channel is as boring as the next.

Le nouvel acteur de ce feuilleton joue aussi bien que les autres.
The new actor in this series acts as well as the others.

Elle ne travaille pas autant que vous.
She doesn't work as much as you do.

Les enfants souffrent autant que les adultes.
Children suffer as much as adults do.

Some adjectives and adverbs have irregular comparative forms:

REGULAR FORM	COMPARATIVE FORM
bon	*meilleur*
mauvais	*plus mauvais* (with concrete nouns)
	pire (with abstract nouns)
bien	*mieux*
mal	*plus mal*
	pis
petit	*plus petit* (with concrete nouns)
	moindre (with abstract nouns)

Il n'y a pas de meilleure émission que celle-là.
There is no better program than this one.

Je n'ai pas la moindre idée de ce qui lui est arrivé.
I don't have the slightest idea what happened to him.

C'est une émission de moindre qualité.
It's a show of lesser quality.

C'est le plus mauvais gâteau que nous ayons jamais mangé.
It's the worse cake we have ever eaten.

b. Le comparatif analytique.
The *comparatif analytique* is used in French as in English. Each clause begins with the comparative term *(plus, moins, aussi/autant).*

Plus ils gagnent d'argent, plus ils en dépensent.
The more money they earn, the more they spend.

Plus le Calvados est vieux, meilleur il est.
The older the Calvados, the better it is.

Plus ce qu'elle mangeait était bon, plus elle se sentait heureuse.[1]
The better the food, the happier she was.

Plus on est de fous, plus on rit.
The more, the merrier.

Moins il en fait, moins il veut en faire.
The less he does, the less he wants to do.

Plus il regarde la télévision, moins ça l'intéresse.
The more he watches television, the less it interests him.

Autant il est sympathique avec nous, autant il est odieux avec eux.
He is as nice with us as he is obnoxious with them.

Autant l'Est est en essor, autant le Nord est en déclin.
The East is expanding as much as the North is declining.

c. Le superlatif.
The superlative is used when comparing three or more things. It is formed with the definite article and the comparative form *(plus, moins, aussi/autant).*

C'est le présentateur le plus aimé du public.[2]
He is the anchor most favored by the public.

C'est le meilleur court-métrage que France 2 ait jamais présenté.
It's the best short film *France 2* has ever shown.

---

[1] Note that in this type of construction *plus . . . bon* should be used instead of *meilleur.*

[2] The adjective will be placed before or after the noun, depending on its length and the sound of the expression.

C'est la pire représentation à laquelle j'aie jamais assisté.
  It's the worst performance I ever attended.

C'est le plus grand écran du[3] monde.
  It's the biggest screen in the world.

As in English, some adjectives are inherently superlative: *unique, principal, favori, mineur, majeur, aîné, cadet.*

Sabine est ma sœur aînée.
  Sabine is my older sister.

Mon metteur en scène favori est Beineix.
  My favorite film director is Beineix.

And some adjectives simply cannot be compared[4] *(premier, dernier, double, triple, parallèle, carré, rectangulaire, superbe, formidable, exquis, excellent . . .).*

C'est une actrice exquise.
  She's an exquisite actress.

The suffix *-issime* also expresses a superlative idea. It is very commonly used and means "of the highest degree." For example: *rarissime, illustrissime, éminentissime, excellentissime, richissime, sérénissime, modernissime.*

Il a rencontré un journaliste illustrissime.
  He met an extremely famous journalist.

C'est un chef-d'œuvre rarissime.
  It is an extremely rare masterpiece.

2. *LES PRONOMS RELATIFS* (RELATIVE PRONOUNS)

a. The simple forms.
qui, que, quoi, dont, où.
The relative pronoun you choose will depend on its function within the relative clause.[5]

Qui (who, which, that) refers to people and things and acts as the subject of the relative clause.

Le feuilleton qui passe sur Canal Plus fait un tabac.
  The series that is on *Canal Plus* is a big hit.

---

[3] With superlatives, use *du, de la, des.*
[4] Unless they are meant as a joke: *Elle est plus enceinte que sa sœur.* (She is more pregnant than her sister.)
[5] A relative clause is a dependent clause introduced by a relative pronoun.

56

L'actrice qui incarne le personnage d'Emma Bovary est trop froide.
The actress who plays the part of Emma Bovary is too cold.

Que (which, whom, that) also refers to people and things but acts as the object of the action in the relative clause.

Le film que nous regardons est sous-titré.
The film that we are watching is subtitled.

La pièce que vous avez vue était diffusée en direct de la Comédie française.
The play you saw was broadcast live from the *Comédie française.*

Quoi (what) only refers to things. It follows a preposition or is used in sentences without verbs.

Quoi de neuf?
What's new?

Acceptez son offre, sans quoi vous le regretterez.
Accept his offer, otherwise you'll regret it.

Chez eux, il y a toujours de quoi boire et manger.
At their house, there is always plenty to drink and to eat.

Dont acts as an object and can refer to people or things. It is used to refer to objects of verbs that are followed by the preposition *de.*

Le documentaire dont il se souvient sera diffusé sur Canal Plus *à vingt-deux heures.*
The documentary he remembers will be broadcast on *Canal Plus* at 10 P.M.

Le journaliste dont vous parlez est actuellement en Afrique.
The journalist you're talking about is presently in Africa.

The pronouns *de qui, duquel, de laquelle, desquels, desquelles* can be used instead of *dont,* but *dont* is more common in modern French.

La présentatrice dont (de laquelle) je parle s'appelle Christine Germain.
The anchorwoman I'm talking about is called Christine Germain.

Dont can also mean "among which/whom."

Cette chaîne a présenté plusieurs spectacles de variétés dont trois étaient de qualité exceptionnelle.
This channel aired several variety shows, three of which were of exceptional quality.

Quatre personnes vous attendent dont Sabine.
Four people are waiting for you, Sabine among them.

The relative pronoun *où* means "where" and is generally used to indicate location. It can sometimes be translated into English by "when" (*le moment où:* "the moment when").

Il rêve d'une télévision où les films ne seraient jamais doublés.
He dreams of a network where films would never be dubbed.

Au train où vont les choses, on verra de plus en plus d'émissions en langue étrangère.
The way things are going, we'll be seeing more and more shows in a foreign language.

Nous cherchons une villa au bord de la mer où passer nos vacances.
We are looking for a villa at the seashore where we can spend our vacation.

Le programme a eu du succès du jour où il a commencé.
The show was successful from the day it started.

The indefinite relative pronouns *ce qui, ce que, ce à quoi, ce dont* translate into English as "what" or "that which." When placed at the beginning of the sentence, they are used for emphasis. They have no specific antecedent and can refer to things, ideas, or situations, but never to people.

Ce qui lui plaît dans ces débats littéraires, c'est la diversité des invités.
What he likes in these literary debates is the diversity of the guests.

Ce que nous regrettons, c'est le manque de variété.
What we regret is the lack of variety.

Ce dont il se plaint, c'est de la bêtise de certains programmes.
What he complains about is the stupidity of some of the shows.

Ce à quoi je m'attendais, c'était à une présentation du sujet beaucoup plus sérieuse.
What I expected was a much more serious presentation of the subject.

J'ignore ce à quoi il s'intéresse.
I don't know what he is interested in.

b. The compound forms.
Lequel is used when a preposition (*à, sur, avec, dans, pour,* etc.) precedes the relative pronoun. In most instances, it refers to things. While it is correct to use *lequel* with people, *qui* is more common.

Le producteur pour qui (pour lequel) il travaille est exigeant.
The producer for whom he works is demanding.

Les feuilletons auxquels Sabine s'intéresse sont souvent doublés.
The series Sabine is interested in are often dubbed.

58

Les émissions sur lesquelles on tombe sont parfois ridicules.
The shows we come across are sometimes ridiculous.

La publicité dans laquelle la panthère se promène dans le Parc Monceau est très drôle.
The commercial in which the panther walks around the *Parc Monceau* is very funny.

After the prepositions *parmi* and *entre,* always use *lequel,* whether referring to people or things.

Les figurants parmi lesquels nous nous trouvions se préparaient à monter sur le plateau.
The extras, among whom we found ourselves, were getting ready to go on the set.

Les candidats entre lesquels ils ont dû choisir n'avaient guère de talent.
The candidates among whom they had to choose did not have much talent.

D. JEU DE MOTS

The verb *ficher* (to fix) and its reflexive counterpart *se ficher* are used in many colloquial expressions.

Qui est-ce qui lui a fichu cette idée dans la tête?
Who put this idea in his/her head?

Il est entré dans son bureau et il a fichu ses dossiers par terre.
He entered his office and chucked all his files on the floor.

Ça fiche tout par terre!
That ruins everything!

Fiche-moi la paix!
Leave me alone!

S'il ne travaille pas plus sérieusement, je le fiche à la porte.
If he doesn't work more seriously, I'm firing him!

Son assistant n'a rien fichu de la journée.
His assistant didn't do a darn thing all day long.

Il est dix heures! Qu'est-ce que tu fichais?
It's ten o'clock! What the heck were you doing?

Qui est-ce qui m'a fichu un imbécile pareil!
How stupid can you get!

Il se fiche pas mal de ce que vous pensez.
He couldn't care less about what you think.

Tu devrais le laisser tomber—c'est évident qu'il se fiche de toi.
You should drop him—it's obvious he's leading you on.

Fais attention! Elle a un fichu caractère.
Watch out! She's got a lousy temper.

Il ne viendra pas ce soir parce qu'il est mal fichu.
He won't come tonight because he feels under the weather.

Tel que je le connais, il est fichu d'arriver en retard.
Knowing him, he's quite likely to arrive late.

E. LE COIN DES AFFAIRES

LA PUBLICITÉ
(PUBLIC RELATIONS / ADVERTISING)

The fields of advertising, marketing, and public relations are fairly new in France. The approach to promoting a product may be quite different and may use different venues from those in the United States. French ads tend to be more abstract and suggestive than ads for the U.S. market, and the name of the product is understated. Humor, especially a play on words, and pop culture are also very popular advertising gimmicks. For example, a male underwear manufacturer used the slogan *Les hommes préfèrent les Jil* (Men prefer "Jils"), alluding to Marilyn Monroe, to promote their line.

The fastest-growing venue for advertising in France is television, but print ads still hold a majority of the market. Magazine ads are very similar to those in America and are featured in nationally circulated publications. Many French magazines are distributed internationally, as well, providing added exposure. Newspapers in France are generally local publications and are not distributed nationwide. Major papers, such as *Le Monde*, have urban and regional editions, providing advertisers with the option of targeting specific regions or groups.

Since the introduction of cable television and privately owned networks in the mid-1980s, France has seen a boom in television advertising, though it remains much more heavily regulated than in the United States. The following industries cannot advertise on television: alcohol, tobacco, publishing (both press and books), cinema, and merchandise distributors (e.g., supermarkets and mail-order businesses). Political parties and candidates are also on this exclusion list. While they cannot air commercials, these groups can sponsor television shows and events. The constraints on what is acceptable on television also extend to the technical aspects of advertising, such as the duration of the commercials, the allowance of only one commercial interruption per show, and in certain cases even censorship of the contents.

Direct-mail services and marketing have exhibited tremendous growth since the early 1980s. All mailings, brochures, instructions, labels, and warranties should be written in French. It is best to hire French copy-writers and consult the U.S. Chamber of Commerce for labeling guidelines, which are rather strict. American manufacturers should also keep in mind, as a possible asset, the environmental symbols that were introduced by the European Union. These markings apply to environmentally friendly and recyclable products and are designed to encourage consumers to purchase products that comply with EU environmental protection policies.

The most underdeveloped sector of communications in France is public relations. This is in great part due to the French perspective on dealing with the media. While contact with the press is prized as one of the major tools for creating a positive corporate image in the United States, in France it is considered a necessary evil. Not surprisingly, the role of communications directors in France is also quite different than in the United States. In most American companies, public relations departments are well- and long-established entities, run by high-level executives specifically trained and educated in communications. In France, these departments are relatively new. Many used to employ former journalists, but today they are run by specialized professionals, many of whom formerly worked as press attachés.

Unlike American communications directors, French *dircoms*—as they are called—do not have the authority to speak for the company. They are seldom quoted in the press and act more as liaisons between the *PDG* and the press. The relative inexperience of the industry may provide a good opportunity for more American public relations firms to offer their expertise and expand their operations to France.

For those Americans interested in advertising their own products in France, there are specialized firms dealing with market research in France. The U.S. Chamber of Commerce also conducts its own market research in fields of interest, and the figures may be obtained by contacting the France desk.

EXERCICES

A. *Comparer comme dans l'exemple.* (Compare as in the example.)

MODÈLE: *La chaîne 1/la chaîne 5/variée. (−)*
La chaîne 1 est moins variée que la chaîne 5.

1. *Les débats/les feuilletons/intéressants. (+)*
2. *Le présentateur de la 2/le présentateur de la 5/séduisant. (−)*
3. *Cet acteur/cette actrice/bon. (−)*

4. *Les films doublés/les films sous-titrés/agaçants.* (+)
5. *Leur publicité/la vôtre/originale.* (−)

B. *Mettre au superlatif comme dans l'exemple.*

MODÈLE: *L'acteur/connu/États-Unis.* (+)
   C'est l'acteur le plus connu des États-Unis.

1. *Le festival/renommé/pays.* (+)
2. *Le film policier/populaire/année.* (+)
3. *Le présentateur/amusant/cette chaîne.* (−)
4. *L'actrice/belle/festival.* (+)
5. *Le magazine hebdomadaire/regardé/toutes les chaînes.* (−)

C. *Compléter en employant des pronoms relatifs.*

1. *Le journal télévisé _____ vous regardez chaque soir est diffusé dans plusieurs pays du monde.*
2. *L'émission _____ tu penses a été remplacée par un feuilleton.*
3. *Voudriez-vous visiter le studio dans _____ cette émission a été tournée?*
4. *Le projecteur _____ il a besoin est au sous-sol.*
5. *Les acteurs _____ vont passer l'audition ont le trac.*
6. *Connais-tu les personnes parmi _____ tu te trouvais hier soir?*
7. *_____ est insupportable, ce sont tous ces films doublés!*
8. *Savez-vous _____ il s'intéresse?*
9. *_____ vous vous plaignez est un problème difficile à résoudre.*
10. *_____ de neuf?*

D. *Traduire.*

1. The more I study, the more I learn.
2. What I need is a television with a larger screen.
3. I don't remember the film you're talking about.
4. When will they broadcast the documentary? I don't have the slightest idea.
5. They are extremely rich.
6. It's the worst series I have ever seen.
7. What I hate is the advertising!
8. Catherine is my younger sister.
9. Can you guess what it's about?
10. This weekly show is a big hit.

LEÇON 5

A. DIALOGUE

RENDEZ-VOUS AVEC UN DÉCORATEUR.

Joan, directrice de marketing à Dallas, a été mutée[1] à Paris. Brice, décorateur, et Romain, ébéniste,[2] lui font quelques suggestions pour la décoration de son logement: un vieil[3] appartement dans le quinzième arrondissement.[4]

BRICE: Un lit en laiton,[5] une housse[6] de couette[7] en coton damassé réversible rouge et jaune, des taies d'oreiller, des doubles rideaux assortis et cette chambre sera digne d'une reine!

JOAN: J'ai vraiment besoin de doubles rideaux?

BRICE: Ces fenêtres ne sont pas des plus étanches.[8] Des rideaux en velours vous protégeront des éventuels[9] courants d'air et habilleront ce coin.

JOAN: La chambre a besoin d'un bon coup de peinture.

BRICE: Il vaudrait mieux poser du papier peint ou tendre du tissu. Une soie sauvage[10] écrue ou rose pâle mettrait en relief vos tableaux et créerait une ambiance plus romantique.

ROMAIN: Brice a le chic[11] pour conjuguer la rigueur et le raffinement.

JOAN: Et où est-ce que je vais mettre toutes mes affaires? Il n'y a pas un seul placard dans cette chambre!

BRICE: Cette chambre mansardée est dotée d'un charme rarissime; je vois très bien un semainier[12] en érable et une armoire en merisier. Qu'en penses-tu, Romain?

ROMAIN: Une armoire picarde[13] mettrait en valeur ce pan de mur.

JOAN: Picarde?

ROMAIN: Ah! Madame! Les Picards sont les virtuoses de la sculpture sur bois. Leurs armoires aux moulures complexes sont d'une finesse exceptionnelle.

JOAN: Mais cela va coûter les yeux de la tête![14]

ROMAIN: Pas du tout! Les reproductions sont "vieillies" dans nos ateliers pour prendre une apparence ancienne: trous de vers, petites taches,[15] traces d'usure, le tout fini à la cire d'abeille. Et nous posons des étagères en châtaignier pour chasser les mites, les araignées et autre vermine!

JOAN: De la vermine?

BRICE: Une mesure de précaution . . . Au fait, j'ai vu une coiffeuse[16] à l'Hôtel Drouot[17] qui irait à la perfection entre ces deux fenêtres. Vous avez l'air surprise, Joan?

JOAN: Je n'ai guère le temps de m'asseoir devant la coiffeuse, mais je vous fais entièrement confiance.

BRICE: Alors, passons au salon.

JOAN: Le coin salle à manger importe peu. J'envisage de donner un cocktail au moins une fois par mois et je voudrais exploiter au maximum l'espace du salon.

BRICE: Dans ce cas, je vous conseille de faire poncer et vitrifier le parquet, puis de mettre un grand tapis[18] devant la cheminée.

JOAN: Un tapis?

BRICE: Votre canapé, vos deux fauteuils crapaud,[19] une fois recouverts de taffetas aux couleurs flamboyantes et deux ou trois poufs[20] feront la joie de vos invités.

ROMAIN: Sans oublier des coussins moelleux[21] assortis au canapé.

JOAN: Quel est le prix de ce taffetas Sully,[22] Brice?

BRICE: Celui-ci coûte environ deux cent vingt francs le mètre en cent trente[23] de large et c'est la bonne largeur . . . Oh! Ce petit secrétaire en noyer ferait plus d'effet dans l'entrée en face du guéridon.

JOAN: Vous ne craignez pas que ça jure?[24]

BRICE: Non, pas du tout. Et il faut oser les contrastes, quitte à choquer les puristes.

JOAN: Au fait, avez-vous réfléchi à ma table basse?[25]

ROMAIN: Ah! Madame! On ne trouve pas de tables basses d'époque!

BRICE: Allons, Romain, ce ne sera pas la première fois que tu coupes les pieds[26] d'une table ancienne!

ROMAIN: Bon, je verrai ce que je peux faire pour vous, Madame.

BRICE: Ce qui me gêne le plus, c'est le manque de lumière. Cette toile de jute tendue sur les murs est trop sombre. Une peinture à l'éponge ocre jaune dynamiserait les murs. Avec cela, quelques appliques et des abat-jour plus clairs et le tour sera joué.

JOAN: Vous avez vraiment pensé à tout!

BRICE: Et je me ferai un plaisir de vous emmener au marché aux puces de Saint-Ouen un dimanche matin pour choisir quelques faïences.

Meeting with an Interior Designer.

Joan, a marketing director from Dallas, has been transferred to Paris. Brice, a decorator, and Romain, a cabinetmaker, give her some suggestions for decorating her home: an old apartment in the fifteenth *arrondissement*.

BRICE: A brass bed, a down quilt cover in reversible red and yellow damask cotton, pillowcases, matching drapes, and this bedroom will be worthy of a queen.

JOAN: Do I really need drapes?

BRICE: These windows are not the most airtight. Velvet drapes will protect you from possible drafts and will dress up this corner.

JOAN: The bedroom does need a paint job.

BRICE: It would be better to put up some wallpaper or fabric. An écru or light pink raw silk would enhance your paintings and create a more romantic ambience.

ROMAIN: Brice has a knack for combining rigor and refinement.

JOAN: Where will I put all my things? There isn't a single closet in this room!

BRICE: The sloping ceiling of this room gives it a rare charm; I see a maple *semainier* and a wild-cherry armoire. What do you think of that, Romain?

ROMAIN: A Picard armoire would enhance this section of the wall.

JOAN: Picard?

ROMAIN: Oh! Madam! The people of Picardy are master woodcarvers. Their armoires with intricate molding are exceptionally refined.

JOAN: That's going to cost an arm and a leg!

ROMAIN: Not at all! The reproductions are "aged" in our workshops to give an antique appearance: wormholes, small stains, wear-and-tear marks, and everything polished with beeswax. We add chestnut shelves to scare away moths, spiders, and other vermin!

JOAN: Vermin!

BRICE: Just to be safe . . . By the way, I saw a dressing table at the Drouot auction house that would fit perfectly between these two windows. Joan, you look surprised?

JOAN: I don't have much leisure time to sit in front of a dressing table, but I trust you completely.

BRICE: So, let's move to the living room.

JOAN: The dining room corner doesn't matter much. I plan to give a cocktail party at least once a month, and I'd like to maximize the living room space.

BRICE: In that case, I would advise you to sand and polyurethane the floors, then place a large rug in front of the fireplace.

JOAN: A rug?

BRICE: Your sofa, your two squat armchairs covered with fiery colored taffeta, and two or three *poufs* will be your guests' delight.

ROMAIN: Let's not forget some soft cushions to match the sofa.

JOAN: Brice, how much does the Sully taffeta cost?

BRICE: This one is about forty-five dollars a yard; it's four feet wide, which is the right width. Oh! This small walnut desk would look nicer in the foyer right across from the pedestal table.

JOAN: You're not worried it would clash?

BRICE: No, not at all. One must be audacious with contrasts, even at the risk of shocking the purists.

JOAN: By the way, have you given some thought to my coffee table?

ROMAIN: Oh! Madam! Period coffee tables do not exist!

BRICE: Come now, Romain! It won't be the first time you cut the legs of an antique table!

ROMAIN: All right, I'll see what I can do for you, Madam.

BRICE: What bothers me the most is the lack of light. This burlap on the walls is too dark. An ochre sponge paint would jazz up the walls. A few lighter-colored wall lamps and shades will do the trick.

JOAN: You really thought of everything!

BRICE: And I'll be delighted to take you to the Saint-Ouen flea market on a Sunday morning to choose a few earthenware pieces.

B. EN BREF

1. "To transfer" can be translated into French in many different ways, depending on the context: *Nous avons transféré des fonds dans une banque française.* (We transferred funds to a French bank.) *Elle n'étudie plus l'histoire de l'art, elle s'est réorientée en anthropologie.* (She transferred from the art history to the anthropology department.) *Son frère a reporté sa colère sur elle.* (Her brother transferred his anger onto her.) *Il a décalqué le dessin.* (He transferred the drawing.)

2. *Un ébéniste* makes expensive furniture, often reproductions of period pieces. *Un menuisier* makes basic cabinetry. *Un charpentier* makes the frame of a building.

3. Remember that *beau, vieux,* and *nouveau* become *bel, vieil,* and *nouvel* in front of a masculine singular noun beginning with a vowel: *un bel assortiment* (a beautiful assortment), *un vieil ébéniste* (an old cabinetmaker), *un nouvel artisan* (a young craftsperson).

4. Paris is divided into twenty *arrondissements,* which start in the center of Paris and spiral outward clockwise. Each *arrondissement,* or administrative subdivision, has its own city hall.

5. The word "brass" can be translated in several ways: *Des lits jumeaux en laiton.* (Brass twin beds.) *Un orchestre de cuivres.* (A brass band.) *Astiquer les cuivres.* (To clean the brass.) *Les grosses huiles assisteront à la soirée.* (The top brass will attend the party.)

6. The term *housse* has many different usages: *Elle emporte toujours une housse à vêtements en voyage.* (She always takes a garment bag when traveling.) *Les draps-housses sont très pratiques.* (Fitted sheets are very practical.) *Ils ont mis des housses sur leurs sièges de voiture à cause de leur chien.* (They placed covers on their car seats because of their dog.)

7. Do not confuse *le duvet* (down) with *une couette* (a down quilt) and *une housse de couette* (a quilt cover, known as a duvet in the United States).

8. *Une montre étanche.* (A waterproof watch.) *Ce manteau est imperméable.* (This coat is waterproof.) *Cette armoire est ignifugée.* (This armoire is fireproof.) *Cette chambre est insonorisée.* (This room is soundproof.)

9. Be sure not to confuse *éventuellement* with its look-alike "eventually." *J'aurais éventuellement besoin de vos conseils.* (It is quite possible I'll need your advice.) *Nous pourrions éventuellement vous prêter notre voiture.* (We could possibly lend you our car.) But: *Ne t'en fais pas, il finira bien par rénover son appartement.* (Don't worry, he'll eventually renovate his apartment.) *Elle s'y est habituée à la longue.* (She eventually got used to it.)

10. *Sauvage* has different meanings, depending on context. *Cet enfant est très sauvage.* (This child is very shy.) *Elle a choisi un papier peint avec des animaux sauvages.* (She chose a wallpaper with wild animals.) *C'est de la concurrence sauvage!* (This is unfair competition!) *Le camping sauvage est illégal dans certaines régions.* (Unauthorized camping is prohibited in some areas.) *Leur dernière grève sauvage a duré quatre mois.* (Their last wildcat strike lasted four months.)

11. *Chic* is widely used in France. It can be used as a noun or an adjective (in which case it is invariable, i.e., it does not agree with the noun to which it refers). *Cette décoratrice porte toujours des robes très chic.* (This decorator always wears elegant dresses.) *Il a été très chic avec nous quand nous avons eu tous ces ennuis.* (He was very nice to us when we had all those problems.) *Chic, on va aux puces!* (Great, we're going to the flea market.) *Ils ont le chic pour décorer leur maison.* (They have a knack for decorating their house.)

12. A *semainier* is a tall, narrow chest with seven drawers. It was designed, as its name suggests, to store a week's supply of clothing (one drawer for each day of the week).

13. *Picardie,* a province north of Paris, is the home of talented woodcarvers. In the sixteenth century, they made the famous choir stalls in the Amiens cathedral. These stalls are considered one of the finest collections of wood sculpture in France.

14. The French have many colorful expressions for saying that something is expensive. *Nous avons dîné dans un nouveau restaurant du Marais; c'était le véritable coup de fusil/coup de barre/coup de bambou.* (We ate in a new restaurant in the *Marais;* the prices were exorbitant.) *Il a failli s'évanouir car la note était salée.* (He almost fainted because the bill was rather steep.) *Cette armoire picarde est hors de portée.* (This Picard armoire is too expensive.)

15. Be careful with homonyms: *la tache* (stain), *la tâche* (task), *Tâche d'y penser.* (Try to remember it.)

16. *Une coiffeuse* is either a woman who does your hair or a small vanity table.

17. The auction house *Hôtel Drouot* was built in 1852. About 350,000 pieces are sold each year. Items are on display the day before an auction between 11 A.M. and noon.

18. *Un tapis.* (A rug.) *Une moquette.* (Wall-to-wall carpeting.)

19. *Crapaud* armchairs appeared in the nineteenth century and were in fashion during the Second Empire. They have short legs, often masked by a skirt with flounces or fringes, and are called "toads" because of their squat shape.

20. *Poufs,* big cushions placed right on the floor, are named after the sound they make when one sits on them.

21. If a cushion is nice and fluffy, it is *moelleux*. If it is nice and soft like satin, it is *doux*. And if it is too soft, i.e., not hard enough to support the back, it is *trop mou*.

22. Fabric is often named after historical figures. The Duke of Sully (1560–1641) was the treasurer under Henry IV. He encouraged agriculture and supported the effort to raise silkworms. He is best known for saying: *"Labourage et pâturage sont les deux mamelles dont la France est alimentée."* (Tilling and grazing are the two breasts that feed France.)

23. The measuring unit is always understood in each field and does not need to be stated. With fabric, 130 refers to 130 centimeters, which has traditionally been the standard width for fabric.

24. *Jurer* (to swear) has a double meaning in French as in English. Be careful how you use it. *Il a juré devant ses parents.* (He cursed in front of his parents.) *Il a juré à ses parents qu'il les aiderait à repeindre la maison.* (He swore to his parents that he would help them repaint the house.)

25. Coffee tables, a modern invention, were popularized by the advent of television. Antique dealers often adapt antique furniture to answer the needs of the modern home, in this case by cutting the legs of a regular table to create a coffee table.

26. *Pied* has several useful meanings. *Le pied de la table est cassé.* (The leg of this table is broken.) *J'ai acheté des verres à pied en cristal.* (I bought some glasses with a crystal stem.) *Le pied de la lampe est en bois.* (The base of the lamp is made out of wood.)

C. GRAMMAIRE ET USAGE

1. *LES ADJECTIFS DÉMONSTRATIFS* (DEMONSTRATIVE ADJECTIVES)

a. The demonstrative adjectives *ce, cet, cette* (this, that) and *ces* (these, those) agree in gender and number with the nouns they modify.

Que pensez-vous de ce papier peint pour votre chambre?
What do you think about this wallpaper for your room?

Il faut exploiter au maximum cet espace.
One must take full advantage of this space.

Cette armoire est en merisier.
This armoire is made of wild cherry wood.

Ces taies d'oreiller sont beaucoup trop grandes.
These pillowcases are far too big.

b. In French, there is usually no distinction made between "this" and "that." When contrast is required, however, *-ci* and *-là* are used.

Ce fauteuil-ci est plus confortable que ce fauteuil-là.
This armchair is more comfortable than that armchair.

Cette céramique-ci est plus ancienne que cette céramique-là.
This pottery is older than that pottery.

c. Demonstrative adjectives are often used in expressions of time; *-ci* then refers to the present, and *-là* to the past.

Les tables en acajou coûtent cher ces temps-ci.
Mahogany tables are expensive nowadays.

Il fait très beau ces jours-ci.
The weather is really beautiful these days.

Ce matin-là, j'ai trouvé une coiffeuse au marché aux puces.
That morning, I found a dressing table at the flea market.

J'ai rencontré Brice ce soir-là.
I met Brice that evening.

d. Demonstrative adjectives can also be used affectionately or sarcastically with proper names.

Ce cher Brice, il ne sait pas quoi faire pour nous aider.
Dear Brice, he does not know what to do to help us.

Ce pauvre Patrick, il lui arrive toujours des ennuis.
Poor Patrick! He always has problems.

Ce bon vieux Michel, on peut toujours compter sur lui.
Good old Michel, we can always count on him.

2. *LES PRONOMS DÉMONSTRATIFS* (DEMONSTRATIVE PRONOUNS)

a. The demonstrative pronoun *ce* is invariable and often appears as the subject of the verb *être*. It refers to a previously introduced event or concept, and the adjective that accompanies it is in the masculine form.

Choisir un papier peint, c'est difficile!
Choosing a wallpaper is difficult!

C'est d'accord.
    It's all right.

    b. The pronouns *celui, celle, ceux,* and *celles* refer to a specific antecedent with which they agree in gender and number.

J'envie ceux qui ont l'œil pour les bonnes affaires.
    I envy those who have an eye for bargains.

Je ne sais pas celui qui vous plaît le plus.
    I don't know which one you like best.

Préférez-vous celui-ci ou celui-là?
    Do you prefer this one or that one?

    c. *Celui-là* and *celui-ci* correspond to the English "former" and "latter." Note that the usual word order in French is different than in English: "the latter" is introduced first, followed by "the former."

Connaissez-vous ces ébénistes? Celui-ci est normand, celui-là est breton.
    Do you know these cabinetmakers? The former is from Brittany, the latter from Normandy.

3. *LES ADJECTIFS COMPOSÉS* (COMPOUND ADJECTIVES)

a. *Les adjectifs de couleur.*
As in English, colors may be combined with other words to create a more specific color definition.

Des tissus rouge foncé mettront en valeur cette pièce.
    Dark red fabric will enhance this room.

Elle a fait capitonner ses fauteuils d'une soie vert pâle.
    She had her armchairs upholstered with a pale green silk.

Ces chaises vert pomme sont parfaites pour la chambre des enfants.
    These apple-green chairs are perfect for the children's room.

    If a compound adjective of color is composed of an adjective + *et* + another adjective and refers to two colors that are indistinguishably combined or intertwined within one pattern, the compound adjective does not agree with the noun it modifies.

Les rideaux cramoisi et or créent une ambiance très chaude.
    These crimson and gold curtains give a very warm feeling.

J'ai trouvé des étoffes indiennes bleu et argent pour les ottomans.
    I found blue and silver Indian fabric for the ottomans.

If, on the other hand, the two colors are clearly distinct from one another, they must agree with the noun to which they refer.

Elle a accroché des rideaux bleus et blancs dans la cuisine.
She hung blue and white curtains in the kitchen.

Où voulez-vous mettre le tableau avec la vache noire et blanche?
Where do you want to put the painting with the black and white cow?

b. Les adjectifs composés dérivés des mots empruntés.
Some compound adjectives are formed using prefixes. With such adjectives (usually of Greek or Latin origin), the prefix does not agree with the noun, but the adjective does.

Cette décoration franco-italienne convient parfaitement à leur villa.
This Franco-Italian decoration suits their villa perfectly.

Ils ne peuvent pas supporter ces œuvres néo-impressionnistes.
They can't stand these neo-impressionist works.

Toi et tes sacro-saints principes de décoration!
You and your sacrosanct decoration principles!

Je suis sûr que cette étoffe extra-fine fera l'affaire.
I am sure that this extra-fine fabric will do the trick.

Brice est un décorateur ultra-sensible.
Brice is an ultrasensitive decorator.

c. Les adjectifs composés employés comme adverbes.
Compound adjectives that are removed or separated from the noun and appear related to the verb act as adverbs. The agreement often varies from case to case. With *amoureux fou, fou furieux,* and *ivre mort,* for example, agreement is required, while with *haut et dru,* no agreement is necessary.

Une coupe en argent, ciselée fin comme de la dentelle.
A silver cup, chiseled as fine as lace.

En voyant la peinture à l'éponge, elle était folle furieuse.
She was raving mad when she saw the sponge painting.

Elles sont toutes amoureuses folles de Romain.
They are all madly in love with Romain.

L'avoine pousse haut et dru.
Oats grow high and thick.

4. *L'EXPRESSION "AVOIR L'AIR"* (THE EXPRESSION *AVOIR L'AIR*)

When *avoir l'air* refers to objects and is used to mean "to seem," the adjective agrees in gender and number with the subject.

Cette couette a l'air toute neuve.
This down quilt seems brand new.

Cette moquette a l'air moelleuse.
This carpet seems soft and fluffy.

When *avoir l'air* describes a momentary impression, the adjective agrees in gender and number with the subject. But when *air* refers to more permanent, physical characteristics, the adjective agrees with *air* and remains masculine singular. Compare the following examples.

Joan avait l'air étonnée par la remarque de Romain.
Joan seemed surprised by Romain's remark.

Joan est très souriante; elle a toujours l'air content.
Joan is always smiling; she always seems happy.

Les chiens qui attendent leur maître devant le magasin ont l'air tristes.
The dogs waiting for their masters in front of the store look sad.

Les pitbulls ont l'air méchant.
Pitbulls look mean.

Christine, tu as l'air trop sérieuse avec ces lunettes!
Christine, you look too serious with these glasses!

À dix ans, Christine avait déjà l'air très sérieux.
When she was ten, Christine already seemed very serious.

When the adjective following *air* is followed by a complement, the adjective remains masculine singular.

L'auberge avait l'air prétentieux d'un hôtel de luxe.
The inn had the pretentious air of a luxury hotel.

La mairie avait l'air délabré d'une vieille ferme abandonnée.
The town hall had the dilapidated air of an old abandoned farm.

5. *L'USAGE DE "QUITTE À"* (USAGE OF *QUITTE À*)

The invariable expression *quitte à* (at the risk of, even if it means) may present some difficulties because it has no English equivalent. It is widely used in written and spoken French and is more idiomatic than *même si*.

Profitons de cette occasion, quitte à le regretter plus tard.
Let's take advantage of this deal, even if we regret it later on.

Elle a acheté un buffet sans savoir s'il tiendrait dans sa cuisine, quitte à le revendre à son antiquaire.
She bought a sideboard not knowing if it would fit in her kitchen, even though it might mean selling it back to her antiques dealer.

Elle restera plus longtemps en France, quitte à sacrifier son séjour en Hollande.
She'll stay longer in France even if it means sacrificing her stay in Holland.

Quitte à se faire des ennemis, il dit toujours ce qu'il pense.
Even at the risk of making enemies, he always says what he thinks.

D. JEU DE MOTS

There is no direct translation for "wrong" in French. It should be translated according to its context.

1. "What's the problem?"

a. With a situation:

Qu'est-ce qu'il y a?
What's wrong?

b. With a specific individual:

Qu'est-ce que vous avez? Vous êtes fatigué?
What's wrong? Are you tired?

Qu'est-ce que tu as? Pourquoi pleures-tu?
What's wrong with you? Why are you crying?

2. Moral wrong or poor judgment.

C'est mal de trahir ses amis.
It is wrong to betray one's friends.

Vous avez eu tort de lui conseiller de résilier son bail.
You were wrong to advise her to cancel her lease.

Qu'est-ce qu'il y a de mal à installer une cloison coulissante?
What's wrong with installing a sliding partition?

3. An error.

Elle s'est trompée sur son compte.
She was wrong about him.

Votre devis est trop élevé; vous vous êtes trompé dans les chiffres.
Your estimate is too high; your figures must be wrong.

Ce n'est pas comme ça qu'il faut s'y prendre.
That's the wrong way to go about it.

4. Most commonly, the idea of "wrong" is expressed by *se tromper* or by negating a positive statement using *pas bon*.

Elle n'a pas acheté la bonne couleur.
Elle s'est trompée de couleur.
She bought the wrong color.

L'antiquaire ne m'a pas donné la bonne clé.
L'antiquaire s'est trompé de clé.
The antiques dealer gave me the wrong key.

Nous ne sommes pas sur la bonne route.
Nous nous sommes trompés de route.
We are on the wrong road.

Elle s'est trompée de numéro.
She dialed the wrong number.

5. Idiomatic expressions.

Vous faites fausse route.
You're on the wrong track. (figuratively)

Elle s'est levée du pied gauche.
She got out on the wrong side of the bed.

Ils ont de mauvaises fréquentations.
They have the wrong kind of friends.

E. LE COIN DES AFFAIRES

LA DISTRIBUTION (DISTRIBUTION)

Perhaps the most important element of launching a product in France is how it will be distributed. France offers a myriad of distribution venues for imported products. In general, French buyers prefer to make purchases through a "middle man (or woman)" and direct sales are fairly rare, with the exception of costly, technically sophisticated goods. An intermediary can be an agent, a distributor, or a salaried representative.

A distributor, known as *un concessionnaire,* can be an individual or an enterprise that purchases products directly from the producer and resells them. Distributors operate independently of the manufacturer and are bound by a contract. Agents do not directly purchase or distribute goods; rather, they match up a manufacturer and a distributor, and are paid a commission for each transaction. Salaried representatives are contracted employees or enterprises, whose commission entails payment of payroll taxes, social security, benefits, and other costs. The U.S. Department of Commerce offers services to help prospective U.S. exporters locate distributors.

Before engaging an intermediary, U.S. firms should be sure to obtain as much information as possible about the representative's status, history, resources, territories covered, sales volume, customer profiles, sales methods, and compatibility with the U.S. firm's requirements. It is advisable to make a very well-informed decision prior to signing a contract, as cancellations of agreements may involve very high severance fees. When drafting the contract, the exporter's interest must be preserved in case the representative's performance is unsatisfactory. It is best to engage a French lawyer for these negotiations.

The main retail outlets in France include department stores *(grands magasins)* such as *Galeries Lafayette* and *Printemps,* "hypermarkets" *(hypermarchés)* such as *Leclerc* and *Carrefour France SNC,* supermarkets *(supermarchés)* such as *Intermarché* and *Casino France,* convenience stores *(centres commerciaux)* such as *Monoprix, Prisunic,* and *Uniprix,* and mail-order marketing *(vente par catalogue)* including *La Redoute* and *CAMIF.*

The mail-order market in France is the fourth largest in the world. Large, specialized stores that emphasize customer service provide another popular venue, especially for the distribution of furniture and do-it-yourself equipment. Finally, there are the relatively new, multi-channel retail groups that own a combination of distribution venues, such as *hypermarchés,* supermarkets, and convenience stores. The largest of these are *Docks de France* and *Promode.*

EXERCICES

A. *Compléter en utilisant l'adjectif démonstratif.*

1. _____ armoire picarde fera beaucoup d'effet.
2. _____ coussins sont extrêmement moelleux.
3. Romain travaille dans _____ atelier de décoration.
4. _____ housse de couette était un cadeau d'anniversaire.
5. Le décorateur a choisi _____ rideaux en velours.
6. Où pensez-vous accrocher _____ tableaux?
7. Si on mettait le petit secrétaire en face de _____ guéridon.
8. Elle envisage de mettre _____ coiffeuse près de la fenêtre.
9. J'ai trouvé _____ faïences aux puces.
10. _____ abat-jour est peint à la main.

B. *Remplacer les mots soulignés par un pronom démonstratif.*

1. Préférez-vous cette lampe-ci ou cette lampe-là?
2. Veut-elle poser ces appliques-ci ou ces appliques-là?
3. Est-ce que Joan désire acheter ce canapé-ci ou ce canapé-là?
4. Prendrez-vous ces coussins-ci ou ces coussins-là?
5. Je suppose que ce taffetas-ci coûte plus cher que ce taffetas-là?

C. *Mettre les mots soulignés au pluriel.*

1. J'ai acheté un tissu bleu pâle pour recouvrir le fauteuil.
2. Romain a choisi une étoffe vermillon et or.
3. Elle a accroché ce tableau néo-réaliste dans le salon.
4. Cette peinture vert foncé jurera avec le reste du décor.
5. Cette housse de couette bleu ciel est en coton damassé.

D. *Traduire en utilisant "quitte à."*

1. Even at the risk of spending too much, she hired two famous decorators.
2. They chose the bright red sofa even at the risk of shocking their friends.
3. They'll spend more time in Joan's apartment at the risk of being late for their next appointment.
4. Joan wants to go to the flea market even if she has to get up very early.
5. Even if she might regret it later, she painted her kitchen bright orange.

LECTURE

In an interview that appeared in *Champs-Élysées* magazine, Évelyne Pagès talked with Yves Berger, a famous French singer, writer, and protector of the French language. Following are excerpts from their dialogue.

Évelyne Pagès: . . . *Vous êtes devenu en fin d'année [19]93, le membre du Conseil supérieur de la langue française, chargé de veiller*[1] *à la sauvegarde*[2] *de notre langue, qui est en péril, et vous parlez même de cancérisation.*

Yves Berger: . . . *Le peuple français, dans son ensemble . . . se rend mal compte*[3] *de la chose pour deux raisons. L'une tient au fait que le mal s'est déjà développé profondément, que les Français sont atteints*[4] *dans leur langue, . . . c'est-à-dire l'influence des lois qui gouvernent l'anglais sur les lois qui gouvernent le français. . . . Toute langue, quelle qu'elle soit, obéit à un fonctionnement qui lui est propre. . . . La langue est une donnée,*[5] *que je dirais génétique mais c'est aussi quelque chose dont on fait l'apprentissage. . . . Et que se passe-t-il aujourd'hui? . . . [P]lus les Français grandissent, plus ils vont dans le temps, et plus ils perdent l'usage de leur langue, c'est-à-dire plus ils contreviennent*[6] *aux lois de l'expression écrite et orale, parce que, de façon sournoise,*[7] *c'est-à-dire inconsciente, les lois du fonctionnement de l'anglo-américain nécrosent,*[8] *repoussent*[9] *et ruinent les lois du fonctionnement du français. . . .*

Et la deuxième raison, c'est qu'ils manquent d'un savoir historique, ils manquent d'une perspective. En effet, ce qui se passe aujourd'hui, c'est . . . une agression dont . . . les Anglo-Américains ne sont pas responsables (ce n'est pas leur faute, ils ne dominent pas, si je puis dire, l'expansion de leur langue), c'est nous qui sommes fautifs[10] *de ne pas répondre à l'offensive par une autre offensive. . . . Et c'est pourquoi tout ce qui se fait actuellement sous ce gouvernement, tout ce que le ministre de la Culture entreprend,*[11] *ce sont des mesures défensives, ce sont des interdictions. Il ne faut pas avoir peur de cela. . . .*

Évelyne Pagès: *Vous êtes bien connu sous le nom de "fou*[12] *d'Amérique" . . . vous êtes américanophile. . . . Alors quand même Yves Berger, on peut de temps en temps saluer*[13] *l'intrusion de certains mots américains dans notre vie courante. Je pense au mot "zapper," que certains académiciens emploient, parce que là il a un but*[14] *précis de concrétiser une idée. On [ne] va pas dire: "Je change rapidement de chaîne de télévision avec ma télécommande," alors que le mot "zapper" résume*[15] *tout. Qu'est-ce que vous pensez de ce phénomène-là?*

Yves Berger: . . . *La langue française est pleine de mots anglais que nous avons adoptés . . . mais ce contre quoi je suis, c'est contre l'adoption, que je dirais facile, que je dirais inconsciente, et souvent d'ailleurs*[16] *résultat de la*

* Yves Berger, interview by Évelyne Pagès in *Champs-Elysées,* March 1994, edited by Terry Lacassin (Nashville, Champs-Elysées, Inc.)

mode, l'invasion d'un mot qui chasse[17] *un autre. Vous avez par exemple l'abominable "solutionner." Qu'est-ce qu'il apporte de plus à "résoudre"? . . . Aujourd'hui tous les gens vous parlent de "solutionner un problème," "solutionner"—quatre syllabes, alors que "résoudre" n'en a que trois et, si je puis dire, est plus modeste, comme il le faut, pour la plupart des mots. . . . [C]ela est grave, mais beaucoup plus que le vocabulaire, ce qui est grave, ce sont les atteintes à la syntaxe. . . . Et quand la syntaxe d'une langue est atteinte, c'est-à-dire la façon de parler, . . . c'est la nature de la langue, et c'est donc l'esprit de la nation qui est atteint. . . . L'américanophile que je suis, le chantre*[18] *de l'Amérique du Nord que je suis, toute mon inspiration d'écrivain venant de l'Amérique du Nord, où j'ai fait cent vingt et un voyages, met aussi sa logique à penser, à vouloir, et à faire que l'expression de son amour de l'Amérique s'exprime dans le français le plus pur, parce que c'est comme ça que le chant sera le plus beau . . .*

VOCABULAIRE

1.	*veiller*	to look after
2.	*la sauvegarde*	safeguard
3.	*se rendre compte*	to realize
4.	*atteindre*	to overtake
5.	*la donnée*	fundamental idea, datum
6.	*contrevenir*	to contravene, infringe
7.	*sournoise*	sly, devious
8.	*nécroser*	to cause necrosis
9.	*repousser*	to push back, repel
10.	*fautif*	faulty, defective
11.	*entreprendre*	to undertake
12.	*le fou*	lunatic, madman
13.	*saluer*	to salute, greet
14.	*le but*	goal
15.	*résumer*	to summarize
16.	*d'ailleurs*	besides
17.	*chasser*	to drive away
18.	*le chantre*	cantor

LEÇON 6

A. DIALOGUE

UN ENTRETIEN.

Lors d'un entretien avec Mme le Goff, M. Deforges explique pourquoi il aimerait travailler pour cette entreprise en tant que directeur commercial.

M. DEFORGES: **J'ai rendez-vous[1] avec madame le Goff.**

RECEPTIONNISTE: **Vous êtes Monsieur . . . ?**

M. DEFORGES: **Monsieur Deforges.**

RECEPTIONNISTE: **Madame le Goff vous attend. Si vous voulez bien me suivre.**

Elle le conduit au bureau de Mme le Goff et annonce son arrivée.

MME LE GOFF: **Bonjour, Monsieur. Asseyez-vous, je vous en prie.[2]**

M. DEFORGES: **Merci.**

MME LE GOFF: *(Elle remue une pile de papiers . . .)* **Comme vous le savez, notre société a retenu votre candidature pour le poste de directeur commercial. Pourriez-vous me dire pour quelles raisons vous avez répondu à notre annonce?**

M. DEFORGES: **L'expansion dont a joui votre société au cours de la dernière décennie[3] et ses brillants résultats à l'exportation sont fort séduisants.**

MME LE GOFF: **Connaissez-vous notre marché à fond?**

M. DEFORGES: **En tant que[4] responsable de l'import-export chez Van Neef, l'un de vos concurrents belges, je suivais de très près vos produits.**

MME LE GOFF: **Pourquoi avez-vous démissionné?[5]**

M. DEFORGES: **Le poste[6] avait peu de débouchés et la société n'offrait guère de possibilités d'évolution de carrière.**

MME LE GOFF: **Pourquoi êtes-vous venu vous installer à Lyon?**

M. DEFORGES: **Nous envisagions de retourner en Aquitaine lorsque l'Université de Lyon a offert une chaire[7] de professeur d'histoire à ma femme.**

MME LE GOFF: **Ah . . . je vois. Et vous avez des enfants?[8]**

M. DEFORGES: **Nous avons une fille de sept ans et un fils de quatre ans et demi.[9]**

MME LE GOFF: En dépit de vos obligations familiales, seriez-vous prêt à effectuer de [10] nombreux déplacements en Orient?

M. DEFORGES: Absolument.

MME LE GOFF: Je dois vous préciser que notre entreprise met l'accent sur le travail d'équipe. Et je ne vous cache pas que le travail est plutôt astreignant.

M. DEFORGES: Je n'y vois aucun inconvénient, au contraire.

MME LE GOFF: Quel rôle envisagez-vous de jouer au sein de notre entreprise?

M. DEFORGES: J'aimerais explorer davantage le marché asiatique et apporter un second souffle à l'exportation en Europe de l'Est.

MME LE GOFF: Comme vous devez vous en douter,[11] ce poste requiert une présentation sans faille et une aptitude à mener des négociations corsées. Quelles étaient vos relations avec vos clients chez Van Neef?

M. DEFORGES: Excellentes. J'ai toujours aimé les contacts humains.

MME LE GOFF: Etes-vous à l'aise lorsque vous devez parler en public?

M. DEFORGES: Ah . . . Mon premier amour était le théâtre! À douze ans, je jouais *L'Avare*[12] devant les cinq cents élèves du lycée Henri IV.

MME LE GOFF: Impressionnant! Quelles sont vos activités extra-professionnelles à l'heure actuelle?

M. DEFORGES: La photographie, l'œnologie et la randonnée.

MME LE GOFF: Et combien de langues parlez-vous?

M. DEFORGES: Je parle couramment l'anglais et l'allemand.[13] Mon italien est un peu rouillé.[14] Et je suis actuellement un cours pour perfectionner mon japonais.

MME LE GOFF: Parfait. . . . À partir de quelle date seriez-vous disponible?

M. DEFORGES: Immédiatement.

MME LE GOFF: Et quelles sont vos prétentions en terme de salaire?

M. DEFORGES: Tout dépend de [15] la charge de travail, des responsabilités, des avantages sociaux: congés payés,[16] primes, indemnités etc.

MME LE GOFF: **Bon, très bien, nous vous en reparlerons. Le poste sera libre d'ici un mois. Vous possédez, semble-t-il,[17] les qualités requises pour le poste à pourvoir.**

M. DEFORGES: **Quand pensez-vous prendre une décision?[18]**

MME LE GOFF: **Nous devrions être à même de[19] vous donner une réponse d'ici une quinzaine.[20] Il est néanmoins nécessaire d'effectuer un test de personnalité[21] et de graphologie[22] ainsi qu'une visite médicale.[23]**

M. DEFORGES: **Je suis à votre entière disposition.**

MME LE GOFF: **Bon, je vais appeler monsieur Maillet, notre graphologue. N'ayez crainte, vous serez en de bonnes mains. Et je vous tiendrai au courant dès que nous aurons pris une décision.**

A JOB INTERVIEW.

During an interview with Mrs. Le Goff, Mr. Deforges explains why he would like to work with this company as marketing director.

MR. DEFORGES: I have an appointment with Mrs. Le Goff.

RECEPTIONIST: Your name is . . . ?

MR. DEFORGES: Mr. Deforges.

RECEPTIONIST: Mrs. Le Goff is expecting you. Please follow me.

She leads him to Mrs. Le Goff's office and announces his arrival.

MRS. LE GOFF: Good morning, sir. Have a seat, please.

MR. DEFORGES: Thank you.

MRS. LE GOFF: As you know, our company is interested in your application for the position of marketing director. Could you tell me why you responded to our ad?

MR. DEFORGES: The expansion your company has been enjoying over the past decade and its outstanding results in exports are very attractive.

MRS. LE GOFF: Do you know our market in depth?

MR. DEFORGES: As import-export manager at Van Neef, one of your Belgian competitors, I followed your products very closely.

MRS. LE GOFF: Why did you resign?

MR. DEFORGES: My position had few prospects and the company offered virtually no opportunities for career advancement.

MRS. LE GOFF: Why did you settle down in Lyon?

MR. DEFORGES: We had planned to go back to the Aquitaine region when the University of Lyon offered my wife a position as the chairperson of the history department.

MRS. LE GOFF: I see . . . Do you have any children?

MR. DEFORGES: We have a seven-year-old daughter and a four-and-a-half-year-old son.

MRS. LE GOFF: In spite of your family obligations, would you be ready to make frequent trips to the Orient?

MR. DEFORGES: Absolutely!

MRS. LE GOFF: I must tell you that our company stresses teamwork. I won't hide from you that the work is rather demanding.

MR. DEFORGES: I have no objection, quite the contrary.

MRS. LE GOFF: What role do you expect to play within our company?

MR. DEFORGES: I'd like to explore the Asian market and give export to Eastern Europe a second wind.

MRS. LE GOFF: As you must suspect, this position requires a flawless appearance and an ability to conduct tough negotiations. How was your relationship with your clients at Van Neef?

MR. DEFORGES: Excellent. I have always thrived on human contact.

MRS. LE GOFF: Are you comfortable speaking in public?

MR. DEFORGES: Oh! Theater was my first love! At the age of twelve, I played *The Miser* in front of five hundred students at the Henri IV high school.

MRS. LE GOFF: Impressive! What are your activities outside the profession at the moment?

MR. DEFORGES: Photography, oenology,[1] and hiking.

MRS. LE GOFF: And how many languages do you speak?

MR. DEFORGES: I am fluent in English and German. My Italian is a bit rusty. And I'm presently taking a course to improve my Japanese.

MRS. LE GOFF: Perfect. . . . When would you be available?

MR. DEFORGES: Immediately.

MRS. LE GOFF: And what are your salary requirements?

MR. DEFORGES: It all depends on workload, responsibilities, benefits: paid vacation, bonuses, allowances, etc.

---

[1] Oenology is the study of wine and winemaking.

MRS. LE GOFF: All right, we'll talk about this again. The position will be open in a month. It seems that you have the skills required to fill it.

MR. DEFORGES: When do you think you'll reach a decision?

MRS. LE GOFF: We should be able to give you an answer in two weeks. However, a personality and a graphology test will be required along with a medical checkup.

MR. DEFORGES: I am entirely at your disposal.

MRS. LE GOFF: All right, I'm going to call our graphology expert, Mr. Maillet. Don't be afraid, you'll be in good hands. I'll let you know as soon as we reach a decision.

B. EN BREF

1. In French, a *rendez-vous* need not have romantic implications. It can refer to any type of appointment: a business meeting, a doctor's appointment, lunch with a friend.

2. *Je vous en prie* means both "please" and "you're welcome."

3. *Décennie:* ten years. Don't confuse it with *décade,* which means ten days.

4. *En tant que* (as) is followed by a noun without an article: *en tant qu'ami* (as a friend), *en tant que spécialiste* (as a specialist).

5. If you resign, *vous démissionnez.* If you are laid off, *vous êtes licencié.* And if your boss fires you, *vous êtes renvoyé* or *mis à la porte.*

6. Masculine, feminine? *Le poste* is a position you hold in a company, while *la poste* is a post office.

7. Watch out for homonyms! *Il occupe la chaire* (chair) *d'archéologie à la Sorbonne. La chair* (flesh) *de ce canard est très tendre.* And if you are really scared, you'll get *la chair de poule* (goose bumps).

8. In France, queries about family are not uncommon in job interviews. So be prepared to answer a wide range of personal questions, such as: Were you happy as a child? Are you married? Do you have children? Do you plan to have some? French employers tend to be very careful about not hiring the wrong person, as the rights of French workers are well protected, and firing someone is much more difficult and expensive than in the United States.

9. When *demi* (half) follows a noun, it agrees in gender with the noun. Compare: *une livre et demie* and *une demi-livre.*

10. Note the use of *de* instead of *des* before plural nouns preceded by an adjective: *des relations excellentes* but *de bonnes relations*.

11. *Douter* (to doubt); but *se douter de* (to suspect, to imagine). *Je ne m'en suis jamais douté.* (I never suspected it.)

12. *The Miser,* a play about human obsession with money and stinginess, is one of Molière's best-known works.

13. If the verb *parler* is modified by an adverb, a definite article is required before the name of the language: *je parle français* but *je parle très bien le français.*

14. If you leave your bicycle out in the rain, *elle sera rouillée,* and if you don't speak French for a long time, your French will also be *rouillé.*

15. Note that verbs often take different prepositions in French and in English. Thus, to depend <u>on</u> is *dépendre <u>de</u>. Tout dépend de toi.* (It all depends on you.)

16. In 1936, Léon Blum's socialist government instituted paid vacation. Today, French workers get five weeks paid vacation a year.

17. When *il semble* (it seems) is inserted in the middle or at the end of a sentence, inversion of subject and verb is required.

18. While in English you "make" a decision, in French you "take" a decision.

19. *À même de:* apt, capable of doing something.

20. Remember: *une quinzaine* (a fortnight) is fourteen days, and *une huitaine* (a week) is seven days.

21. In France, a psychological examination is a routine part of the job application process. Typical questions include: *Vous est-il difficile de vous lever le matin? Quand vous voyagez, qu'emportez-vous comme bagages à main? Quel film avez-vous revu plus de trois fois? Que pensez-vous de votre ancien patron?*

22. For many French companies, a job applicant's handwriting is a key indicator of temperament, intellectual aptitude, and personal traits. Graphology test results often play a deciding role in the hiring process. If your handwritten cover letter proves insufficient, you may be asked to produce another writing sample during the interview.

23. Prospective employees in France must undergo a medical exam.

C. GRAMMAIRE ET USAGE

1. *LE PASSÉ COMPOSÉ* (THE PRESENT PERFECT)

The *passé composé* expresses a completed action in the past. It is formed with the present indicative of *être* or *avoir* and the past participle of the verb. The past participle of regular verbs is formed by dropping the infinitive *-er*, *-ir*, and *-re* endings, and replacing them with *-é, -i,* and *-u,* respectively. Some verbs have an irregular past participle that must be memorized.[2]

	TRAVAILLER	PARTIR
je	ai travaillé	suis parti(e)
tu	as travaillé	es parti(e)
il/elle/on	a travaillé	est parti(e)
nous	avons travaillé	sommes parti(e)s
vous	avez travaillé	êtes parti(e)(s)
ils/elles	ont travaillé	sont parti(e)s

Most verbs take *avoir* as their auxiliary verb, but a small group take *être*.[3] All reflexive and reciprocal verbs are also conjugated with *être*. Remember that verbs conjugated with *être* must agree in gender and number with the subject, unless they are preceded by a direct object, in which case they agree with that direct object.

A-t-elle dû passer un test psychologique?
Did she have to take a psychological test?

Elle n'est pas allée à la réunion.
She did not go to the meeting.

Ils n'ont jamais répondu.
They never answered.

Mme Le Goff s'est assise près de la fenêtre.
Mrs. Le Goff sat down next to the window.

Note that when a pronominal verb is followed by a complement, the past participle does not agree with the subject.

Ils se sont serré la main.
They shook hands.

---

[2] For the forms of irregular past participles, please refer to Appendix I, p. 347.
[3] The verbs that are conjugated with *être* are: *aller, venir, monter, descendre, arriver, partir, sortir, naître, mourir, entrer, rester, retourner, revenir,* and *tomber*.

Ils se sont parlé au téléphone.
They talked to each other on the phone.

Elle s'est cassé un ongle.
She broke a nail.

2. *L'IMPARFAIT* (THE IMPERFECT)

The imperfect is used to describe a state of mind or a state of being in the past, as well as continuous or habitual past actions. It is formed with the root of the present indicative *nous* form of a verb (e.g., *parlons* → *parl-*) and the imperfect endings, which are the same for all three verb groups: *-ais, -ais, -ait, -ions, -iez, -aient.*

	DONNER	FAIRE	FINIR
je	donnais	faisais	finissais
tu	donnais	faisais	finissais
il/elle/on	donnait	faisait	finissait
nous	donnions	faisions	finissions
vous	donniez	faisiez	finissiez
ils/elles	donnaient	faisaient	finissaient

Tu avais peur de rater son examen de graphologie?
Were you afraid of failing his graphology test?

La société était au bord de la faillite.
The company was on the verge of bankruptcy.

Le directeur prenait des notes pendant que je parlais.
The director was taking notes while I was talking.

Si on + a verb in the imperfect expresses "What about?" or "How about."

Si on envoyait notre C.V. au nouveau PDG?
What about sending our résumé to the new CEO?

Si on fêtait ta promotion?
What about celebrating your promotion?

Si + a verb in the imperfect is used to express "if only . . ."

Si j'avais plus d'argent!
If only I had more money!

Si vous pouviez décrocher ce poste!
If only you could get this position!

The imperfect is often used in French where the past conditional is used in English: to express something that should have happened but didn't.

Il n'avait qu'à parler et je lui offrais le poste.
If only he had said something. I would have offered him the position.

Un mot de plus et le contrat était annulé.
One more word and the contract would have been cancelled.

Votre absence à la réunion pouvait tout gâcher!
Your absence from the meeting could have spoiled everything!

The imperfect is also used to make a statement more polite or mild.

Caroline, avant que vous nous donniez votre démission, je voulais vous poser quelques questions.
Caroline, before you resign, I would like to ask you a few questions.

Caroline, je veux vous poser quelques questions would be much more peremptory.

Mesdames et Messieurs, en entamant cette conférence, je souhaitais vous faire part de mes projets.
Ladies and gentlemen, on opening this conference, I wish to inform you about my plans.

3. *L'IMPARFAIT OU LE PASSÉ COMPOSÉ?* (IMPERFECT OR PRESENT PERFECT?)

When one past action interrupts an ongoing past action, the ongoing or background action should be in the *imparfait,* while the interrupting or sudden action should be in the *passé composé.*

Carole allait démissionner lorsque son patron l'a promue vice-présidente.
Carole was going to resign, when her boss promoted her to vice president.

Je parlais au contremaître quand tout à coup l'alarme a retenti.
I was talking to the foreman when suddenly the alarm rang.

4. *LE PLUS-QUE-PARFAIT* (THE PAST PERFECT)

The *plus-que-parfait* is formed with the imperfect of *être* or *avoir* plus the past participle of the verb. It is used to express a past action that occurred prior to another past action or event.

	CONSEILLER	*RENTRER*
je	*avais conseillé*	*étais rentré(e)*
tu	*avais conseillé*	*étais rentré(e)*
il/elle/on	*avait conseillé*	*était rentré(e)*
nous	*avions conseillé*	*étions rentré(e)s*
vous	*aviez conseillé*	*étiez rentré(e)(s)*
ils/elles	*avaient conseillé*	*étaient rentré(e)s*

Mme Le Goff s'est rappelée qu'elle avait oublié l'entretien de quatorze heures.
Mrs. Le Goff remembered she had forgotten the two P.M. interview.

Je lui ai expliqué pourquoi j'avais démissionné.
I explained to him/her why I had resigned.

Pierre était déprimé parce que son patron l'avait mis à la porte.
Pierre was depressed because his boss had fired him.

5. *LA PRÉPOSITION "CHEZ"* (THE PREPOSITION *CHEZ*)

The preposition *chez* can mean "in," "at," or "with," depending on the context.

Ils sont rentrés chez eux à minuit.
They went home (to their house) at midnight.

Il était à la tête du service publicité chez Van Ness.
He was head of the advertising department at Van Ness.

Chez Émile Zola, la lutte ouvrière joue un rôle clé.
With Émile Zola, the workers' struggle plays a key role.

Chez cet employé, tout est psychosomatique.
With this employee, everything is psychosomatic.

On remarque ces manières chez les bourgeois.
These manners are noticeable in the middle class.

D. JEU DE MOTS

Souffle (breath), like its English counterpart, appears in many idiomatic expressions.

Il n'y avait pas un souffle de vent.
There wasn't a breath of air.

Ça lui a coupé le souffle.
That took his breath away.

C'est à vous couper le souffle.
It's breathtaking.

Pour jouer du saxophone, il faut du souffle.
To play the saxophone, you need a lot of wind.

Sa vie ne tient qu'à un souffle.
His/her life hangs by a thread.

Elle est arrivée dans la salle de conférence à bout de souffle.
She arrived in the conference room completely out of breath.

Il ne manque pas de souffle!
He's got some nerve!

Leur entreprise a trouvé son deuxième souffle.
Their company found its second wind.

Son patron a un souffle au cœur.
His boss has a heart murmur.

Quel souffle du génie chez ce poète!
This poet is so very inspired!

Il a exhalé son dernier souffle.
He breathed his last.

E. LE COIN DES AFFAIRES

TROUVER UN EMPLOI (FINDING A JOB)

There are different ways of getting a job interview in France. If you don't know someone *qui a le bras long* (with connections), you'll just have to leaf through the classified ads.

Loueur de Systèmes informatiques et distributeur de micro-ordinateurs, nous sommes aujourd'hui leader en Europe.

Responsable de gestion

Rattaché à la Direction Financière, vous assurez le contrôle et la gestion (CA, achats, coûts de ventes, stocks . . .) de notre activité. Pour ce faire, vous encadrez une équipe de 10 personnes. De formation supérieure, vous avez une expérience d'au moins 3 ans en contrôle de gestion, si possible en milieu industriel. Actif, précis, autonome, vous avez le sens des initiatives.

Adresser lettre et CV à l'attention de
Dominique Tessier, Direction des Ressources Humaines, 25, rue des Halles. 94322 Rungis.

As a computer system rental and personal computer distribution company, we are today's leader in Europe.

Administration Manager

Reporting to the Director of Finance, you would provide supervision and management (turnover, purchasing, sales costs, stock . . .) for our business. To do so, you will supervise a team of 10 people. You should have advanced training and at least 3 years' experience in supervision and management, preferably in the industrial field. Hardworking, precise, and self-sufficient, you should be used to taking the initiative.

Send your letter and résumé to the attention of
Dominique Tessier, Director of Human Resources, 25, rue des Halles. 94322 Rungis.

Une Agence indépendante, spécialisée dans la communication des ressources humaines, vous propose de suivre des voies jamais empruntées . . . Résolument tournés vers la volonté d'innover, nous offrons l'opportunité à un

Chef de publicité h/f

d'intégrer notre structure commerciale à dimension humaine. Pour développer et suivre notre clientèle, nous souhaitons adjoindre la pertinence et le sourire d'un chef de publicité autonome, et totalement investi dans son travail.

Fort d'une expérience de 2 à 6 ans en Agence, vous avez su consolider un savoir-faire et un portefeuille clients.

Laissez-nous votre carte de visite sur Minitel 3689 Perspective 20001

An independent agency, specializing in human resource communications, proposes that you follow a path never taken . . . Determined to innovate, we offer the opportunity for a

Head of Advertising m/f

to integrate our commercial structure on a human dimension. To develop and maintain our client base, we hope to join the competence and smile of an independent Head of Advertising, completely devoted to his/her work.

Backed by 2 to 6 years of experience in an agency, you should be able to consolidate know-how and a client portfolio.

Leave us your business card on Minitel 3689 Perspective 20001

Nous serons ravis de faire votre connaissance. Réponse assurée à chaque candidat.

Secrétaire bilingue (français-anglais)

- âgé(e) de plus de 25 ans
- titulaire d'un diplôme de secrétariat de direction
- 3 années d'expérience minimum
- bonne connaissance du traitement de texte
- rémunération 11 000 x 13

Contactez M. Leduc au 47 35 78 00, poste 24

We would be glad to meet you. A response is guaranteed to each candidate.

Bilingual Secretary (French-English)

- age 25 or older
- secretarial diploma
- minimum 3 years' experience
- good knowledge of word processing
- Salary: 11,000/month plus 1 month bonus

Contact Mr. Leduc at 47 35 78 00, ext. 24

DIRECTEUR COMMERCIAL

Près du président de ce groupe fabriquant et commercialisant des produits de grande consommation, réalisant un CA de plus de 800 MF avec une marge en constante progression, venez donner une nouvelle dimension à votre carrière:

La Direction Commerciale

Nos produits sont vendus en France et à l'étranger par le biais de canaux de distribution différents nécessitant la mise en place d'équipes commerciales spécifiques et la prolongation de nos actions commerciales existantes en renforçant leur pénétration. Vous proposez au Président une stratégie de développement commercial, puis mettez en oeuvre l'ensemble des actions nécessaires, allant du plan marketing à l'administration des ventes.
35/40 ans - Diplômé d'une Grande École, vous avez réussi un parcours commercial dans les produits de grande consommation et le moment est venu pour vous de prendre des responsabilités globales au sein d'une entreprise indépendante qui cherche un homme ou une femme d'envergure.

Nous vous garantissons la plus grande discrétion. Adresser votre dossier de candidature accompagné d'une photo et de vos prétensions sous la référence de SILA Service Ressources Humaines - 30 boulevard Béranger, Lyon. Tapez 3615 NW17 réf. AVA.

MARKETING DIRECTOR

Close to the president of this manufacturing and marketing group for mass-market products, realizing a turnover of more than 800 million francs with an ever-increasing margin, come and give a new dimension to your career:

Marketing Director

Our products are sold in France and overseas through various channels of distribution which require the placement of specific marketing teams as well as the extension of our existing marketing efforts to reinforce their effectiveness. You will propose a strategy for marketing development to the president, and implement the necessary steps, in accordance with the sales administration's marketing policy.
35-40 years old, a graduate of a Grande École, you have succeeded in marketing mass-consumption products, and the time has come for you to undertake global responsibilities, within an independent enterprise seeking a man or woman of caliber.

We will guarantee you the greatest discretion. Send your application accompanied by a photo and your objectives to IPCO Service Human Resources, 30 boulevard Béranger, Lyon. Tapez 3615 NW17 réf. AVA.

Once you find an interesting position in the want ads, apply for the job by sending in your resumé with a cover letter. The cover letter should be handwritten, not typed, and a recent photograph is generally attached to the upper right-hand corner of your résumé/curriculum vitae.

Bruno Deforges
15, rue Arthur Rimbaud
69000 Lyon
Tél: 33.59.60.62

            Madame Jacqueline Le Goff
            S.I.L.A.
            30, boulevard Béranger
            69000 Lyon

Madame,

    Suite à votre annonce dans le Nouvel Économiste du 5 mars, je me permets de solliciter le poste de directeur commercial. Attiré par la réputation de votre société, j'aimerais me joindre à votre équipe.

    Grâce à ma formation, j'ai acquis des bases solides en gestion et mon expérience en Belgique m'a permis de connaître de nombreux aspects de l'import-export et de suivre des dossiers sur le plan international. Actif et dynamique, je suis à même d'assumer de hautes responsabilités.

    Vous trouverez ci-joint mon curriculum vitae ainsi que les photocopies de mes diplômes.

    En espérant que ma candidature retiendra votre attention, je reste à votre entière disposition pour vous fournir les renseignements complémentaires que vous pourriez souhaiter.

            Je vous prie de croire, Madame,
            à l'assurance de mes sentiments.

            Bruno Deforges

Bruno Deforges
15, rue Arthur Rimbaud
69000 Lyon
Tél. 33.59.60.62

> Mrs. Jacqueline Le Goff
> S.I.L.A.
> 30, boulevard Béranger
> 69000 Lyon

Mrs. Le Goff:

Following your announcement in the Nouvel Économiste of March 5th, please accept my application for the position of Marketing Director. Drawn to the reputation of your company, I would love to join your team.

Thanks to my training, I have acquired a solid foundation in management, and my experience in Belgium has enabled me to become familiar with a number of aspects of import-export and to keep up with documents on international policies. Hardworking and dynamic, I am ready to take on greater responsibilities.

Please find enclosed my résumé as well as copies of my diplomas.

Hoping that my application will keep your attention, I remain available to provide you with the letters of recommendation you may need.

> I remain, sincerely yours
>
> Bruno Deforges

Bruno Deforges
15, rue Arthur Rimbaud
69000 Lyon
Tél: 33.59.60.62
Fax: 33.59.60.80

EXPÉRIENCE PROFESSIONNELLE

De 1988 au présent: VAN NEEF, Bruxelles. CA: 850 millions de francs belges.

- Responsable de l'import-export de matériel pour le traitement des eaux.
- Résultats moyens: +8% par rapport aux objectifs.

Dans le cadre de cette mission, j'ai notamment:

- fait évoluer la notoriété de nos produits à l'étranger.
- coordonné les divers services (ventes, production, marketing).
- mis en place un nouveau système informatique en Afrique.
- développé le marché international.

De 1981 à 1987: RÉSEAU VERT DU NORD-EST, Lille.

Responsable du marketing, j'ai:

- lancé une stratégie de protection de l'environnement dans le nord-est.
- développé la cohésion du réseau européen.
- réorganisé nos campagnes publicitaires sur le plan national.

FORMATION

- Diplômé avec mention de l'Institut des Hautes Études Commerciales.
- Maîtrise d'économie.

LANGUES

Anglais et allemand: parlé, lu et écrit.
Séjour de 6 mois aux États-Unis.
Italien: parlé.
Japonais: niveau intermédiaire.

DIVERS

Hobbies: œnologie, randonnée, photographie.

Bruno Deforges
15, rue Arthur Rimbaud
69000 Lyon
Tél: 33.59.60.62
Fax: 33.59.60.80

PROFESSIONAL EXPERIENCE

1988–present: VAN NEEF, Brussels. Turnover: 850 million
Belgian francs.
- Import-export manager for water treatment materials.
- Average results: 8% above projections.

In the scope of this assignment, I have notably:
- developed our product recognition overseas.
- coordinated various services (sales, production, marketing)
- put in place a new computer system in Africa.
- developed the international market.

1981–1987: RÉSEAU VERT DU NORD-EST, Lille./GREEN
NETWORK

As Marketing Manager, I:
* launched a strategy for environmental protection in the
  Northeast.
* developed a cohesive European network.
* reorganized our corporate advertisements in conjunction
  with national policy.

EDUCATION

* Graduated with honorable mention from the *Institut des
  Hautes Études Commerciales.*
* M.A. in Economics.

LANGUAGES

English and German: speak, read, and write.
6-month stay in the United States.
Italian: speak.
Japanese: intermediate level.

OTHER

Hobbies: oenology, hiking, photography.

Business etiquette in France is fairly strict as compared with that of the United States. Interviewers will go over your résumé, ask for clarification, and evaluate your motivation. They will try to determine your reasons for applying for the position and whether you can be an asset to the team. If the position requires international travel, expect questions on flexibility and adaptation to other cultures. So, don't go unprepared. Dress appropriately, make sure you have extra copies of your résumé, and don't forget your favorite pen in case you have to take that graphology test again!

EXERCICES

A. *Mettre les phrases suivantes au passé composé.*

1. *Elle doit poser sa candidature avant le 15 mai.*
2. *Ils répondent à une annonce dans le journal.*
3. *Il ne prend pas ces décisions.*
4. *Julien ne s'asseoit pas dans son bureau.*
5. *Retournez-vous en Aquitaine?*

B. *Mettre les phrases suivantes à l'imparfait.*

1. *M. Deforges travaille en Belgique.*
2. *Il est élève au Lycée Charlemagne.*
3. *Nous habitons dans une grande ville.*
4. *Ils envisagent de s'installer à l'étranger.*
5. *Vous suivez nos produits de très près?*

C. *Mettre les verbes au passé composé ou à l'imparfait selon le sens.*

1. *Quand j'étais contremaître, je (avoir) de nombreuses responsabilités.*
2. *Yves (passer) un test de graphologie hier.*
3. *Elles (explorer) l'Aquitaine pendant leurs vacances l'été dernier.*
4. *Nous rédigions le rapport quand le téléphone (sonner).*
5. *Autrefois, Christine (avoir) toujours peur de passer un entretien.*
6. *À Bruxelles, nous (habiter) dans une vieille maison.*
7. *L'entreprise (offrir) un poste à M. Benoît.*
8. *Je regardais les petites annonces pendant qu'il (parler) au téléphone.*
9. *Ils (être) sur le point de l'engager quand le graphologue (apporter) un rapport défavorable.*
10. *Après des négociations corsées, ils (finir) par signer le contrat.*

D. *Reformuler les phrases comme dans l'exemple.*

EXEMPLE: *Nous téléphonons à ce concurrent.*
Si on téléphonait à ce concurrent?

1. *Nous posons notre candidature pour ce poste.*
2. *Nous invitons le directeur commercial à déjeuner avec nous.*
3. *Nous explorons davantage le marché chinois.*
4. *Nous célébrons les succès de cette décennie.*
5. *Nous prenons rendez-vous avec le vice-président.*

LEÇON 7

A. DIALOGUE

UN NOUVEAU BOULOT.

Pascal vient d'être embauché[1] à l'essai comme mécanicien chez Airbus.[2] Pour son premier jour, Didier, un de ses futurs collègues, lui sert de[3] guide.

DIDIER: **Vous permettez que je vous appelle par votre prénom?[4] Moi, je m'appelle Didier.**

PASCAL: **Je vous en prie.**

DIDIER: **Je suis chargé aujourd'hui de votre orientation, de répondre à toute question éventuelle et de passer en revue le règlement intérieur.[5]**

PASCAL: **C'est très gentil de votre part, Didier. Depuis combien de temps travaillez-vous ici?**

DIDIER: **Depuis plus de trois ans. Quand je suis arrivé, le mécanicien qui occupait mon poste depuis quinze ans venait d'être mis à la porte.**

PASCAL: **Pour quelle raison?**

DIDIER: **On avait retrouvé des documents secrets dans son armoire-vestiaire.[6] Il aurait divulgué[7] des procédés de fabrication à des entreprises étrangères.**

PASCAL: **Plutôt grave!**

DIDIER: **À qui le dites-vous! Notre entreprise est en plein essor, riche en équipes performantes mais au moindre écart . . .**

PASCAL: **Par exemple?**

DIDIER: **La direction imposera l'alcootest aux salariés affectés à une machine dangereuse et dont l'état d'ivresse constituerait une menace pour eux-mêmes ou leur entourage.**

PASCAL: **Toute boisson alcoolisée est donc interdite?**

DIDIER: **Dans les locaux de travail sauf dans des circonstances exceptionnelles et avec l'accord de la Direction. Seuls du vin, du cidre et de la bière peuvent être consommés lors des repas, en quantité raisonnable. Au fait, est-ce que vous fumez?**

PASCAL: **Beaucoup moins qu'avant.**

DIDIER: **Il est interdit de fumer dans les ateliers vu les risques d'incendie mais vous pouvez fumer dans les salles réservées à cet effet.**

PASCAL: **Ma femme a cessé de fumer il y a deux ans; elle essaie de me convaincre d'en faire autant.**

DIDIER: **Nous avons mis en place, au sein même de l'entreprise, un programme visant à lutter contre le tabagisme. Si cela vous intéresse, le médecin vous en parlera lors de votre prochaine visite médicale.**

PASCAL: **Très bien. Vous ne m'avez pas montré l'horloge pointeuse!**

DIDIER: **Ah! Nous sommes passés devant il y a un instant. Comme vous le savez, le salarié doit se trouver en tenue à son poste aux heures fixées.[8] Le temps de travail ne comprend pas les autres occupations telles que l'habillage, le casse-croûte et la pause.[9] Et il est formellement interdit, sous peine de sanction, de pointer pour un autre salarié . . .**

PASCAL: **. . . qui souhaiterait prolonger son week-end!**

DIDIER: **Toute absence autre que l'absence résultant d'une maladie ou d'un accident doit être justifiée dans les trois jours maximum, sauf en cas de force majeure.[10]**

PASCAL: **De force majeure! Ça ne rigole pas!**

DIDIER: **On ne peut quand même pas se plaindre, on bénéficie de nombreux avantages: cinq semaines de congés, une prime de rendement, des indemnités de transport et une formation continue très appréciable que notre direction en collaboration avec le C.E.[11] ont mis sur pied il y a une dizaine d'années.**

PASCAL: **La formation a-t-elle lieu sur place?**

DIDIER: **La plupart des stages de formation continue sont effectués dans nos locaux toulousains.[12] Ils ont pour but de nous familiariser avec les nouvelles technologies et d'élargir nos connaissances en informatique. C'est aussi une occasion pour faire la connaissance de nos collègues.**

PASCAL: **Et le contremaître? Il est sympathique?**

DIDIER: **Il tient les rênes[13] avec une certaine souplesse. Si vous faites votre travail correctement et si vous respectez les consignes,[14] il peut être plutôt sympa. Mais s'il est mal luné,[15] n'allez pas vous frotter à lui pour lui demander une augmentation.**

PASCAL: **Et le grand patron? Est-ce qu'il fait le tour des ateliers?**

DIDIER: À vrai dire, il a d'autres chats à fouetter! Il est la figure de proue[16] de notre industrie: un visionnaire qui déborde d'énergie et bouillonne d'idées! Il ne faut pas compter le voir trop souvent, par contre, vous et moi, on va se voir tous les jours . . .

A NEW JOB.

Airbus has just hired Pascal on a trial basis as a mechanic. On his first day, Didier, one of his future colleagues, serves as his guide.

DIDIER: May I call you by your first name? Mine is Didier.

PASCAL: Please do.

DIDIER: Today, I'm in charge of your orientation, answering any possible questions, and going over the in-house regulations.

PASCAL: That's very nice of you, Didier. How long have you been working here?

DIDIER: Over three years. When I arrived, the mechanic who had my position for fifteen years had just been fired.

PASCAL: Why?

DIDIER: Secret documents had been found in his locker. He reportedly revealed some manufacturing processes to foreign companies.

PASCAL: Rather serious!

DIDIER: You're telling me! Our company is expanding rapidly, has a wealth of productive teams, but one mistake and . . .

PASCAL: What, for instance?

DIDIER: The management requires a breathalizer test for workers who are assigned to dangerous machines and whose drunken state would present a threat to themselves and the people around them.

PASCAL: So, every alcoholic beverage is prohibited?

DIDIER: On the premises, yes, except in special circumstances and with the management's authorization. Only wine, cider, and beer can be drunk during meals and only in reasonable quantities. By the way, do you smoke?

PASCAL: Much less than before.

DIDIER: It is forbidden to smoke in the shops, given the fire hazards, but you can smoke in the rooms reserved for that purpose.

PASCAL: My wife quit smoking two years ago; she is trying to convince me to do the same.

DIDIER: We have set up, within the company itself, a program aimed at combatting smoking. If you're interested, the doctor will talk to you about it during your next medical exam.

PASCAL: Very good. You didn't show me the time clock!

DIDIER: Oh! We passed it a minute ago. As you know, every worker must be at his station, in uniform, at a set time. Work time does not include other activities, such as getting dressed, having a snack or a break. And it is strictly forbidden, at the risk of a penalty, to punch in for another worker . . .

PASCAL: . . . who would like to extend his weekend.

DIDIER: Any absence other than one due to illness or accident has to be accounted for within three days at most, except in the case of an act of God.

PASCAL: An act of God! You mean business here!

DIDIER: We can't complain, though; we are entitled to a lot of benefits: five weeks' paid vacation, a productivity bonus, transportation allowance, and valuable professional training that our management set up about ten years ago in collaboration with the workers' council.

PASCAL: Is the training done on the premises?

DIDIER: Most of the training takes place in our Toulouse headquarters. The goal is to familiarize us with new technology and to enhance our knowledge of computer science. It also gives us the opportunity to get acquainted with our colleagues.

PASCAL: What about the foreman? Is he pleasant?

DIDIER: He holds the reins with some slack. If you do your job properly and if you follow orders, he can be nice enough. But if he is in a bad mood, don't go near him to try asking for a raise.

PASCAL: What about the big boss? Does he come around the shops?

DIDIER: To be honest, he has other fish to fry. He is the captain of our industry . . . a visionary who bubbles over with energy and whose mind is teeming with ideas! Don't count on seeing him too often! On the other hand, you and me, we're going to see each other every day!

B. EN BREF

1. Different words are used for hiring, depending on the nature of the work: *L'usine a embauché 100 ouvriers.* (The factory hired 100 workers.) *Allez-vous engager un nouveau comptable?* (Are you going to hire a new accountant?) *Le gouvernement l'a nommé au poste de secrétaire général.* (The government appointed him secretary general.)

2. *Airbus Industrie,* an international consortium founded in 1969, is based in Toulouse. It controls 40 percent of the medium-size jet market and is the second largest jet manufacturer after Boeing.

3. *Servir* has several common usages. *Il sert le café.* (He serves coffee.) *À quoi ça sert?* (What's that for?/What's the point?) *Nous nous servons de cet ingrédient.* (We use this ingredient.) *Son bureau sert de laboratoire.* (His office serves as a lab.)

4. The *vous* form is used among employees of upper and middle management level. Generally, people are addressed with *Monsieur* or *Madame.* At the lower level, workers tend to use the *tu* form when they work closely together. Some workers with several years' seniority may use *tu* with the "younger" workers, as well. There is no set rule, so it is best to use *vous* until someone suggests using *tu.*

5. The workers must be knowledgeable about in-house regulations. Each company must have a copy of these regulations on its premises accessible to the workers.

6. A locker is assigned to each worker, who must keep it clean and in good condition. It is, however, considered to be property of the management and may be opened at any time in the presence of witnesses.

7. To convey an idea that has not been confirmed by an official source, use the conditional or the past conditional. *L'entreprise serait au bord de la faillite.* (The company is reportedly on the verge of bankruptcy.) *Il aurait vendu toutes ses actions.* (He reportedly sold all his stocks.) For more on the usage of the conditional, see *Leçon* 12.

8. Flexible hours are more and more common in France and are greatly appreciated by workers. Typically, workers have the option of starting at 8:00 or 9:00 A.M. and leaving at 4:00 or 5:00 P.M.

9. Usually there are two ten- to fifteen-minute coffee breaks during the day. In most industrial companies, workers must take their breaks away from their field of operation in order not to distract the other workers and to minimize hazards.

10. *Le tremblement de terre* (earthquake), *l'incendie* (fire), *l'inondation* (flood), *l'ouragan* (hurricane), *le typhon* (typhoon), *le cyclone* (cyclone), *la tornade* (tornado), *l'orage tropical* (tropical storm), *l'éruption volcanique* (volcanic eruption), and *le glissement de terrain* (landslide) are all considered acts of God.

11. Workers' councils were created in 1945. They are mandatory in every company of fifty or more workers. The councils are elected for two years by all the workers to fulfill a professional, economic, and social mission to improve working conditions, guarantee safety, and provide information and training.

12. When referring to residents of a particular city or province, there are no set rules regarding the endings. Therefore, the inhabitants of Toulouse are called *Toulousains,* those from Lyon are *Lyonnais,* and those from Brittany are *Bretons.*

13. Don't confuse *la reine* (the queen), *le renne* (the reindeer), and *les rênes* (the reins).

14. *La consigne* has several different meanings: *Il respecte les consignes du contremaître.* (He follows the foreman's orders.) *Nous avons déposé nos bagages à la consigne.* (We dropped our luggage at the luggage check.) *La consigne de cette bouteille vous sera remboursée quand vous rapporterez la bouteille.* (The deposit on this bottle will be returned to you when you return the bottle.)

15. Someone may be *bien ou mal luné,* which means "in a good or bad mood." A *lunatique* is someone who is unpredictable and has frequently changing moods, similar to the phases of the moon.

16. Literally a carved figure on the bow of a ship, reputedly bringing good luck during the voyage. In modern language, it means the key person or the inspiration behind a venture.

C. GRAMMAIRE ET USAGE

1. *ÊTRE OU AVOIR? (ÊTRE OR AVOIR?)*

A number of verbs can be conjugated with either *être* or *avoir,* depending on how they are used. When they are transitive (i.e., have a direct object), they are conjugated with *avoir;* when they are intransitive (i.e., have no direct object), they are conjugated with *être.* Note that the meaning also changes according to usage. Compare:

Elle a passé ses vacances à Toulouse en juin dernier.
She spent her vacation in Toulouse last June.

Nous sommes passés par Toulon pour aller à Perpignan.
We went through Toulon to go to Perpignan.

Ils ont descendu les caisses de l'étagère du haut.
They took the cartons down from the top shelf.

À quelle heure est-il descendu?
   At what time did he come down?

Avez-vous monté les caisses au deuxième étage?
   Did you take the cases up to the third floor?

Est-ce que tu es jamais monté en haut de la Tour Montparnasse?
   Did you ever go to the top of the Montparnasse Tower?

Avez-vous sorti les documents du coffre-fort?
   Did you take the documents out of the vault?

Monsieur Bernardin est sorti.
   Mr. Bernardin stepped out.

J'ai rentré la voiture.
   I took the car in.

À quelle heure êtes-vous rentré chez vous?
   At what time did you get home?

Il a retourné la crêpe.
   He flipped the crêpe.

Pourquoi n'êtes-vous jamais retourné chez eux?
   Why didn't you ever go back to their house?

2. *LES EXPRESSIONS DE TEMPS II* (EXPRESSIONS OF TIME II)

To express how long an action has been going on, use *il y a . . . que, depuis,* or *voici/voilà . . . que* with a verb in the present tense (because the action is still going on in the present). Note that in English, the verb is in the past.

Cette usine fait les trois-huit depuis plusieurs années.
   This factory has been operating three shifts for several years.

Il y a huit jours qu'il essaie de réparer ce moteur.
   He has been trying to repair this engine for a week.

Voilà trois mois qu'elle travaille avec nous.
   She has been working with us for three months.

Nous fabriquons ces produits depuis 1920.
   We have been making those products since 1920.

In a negative sentence, the French verb is in the *passé composé* (because the action no longer occurs in the present).

Elle n'a pas fumé une seule cigarette depuis trois mois.
   She has not smoked a single cigarette in the past three months.

Je ne suis pas retournée à Toulouse depuis des mois.
   I have not been in Toulouse for months.

To express that an action had been going on before another one began, the verb should be in the imperfect.

Il travaillait ici depuis quinze ans quand il a décidé de donner sa démission.
He had been working here for fifteen years when he decided to resign.

J'étais dans cet atelier depuis six mois lorsque le contremaître a décidé de m'envoyer ailleurs.
I had been in this workshop for six months when the foreman decided to send me elsewhere.

To ask a question about the duration of an action, use *depuis quand* (since when) or *depuis combien de temps* (how long).

Depuis quand utilisez-vous ce procédé de fabrication? Depuis 1920.
Since when have you been using this manufacturing process? Since 1920.

Depuis combien de temps travaille-t-elle chez Airbus? Depuis deux ans.
How long has she been working for Airbus? For two years.

To express how long ago an action occurred, use *il y a.*

Elle a fait un stage intensif il y a six mois.
She went through intensive training six months ago.

Il y a cent ans, les congés payés n'existaient pas.
A hundred years ago, paid leave did not exist.

Other expressions used to indicate the duration of an action include *pendant* and *en.*[1] Remember that *pendant* can often be omitted (as in English).

Le syndicat a débattu la question pendant des semaines.
The union debated the question for weeks.

Les ouvriers ont revendiqué leurs droits pendant des années avant d'obtenir satisfaction.
The workers claimed their rights for years before getting satisfaction.

La pause-café dure (pendant) quinze minutes.
The coffee break lasts fifteen minutes.

[1] Be sure not to confuse *en* and *dans*. Use *en* to express the duration of an action and *dans* to indicate when something will take place. Compare:

Notre atelier peut fabriquer mille pièces en vingt minutes.
Our shop can make a thousand parts in twenty minutes.

Nous vous enverrons le produit fini dans trois jours.
We'll send you the finished product in three days.

D. JEU DE MOTS

Cats seem to have the tongues of the French . . .

On est arrivé à Toulouse très tard et il n'y avait pas un chat dans la rue.
   We arrived in Toulouse very late, and there wasn't a soul in the street.

Je ne connais pas la réponse, je donne ma langue au chat.
   I don't know the answer; I give up.

Il a un chat dans la gorge.
   He has a frog in his throat.

Il ne faut pas réveiller le chat qui dort.
   Let sleeping dogs lie.

Chat échaudé craint l'eau froide.
   Once bitten, twice shy.

Il faut appeler un chat un chat.
   Call a spade a spade.

Quand le chat n'est pas là, les souris dansent.
   When the cat's away, the mice will play.

E. LE COIN DES AFFAIRES

ORGANISATION DU TRAVAIL (COMPANY STRUCTURE)

Most French companies are organized according to one of two principles. Older, family-owned firms are structured hierarchically and are usually located in cities such as Bordeaux, Rouen, and Lyon, which tend to be more traditional than Paris. The head of such a company, the *PDG* or *président directeur général* (the CEO), has executive power over the *cadres supérieurs* (upper management) and *cadres moyens* (middle management). While managers all have specific duties, responsibilities, and authority, it is the *PDG* who has final say on all company decisions. Other, more modern companies, specializing in newer fields such as marketing, advertising, electronics, and media, are characterized by high-tech facilities as well as an emphasis on group responsibility and shared decision making.

In the older companies, the atmosphere is generally very formal, and traditional forms of address and dress codes must be strictly respected. In such environments, address your immediate superiors and colleagues as *Monsieur* or *Madame,* and the *PDG* or a high-level executive as *Monsieur le Directeur, Madame la Présidente,* etc., depending on his or her official title. After many years in a company, some employees may address each other on a first-name basis, but they would nevertheless continue using *vous* in the office to show respect for company code and hierarchy (or because they wish to conceal that they're having an affair!). *Tu* may be used outside the office. As a foreigner, you should always use *vous,* unless asked to use *tu.* Common phrases used to suggest moving from *vouvoiement* (using *vous*) to *tutoiement* (using *tu*) include: *Vous pouvez me tutoyer.* (You may use *tu* with me.) and *Et si on se tutoyait?* (How about using *tu* with each other?). As previously mentioned, the dress code in more traditional companies is, as can be expected, very conservative. Men always wear suits and subtle ties. Women generally wear dresses or suits. Pants are acceptable only if they are part of a suit, and an air of elegance is expected.

In more modern companies, as in the United States, you will find a much more relaxed atmosphere. *Tutoiement* among colleagues is more common and dress codes are more lenient. Men can wear pants and a shirt, and their ties are sometimes colorful and humorous; women, too, tend to be more casual, though never sloppy. In either case, Americans visiting France should prepare to dress formally, regardless of the company with which they're doing business, as underdressing may be taken as a sign of disrespect.

WOMEN IN BUSINESS

French women did not gain the right to vote until 1945 (much later than in many other European countries), and it was not until the 1970s that property, employment, and divorce rights were equalized between the sexes. While there are still few women at the top of traditional industries, the role of women in French business life has improved dramatically. They hold management positions in government, finance, retailing, media, advertising, and other fields, but they are still often the victims of prejudice.

French businesswomen have traditionally been expected to be feminine and not overly aggressive. Flirtation still plays a great role in office relations, and the French are much more tolerant on sexual matters. In recent years, however, as women have been moving up the social ladder and assuming traditionally male positions, sexual harassment suits are becoming more common. According to a recent poll, one out of five working women is the victim of sexual harassment (twenty-nine percent by a high-level executive, twenty-six percent by their immediate superior, and twenty-two percent by a colleague). The Anita Hill affair had a great impact on France. Less than a year later, the *Code pénal* was amended, and sexual harassment by a superior is now an offense that can lead to a fine of 200,000 francs and up to two years imprisonment.

The long-standing French tradition of flirting, even in an office environment, may be a bit confusing for Americans. If faced with a situation that makes you uncomfortable, you may say: *Je suis désolé(e), je ne sors jamais avec mes collègues.* (I'm sorry, I never go out with my co-workers.). If someone is very insistent, be firm and say: *Cette situation est vraiment désagréable, je vous prie de me laisser tranquille.* (This situation is very unpleasant; please leave me alone.)

MAJOR HOLIDAYS

When scheduling appointments, it is important to keep in mind that all French companies are closed on the following holidays:

le 1er janvier	January 1st—New Year's Day
le lundi de Pâques	Monday following Easter Sunday
le 1er mai	May 1st—Labor Day
le 8 mai	May 8th—Armistice Day for WWII
l'Ascension	Ascension Day
le lundi de Pentecôte	Pentecost Monday
le 14 juillet	July 14th—Bastille Day
l'Assomption	August 15th—Assumption
la Toussaint	November 1st—All Saints' Day
le 11 novembre	November 11th—Armistice Day for WWI
le jour de Noël	December 25th—Christmas Day

The French are also known for "bridging the gap" *(faire le pont)* between mid-week holidays and weekends by taking additional days off. Remember, too, that the French generally take five weeks of vacation a year, and that August tends to be a slow month for many companies.

JOB TITLES

Following are the French equivalents of some common job titles.

CEO (Chief Executive Officer) and/or Chairman	*PDG (Président Directeur Général)*
President	*le directeur général*
Vice President	*le directeur général adjoint*
Executive Director	*le directeur opérationnel*
Marketing Director	*le directeur du marketing*
Sales Manager	*le directeur des ventes*
Assistant Manager	*le directeur adjoint*
Executive Secretary	*le/la secrétaire de direction*
Head of the Accounting Department	*chef du service de la comptabilité*
a trainee	*un stagaire*

A. *Mettre les phrases suivantes au passé composé.*

1. *L'équipe de nuit passe une demi-heure à nettoyer ses machines.*
2. *Je rentre à la maison épuisé après le travail.*
3. *Le patron sort le rapport du tiroir.*
4. *Didier rentre sa bicyclette dans l'atelier.*
5. *Les deux mécaniciens passent devant l'horloge pointeuse sans s'arrêter.*
6. *Le contremaître démonte une machine dangereuse.*
7. *Pascal et Jacques sortent pour fumer une cigarette pendant la pause.*
8. *Les ouvriers descendent les cartons au sous-sol.*
9. *Tu retournes la caisse pour voir l'autre étiquette.*
10. *À quel arrêt descendez-vous?*

B. *Réécrire les phrases en remplaçant "il y a . . . que" par "depuis."*

1. *Il y a trois mois qu'il travaille chez Renault.*
2. *Il y a deux ans que Patrick habite à Toulouse.*
3. *Il y a une vingtaine d'années que l'entreprise utilise ces machines.*
4. *Il y a trente ans que mon père est contremaître.*
5. *Il y a dix ans que nous fabriquons ces produits.*

C. *Traduire.*

1. She stopped smoking ten years ago.
2. Our union fought against shorter coffee breaks for weeks.
3. These benefits did not exist twenty years ago.
4. Our team had been complaining about this mechanic for weeks when the management fired him.
5. She has not received a raise for two years.
6. The management set up a new training program a year ago.
7. The company has not changed its manufacturing processes for a long time.
8. He had been using the machine for months when it suddenly broke down.
9. The mechanics have been threatening for a month to go on strike.
10. Airbus hired him last week.

LEÇON 8

A. DIALOGUE

UNE HISTOIRE D'AMOUR.

Jeremy assiste à la répétition[1] d'une pièce dans un théâtre parisien.

OENONE: **Aimez-vous?**

PHÈDRE: **De l'amour, j'ai toutes les fureurs.**

OENONE: **Pour qui?**

PHÈDRE: **Tu vas ouïr[2] le comble des horreurs. J'aime . . . À ce nom fatal, je tremble, je frissonne.[3] J'aime . . .**

OENONE: **Qui?**

PHÈDRE: **Tu connais ce fils de l'Amazone, ce prince si longtemps par moi-même opprimé?**

OENONE: **Hippolyte? Grands dieux!**

PHÈDRE: **C'est toi qui l'a nommé!**

OENONE: **Juste ciel! Tout mon sang dans mes veines se glace! O désespoir! O crime! O déplorable race! Voyage infortuné! Rivage malheureux, fallait-il approcher de tes bords dangereux!**

L'auditoire applaudit avec enthousiasme.

BENJAMIN: **Jeremy, je suis à vous dans un instant.**

JEREMY: **Prenez votre temps, je vous en prie.**

Benjamin, metteur en scène,[4] parle aux acteurs.

BENJAMIN: **Répétition demain à quatorze heures précises. Nous reprendrons à partir de l'acte deux. Soyez à l'heure car on a du pain sur la planche![5]**

JEREMY *(parlant à Benjamin):* **Félicitations! C'est vraiment fantastique!**

BENJAMIN: **Ce n'est pas encore au point[6] et je ne suis pas entièrement satisfait des[7] décors. De plus, la costumière est en mal[8] d'inspiration car elle n'a pas reçu les étoffes qu'elle a commandées à Madras.**

JEREMY: **Oh, tout cela finira bien par[9] s'arranger!**

BENJAMIN: **Vous croyez vraiment qu'une adaptation si moderne de Phèdre[10] plaira au public américain? La sensibilité[11] est si différente!**

JEREMY: Croyez-moi, ce sera le coup de foudre! Cette mise en scène très audacieuse fera un tabac.

BENJAMIN: Où en êtes-vous[12] dans la traduction?

JEREMY: Ça avance. Nous voulons assurer une fidélité sans faille à votre interprétation. Je vous préviendrai dès que les surtitres[13] seront au point.

BENJAMIN: Attendez un instant, j'ai quelques mots à dire à l'éclairagiste. Après cela, voulez-vous prendre un café avec moi?

JEREMY: Euh . . .

À cet instant même, Carole s'avance vers Jeremy d'un pas assuré.

BENJAMIN: Ah, je vois . . . Carole m'a devancé.

JEREMY: Carole m'a promis de me faire découvrir un quartier de Paris que je ne connais pas.

CAROLE: Ce serait dommage que Jeremy quitte Paris sans avoir vu le Canal St-Martin.[14]

BENJAMIN: Vous êtes en bonnes mains, Jeremy. Carole connaît Paris comme sa poche.[15] Amusez-vous bien!

JEREMY: Je vous appelle dans le courant de la semaine.

Carole et Jeremy quittent le théâtre et se dirigent vers le Canal.

JEREMY: Tu sais, tu étais vraiment géniale. Le rôle de Phèdre te va comme un gant. Quelle présence sur scène! Je . . .

CAROLE: . . . Et au bord de la Seine?[16]

JEREMY: Vous les acteurs, vous blaguez tout le temps. Vous ne prenez rien au sérieux!

CAROLE: Qu'y a-t-il de si sérieux?

JEREMY: Carole . . .

CAROLE: À ce nom fatal, je tremble, je frissonne . . .

JEREMY: Tu n'as aucune pitié pour un infortuné Américain qui . . .

CAROLE: Voyage infortuné! Rivage malheureux, fallait-il approcher de tes bords dangereux!

JEREMY: Je capitule!

CAROLE: Vais-je ouïr le comble des horreurs?

JEREMY: Carole!

CAROLE: **Oui, Jeremy?**

JEREMY: **Carole, sais-tu que je t'aime?**

A LOVE STORY.

Jeremy attends the rehearsal of a play in a Parisian theater.

OENONE: Are you in love?

PHÈDRE: I feel all love's wild ecstasies.

OENONE: For whom?

PHÈDRE: Now hear the crowning horror. Yes, I love . . . I shake, I tremble at his very name. I love . . .

OENONE: Whom?

PHÈDRE: You know him, son of the Amazon, that prince whom I myself have so long oppressed.

OENONE: Hippolyte? Good heavens!

PHÈDRE: It's you who said his name.

OENONE: Great Heavens, my blood now freezes in my veins! Oh despair! Oh crime! Oh cursed race! Oh ill fated voyage! Why were we doomed ever to approach your dangerous shores!

The audience applauds enthusiastically.

BENJAMIN: Jeremy, I'll be with you in a moment.

JEREMY: Please take your time.

Benjamin, the director, talks to the actors.

BENJAMIN: We'll have a rehearsal tomorrow at two P.M. sharp. We'll start from Act Two. Be on time because we'll have plenty to do!

JEREMY (talking to Benjamin): Congratulations! It was really great!

BENJAMIN: It is not quite there yet, and I'm not fully satisfied with the sets. Also, the costume designer doesn't feel inspired because she hasn't received the fabric she ordered from Madras.

JEREMY: Oh, everything will work out!

BENJAMIN: Do you really think that the American audience will enjoy such a modern adaptation of *Phèdre?* Their sensibility is so different!

JEREMY: Believe me, it'll be love at first sight! This very daring production will be a big hit!

BENJAMIN: At what stage are you in the translation?

113

JEREMY: It's moving along. We want to make sure we'll be completely faithful to your interpretation. I'll let you know as soon as the supertitles are ready.

BENJAMIN: Wait a minute, I have a few things to say to the lighting engineer. After that, would you like to go for coffee with me?

JEREMY: Uh . . .

At that very moment, Carole approaches Jeremy, with a firm, steady step.

BENJAMIN: Oh, I see . . . Carole beat me to it.

JEREMY: Carole promised to help me discover a neighborhood in Paris that I don't know yet.

CAROLE: It would be a shame if Jeremy left Paris without seeing the St. Martin Canal.

BENJAMIN: You'll be in good hands, Jeremy. Carole knows Paris like the back of her hand. Have a great time!

JEREMY: I'll call you during the week.

Carole and Jeremy leave the theater and walk toward the canal.

JEREMY: You know, you were really fantastic. Phèdre's part fits you like a glove. What presence on stage! I . . .

CAROLE: . . . and by the Seine?

JEREMY: You actors are always joking. You don't take anything seriously!

CAROLE: What's so serious?

JEREMY: Carole . . .

CAROLE: "I tremble at that very name."

JEREMY: You have no pity for this poor American who . . .

CAROLE: "Oh, ill fated voyage! Why were we doomed ever to approach your dangerous shores!"

JEREMY: I give up!

CAROLE: "Now hear the crowning horror."

JEREMY: Carole!

CAROLE: Yes, Jeremy?

JEREMY: Carole, do you know I love you?

B. EN BREF

1. *Il y a trop de répétitions dans votre article.* (There is too much repetition in your article.) *Vingt répétitions dans le théâtre sont exigées avant le début du spectacle.* (Twenty rehearsals in the theater are required before the opening of the show.) *La répétition générale commence à 18 heures.* (The dress rehearsal will start at 6 P.M.)

2. *Ouïr* is a literary verb that is rarely used today, but it has modern noun and adjective derivatives. *Elle a l'ouïe fine.* (She has a good ear.) *Ce ne sont que des ouï-dire.* (These are only rumors.) *Je l'ai appris par ouï-dire.* (I found out by hearsay.) *Je suis tout ouïe.* (I'm all ears.) *Elle a vécu une expérience inouïe.* (She had an extraordinary experience.) *La violence de cette pièce est inouïe!* (The violence in this play is unheard of.)

3. In French, as in English, people often tremble with joy or fear. *Jeremy a tressailli de joie en voyant Sabine.* (Jeremy trembled with joy when he saw Sabine.) *Cette pièce me fait frémir.* (This play makes me shiver.) *Tu frissonnes, mets donc une veste!* (You're shivering, put on a jacket!) *Il tremblait de tous ses membres avant de monter sur scène.* (He was shaking all over before going on stage.)

4. *Le metteur en scène* (the director), *le scénariste* (scriptwriter), *le cadreur* (the cameraperson), *l'ingénieur du son* (the sound engineer), *le costumier* (the costume designer).

5. *Sabine est montée sur les planches à l'âge de cinq ans.* (Sabine has been on stage since she was five.) *Elle a brûlé les planches hier soir.* (She shook the house last night.) *Vous avez du travail sur la planche avant la première.* (You have a lot of work to do before the première.—colloquial.) *Carole voudrait faire de la planche à voile.* (Carole would like to go windsurfing.)

6. *Au point* can take on different meanings depending on how it is used: *Votre appareil-photo n'est pas au point.* (Your camera is out of focus.) *Il faut mettre cette affaire au point avant de signer le contrat.* (We have to finalize all the details before signing the contract.) *Cette machine n'est vraiment pas au point.* (This machine is not quite up to snuff yet.) *Nous avons eu une mise au point; depuis, tout va bien.* (We had a discussion; since then, everything is going fine.)

7. The English preposition "with" is often translated into French by another preposition. *Nous sommes satisfaits de la qualité.* (We are satisfied with the quality.) *Elle est contente d'elle-même.* (She is happy with herself.) *Chez Racine, la psychologie joue un rôle important.* (With Racine, psychology plays an important part.)

8. *En mal de* is used like *en manque de*. *Le journaliste est en mal de copie.* (The journalist is short of copy.) *L'auteur dramatique est en mal d'inspiration.* (The playwright is looking for inspiration.)

9. *Finir* can take either *de* or *par* when followed by another verb. *Elle finira d'écrire le scénario d'ici la fin du mois.* (She'll finish writing the scenario by the end of the month.) *Après avoir longuement hésité, il a fini par accepter le rôle principal.* (After hesitating for a long time, he finally accepted the lead.)

10. *Phèdre* is one of Racine's famous tragedies. Although the plot is simple, the characters tend to be complex. Phèdre is passionately in love with her stepson, which is a cause of great suffering, as she believes the passion to be a curse sent by the gods.

11. Be sure to distinguish between *la sensibilité* (sensitivity) and *le bon sens, la raison* (reason).

12. *En être* means to have reached a point. *Où en êtes-vous dans vos recherches?* (How far along are you with your research?) *J'en suis à la moitié.* (I am halfway there.) *J'en suis à la page cinquante.* (I'm on page fifty.) *Il ne sait plus où il en est.* (He does not know where he stands anymore.)

13. *Les surtitres* (supertitles), *les sous-titres* (subtitles), *le doublage* (dubbing).

14. A boat tour of Paris can be taken along the St. Martin Canal starting near the *Parc de la Villette* in the northern section of the city. The full tour takes three hours and features great views of areas unknown to many tourists.

15. The word *poche* appears in many idiomatic expressions. *Elle lui a donné cent francs d'argent de poche.* (She gave him a hundred francs as pocket money.) *Il a payé de sa poche.* (He paid out of his own pocket.) *C'est dans la poche!* (It's in the bag!) *Elle en a été de sa poche.* (She lost out.) *Tout le monde sait qu'il s'est rempli les poches.* (Everyone knows he pocketed a lot of money.) *Sa tante n'a pas sa langue dans sa poche.* (Her aunt is a real chatterbox.)

16. Don't confuse the homonyms *la Seine* (the Seine River), *la scène* (the stage), and *la Cène* (the Last Supper).

C. GRAMMAIRE ET USAGE

1. *LE FUTUR* (THE FUTURE TENSE)

The simple future is formed by adding the future endings *(-ai, -as, -a, -ons, -ez, -ont)* to the infinitive or, for irregular verbs, to the future stem.[1]

	RÉCITER	*APPLAUDIR*	*PRENDRE*
je	*réciterai*	*applaudirai*	*prendrai*
tu	*réciteras*	*applaudiras*	*prendras*
il/elle/on	*récitera*	*applaudira*	*prendra*
nous	*réciterons*	*applaudirons*	*prendrons*
vous	*réciterez*	*applaudirez*	*prendrez*
ils/elles	*réciteront*	*applaudiront*	*prendront*

This tense has many different usages:

a. As in English, it is used to describe events in the future.

Leur troupe jouera Phèdre *à Avignon cet été.*
Their company will stage *Phèdre* in Avignon this summer.

Cette adaptation moderne plaira au public américain.
The American public will enjoy this modern adaptation.

b. In a compound sentence, if the main clause is in the future tense, the dependent clause, introduced by *quand/lorsque* (when), *dès que/aussitôt que* (as soon as), or *tant que* (as long as), will also be in the future. Note that in English, the dependent clause is in the present tense.

Je vous préviendrai dès que les costumes arriveront.
I'll inform you as soon as the costumes arrive.

M'emmènerez-vous au Canal St-Martin quand je serai à Paris?
Will you take me to the St. Martin Canal when I am in Paris?

c. The simple future can be used instead of the imperative to achieve a less peremptory tone.

Vous voudrez bien m'excuser.
Veuillez m'excuser.
Please excuse me.

---

[1] For the conjugation of irregular verbs, consult Appendix I, page 347.

Carole, vous enverrez ce document à Benjamin Lépinay.
Carole, envoyez ce paquet à Benjamin Lépinay.
    Carole, send this document to Benjamin Lépinay.

    d. The simple future can be used to show tact and politeness.

Je vous demanderai d'être très gentil avec lui.
    I am asking you to be very nice to him.

Nous vous serons reconnaissants de ne pas faire de bruit.
    We'll be grateful if you wouldn't make any noise.

    e. The future tense of *avoir* and *être* is sometimes used to express
probability in the present, to indicate something that is likely to be true.

L'acteur a manqué la répétition; il sera encore au lit.
    The actor missed the rehearsal; he is probably still in bed.

Alain n'était pas à la représentation; il aura encore son arthrose!
    Alain was not at the performance; it's probably his arthritis again!

    f. In narration, the simple future can be used to express a future idea
from the standpoint of the past.

Un des plus grands poètes du dix-neuvième et il mourra dans la misère.
    One of the greatest poets of the nineteenth century, and he would die in
misery.

Cet auteur dramatique ne connaîtra la célébrité qu'à un âge avancé.
    This playwright would not become famous until his old age.

2. *LE FUTUR ANTÉRIEUR* (THE FUTURE PERFECT)

To form this compound tense, use the future tense of the auxiliary *avoir*
or *être* and the past participle of the main verb. Although this tense is
rarely used in English, it must be used in French under certain
circumstances.

	JOUER	PARTIR
je	aurai joué	serai parti(e)
tu	auras joué	seras parti(e)
il/elle/on	aura joué	sera parti(e)
nous	aurons joué	serons parti(e)s
vous	aurez joué	serez parti(e)(s)
ils/elles	auront joué	seront parti(e)s

The future perfect describes an action that will have occurred prior to another action or moment in the future.

Je vous appellerai dès que vous serez rentré aux États-Unis.
I'll call you as soon as you return to the United States.

Nous aurons réglé tous les problèmes avant le 15 septembre.
We'll have worked out all the problems before September 15th.

The future perfect can also be used to express probability in the past, in the same way that the simple future is used to express probability in the present.

Elle aura encore fait des bêtises!
She probably got into trouble again!

Il aura laissé ses clés dans la voiture. Allez vite les chercher!
He probably left his keys in the car. Go get them, and fast!

3. *LES PRONOMS DISJOINTS* (DISJUNCTIVE PRONOUNS)

In French, the disjunctive pronouns are: *moi, toi, lui, elle, nous, vous, eux,* and *elles.* They can be used:

a. for emphasis.

Toi seule pouvais incarner le rôle de Phèdre.
You alone could play the role of Phèdre.

Lui aussi savait qu'une telle pièce présentait des risques.
He, too, knew that such a play was risky.

Ce prince si longtemps par moi-même opprimé.
This prince so long oppressed by me.

b. with *c'est . . . qui . . .* (it's . . . who). Note that where English usually uses tone for emphasis, French uses repetition.

C'est lui qui a obtenu le rôle principal.
He got the lead. (literally: It's he who got the lead.)

C'est vous qui devez régler l'éclairage.
You must set the lighting. (literally: It's you who must set the lighting.)

c. in conjunction with another subject.

Carole et moi, nous allons faire un tour en péniche sur le canal.
Carole and I are going for a barge ride on the canal.

Lui et ses copains ne cessent de blaguer.
He and his friends never stop joking.

d. after a first- or second-person affirmative imperative (unless *y* and *en* are used as well).

Amuse-toi bien!
Enjoy yourself!

Prévenez-moi dès que les surtitres seront prêts.
Let me know as soon as the supertitles are ready.

Va-t-en!
Go away!

e. in short responses where the verb is omitted. (Notice that the verb often appears in English.)

Qui a vu le nouveau spectacle au Palais des Congrès?—Moi!
Who's seen the new show at the *Palais des Congrès?*—I have!

Il aime les comédies. Nous aussi.
He likes comedies. So do we.

Elle n'est jamais allée au Théâtre de l'Atelier. Eux non plus.
She has never been at the *Théâtre de l'Atelier.* Neither have they.

f. after prepositions.

Je suis à vous dans un instant.
I'll be with you in a moment.

Phèdre s'avança vers lui.
Phèdre moved toward him.

Nous irons au théâtre avec eux vendredi en huit.
We'll go to the theater with them a week from Friday.

Le metteur en scène a vraiment confiance en eux.
The director really trusts them.

g. with *ne . . . que.*

Les spectateurs n'avaient d'yeux que pour elle.
The audience only had eyes for her.

Au premier acte, il n'y avait que lui sur la scène.
In the first act, there was no one but him on stage.

120

4. *SAVOIR ET CONNAÎTRE* (*SAVOIR* AND *CONNAÎTRE*)

Savoir is used:

a. when referring to knowledge of a fact or thorough knowledge of a subject.

Elle sait ce poème par cœur.
She knows this poem by heart.

Nous savons notre leçon.
We know our lesson.

b. when referring to the ability (knowing how) to do something, usually acquired after practice and repetition. Note that "how" is implied and not translated.

Il sait mettre au point l'éclairage.
He knows how to set the lighting.

Notre ingénieur du son sait tout faire.
Our sound engineer can do anything.

Savez-vous[2] jouer au tennis.
Can you (do you know how to) play tennis?

If "to know how" is followed by an infinitive and explicitly refers to the manner in which something is done (*par quel moyen, de quelle façon, de quelle manière),* "how" needs to be stated.

Je ne sais vraiment pas comment vous expliquer.
I really don't know how to explain.

Elle ne sait pas comment exprimer sa gratitude.
She doesn't know how to express her gratitude.

c. with conjunctions.

Il ne sait pas pourquoi le souffleur n'est pas dans la fosse.
He does not know why the prompter is not in the pit.

On ne sait pas si le remplaçant sera à la hauteur.
We do not know if the understudy will be up to the task.

La maquilleuse ne sait pas qui a pris sa poudre de riz.
The makeup artist does not know who took her face powder.

---

[2] Note the difference between physical ability and permission: *savoir* versus *pouvoir.*

Je ne peux pas jouer au tennis aujourd'hui parce que je suis enrhumée.
I can't play tennis today because I have a cold.

Connaître is used:

    a. to express knowledge of or acquaintance with a person or place, or to indicate only cursory knowledge of a subject.

Connaissez-vous le metteur en scène de cette pièce?
Do you know this play's director?

Il connaît Paris comme sa poche.
He knows Paris like the back of his hand.

Je connais ce poème mais je ne pourrais pas vous le réciter.
I am familiar with this poem, but I would not be able to recite it for you.

    b. in the past tense to mean "to meet," although this is an old-fashioned usage. Today, *rencontrer* is preferred.

Il a connu/rencontré sa femme à une soirée.
He met his wife at a party.

Elle l'a connu/rencontré dans un cinéma.
She met him in a movie theater.

    c. in a figurative way to mean "to have, to enjoy, to feel, to experience."

Ce théâtre connaît un succès inattendu.
This theater is enjoying unexpected success.

Leur bonté ne connaît pas de bornes.
Their kindness knows no limits.

La plupart des acteurs connaissent la misère avant la célébrité.
Most actors know poverty before fame.

De nos jours, bon nombre de pays connaissent la famine.
Nowadays, many a country knows famine.

D. JEU DE MOTS

It's not surprising that the word *amour* is heard often in France.

Jeremy était fou d'amour.
Jeremy was madly in love.

On ne peut pas vivre d'amour et d'eau fraîche.
One cannot live on love alone.

L'amour libre était à la mode dans les années 60.
Free love was in fashion in the 1960s.

À tes amours!
    Here's to you!

Elle l'a fait pour l'amour de l'art.
    She did it for the love of it.

Son manque d'amour-propre a déçu Carole.
    His lack of self-esteem disappointed Carole.

Son mal d'amour l'isolait de ses amis.
    His lovesickness isolated him from his friends.

C'est une enfant de l'amour.
    She is a love child.

L'amour est aveugle.
    Love is blind.

Comment vont les amours?
    How is your love life?

C'est un amour de petit bébé.
    It's a darling little baby.

C'est un remède à l'amour.
    It's a remedy for love.

C'est une de mes anciennes amours.
    He is one of my old flames.

E. LE COIN DES AFFAIRES

ÉTIQUETTE (ETIQUETTE)

Your knowledge of French may prove to be one of your most effective tools when doing business in France. Addressing your business partners in French will help to establish a positive relationship from the start. Don't be surprised or insulted if they respond in English—it's not a reflection of your speaking ability, but rather an eagerness on their part to practice their English. Feel free to revert back to French, and don't be embarrassed about your mistakes. Politely say: *Veuillez excuser mes fautes mais cela me fait tellement plaisir de parler votre langue.* (Please excuse my mistakes, but I like to speak your language.) Don't be afraid to joke about your mistakes. Saying *je suis chaud/e* ("I'm hot"—sexually), when you mean to say *j'ai chaud* ("I'm hot," i.e., "it's warm in here"), may help to elicit a smile even from the most conservative audience.

Whether traveling abroad, or receiving a French visitor on home ground, having your business cards printed in French as well as in English will avoid any misunderstandings and communicate respect for your foreign partners. If you have a written agenda prepared for your meeting, it, too, should be in both French and English. When introducing American associates to your French partners, be sure to state not only their name, but their title as well. If talks are conducted in English and your French partner is not fluent, try to have an interpreter available. If none is available, be sure to stop periodically and summarize the content of the discussions in French. Encourage your partner to ask questions and participate in the discussions (with or without your help) at any time.

When in France, knowledge of the language will enable you to read the local papers, watch television, enjoy the theater, generally keep abreast of local politics and gossip, and get an inside look at the social fabric of French society. Your familiarity with French culture will impress your partners and open many doors for you. The French are renowned conversationalists and appreciate well-informed "sparring partners." The ability to hold your own in a heated debate will be respected, though such arguments should be avoided in an office environment.

While strong opinions are encouraged, it is never appropriate to lecture people on their habits or way of life. A common *faux-pas* made by Americans is to denounce smokers. While the anti-smoking campaign is gaining much ground in France, it is still considered inappropriate to try to educate the French on the dangers of smoking. Your *Eteignez votre cigarette, s'il vous plaît.* (Please put out your cigarette.) or *La fumée me dérange.* (The smoke bothers me.) may be met with a harsh stare.

Finally, remember that understatement is the norm in France. While in the United States, you would be expected to act self-assured and to let your partners know what makes you the best person to do business with. In France, people will never openly "sing their own praises," but they will make you aware of them.

Try not to overemphasize anything, especially the size of your country as compared to France, or the superiority of your technology over your partners'. Furthermore, try to use your hosts' measurement and monetary systems; that is, talk in francs, liters, and meters, instead of dollars, gallons, and yards. For example, while blocks are a very common measurement of distance here, no such concept exists in French. Thus, to say "My office is fifteen blocks away from my house," you would have to translate your idea into minutes, meters, or subway stations: *Mon bureau est à quinze minutes (trois stations de métro) de chez moi.* Finally, be open to the different culture and aware that there simply won't be a parallel in France for everything you are accustomed to in the United States.

EXERCICES

A. *Mettre les phrases suivantes au futur.*

1. *Cette nouvelle pièce fait un tabac.*
2. *Jeremy connaît Paris comme sa poche.*
3. *Elle frissonne de peur avant de monter sur scène.*
4. *L'auteur dramatique est à court d'idées.*
5. *Le scénariste envoie le dernier acte au metteur en scène.*
6. *Vous mettez au point la dernière scène.*
7. *Est-ce que tu as le trac?*
8. *Nous pouvons faire une adaptation plus audacieuse.*
9. *Vous nous prévenez de votre retard.*
10. *La troupe part pour Tokyo la semaine prochaine.*

B. *Conjuguer les verbes entre parenthèses.*

1. *L'emmèneras-tu au café-théâtre quand elle (être) à Paris?*
2. *Les parents de Carole assisteront à une répétition lorsqu'ils (venir) à Paris.*
3. *L'auteur m'enverra la scénario dès qu'il (pouvoir).*
4. *Tant qu'elle sera actrice, elle (devoir) suivre des cours de danse.*
5. *Ils iront à Shanghai quand ils (faire) une tournée en Chine.*

C. *Traduire en employant les pronoms disjoints.*

1. *Moi, je vais à la répétition et (you) où vas-tu?*
2. *Voulez-vous faire un tour en péniche avec (them)?*
3. *Je n'aime pas les comédies.* (Neither does he.)
4. *L'acteur s'est dirigé vers (us).*
5. *C'est (her) qui fait la traduction de la pièce.*

D. *Traduire.*

1. Do you know Émilie, the new understudy?
2. Do you know if Carole will play the role of Phèdre?
3. The lighting engineer will create a romantic mood.
4. The actors know their parts by heart.
5. The costume designer does not know if Phèdre will like her dress.
6. The play will enjoy great success in the United States.
7. Young actors experience poverty at the beginning of their career.
8. Do all actors know how to sing?

LEÇON 9

A. DIALOGUE

LA CUISINE.

Michael fait un stage au Cordon Bleu[1] à Paris.

LE CHEF: Assurez-vous que vous avez devant vous tous les ingrédients nécessaires pour le soufflé[2] au chocolat à la Proust:[3] 125 grammes de chocolat amer,[4] 350 millilitres de lait, 150 grammes de beurre, 60 grammes de farine, 200 grammes de sucre en poudre, 6 œufs, une cuillère à café d'extrait de vanille, un demi-verre de rhum.

MATHILDE *(à son voisin):* Un vrai dessert minceur![5]

LE CHEF: Pendant que le chocolat fond[6] doucement dans le lait, mélangez la farine et le sucre dans un bol de taille moyenne.

MICHAEL: Avec une cuillère?

LE CHEF: Non, avec une spatule[7] en bois.

MICHAEL: Puis on ajoute la farine et le sucre au beurre fondu?

LE CHEF: Et vous fouettez énergiquement.

MATHILDE: Et ensuite on sépare les jaunes des blancs?

LE CHEF: Non, non, non! . . . D'abord vous versez le chocolat fondu sur le mélange beurre-sucre-farine en remuant jusqu'à ce que tout soit bien lisse. Vous reversez le tout dans la casserole en cuivre[8] et vous ajoutez le reste des ingrédients.

MATHILDE: Et c'est ça, le soufflé au chocolat à la Proust?

LE CHEF: "Mais à l'instant même où la gorgée mêlée de miettes de gâteau toucha mon palais, je tressaillis, attentif à ce qui se passait d'extraordinaire en moi. Un plaisir délicieux m'avait envahi, isolé, sans la notion de sa cause . . ."[9]

MICHAEL: Impressionnant! Notre chef est un véritable poète!

LE CHEF: Monsieur, Marcel Proust nous a légué une œuvre littéraire remarquable mais aussi des recettes,[10] des menus et des décors de table de la Belle Époque[11]—un trésor inestimable! Qui n'a jamais rêvé de dîner avec la duchesse de Guermantes?[12]

MATHILDE: Zut![13] Ça brûle![14] Ah! C'est tout collé au fond![15]

LE CHEF: En cuisine, Mademoiselle, il faut faire preuve d'une vigilance sans faille. Recommencez en suivant la recette.

MICHAEL: **Je peux vous aider?**

MATHILDE: **Volontiers. Vous seriez gentil de me relire la recette.**

MICHAEL: **Mettre les carrés de chocolat dans une casserole. Ajouter le lait et faire chauffer à feu doux. Faire fondre le beurre. Après avoir mélangé la farine et le sucre, verser . . .**

MATHILDE: **Séparer les jaunes des blancs. Ça y est! Je m'en souviens . . . Cette fois, je vais surveiller pour ne rien brûler.**

LE CHEF: **Un peu plus d'énergie pour battre vos œufs en neige! C'est de l'huile de coude**[16] **qu'il vous faut!**

MICHAEL: **Ça va comme ça?**

LE CHEF: **C'est mieux . . . Bon, maintenant, beurrez vos ramequins et surtout ne lésinez pas sur le beurre, sinon . . .**

MICHAEL: **On laisse le four à 200°**[17] **pendant toute la cuisson?**

LE CHEF: **Absolument! Les soufflés doivent cuire**[18] **à température constante pendant 20 minutes.**

MATHILDE: **Et est-ce qu'il y a un truc**[19] **pour les empêcher de s'effondrer?**

LE CHEF: **Le truc, c'est l'expérience et la persévérance, Mademoiselle.**

MATHILDE: **Alors, on n'est pas au bout de nos peines!**

LE CHEF: **Bon, nous allons maintenant parler de la présentation. Présenter un plat, comme à l'époque de Monsieur Proust, c'est tout un art.**

MATHILDE *(à Michael):* **Pourquoi en faire tout un plat?**[20] **C'est vraiment le goût qui compte, non?**

LE CHEF: **Le meilleur soufflé au chocolat qui n'est pas présenté dans de la faïence sur une nappe pimpante et dégusté avec la plus belle argenterie, n'est pas digne de ce nom.**

MICHAEL: **Et Proust était très sensible au parfum des fleurs, si j'ai bonne mémoire.**

LE CHEF: **Il s'en entourait toujours: des roses, des pivoines, des hortensias, des chrysanthèmes**[21] **japonais . . . Si les fleurs n'embellissaient pas la table, elles décoraient les mets exquis.**

MICHAEL: **Quel parfum! Nos soufflés embaument**[22] **la cuisine.**

LE CHEF: **L'heure de vérité . . . Tout le monde à table! Marc, apportez-nous le Vouvray**[23] **pour accompagner ces succulents desserts.**

COOKING.

Michael is studying at the *Cordon Bleu* in Paris.

THE CHEF: Make sure you have all the necessary ingredients in front of you for Proust's chocolate soufflé: 4½ ounces of bittersweet chocolate, 1½ cups of milk, 5 ounces of butter, ½ cup of flour, a cup of powdered sugar, 6 eggs, a teaspoon of vanilla extract, half a glass of rum.

MATHILDE (to her neighbor): A real low-calorie dessert!

THE CHEF: While the chocolate slowly melts in the milk, mix in the flour and the sugar in a medium-size bowl.

MICHAEL: With a spoon?

THE CHEF: No, with a wooden spatula.

MICHAEL: Then we add the flour and the sugar to the melted butter?

THE CHEF: And whip energetically.

MATHILDE: And then do we separate the egg yolks from the whites?

THE CHEF: No, no, no! First you pour the melted chocolate over the butter-sugar-flour mixture, stirring until smooth. You pour everything back into the copper pan and you add the rest of the ingredients.

MATHILDE: And that's what Proust's chocolate soufflé is all about?

THE CHEF: "No sooner had the warm liquid mixed with the crumbs touched my palate than a shudder ran through me and I stopped, intent upon the extraordinary thing that was happening to me. An exquisite pleasure had invaded my senses, something isolated, detached, with no suggestion of its origin . . ."

MICHAEL: Impressive! Our chef is a real poet!

THE CHEF: Sir, Marcel Proust bequeathed us a remarkable body of literary work but also recipes, menus, and Belle Époque table settings—a priceless treasure! Who has never dreamed of dining with the Duchess of Guermantes?

MATHILDE: Shoot! It's burning! Oh! It's all stuck to the bottom!

THE CHEF: With gourmet cooking, miss, one must exercise a flawless vigilance. Start all over, following the recipe.

MICHAEL: Can I help you?

MATHILDE: Please. It would be very nice of you to read the recipe over for me.

MICHAEL: Put the chocolate pieces into a pan. Add the milk and heat over a low flame. Melt the butter. After mixing in the flour and the sugar, pour . . .

MATHILDE: Separate the yolks from the whites. That's it! I remember . . . This time, I'm going to keep an eye on it in order not to burn anything.

THE CHEF: A little more energy to whip the egg whites to stiff peaks! What you need is elbow grease!

MICHAEL: Is it all right like this?

THE CHEF: It's better . . . So, now, butter your soufflé dishes and don't skimp on the butter, or . . .

MICHAEL: Do we leave the oven at 400° the entire time it's cooking?

THE CHEF: Absolutely! Soufflés must cook at a constant temperature for 20 minutes.

MATHILDE: And is there a trick to prevent them from collapsing?

THE CHEF: The trick is experience and perseverance, miss.

MATHILDE: We still have a long way to go then, don't we?

THE CHEF: So, now we're going to talk about presentation. To present a dish as in Monsieur Proust's time is really an art.

MATHILDE (to Michael): Why make such a fuss about it? It's really the taste that counts, right?

THE CHEF: The best chocolate soufflé not presented on fine china with a spanking clean tablecloth and eaten with the finest silverware, is not worthy of its name!

MICHAEL: And Proust was sensitive to the fragrance of flowers, if I remember well.

THE CHEF: He always surrounded himself with flowers: roses, peonies, hydrangeas, Japanese chrysanthemums. If the flowers were not used to embellish the table, they decorated the exquisite foods.

MICHAEL: It smells so good . . . Our soufflés are filling the kitchen with a wonderful aroma!

THE CHEF: The moment of truth . . . Everyone to the table! Marc, bring us the Vouvray to go with these delicious desserts.

B. EN BREF

1. *Le Cordon Bleu,* located in Paris, is one of the most renowned cooking schools in the world.

2. A *soufflé* gets its name from the verb meaning "to blow" because it puffs up in the oven. You can savor *un soufflé au fromage* (a cheese soufflé), *un soufflé au chocolat* (a chocolate soufflé), or *un soufflé aux moules* (a soufflé with mussels).

3. Proust's *À la recherche du temps perdu (Remembrance of Things Past)* was originally published in eight parts, of which *Du côté de chez Swann* (1913) is probably the best known.

4. The word "bitter" can be translated in different ways according to the context: *une orange amère* (a bitter orange), *un hiver rigoureux* (a bitter winter), *un vent cinglant* (a bitter wind), *une violente opposition* (a bitter opposition), *des critiques acerbes* (bitter criticism). But to describe a bitter taste, *amer* is always used.

5. *La cuisine minceur* or *la cuisine légère* was popularized by the famous chef Michel Guérard, who hosted a successful television show and published many best-selling cookbooks.

6. The following verbs are often confused: *fondre* (to melt), *fendre* (to crack), *feindre* (to pretend). *Le chocolat est fondu.* (The chocolate is melted.) *L'assiette est fendue au milieu.* (The plate is cracked in the middle.) *Elle feint de ne pas savoir faire la cuisine.* (She pretends she can't cook.)

7. Here are the names of a few utensils that will come in handy when cooking: *la casserole* (pan), *la poêle* (frying pan), *le fouet* (whip), *le tamis* (sieve), *la louche* (ladle), *l'écumoir* (skimmer), *la planche à découper* (cutting board), *le saladier* (salad bowl), *le batteur* (whisk), *le rouleau à pâtisserie* (rolling pin), *l'égouttoir* (colander).

8. Although stainless steel is widely used, serious chefs still use copper pans to prepare certain sauces that require slow and constant cooking.

9. This is a quotation from *À la recherche du temps perdu* in which the narrator tries to relive the past. The flavor of a *madeleine* (a small cake in the shape of a shell) dipped in tea reminds him of a childhood moment.

10. The word *recette* takes on different meanings according to the context: *C'est la meilleure recette pour les chaussons aux pommes.* (This is the best recipe for apple turnovers.) *L'épicier a fait une bonne recette aujourd'hui.* (The grocer's cash receipts were good today.) *Elle réussit tout ce qu'elle entreprend, je voudrais bien avoir la recette.* (She is successful with everything she undertakes; I'd love to know her secret.) *Son idée a fait recette.* (His idea is a winner.)

11. *La Belle Époque* (1871–1914) was the era of elegance and gaiety that characterized fashionable Parisian life in the period preceding World War I.

12. *La duchesse de Guermantes* is a character in *Du côté de chez Swann* with whom the narrator falls in love. By satirizing the selfishness of that world, Proust analyzes the mechanism of creativity.

13. Another non-vulgar exclamation, expressing discontent or annoyance, is *flûte!*

14. The verb *brûler* is used in many idiomatic expressions. *Brûler la chandelle par les deux bouts.* (To burn the candle at both ends.) *Brûler des étapes.* (To skip steps.) *Brûler les planches.* (To light up the stage.) *Brûler un feu.* (To run a red light.) *Le torchon brûle!* (The battle rages!) *Brûler de faire quelque chose.* (To be dying to do something.)

15. *Au fond* is an expression that may come in handy. *Au fond du cinéma.* (In the back of the theater.) *Au fond de mon coeur.* (From the bottom of my heart.) *Au fond.* (In reality.) *Au fond du couloir.* (Down the hall.)

16. The word *huile* appears in many idiomatic expressions—*une grosse huile* (a big shot), *jeter de l'huile sur le feu* (to add fuel to the fire), *ça baigne dans l'huile* (everything is looking great), *faire tache d'huile* (to spread).

17. In Europe, temperature is measured in centigrade.

18. Be careful with the verbs *cuire* and *bouillir:* they must be used with *faire* when the action is carried out by a person but without *faire* when their subject is the thing being cooked or boiled. *Le rôti cuit dans le four.* (The roast is cooking in the oven.) *Je fais cuire le rôti.* (I cook the roast.) *L'eau bout.* (The water is boiling.) *Je fais bouillir de l'eau.* (I am boiling some water.) The only time *bouillir* is used without *faire* when its subject is a person is in the figurative sense: *Je bous de colère.* (I am fuming.)

19. If you're not sure what to call something or how to refer to a trick or an unclear situation, you can always use *truc*. *Où as-tu acheté ce truc?* (Where did you buy this thing?) *Pierre m'a raconté un truc incroyable.* (Pierre told me an incredible thing.) *Elle a trouvé le truc pour le faire arriver à l'heure.* (She found the trick for making him come on time.) *Je connais son truc.* (I know what he's up to.)

20. In addition to meaning "dish," *plat* has some creative usages. *Il lui mijote toujours des petits plats.* (He always cooks the most delicious dishes for her.) *Elle en a fait tout un plat.* (She made a fuss about it.) *Ils ont mis les petits plats dans les grands pour son 30ᵉ anniversaire.* (They made a big splash for her 30th birthday.) *Elle voudrait qu'on lui apporte tout sur un plat d'argent.* (She wants everything handed to her on a silver platter.) *Il a encore mis les pieds dans le plat!* (He put his foot in his mouth again!)

21. Flowers, which were associated with various divinities in ancient times, still have a symbolic meaning in different cultures. In France, an anemone means a break-up; a nasturtium, indifference; a daisy, innocence; and a chrysanthemum, death. One should never send *les œillets* (carnations), as they are suspected of having *le mauvais œil* (the evil eye). Watch out for colors, too: yellow, for example, implies you've been the victim of infidelity. Whichever flowers you choose, make sure you give an odd number.

22. The verb *embaumer* presents a few problems in translation: *Les roses embaument la chambre.* (The roses fill the room with a wonderful scent.) *L'air embaume le jasmin.* (The air is fragrant with jasmine.) *Les Égyptiens embaumaient leurs morts.* (Egyptians embalmed their dead.)

23. Vouvray, a town near Tours, in the Loire Valley, is famous for its dry white wine.

C. GRAMMAIRE ET USAGE

1. *L'INFINITIF* (THE INFINITIVE)

In French, the infinitive is rather versatile and has a wide range of uses:

a. The injunctive infinitive.
The injunctive infinitive is used in general instructions, public notices, and proverbs.

Égoutter les légumes et ajouter une gousse d'ail.
Drain the vegetables and add a clove of garlic.

Ne pas se pencher par la fenêtre.
Do not lean out of the window.

Voir Venise et mourir.
To see Venice and die.

b. The interrogative infinitive.

Comment résister à une pareille tentation?
How (am I) to resist such a temptation?

Que dire?
What else (is there) to say?

Pourquoi en faire tout un plat?
Why make a fuss about it?

c. The infinitive after verbs of perception.
In French, verbs of perception are followed by the infinitive, while in English we generally use the present participle.

Mathilde entend le chef crier du fond de la cuisine.
 Mathilde hears the chef shouting from the back of the kitchen.

Michel voit le soufflé monter dans le four.
 Michel sees the soufflé rising in the oven.

Les étudiants l'écoutent expliquer en détail la recette.
 The students are listening to him explain the recipe in detail.

d. The infinitive after *faire* and *laisser*.

Ils nous ont fait entrer dans le salon.
 They showed us into the living room.

Le chef l'a laissé pétrir la pâte.
 The chef allowed him to knead the dough.

e. Verbs directly followed by the infinitive.
While the infinitive is often introduced by a preposition, a number of verbs are followed directly by the infinitive. These include: *aller, courir, descendre, désirer, devoir, envoyer, falloir, monter, oser, pouvoir, savoir, valoir,* and *vouloir.*

L'apprenti doit broyer les amandes pour faire le gâteau.
 The apprentice must grind the almonds to make the cake.

Il faut hacher la viande pour faire des hamburgers.
 One must mince meat to make hamburgers.

f. Infinitives introduced by prepositions.
A great many verbs are followed by prepositions,[1] but there are absolutely no set rules guiding your choice. It is simply a matter of memorization.

After certain verbs, such as *aider, réussir, s'intéresser,* and *s'attendre,* the infinitive is introduced by *à.* After other verbs and expressions, such as *éviter, permettre, projeter,* and *avoir peur,* it is introduced by *de.*

Il nous a appris à faire une vraie mayonnaise française.
 He taught us how to make a real French mayonnaise.

---

[1] For more on the usage of prepositions with infinitives see *Leçon* 14.

Michael l'a aidée à démouler la Charlotte aux poires.
Michael helped her remove her Pear Charlotte from the mold.

Tu as peur de râper le fromage trop fin.
You're afraid of grating the cheese too finely.

Il faut éviter de mettre trop de sel dans la ratatouille.
One must avoid putting too much salt in the ratatouille.

With certain verbs, the infinitive can follow *à* or *de,* but the meaning of these verbs changes with the preposition (e.g., *décider de, se décider à; s'occuper de, s'occuper à*). Compare:

Le chef a décidé de faire un saumon poché.
The chef decided to make poached salmon.

Elle s'est finalement décidé à apprendre à faire la cuisine!
She finally made up her mind to learn how to cook.

g. The past infinitive.
When introducing a past action (with the preposition *après*), the past infinitive (the infinitive of *avoir* or *être* + the past participle of the main verb) should be used in French. Note that this form is seldom used in English, where the -ing form of a verb is generally preferred.

T'es-tu excusé après avoir renversé la poêle?
Did you apologize after knocking (having knocked) over the frying pan?

Le chef a mis le gigot d'agneau au four après l'avoir fait mariner.
The chef put the leg of lamb in the oven after marinating (having marinated) it.

2. *LE PRONOM "EN"* (THE PRONOUN *EN*)

When *en* precedes a verb in a compound tense, the past participle never agrees with it.

Elle a mis trois tranches fines de jambon dans l'assiette.
She put three thin slices of ham on the plate.

Elle en a mis trois dans l'assiette.
She put three (of them) in the plate.

Le chef a râpé une livre de fromage.
The chef grated one pound of cheese.

Le chef en a râpé une livre.
The chef grated one pound (of it).

D. JEU DE MOTS

The verb "to show" can be translated into French in many different ways, depending on context.

Elle fait preuve de beaucoup de courage.
She shows a lot of courage.

Le chef est fatigué et ça se voit.
The chef is tired, and it shows.

Ils passeront un film sur la cuisine.
They'll show a film on cooking.

Fais-moi voir ta tarte aux prunes.
Show me your plum pie.

Sa façon de s'habiller témoigne de son bon goût.
Her choice of clothes shows her good taste.

Les efforts qu'il y a consacrés n'ont rien donné.
He has nothing to show for all the effort he put into it.

Il faudrait qu'elle fasse acte de présence à la soirée de Stéphane.
She ought to show (make an appearance) at Stéphane's party.

Tu dois abattre tes cartes.
You have to show your hand.

E. LE COIN DES AFFAIRES

LES REPAS D'AFFAIRES (BUSINESS MEALS)

The business breakfast is fairly new to the French, who have always enjoyed spending their mornings alone or with their families, with a good cup of coffee, fresh croissants, and the daily paper. *Le power breakfast,* as it's commonly referred to, is now the trend, but its future remains uncertain.

Business lunches are a long-standing French tradition, though their duration is decreasing to accommodate the fast pace of modern living. It may not be uncommon, however, for your French host to take you to a fine restaurant for a meal that lasts for hours. It is customary to begin with small talk about topics of general interest, and then gradually ease into business discussions. It is not inappropriate for you, as the foreigner, to initiate talk of business, but don't expect to close a deal or sign a contract over lunch. The check should be paid by the person who extended the invitation.

If you wish to take someone to lunch, you should make your intentions clear to avoid quarreling over the check. A common invitation is: *Cela me ferait plaisir de vous inviter à déjeuner.* (It would be a great pleasure to treat you to lunch.) You should always suggest a good restaurant, but don't be surprised to hear your host suggest: *Et si on déjeunait à la brasserie du coin?* (What about having lunch at the *brasserie* on the corner?) If you insist on a fine restaurant, be sure to make reservations in advance and to arrive ten to fifteen minutes ahead of time to welcome your guests. Once you are shown to your table, it is your responsibility to seat your guests, generally according to seniority, gender (alternate men and women), or your own personal interest. Keep in mind that fancy, extended lunches should be reserved for special occasions: to make a good first impression or to celebrate an important deal. The simpler lunches at a *brasserie* are more common.

Business dinners are less common than lunches, as the business day ends later in France than in the United States, and the French are very protective of their private time. If a dinner is most convenient for both parties, the conventions are the same as for business lunches. If you are invited to dinner, it is not uncommon for the host's spouse to join you. However, if you extend the invitation, you should not invite his or her spouse unless you already know them.

Although you are unlikely to be invited to your host's home—the French like to keep their private and business lives separate—if by chance you do get an invitation, there are a few rules to follow. Avoid discussing business before coffee is served, and do not smoke before the end of the meal. It is considered improper to comment about the food being served. It is assumed that you would never be served anything sub-standard, and thus any comments, even complimentary ones, are superfluous. A thank-you note to the hosts, however, will be appreciated: *Je tiens à vous remercier de cette très agréable soirée. Cela m'a fait plaisir de faire la connaissance de votre famille et de vos amis. Je vous prie de croire à l'assurance de mes sentiments.* (I wish to thank you for this wonderful evening. It was a pleasure to meet your family and friends. Sincerely.)

Once they welcome you into their home, the French are extremely hospitable and social. Your business connections may lead to some lasting friendships, and you may find yourself invited to many social and cultural events, or to a private country home. It would then be poor form to decline the invitation without a legitimate reason.

EXERCICES

A. *Compléter avec les verbes suivants au présent ou à l'infinitif: éplucher, égoutter, battre, pétrir, broyer, bouillir, hacher, mariner, râper, démouler.*

1. *Mathilde doit _____ les amandes amères pour faire le dessert.*
2. *L'apprenti _____ 500 grammes de gruyère pour le soufflé.*
3. *Est-ce qu'il faut _____ les pommes de terre nouvelles?*
4. *Michael _____ le flan avant de le servir.*
5. *Le boulanger _____ la pâte.*
6. *Est-ce que tu pourrais _____ les spaghettis?*
7. *Fais _____ de l'eau pour faire du thé.*
8. *Elle _____ cinq œufs pour faire une omelette.*
9. *Le chef lui a dit de _____ la viande.*
10. *Il vaut faire _____ ce morceau de bœuf plusieurs heures.*

B. *Traduire les verbes entre parenthèses.*

1. *Mathilde* (succeeded) *démouler le gâteau au chocolat.*
2. *Il vaudrait mieux* (to take) *un cours dans cette école de cuisine.*
3. *Le chef leur* (allows) *se servir d'une spatule en plastique.*
4. *Après des mois d'hésitation, Mathilde* (decided) *s'inscrire au Cordon Bleu.*
5. *Le sous-chef me* (helped) *décorer les plats.*
6. *Michel Guérard* (plans) *ouvrir un nouveau restaurant.*
7. *Est-ce que tu* (dared) *demander la recette au patron?*
8. *Nous* (expect) *recevoir un diplôme à la fin de notre stage.*
9. *Ce critique culinaire* (is interested in) *trouver des recettes inconnues.*
10. *Nous* (decided) *faire un gigot d'agneau.*

C. *Traduire.*

1. Michael is having fun learning how to make a chocolate mousse.
2. Add a clove of garlic, and cook for an hour.
3. In order to avoid burning the sauce, one must stir it slowly.
4. He peeled the potatoes and put them in the frying pan.
5. She melted the butter before pouring it in the pan.

LEÇON 10

A. DIALOGUE

DANS UNE PARFUMERIE.

Mme Moore, rédactrice[1] d'un magazine de mode,[2] fait des recherches[3] pour rédiger un article sur l'industrie de la parfumerie. Sa première étape:[4] une parfumerie[5] à Chartres[6] que M. Amaury lui fait visiter.

MME MOORE: **Ces machines sont impressionnantes! À quoi servent-elles?**

M. AMAURY: **C'est dans ces centrifugeuses que l'on[7] mélange les ingrédients.**

MME MOORE: **Où vous procurez-vous tous les ingrédients?**

M. AMAURY: **Peut-être avez-vous aperçu notre serre en arrivant.[8]**

MME MOORE: **Ah! Cette énorme bulle?[9] Qu'est-ce que vous y faites pousser?**

M. AMAURY: **Des myriades de plantes: des violettes, des iris, du mimosa, des narcisses, de la lavande, de la sauge et bien d'autres . . .**

MME MOORE: **Vous faites tout pousser sur place?**

M. AMAURY: **Non, nos chercheurs sillonnent le monde en quête de senteurs exotiques: le bois de santal en Inde, les roses en Bulgarie etc.**

MME MOORE: **Alors, tous vos ingrédients sont naturels?**

M. AMAURY: **Non, certaines senteurs, comme le muguet, sont issues de produits de synthèse.**

MME MOORE: **Quel est le processus de fabrication?**

M. AMAURY: **D'abord les matières premières sont pesées, puis mélangées. Ensuite on ajoute de l'alcool.[10] Une fois dilué, le jus est placé dans une cuve où il macérera à température constante avant d'être filtré.**

MME MOORE: **Mais comment pouvez-vous toujours reproduire le même parfum?**

M. AMAURY: **Nous suivons scrupuleusement une recette.**

MME MOORE: **Comme en gastronomie?**

M. AMAURY: **Exactement. Il ne faut pas oublier qu'un contrôle qualité et une analyse chromatique sont effectués régulièrement. Et notre "nez"**[11] **est d'une vigilance à toute épreuve.**

MME MOORE: **Votre nez?**

M. AMAURY: **Oui, c'est l'expert qui peut distinguer des milliers de fragrances. Je vais vous emmener dans le laboratoire où il fait ses expériences.**[12]

M. VILLIERS: **Ah, monsieur Amaury, vous êtes toujours accompagné de jolies dames . . .**

M. AMAURY: **Madame Moore, je vous présente monsieur Villiers, notre "nez."**

MME MOORE: **Enchantée.**

M. AMAURY: **Madame Moore est rédactrice à San Francisco. Pourriez-vous lui dévoiler quelques-uns de vos secrets?**

M. VILLIERS: **Avec plaisir.**

MME MOORE: **Qu'est-ce que vous faites de toutes ces fioles?**

M. VILLIERS: **Ah . . . ça c'est mon orgue à parfum. Comme un musicien se sert de son clavier, je joue avec ces senteurs pour évaluer, composer, inventer. Sentez . . .**

MME MOORE: **Oh! Que ça sent bon!**[13]

M. VILLIERS: **Nous conservons précieusement tous les échantillons et nos données sont informatisées**[14] **car le parfum, c'est la mémoire.**

MME MOORE: **Mais qu'est-ce qui vous inspire pour créer un parfum?**

M. VILLIERS: **Au siècle dernier, j'aurais créé un parfum pour l'Impératrice Eugénie**[15] **ou pour le bal du baron de Nucingen.**[16] **Aujourd'hui, je vais créer un mélange d'algues, de pêche et de vanille pour la femme d'affaires dynamique et raffinée qui vit entre deux avions. On l'appellera San Francisco . . .**

M. AMAURY: **Monsieur Villiers, vous semblez fort inspiré ce matin! Nous vous laissons car madame Moore souhaite voir tous nos ateliers.**

MME MOORE: **Merci beaucoup. Je suis ravie d'avoir fait votre connaissance.**

M. VILLIERS: **Moi de même.**

MME MOORE: **J'avais l'impression d'être dans le laboratoire d'un alchimiste au Moyen-Age.**

M. AMAURY: **Vous savez, même si les moyens se sont modernisés, le processus demeure inchangé.**

MME MOORE: **Quels sont les progrès réalisés récemment dans votre industrie?**

M. AMAURY: **De nos jours, nous sommes à même de prévenir les allergies et de nous assurer du bon vieillissement des produits. Nous essayons toujours de mettre au point de nouveaux parfums qui durent plus longtemps[17] et nous effectuons de nombreuses expériences[18] pour évaluer l'importance du parfum au quotidien. Entrez.**

MME MOORE: **Cet atelier est immense!**

M. AMAURY: **On remplit les flacons sur cette chaîne,[19] puis on place les bouchons. Ensuite, les flacons[20] sont étiquetés.**

MME MOORE: **Et tout est conditionné sur place?**

M. AMAURY: **Après une série de contrôles, le conditionnement des flacons se fait dans notre annexe.**

MME MOORE: **La contrefaçon vous touche toujours autant?**

M. AMAURY: **Nous faisons notre possible pour y remédier.[21] Suivez-moi, je vous prie, je vais vous montrer un film sur l'histoire de la parfumerie qui répondra à toutes vos questions.**

IN A PERFUME FACTORY.

Mrs. Moore, editor of a fashion magazine, is doing research in order to write an article on the perfume industry. Her first stop: a perfume factory in Chartres where Mr. Amaury gives her a tour.

MRS. MOORE: These machines are impressive! What are they used for?

MR. AMAURY: It is in these blending vats that we mix the ingredients.

MRS. MOORE: Where do you get all the ingredients?

MR. AMAURY: Maybe you noticed a greenhouse when you arrived?

MRS. MOORE: Oh, that huge bubble? What do you grow in there?

MR. AMAURY: A myriad of plants: violets, irises, mimosa, narcissus, lavender, sage, and many others.

MRS. MOORE: Do you grow everything on the premises?

MR. AMAURY: No, our researchers comb the world in search of exotic fragrances: sandalwood in India, roses in Bulgaria, etc.

MRS. MOORE: So, all your ingredients are natural?

MR. AMAURY: No, certain fragrances, such as lily-of-the-valley, are synthetic byproducts.

MRS. MOORE: What is the manufacturing process like?

MR. AMAURY: First the raw materials are weighed and mixed. Then we add the alcohol. Once diluted, the juice is placed in a vat where it will steep at a constant temperature before being filtered.

MRS. MOORE: But how can you always reproduce the same fragrance?

MR. AMAURY: We follow a recipe scrupulously.

MRS. MOORE: As in gastronomy?

MR. AMAURY: Exactly. Don't forget that a quality control test and a chromatic analysis are performed regularly. And our "nose" is foolproof.

MRS. MOORE: Your nose?

MR. AMAURY: Yes, that's the expert who can distinguish thousands of fragrances. I'm going to take you to the lab where he does his experiments.

MR. VILLIERS: Oh! Mr. Amaury, you're always with pretty women!

MR. AMAURY: Mrs. Moore, I would like to introduce Mr. Villiers, our "nose."

MRS. MOORE: Pleased to meet you.

MR. AMAURY: Mrs. Moore is an editor from San Francisco. Would you reveal a few of your secrets to her?

MR. VILLIERS: With pleasure.

MRS. MOORE: What do you do with all these vials?

MR. VILLIERS: Oh, that's my fragrance organ. Just as a musician uses a keyboard, I play with these scents to appreciate, to compose, to create. Smell this . . .

MRS. MOORE: Oh! That smells so good.

MR. VILLIERS: We jealously guard all the samples and our data is computerized because fragrance is memory.

MRS. MOORE: What inspires you to create a perfume?

MR. VILLIERS: Had I worked in the last century, I would have created a perfume for the Empress Eugénie or for the Baron of Nucingen's ball. Today, I'm going to create a combination of seaweed, peach, and vanilla for the refined, dynamic businesswoman who lives "between two airplanes." And we'll call it San Francisco.

MR. AMAURY: Mr. Villiers, you seem very inspired this morning. We're going to leave you because Mrs. Moore wants to see all our workshops.

MRS. MOORE: Thank you very much. I am very pleased to have met you.

MR. VILLIERS: So am I.

MRS. MOORE: I had the feeling I was in an alchemist's lab during the Middle Ages.

MR. AMAURY: You know, even if the methods have been modernized, the process remains unchanged.

MRS. MOORE: What are the most recent achievements of your industry?

MR. AMAURY: Nowadays, we are in a position to prevent allergies and to guarantee products with a long shelf life. We always try to create new fragrances that last longer and we do numerous experiments to evaluate the importance of perfume in daily life. Come in.

MRS. MOORE: This workshop is huge.

MR. AMAURY: We fill the bottles on this assembly line, cap them, then label them.

MRS. MOORE: And everything is packaged on the premises?

MR. AMAURY: After a series of controls, the packaging of the bottles takes place in our annex.

MRS. MOORE: Does counterfeiting still affect you a lot?

MR. AMAURY: We do our best to remedy it. Follow me, please. I'm going to show you a film on the history of perfume making that will answer all your questions.

B. EN BREF

1. *Le rédacteur, la rédactrice* (the editor); *l'éditeur, l'éditrice* (the publisher).

2. As always, be careful with gender. Don't confuse *la mode* (fashion, style) with *le mode* (form, method).

3. *La recherche* (singular) refers to research on a grand scale. *Elle travaille au Centre national de la recherche scientifique.* (She is working at the National Center for Scientific Research.) But *les recherches* (plural) refers to individual study for a personal or school project: *Nous faisons des recherches dans la bibliothèque pour écrire un livre.* (We are doing library research for our book.)

4. *Une étape* is a stop in the general sense. Planes and ships make *une escale.*

5. *La parfumerie* can refer to a factory as well as to a perfume shop or department.

6. Chartres, southwest of Paris, is famous for its Gothic cathedral with its numerous stained-glass windows and three *rosaces* (rose windows).

7. *Le* can be used in front of *on* to facilitate pronunciation. It has no grammatical function.

8. Do not forget to invert the subject and the verb when *peut-être* appears at the beginning of a sentence.

9. *La bulle de savon, de champagne, du verre:* bubble. *La bulle d'une bande dessinée:* dialogue bubble in a comic strip.

10. Alcohol is added so that perfume dries faster once it is applied.

11. *Le nez* is a chemical engineer. Some believe that a "nose" is naturally gifted, while others claim the skill can be learned. As the olfactory sense stops developing at the age of fifteen, extreme vigilance is required at a young age. The profession is, therefore, often passed from one generation to the next. Some "noses" can recognize more than 6,000 fragrances and do daily exercises to maintain their keen sense of smell.

12. *Le chimiste a fait une expérience scientifique.* (The chemist performed a scientific experiment.) *Cet ingénieur a beaucoup d'expérience.* (This engineer has a lot of experience.)

13. Note that *bon* acts as an adverb here.

14. The *Osmothèque,* located in Versailles and open to the public, is the first library of fragrances. Its task is to recreate perfumes that have disappeared over the centuries.

15. The Empress Eugénie (1853–1870) played a key role in developing the fragrance industry. She ordered many fragrances for special occasions and had a personal perfumer. Royal courts all over Europe often had their own perfumes.

16. Madame de Nucingen is one of the daughters in Balzac's *Père Goriot.*

17. *Amber-gris,* the digestive stone from a whale's stomach, is used to extend the fragrance of luxurious perfumes.

18. The role of scents in everyday life is a subject of continual study in France. Many experiments are conducted in classrooms, offices, and prisons to test the impact of fragrance on body and mind. For example, students taking a test in a room filled with a specific fragrance will score higher than students taking the same test in a fragrance-free room. The association of fragrance with wine and music is also gaining in popularity all over the world. The Fragrance Foundation in New York City hosts wine tastings and fragrance testings, while the *Musée des Arts Décoratifs* in Paris features an electronic perfume keyboard that allows visitors to experiment with sound, image, and scent.

19. Note the different usages of *chaîne. Quelle chaîne regardes-tu?* (What channel are you watching?) *Il a travaillé à la chaîne pendant dix ans.* (He worked on an assembly line for ten years.) *Cette chaîne de montagne est splendide.* (This mountain range is magnificent.) *J'ai perdu ma chaîne en or.* (I lost my gold chain.)

20. Perfume bottles have become as important as the fragrance itself. They are often created by famous designers or glass makers and are considered collection pieces.

21. Counterfeiting is prevalent in this industry, which is forced to fight the problem with ingenuity. In some cases a special computerized code on the cap identifies the authentic product; in other cases the shape of the glass or the cap cannot be reproduced. The recipe for a fragrance is locked in a vault to which only a handful of people have access. In some cases, the original recipe created decades ago may still exist handwritten on parchment.

C. GRAMMAIRE ET USAGE

1. *LES PRONOMS INTERROGATIFS* (INTERROGATIVE PRONOUNS)

a. Simple forms: *qui, que, quoi, lequel.*

Qui a découvert cette nouvelle technique?
Who discovered this new technique?

Que va-t-elle faire de tous ces échantillons?
What will she do with all these samples?

À quoi sert cette machine?
What is this machine used for?

Laquelle de ces femmes porte Magie Noire de Lancôme?
Which one of these women is wearing Lancôme's *Magie Noire?*

b. Compound forms.

As with other interrogatives, interrogative pronouns are often followed by *est-ce qui* (if the pronoun is the subject) or *est-ce que* (if the pronoun is the object) in spoken language and sometimes in written language.

Qui est-ce qui a contrôlé les cuves ce matin?
Who checked the vats this morning?

À qui est-ce que vous voudriez parler?
To whom would you like to talk?

Qu'est-ce qui se passerait si vous brûliez cette étape?
What would happen if you skipped this step?

Qu'est-ce que vous ajoutez pour prolonger la senteur?
What do you add to make the fragrance last longer?

2. *LES ADVERBES* (ADVERBS)

Adverbs are generally formed by adding the suffix *-ment* to the feminine form of an adjective; for adjectives ending in *-ent* and *-ant,* the ending should be replaced by *-emment,* and *-amment,* respectively *(fou →
follement, actif → activement, artisanal → artisanalement, élégant →
élégamment, violent → violemment).* Some adverbs present minor irregularities in spelling and must simply be memorized.[1]

Il a rapidement expliqué la processus de fabrication.
He quickly explained the manufacturing process.

Elle a été profondément touchée par sa gentillesse.
She was deeply moved by his kindness.

As in English, there are special forms for adverbs of location and quantity.

ici	here	*devant*	in front
là	there	*derrière*	behind
dehors	outside	*près*	near
dedans	inside	*loin*	far
dessus	on top	*partout*	everywhere
dessous	under	*ailleurs*	elsewhere

Il a mis une note dedans.
He placed a note inside.

Il y avait des flacons partout.
Perfume bottles were everywhere.

[1] For a list of common adverbs with spelling irregularities, please refer to Appendix D (page 320).

146

There are also adverbs of quantity that express intensity or degree.

beaucoup	much	*presque*	almost
trop	too much	*guère*	hardly
assez	enough	*tellement*	so much
davantage	more	*à peine*	barely
peu	little	*combien*	how much
si	so	*fort*	very

Il est fort occupé en ce moment.
    He is very busy at the moment.

Elle a presque fini.
    She's almost finished.

Some adjectives can take on an adverbial function.

Comme ce parfum sent bon!
    This perfume smells so good!

Ces herbes sauvages sentent mauvais.
    This wild grass smells bad.

On ne voit pas très clair dans cette pièce.
    We can't see very clearly in this room.

Cette essence coûte cher.
    This essence costs a lost.

Parlez plus fort pour qu'on vous entende!
    Speak more loudly so that we can hear you!

Elle chante faux.
    She sings off key.

Il prit ses fioles et les posa droit sur la table.
    He took his vials and placed them straight on the table.

Many common French adverbial phrases are borrowed from Latin, Italian, or regional usage.

Expliquez grosso modo comment ça marche. (Italian)
    Explain roughly how it works.

Elle veut s'en assurer de visu. (Latin)
    She wants to check it for herself.

La police a évacué la salle manu militari. (Latin)
    The police evacuated the room by force.

Le chimiste s'est mis au travail illico. (Italian)
    The chemist got to work right away.

Nous partageons les bénéfices moitié-moitié. (Québec)
Nous partageons les bénéfices fifty-fifty. (English)
    We split the profits fifty-fifty.

3. *LA FORME CAUSATIVE* (THE CAUSATIVE)

The causative form expresses the notion of having something done by someone, or of causing something to happen. Compare:

Nous fabriquons ces produits.
    We make these products.

Nous faisons fabriquer ces produits par des sous-traitants.
    We have these products made by subcontractors.

Elle remplit les flacons.
    She fills the bottles.

Elle fait remplir les flacons par son assistant.
    She has the bottles filled by her assistant.

Le directeur adjoint visite la parfumerie.
    The assistant director visits the perfume factory.

Le directeur adjoint nous fait visiter la parfumerie.
    The assistant director shows us around the perfume factory.

Ces matières premières macèrent pendant des semaines.
    This raw material macerates for weeks.

Nous faisons macérer ces matières premières dans une cuve en acier inoxydable.
    We macerate this raw material in a stainless-steel vat.

Ces roses poussent dans notre région.
    These roses grow in our region.

Nous faisons pousser ces iris en serre.
    We grow these irises in a greenhouse.

D. JEU DE MOTS

Noses are quite popular in French idioms.

En quittant l'entreprise de cette façon, il a fait un pied de nez au PDG.
    By leaving the company this way, he thumbed his nose at the CEO.

Il nous a ri au nez.
    He laughed in our faces.

À vue de nez, il y a une erreur dans ce rapport.
    At first glance, there is a mistake in this report.

148

Ils sont toujours en train de se bouffer le nez.
They are always at each other's throats.

Sa secrétaire le mène par le bout du nez.
His secretary is leading him by the nose.

Elle lui a claqué la porte au nez.
She slammed the door in his face.

Elle a eu le nez fin en achetant cette entreprise.
She had flair when she bought this company.

On est passé chez lui pour lui dire bonjour mais on s'est cassé le nez.
We stopped by his house to say hello, but no one was in.

L'affaire lui est passée sous le nez.
The deal slipped through his fingers.

Elle a fait un drôle de nez toute la soirée.
She pulled a funny face the whole evening.

Le chimiste épuisé commençait à piquer du nez sur ses échantillons.
The exhausted chemist started falling asleep on his samples.

Ce n'est pas le genre à se piquer le nez.
He is not the boozing kind.

La moutarde lui monta au nez!
He lost his temper!

Ne fourre pas ton nez dans mes affaires.
Mind your own business.

Ça se voit comme le nez au milieu de la figure.
It's as clear as day.

Il faut toujours lui tirer les vers du nez.
One always has to worm some information out of him.

Ton nez remue, tu mens.
I can tell that you are lying.

E. LE COIN DES AFFAIRES

L'INDUSTRIE FRANÇAISE (FRENCH INDUSTRY)

French industry has been changing steadily over the past two decades. Industrial employment fell by more than 15 percent by the mid-1980s, as traditional sectors of industry, such as steel, shipbuilding, and textile manufacturing, suffered great losses. Meanwhile, a profusion of new jobs emerged in the service sector. Industries on the rise throughout the 1980s and early 1990s include health care, telecommunications, software development, and long-distance railroad service. Other major sectors of French industry include defense, aerospace, automotive, tourism, pharmaceuticals, and processed foods.

The French defense budget saw an increase in the late 1980s and began allocating more funds for equipment purchasing and development than for service personnel. One of France's major undertakings is its commitment to renew its aircraft, missile, and nuclear fleet, which will ensure continued spending and production through the end of the twentieth century. Coupled with its commitment to defense development is France's role as the European leader in the aerospace program. Its domination of the market has led to increased aerospace exports, totaling 10 percent of sales by the late 1980s.

The French automotive industry was in great turmoil in the 1980s but has since experienced a revival. Peugeot-Citroën leads the market. After launching an aggressive marketing campaign for Europe, including a new model each year, it ranked fourth on the European Market by the mid-90s.

France is a European leader in software development, and the industry is most likely to continue to grow. The development of the high-tech and software industries has led to the revival of underdeveloped regions in southern and southeastern France. The traditional industries are centered in the northeast and around Paris.

Although the traditional sectors of industry have been on the decline, they remain an integral part of the French economy. A quarter of the working population *(la population active)* is employed in the manufacturing industry. Some sectors have had to restructure and change their focus. For example, French textiles from Lyon are still world renowned and constitute a substantial French export to the United States. The industry stresses quality versus quantity and caters to the high-end design market. Some of the leading French companies include: *Peugeot, LVMH (Louis Vuitton— Moët Hennessy), BSN* (France's largest food company), *Michelin* (the world's second largest producer of automobile tires, following Goodyear), and *L'Oréal* (the world's largest cosmetics company).

EXERCICES

A. *Compléter en utilisant des pronoms interrogatifs.*

1. À _____ sert l'énorme bulle à côté de la parfumerie?
2. _____ fait visiter l'atelier à Mme Moore?
3. _____ de ces deux hommes est le meilleur "nez"?
4. De ces deux essences, _____ se rapproche le plus du mimosa?
5. _____ faites-vous pousser dans le jardin?
6. _____ a mis au point ce nouveau parfum?
7. En _____ est ce flacon?
8. Parmi toutes ces senteurs exotiques, _____ sont issues de produits de synthèse?
9. _____ fait-on macérer dans cette cuve?
10. En _____ l'orgue vous est utile?

B. *Reformuler les questions en utilisant les formes longues des pronoms interrogatifs.*

1. Qui a sillonné la France à la recherche de plantes rares?
2. Que faut-il faire pour reproduire les mêmes senteurs?
3. À qui pensait-il en créant ce nouveau parfum?
4. Que faisaient-ils au Moyen-Age?
5. Pour qui travaille-t-il?

C. *Former les adverbes correspondant aux adjectifs suivants.* (Form adverbs corresponding to the following adjectives.)

1. *Scrupuleux*
2. *Récent*
3. *Doux*
4. *Passif*
5. *Lent*
6. *Profond*
7. *Suffisant*
8. *Mou*
9. *Vif*
10. *Gentil*

PREMIÈRE RÉVISION

A. *Mettre les phrases suivantes au passé composé.*

1. *Le directeur explique les qualités requises pour le poste.*
2. *Elle sort du théâtre pour téléphoner.*
3. *M. Duvallon bavarde avec l'hôtesse de l'air.*
4. *Il se débrouille pour trouver un nouveau boulot à Bruxelles.*
5. *Le règlement intérieur protège les employés de l'usine.*
6. *Il choisit un parfum pour sa femme.*
7. *Nous procurons les meilleurs ingrédients pour le soufflé.*
8. *Ils attendent l'arrivée des invités.*
9. *Vous souvenez-vous de ce vieux film américain?*
10. *Ils passent devant le vieux moulin.*

B. *Mettre les phrases suivantes au futur.*

1. *À quoi ça sert?*
2. *Ils mélangent les matières premières dans une cuve.*
3. *Ils vont en Belgique cet été.*
4. *Elle sait la réponse.*
5. *Est-ce que ce chocolat fond facilement?*
6. *Nous pouvons vendre ces produits sur le marché international.*
7. *Ils doivent apporter du champagne pour son anniversaire.*
8. *Elle reçoit une lettre de lui toutes les semaines.*
9. *Mon chef veut retrouver les documents secrets.*
10. *L'industrie lutte contre les produits de synthèse.*

C. *Mettre les phrases suivantes à la forme interrogative en employant l'inversion.*

1. *Ils ont rendez-vous à Paris avec le PDG de Peugeot.*
2. *Elle pense que les ouvriers se mettront en grève demain.*
3. *Les chanteurs voulaient des chambres non-fumeur.*
4. *Tu connais Fontainebleau comme ta poche.*
5. *Je jette un coup d'œil aux gâteaux toutes les quinze minutes.*
6. *Scarlett a fouetté le cheval fatigué.*
7. *Vous devez utiliser ces centrifugeuses.*
8. *Il a raccroché parce que la discussion devenait enflammée.*
9. *Vous diffuserez un feuilleton à vingt heures.*
10. *Elle emmènera Hervé dans un café très branché.*

D. *Réécrire les phrases en remplaçant les mots soulignés par un pronom.*

1. *L'objectif est de promouvoir les livres.*
2. *Michael s'inscrit à une stage au Cordon Bleu.*
3. *Nos jardiniers plantent des violettes, des iris et du mimosa.*
4. *Karen a envoyé la liste des invités.*
5. *Jeremy va au théâtre pour assister à la répétition.*

6. *Les voyageurs ont rattrapé le retard.*
7. *Ils veulent vendre ces machines à leur concurrents.*
8. *Brice emmènera Catherine et Sandrine au marché aux puces.*
9. *Le médecin parlera à Pascal du tabagisme.*
10. *Elle a remercié sa tante.*

E. *Traduire.*

1. We're supposed to arrive at noon.
2. Don't worry—the editor will be here in five minutes.
3. He resigned yesterday.
4. Where do you buy your raw material?
5. He poured the secret ingredients into the vat.
6. I'm not in a position to help you.
7. This chair is more comfortable than that one.
8. She bought a mahogany table for her living room.
9. Bring me the contracts you just sent them.
10. May I introduce you to my mother, Madame Fontanelle?

LECTURE

EUGÉNIE GRANDET de Honoré de Balzac

The title character in Honoré de Balzac's *Eugénie Grandet* is a woman whose father, a miser, made his fortune through hard work in the provinces. Eugénie gives every penny she received from her father to her cousin Charles, with whom she is in love. Here is her father's reaction when he discovers what she's done.

—*Ma fille, lui dit Grandet, vous allez me dire où est votre trésor.*

—*Mon père, si vous me faites des présents dont je ne sois pas entièrement maîtresse, reprenez-les, répondit froidement Eugénie en cherchant le napoléon sur la cheminée[1] et le lui présentant.*

Grandet saisit vivement le napoléon et le coula[2] dans son gousset.[3]

—*Je crois bien que je ne te donnerai plus rien. Pas seulement ça! dit-il en faisant claquer l'ongle[4] de son pouce[5] sous sa maîtresse dent. Vous méprisez[6] donc votre père, vous n'avez donc pas confiance en lui, vous ne savez donc pas ce que c'est qu'un père. S'il n'est pas tout pour vous, il n'est rien. Où est votre or?*

—*Mon père, je vous aime et vous respecte, malgré votre colère;[7] mais je vous ferai fort humblement observer que j'ai vingt-deux ans. Vous m'avez assez souvent dit que je suis majeure, pour que je le sache. J'ai fait de mon argent ce qu'il m'a plu d'en faire, et soyez sûr qu'il est bien placé . . .*

—*Où?*

—*C'est un secret inviolable, dit-elle. N'avez-vous vos secrets?*

—*Ne suis-je pas le chef de ma famille, ne puis-je avoir mes affaires?*

—*C'est aussi mon affaire.*

—*Cette affaire doit être mauvaise si vous ne pouvez pas la dire à votre pére, Mademoiselle Grandet.*

—*Elle est excellente, et je ne puis pas la dire à mon père.*

—*L'or est une chose chère. Les plus honnêtes filles peuvent faire des fautes, donner je ne sais quoi, cela se voit chez les grands seigneurs et même chez les bourgeois; mais donner de l'or, car vous l'avez donné à quelqu'un, hein? Eugénie fut impassible. A-t-on vu pareille[8] fille! Est-ce moi qui suis votre père? Si vous l'avez placé, vous en avez un reçu . . .*

—*Étais-je libre, oui ou non, d'en faire ce que bon me semblait? Était-ce à moi?*

—*Mais tu es une enfant.*

—*Majeure.*

—*Abasourdi[9] par la logique de sa fille, Grandet pâlit, trépigna,[10] jura; puis trouvant enfin des paroles, il cria: —Maudit[11] serpent de fille! ah! mauvaise graine, tu sais bien que je t'aime et tu en abuses. Elle égorge[12] son père! Pardieu, tu auras jeté notre fortune aux pieds de ce va-nu-pieds[13] qui a des bottes de maroquin. Par la serpette[14] de mon père, je ne peux pas te déshériter, nom d'un tonneau! mais je te maudis, toi, ton cousin et tes enfants! Tu ne verras rien arriver de bon de tout cela, entends-tu? Si c'était*

à Charles, que . . . Mais non, ce n'est pas possible. Quoi! Ce méchant[15]
mirliflor[16] *m'aurait dévalisé*[17] *. . . Il regarda sa fille qui restait muette et
froide.*

—Elle ne bougera pas, elle ne sourcillera[18] *pas, elle est plus Grandet que
je ne suis Grandet. Tu n'as pas donné ton or pour rien, au moins. Voyons
dis? Eugénie regarda son père, en lui jetant un regard ironique qui
l'offensa. Eugénie, vous êtes chez moi, chez votre père. Vous devez, pour y
rester, vous soumettre*[19] *à ses ordres. Les prêtres vous ordonnent de
m'obéir. Eugénie baissa la tête. Vous m'offensez dans ce que j'ai de plus
cher, reprit-il, je ne veux vous voir que soumise. Allez dans votre chambre.
Vous y demeurerez jusqu'à ce que je vous permette d'en sortir. Nanon vous
portera du pain et de l'eau. Vous m'avez entendu, marchez!*

VOCABULAIRE

1.	*la cheminée*	chimney, fireplace, mantelpiece
2.	*couler*	to slip
3.	*le gousset*	waistcoat pocket
4.	*l'ongle*	nail
5.	*le pouce*	thumb
6.	*mépriser*	to despise, scorn
7.	*colère*	anger
8.	*pareille*	such, similar
9.	*abasourdi*	flabbergasted
10.	*trépigner*	to tremble
11.	*maudire*	to curse
12.	*égorger*	to slaughter, massacre
13.	*le va-nu-pieds*	barefoot tramp, urchin
14.	*la serpette*	bill hook, pruning knife
15.	*méchant*	nasty
16.	*le mirliflor*	braggard, dandy
17.	*dévaliser*	to rob, strip
18.	*sourciller*	to frown, blink
19.	*soumettre*	to submit, obey

LEÇON 11

A. DIALOGUE

L'ÉCONOMIE.

Corinne et Hervé présentent la rubrique économique au journal télévisé de vingt heures.

HERVÉ: **Merci Yves. C'était Yves Maurisseau, en direct de Moscou.**

CORINNE: **Et maintenant, l'actualité économique. Le baromètre[1] semble être à la hausse dans l'Hexagone, Hervé?**

HERVÉ: **Eh bien oui, la zone de turbulence est derrière nous, la croissance s'accélère, l'inflation recule et le marché de l'emploi se stabilise. L'embellie de l'emploi profite surtout au secteur tertiaire:[2] plus de 80 000 nouveaux emplois au cours du second trimestre—une augmentation de 0,4%. Il faut, cependant, noter une progression sensible[3] du sous-emploi. L'objectif actuel du gouvernement: un taux de chômage qui ne dépasserait pas 8% de la population active.**

CORINNE: **Lors de sa dernière conférence de presse, le ministre de l'économie a déclaré que le pire était passé. A-t-il raison de se montrer si satisfait?**

HERVÉ: **Absolument. L'inflation étant partiellement maîtrisée, la reprise se confirme. La croissance[4] a été de 0,75%, un chiffre supérieur au 0,5% attendu. Un recul de plus de 2,5% par rapport à juin a été enregistré[5] dans l'industrie mais ses effectifs[6] restent invariables. Les prix à la consommation sont restés stables en août; selon une enquête réalisée par l'INSEE,[7] ils pourraient baisser de 0,1%. Toutefois, les bons indicateurs se multiplient un peu partout et même les Français ont retrouvé un grain d'optimisme. Qu'en est-il outre-Atlantique, Corinne?**

CORINNE: **La Réserve fédérale vient d'augmenter ses taux d'intérêt à court terme. La décision étant attendue, les marchés financiers ont réagi de façon épidermique.[8] Tout en gardant son optimisme, le vieux continent s'interroge toujours sur les répercussions que cette mesure risque d'avoir sur la reprise européenne.**

HERVÉ: **Que comptent faire les autres banques centrales?**

CORINNE: **Pour l'instant, les experts estiment que l'Europe ne va pas suivre la hausse des taux américains. En revanche, bon nombre pensent que ce sont les devises qui bougeront, avec un Deutsche Mark de plus en plus maître du jeu.**

HERVÉ: Passons aux finances: les tendances hebdomadaires. Nous retrouvons Julie, notre gourou financier, en direct de la Bourse.[9] Bonjour Julie.

JULIE: Bonjour. Les actions sont en hausse à Paris comme dans les deux autres grandes places financières européennes, Francfort et Londres.[10] L'indice CAC 40[11] affiche une progression de 1%, à 2 033 points, l'indice britannique Footsie gagne 1,2% et le Nikkei japonais 0,8%. Sur le front des valeurs, Moulinex remporte la palme de la plus forte hausse, plus 3,3%. Rhône Poulenc bénéficie également d'un rattrapage et gagne 2,2%. À Paris, parmi les plus fortes hausses, Club Méditerranée qui progresse de 2,2% à 411 francs. Le titre est soutenu par des déclarations encourageantes de Serge Trigano, son président, qui a déclaré que la saison était assez bonne et que les villages étaient pratiquement tous pleins.

HERVÉ: Un mot sur le marché de l'or[12] pour terminer.

JULIE: L'once[13] du métal simple progresse de $1,50 au fixing du matin de Londres à $377,80. À Paris, le lingot perd 400 francs à 65 100 francs. Le napoléon,[14] en revanche, gagne 4 francs à 380 francs.

HERVÉ: C'était Julie Vilmorin en direct de la Bourse de Paris.

ECONOMICS.

Corinne and Hervé present the economic report on the eight-o'clock news.

HERVÉ: Thank you, Yves. That was Yves Maurisseau, live from Moscow.

CORINNE: And now, the economic report. Hervé, does the barometer seem to be rising in France?

HERVÉ: Well, yes. The turbulent zone is behind us, growth is accelerating, inflation is shrinking, and the job market is stabilizing. The improvement in employment opportunities benefits the service industry in particular, with more than 80,000 new jobs in the second quarter—an increase of 0.4%. A slight increase in underemployment, however, should be noted. The current goal of the government: an unemployment rate not exceeding 8% of the labor force.

CORINNE: During his last press conference, the secretary of the economy indicated that the worst is behind us. Is he right to feel so pleased?

HERVÉ: Absolutely! With inflation partly under control, the recovery is well under way. Growth reached a rate of 0.75%—a figure exceeding the projected 0.5%. A decline of over 2.5% compared to June was recorded in industry, but the labor force remains unchanged. The consumer price index remained stable in August; according to an INSEE survey, it could go down 0.1%. Nevertheless, positive indicators are springing up everywhere, and even the French have rediscovered a touch of optimism. What's happening in the United States?

CORINNE: The Federal Reserve has just increased short-term interest rates. Since the decision was expected, the financial market rushed to react. While remaining optimistic, the old continent is continually weighing the repercussions of this measure on the European economic revival.

HERVÉ: What do the other major banks plan to do?

CORINNE: For the moment, experts don't think that Europe will follow the Americans in raising the rates. By contrast, many think that currencies will fluctuate, with the Deutsche Mark gaining more and more of an upper hand.

HERVÉ: Let's move to finances: the weekly trends. We go to Julie, our financial guru, live at the Stock Exchange. Hi, Julie!

JULIE: Hi! Stocks are up in Paris as in the other two major European financial centers, Frankfurt and London. The CAC 40 index shows a 1% rise, up to 2033 points, the Footsie index gains 1.2% and the Nikkei 0.8%. On the securities front, Moulinex takes the prize, with the biggest increase, more than 3.3%. Rhône Poulenc is also on the rise, gaining 2.2%. In Paris, among the highest gains, Club Med, which rose 2.2% to 441 francs. The stock is bolstered by encouraging declarations made by Serge Trigano, the company's president, who stated that the season was fairly good and that the resorts were practically all full.

HERVÉ: To wrap it up, a word on the gold market.

JULIE: One ounce of base metal has gone up $1.50 at the London morning fixing, reaching the price of $377.80. In Paris, the gold bar loses 400 francs, ending at 65,100 francs. The Napoleon, on the other hand, gained 4 francs, ending at 380 francs.

HERVÉ: That was Julie Vilmorin, live from the Paris Stock Exchange.

B. EN BREF

1. As in English, many climatic expressions are used to describe the state of the economy: *une tempête* (storm), *une accalmie* (lull, calm spell), *une éclaircie* (sunny spell), *un frémissement* (shivering), *la turbulence* (turbulence), *un glissement* (swing, landslide), *le réchauffement* (warming up), *le refroidissement* (cooling-off, temperature drop), *le cyclone* (cyclone), *un rayon de soleil* (ray of sun), *la nébulosité* (cloudiness), *le dégel* (thawing), *l'agitation* (restlessness).

2. *Le secteur primaire* (primary sector), *le secteur secondaire* (secondary sector: processing) *le secteur tertiaire* (tertiary sector: raw materials/service industries).

3. *Il est très sensible à votre gentillesse.* (He is very sensitive to your kindness.) *La différence n'est pas sensible.* (The difference is hardly noticeable.) *Une baisse sensible du dollar a eu de graves répercussions la semaine dernière.* (A noticeable drop of the dollar had serious repercussions last week.)

4. *L'économiste a prévu une baisse de la croissance économique.* (The economist forecast a drop in the economic growth.) *Cet enfant (cette plante) est en pleine croissance.* (This child [this plant] is growing rapidly.)

5. The verb *enregistrer* can take on different meanings: *Claude a enregistré ses bagages.* (Claude checked his luggage.) *Le franc a enregistré une forte baisse.* (The franc suffered a great loss.) *Nous avons enregistré sa conférence.* (We recorded his conference.) *L'employé de la mairie a enregistré la naissance des jumeaux.* (The town clerk registered the birth of the twins.)

6. *Nous avons une crise d'effectifs.* (We have a shortage of manpower.) *L'effectif des classes a été réduit à vingt.* (The size of the classes was reduced to twenty.) *L'effectif est au complet.* (We are at full military strength.)

7. The French love polls and have a few agencies to keep them happy. *INSEE* is the *Institut national de statistiques et d'études économiques* (National Institute for Statistics and Economic Studies). *IFOP, Institut français d'opinion publique* (French Public Opinion Institute) was created in the 1940s. *SOFRES, Société française d'études par sondage* (French Society of Poll Studies), is the other main polling organization, in existence since 1962.

8. *Une lésion épidermique* (skin lesion). *Un test épidermique* (patch-test). *Une colère épidermique* (outburst). *Une blessure épidermique* (surface scratch).

9. There are different kinds of *Bourses: la Bourse du Travail* (Labor Exchange), *la Bourse du Commerce* (Commodity Exchange), *la Bourse des Valeurs* (Stock Exchange).

10. The main trading cities are Paris, London, Frankfurt, Brussels, Amsterdam, Milan, Tokyo, and, of course, New York City (Wall Street).

11. *CAC, Compagnie des agents de change,* is an indicator similar to the Dow Jones.

12. *L'or blanc* (white gold), *l'or noir* (oil), *l'or brut* (gold in nuggets), *un bracelet plaqué or* (gold-plated bracelet). *Une affaire en or* (excellent bargain). *Ils roulent sur l'or, ils sont cousus d'or* (they are very rich). *Elle a acheté cette entreprise à prix d'or.* (She bought this company at an exorbitant price.)

13. The ounce measure is rarely used in French, except for measuring a few precious items or in idiomatic expressions: *Elle a acheté ces perles à l'once.* (She bought these pearls by weight.) *Il n'a pas une once de bon sens.* (He does not have an ounce of common sense.)

14. Napoleons are old 20-franc gold coins with the effigy of Napoleon I or Napoleon III.

C. GRAMMAIRE ET USAGE

1. *LA VOIX PASSIVE* (THE PASSIVE VOICE)

A sentence can be in either the active or the passive voice. In the active voice, the subject performs an action, and the object is "acted upon." In the passive voice, subject and object exchange roles, and the subject no longer performs the action, but is acted upon. It is important to note that the passive voice is much more common in English than in French. You will have to acquire the reflex of switching back and forth on many occasions.

The passive voice is formed with *être* in the desired tense plus the past participle of the main verb. The agent of the action (i.e., the subject in the active sentence that becomes the object in the passive sentence) is introduced by *de* or *par*.[1] Compare the following active and passive sentences:

Tout le monde respecte cet analyste financier.
Everybody respects this financial analyst.

Cet analyste financier est respecté de tout le monde.
This financial analyst is respected by everybody.

Le directeur adjoint a rédigé ce rapport sur le déficit.
The assistant director wrote this report on the deficit.

Ce rapport sur le déficit a été rédigé par le directeur adjoint.
This report on the deficit was written by the assistant director.

---

[1] As in English, the agent can be omitted altogether. For example:

Ce projet de loi est actuellement discuté.
This bill is currently being discussed.

Note that the tense of *être* in the passive sentence corresponds to the tense of the main verb in the active sentence.

La société publiera les résultats trimestriels.
The company will publish the quarterly results.

Les résultats trimestriels seront publiés par la société.
The quarterly results will be published by the company.

L'ancien PDG justifiait toujours les dépenses.
The former CEO always justified the expenses.

Les dépenses étaient toujours justifiées par l'ancien PDG.
The expenses were always justified by the former CEO.

In most cases, the agent is introduced by *par*.

Cette article est écrit par un expert allemand.
This article is written by a German expert.

However, *de* should be used after verbs that express:

a. emotion or opinion, such as *aimer, estimer, détester.*

Il est détesté de ses employés.
He is hated by his employees.

b. habitual action or common occurrence where the agent of the action plays a less active role: *être suivi, précédé, accompagné.*

Cette expression est suivie du subjonctif.
This expression is followed by the subjunctive.

Le président était suivi de ses ministres.
The president was followed by his ministers.

But if the president is "actively" followed:

Le président était suivi par un espion.
The president was followed by a spy.

c. Other verbs with a more stationary sense, for example, *couvrir, remplir, entourer,* are followed by *de* or *par* depending on the degree of action indicated by the verbs.

La maison était entourée d'une haute clôture.
The house was surrounded by a high fence.

La maison était entourée par une vingtaine de policiers.
The house was surrounded by some twenty policemen.

The passive voice is also used:

a. to emphasize the passive subject.

Le débat sur la privatisation a été suivi par des millions de Français.
The debate on private ownership was followed by millions of French people. (The stress is on debate.)

Ce précieux tuyau a été communiqué par un agent sans scrupules.
This precious tip was communicated by an unscrupulous agent. (The stress is on tip.)

b. to avoid using *on* as the subject of an active sentence or to avoid having to specify the agent of the action.

L'incompétence des investisseurs a été très remarquée.
The investors' incompetence was noticed by everyone.

Aucune décision ne sera prise avant la fin septembre.
No decisions will be made before the end of September.

c. with pronominal verbs (i.e., the impersonal *"se"* verbs) to describe customs or general rules. Note that the subject of these sentences is an inanimate object and, therefore, cannot be the agent of the action.

Les actions d'Eurotunnel se vendent très bien en ce moment.
Eurotunnel stocks sell very well these days.

L'arabe se lit de droite à gauche.
Arabic is read from right to left.

Le vin rouge se sert chambré.
Red wine is served at room temperature.

d. with the following reflexive verbs: *se laisser, se faire, se voir, s'entendre,* when followed by an infinitive.

Il s'est laissé influencer trop facilement.
He let himself be influenced too easily.

Nous nous sommes entendu dire qu'il faudrait changer de méthode.
They went so far as to tell us that we would have to change our method.

It is important to note that the passive voice is used more in English than in French, and that, even under many of the circumstances listed above, the active voice is preferred.

In French, the passive should be avoided when:

a. the agent is expressed.

Notre agence a publié ces chiffres.
These figures were published by our agency.

b. the understood agent is a person. In that case *on* is used.

On peut acheter ces actions à la Bourse.
These stocks can be bought at the Stock Exchange.

c. a habitual action or custom is described.

Ça ne se fait pas.
This is not to be done.

In some cases, it is absolutely impossible to use the passive voice in French.

On ne leur a pas permis de spéculer.
They were not allowed to speculate.

On a donné un nouveau portefeuille d'actions à Christine.
Christine was given a new stock portfolio.

2. *LE PARTICIPE PRÉSENT* (THE PRESENT PARTICIPLE)

The present participle is formed by adding *-ant* to the present indicative stem of the *nous* form of a verb. For example, *attendre → attend-ons → attendant; boire → buv-ons → buvant.* Only *avoir, être,* and *savoir* have irregular present participles: *ayant, étant,* and *sachant,* respectively.

The present participle can be used as an adjective or a noun: *un commerçant* (a shopkeeper), *un assistant* (an assistant), *un gagnant* (a winner).

L'assistant de l'agent de change nous a proposé un portefeuille séduisant.
The broker's assistant offered us an attractive portfolio. (noun and adjective)

L'ALENA est un sujet de discussion toujours fascinant.
NAFTA is still a fascinating subject for discussion. (adjective)

L'enjeu économique est impressionnant.
The economic stakes are high. (adjective)

Ces transactions nous semblent intéressantes.
These transactions seem interesting. (adjective)

Note that the spelling of some present participles changes according to whether they are used as nouns or as adjectives. For example, *adhérant* becomes *adhérent* when used as a noun, and *excellant* becomes *excellent* when used as an adjective. Other examples include: *affluant* → *affluent* (n.); *différant* → *différent* (adj.); *communiquant* → *communicant* (adj.); *fabriquant* → *fabricant* (n.); *fatiguant* → *fatigant* (adj.).

Il a sauvé son entreprise de la faillite en fabriquant de nouveaux produits.
He saved his company from bankruptcy by making new products.

Vous lui ferait plaisir en lui communiquant cette nouvelle.
You'll make him happy by communicating this piece of news to him.

The present participle is generally used alone to indicate an action that is occurring simultaneously with the main verb. It generally modifies or emphasizes a noun or a pronoun, rather than a verb.

J'ai vu le cambiste sortant de la Bourse.
I saw the trader leaving the Stock Exchange.

Ne sachant que faire, l'agent de change nous a appelés.
Not knowing what to do, the broker called us.

3. *LE GÉRONDIF* (THE GERUND)

When the present participle is introduced by *en,* it is referred to as *le gérondif.* Its emphasis is on the verb in the sentence. This structure is used to describe the relationship between two actions:

a. simultaneity.

Il a appris le montant de ses pertes en rentrant de vacances.
He found out how much he had lost when he came back from vacation.

b. manner.

Hervé a fait faillite en investissant dans cette entreprise.
Hervé went bankrupt by investing in this company.

c. condition.

En adoptant cette mesure fiscale, le président s'attirerait les foudres du public.
If he adopted (by adopting) this tax policy, the president would anger the public tremendously.

d. causality.

Corinne a fait une erreur en vendant ses lingots d'or.
Corinne made a mistake when she sold her gold ingots.

165

To stress the simultaneity of two actions, use *tout* preceding the gerund form. This form is also used to underscore a contradiction.

Tout en parlant avec moi au téléphone, l'agent de change négociait un contrat.
While he was talking to me on the phone, the broker was negotiating a contract.

Tout en proposant un accord de paix, ils se préparaient à faire la guerre.
While proposing a peace plan, they were preparing for war.

4. *DIFFICULTÉS DE TRADUCTION* (TRANSLATION PROBLEMS)

Though it technically corresponds to the French present participle, the English *-ing* form of a verb cannot always be translated as such. When acting as a subject or object, it can be translated into French with an infinitive or a noun.

Voir, c'est croire.
Seeing is believing.

Aimez-vous nager?
Do you like swimming?

La lecture de ce document de la première à la dernière page est essentielle.
Reading this report from first to last page is essential.

After verbs of perception such as *voir, entendre,* and *sentir,* there are several options:

On voyait le taux du dollar chuter (qui chutait/en train de chuter) pendant la récession.
We could see the dollar's rate of exchange falling during the recession.

After expressions indicating the passage of time and physical position, the infinitive introduced by *à* is used in French, where the present participle is used in English.

Les actionnaires passent leur temps à surveiller la cote de leurs valeurs.
Stockholders spend their time reading quotations.

Le ministre a passé des mois à essayer de résoudre la crise monétaire.
The minister spent months trying to solve the monetary crisis.

Il était assis à caresser ses lingots d'or.
He was sitting stroking his gold ingots.

Elle était à genoux à trier ses dossiers.
She was kneeling sorting her files.

Finally, if the main verb and the gerund have different subjects in English, the gerund is usually translated by a subordinate clause in French.

Il ne peut pas dire une parole sans que tout le monde se moque de lui.
He cannot utter a word without everyone making fun of him.

D. JEU DE MOTS

Grain can be used in many different and sometimes playful ways.

Comment voulez-vous votre café? Moulu ou en grains?
How would you like your coffee? Ground or whole?

Ce poulet de grain est délicieux.
This corn-fed chicken is delicious.

J'ai trouvé des grains de sable sur mes lunettes de soleil.
I found some grains of sand on my sunglasses.

Il faut toujours qu'elle mette son grain de sel!
She always has to put in her two cents' worth!

Il faut séparer le bon grain de l'ivraie.
One must separate the wheat from the chaff.

Il faut toujours veiller au grain.
One must always keep an eye out for trouble.

Je crois qu'il a un grain.
I think he has a screw loose.

Il n'a pas un grain de bon sens.
He doesn't have an ounce of common sense.

Il faut parfois un petit grain de folie.
It sometimes helps to be a bit eccentric.

Qui sème bon grain recueille bon pain.
You reap what you sow.

E. LE COIN DES AFFAIRES

LA BANQUE (BANKING)

In addition to offering cash management services for individuals and commercial entities, French banks assist in public offerings of shares and debentures, as well as in placements in international markets, mergers, acquisitions, and takeovers. France's central bank is *La Banque de France* (the Bank of France). It possesses powers much like the U.S. Federal Reserve Bank. It issues all national bank notes. As a central bank, it supervises and licenses credit institutions. The Bank of France was controlled by the French government until January 1994, when it was established as an independent central bank, to comply with the Maastricht Treaty and in anticipation of European monetary union.

There are more than 500 commercial banks licensed in France, including *Société Générale, Crédit Lyonnais, Crédit Agricole,* and *Banque Nationale de Paris,* which constitute four of the five largest banks in all of Europe. Savings banks, which include the Post Office, have the authority to finance small businesses directly. In addition there are more than 150 foreign banks in France, including several major U.S. banks, such as Bank of America, Citibank, J.P. Morgan, and Chase Manhattan Bank.

With the unification of Europe, France set out to establish Paris as Europe's number one financial center. Major steps in this direction were made in the late 1980s with the establishment of *MATIF,* a futures and options market, and *MONEP,* a stock and index options market, and with the integration of regional stock markets into the Paris Bourse in 1991. Securities on the Paris Bourse can appear under the official list (for which the company must have 25% of its capital), the second market (availability of 10% of the capital), or the unlisted market—the *hors-cote.* The *CAC* system used in France is similar to those used in Tokyo. Bonds constitute the majority of transactions on the French Bourse, but financial authorities have been trying to reverse this trend in favor of stocks. Americans are free to invest or sell on the French Bourse and may open an account at a French bank or with a French broker.

Naturally, French banks also offer private checking or savings accounts for individuals. Following are the types of forms you might encounter in a French bank.

CRÉDIT DE TOURAINE

3 Boulevard Béranger - 75011 Paris

PAYEZ CONTRE CE CHÈQUE NON ENDOSSABLE
SAUF AU PROFIT D'UN ÉTABLISSEMENT BANCAIRE

somme en toutes lettres

PAYABLE À

Nº de compte

Compensable à Paris

lieu de création

LE _____ ,19 ____

PAYABLE À

Nº CHÈQUE

la signature ne doit pas atteindre la marge

928650007 9806540032101 ⌃ 313962150001

CRÉDIT DE TOURAINE

3 Boulevard Béranger - 75011 Paris

PAYMENT WILL BE ISSUED AGAINST THIS CHECK
ONLY IF ENDORSED BY A BANKING ESTABLISHMENT

AMOUNT IN WORDS

PAYABLE TO

ACCOUNT NO.

TO BE CLEARED IN PARIS

ISSUED AT

ON _____ ,19 ____

PAYABLE TO

CHECK NO.

SIGNATURE MAY NOT EXCEED MARGIN

928650007 9806540032101 ⌃ 313962150001

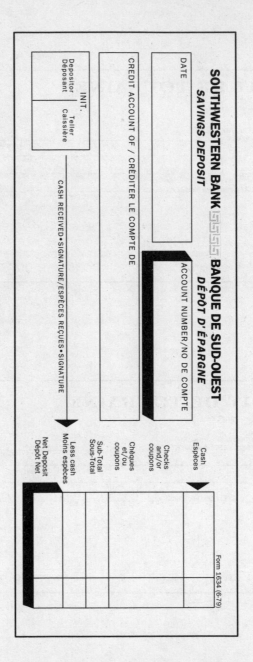

SOUTHWESTERN BANK 5555 BANQUE DE SUD-OUEST
SAVINGS DEPOSIT   DÉPÔT D'ÉPARGNE

DATE

ACCOUNT NUMBER/NO DE COMPTE

CREDIT ACCOUNT OF / CRÉDITER LE COMPTE DE

INIT.

Depositor   Teller
Déposant   Caissière

CASH RECEIVED•SIGNATURE/ESPÈCES REÇUES•SIGNATURE

Cash
Espèces

Checks
and/or
coupons

Chèques
et/ou
coupons

Sub-Total
Sous-Total

Less cash
Moins espèces

Net Deposit
Dépôt Net

Form 1634 (6-79)

170

EXERCICES

A. *Mettre à la voix passive.*

1. *Hervé et Corinne présentent la rubrique économique.*
2. *Le ministre de l'économie a annulé la conférence de presse.*
3. *Les experts financiers annonceront une baisse du dollar.*
4. *La Réserve fédérale a augmenté les taux d'intérêt.*
5. *Les Canadiens fréquentent les villages du Club Med au Mexique.*

B. *Mettre à la voix active.*

1. *Les tendances hebdomadaires sont présentées par Julie.*
2. *Nous avons été déçus par leur manque de compétence.*
3. *La Palme sera sans doute remportée par Eurotunnel.*
4. *Ces déclarations ont été faites par le président.*
5. *Ce gourou financier est aimé des téléspectateurs.*
6. *La reprise est confirmée.*
7. *Le bureau du présentateur est couvert d'une montagne de dossiers.*
8. *Cette rubrique financière est reçue chaque jour par le Japon.*
9. *La valeur des devises est influencée par l'état de l'économie allemande.*
10. *Le rapport annuel sera rédigé par notre équipe avant la fin du mois.*

C. *Traduire en utilisant la voix active.*

1. This financial expert is respected by the consumers.
2. The report was written by both journalists.
3. Stocks are often bought by phone.
4. Gold bars sell well in a period of recession.
5. They were not allowed to publish these figures.
6. This is not said in English.
7. At the economic conference in Geneva, at least four languages are spoken.
8. This piece of advice was given to me by a trader.
9. She let herself be influenced by her broker.
10. The stock exchange was full of investors.

D. *Compléter les phrases suivantes avec la forme qui convient.* (You may add "en" or "tout en" when you think it is appropriate.)

1. *(Savoir) qu'il n'avait pas beaucoup d'argent, il a investi avec prudence.*
2. *Il écoutait la radio (rédiger) son rapport.*
3. *(Fatiguer) tout le monde, l'analyste a recommencé sa présentation.*
4. *(Être) en colère contre son secrétaire, le PDG ne l'a pas renvoyé.*
5. *Leur compagnie a fait fortune (fabriquer) des pièces en plastique.*

171

6. *(Rejeter) cette mesure, le président risque de perdre les élections.*
7. *Le cambiste ira directement à la Bourse (arriver) à Paris.*
8. *Il s'est rendu compte de ses erreurs (finir) son rapport.*
9. *(Être) très strict, le PDG était estimé de ses employés.*
10. *(Profiter) du marché favorable, il a acheté de nombreuses actions.*

LEÇON 12

A. DIALOGUE

LA MODE, TOUJOURS LA MODE.[1]

Christian Lacroix,[2] l'un des plus grands couturiers[3] français, a insufflé une nouvelle vie à la couture[4] française par ses somptueux plissés, ses énormes cols, ses jupes bouffantes et une nostalgie insolente pour une féminité romantique. Pour lui, l'élégance n'est pas toujours synonyme de simplicité.

DIANE RAFFERTY: Qu'est-ce qui a inspiré votre collection[5] de printemps?

CHRISTIAN LACROIX: Je ne souhaitais pas imposer un thème trop précis. C'est trop commercial. Je voulais jouer avec les formes, les couleurs, les tissus et les imprimés. Mais à force de travailler aussi instinctivement que possible, j'ai découvert que ce qui s'insinuait dans mes croquis était une nostalgie de l'insouciance de mes belles années universitaires. En même temps, je voulais réconcilier cette nostalgie avec la façon dont on s'habille aujourd'hui. Le prêt-à-porter,[6] c'est une sublimation de la rue. Il faut dire que j'adore mélanger les cultures.

DIANE RAFFERTY: Dans votre collection prêt-à-porter, l'influence de la mode anglaise des années 70 saute aux yeux.

CHRISTIAN LACROIX: C'est exact, mais n'oubliez pas que les années 70 à Londres reflétaient la nostalgie des années 30 et 40. La mode, c'est comme les poupées russes: on en ouvre une et il y en a une autre à l'intérieur et encore une autre . . . Il serait prétentieux de dire qu'une collection est pareille à un roman, c'est plutôt un album de photos avec des souvenirs de vacances de ma mère et de ma sœur à Arles.[7] Et ce genre de création est aussi moderne que tout ce que l'on qualifie de[8] "moderne" aujourd'hui.

DIANE RAFFERTY: Faites-vous vos croquis en couleur?

CHRISTIAN LACROIX: Non, en noir et blanc. Toujours. D'abord, je me demande quelles couleurs je désire. Je fais tout séparément: les couleurs, les tissus. Ensuite, je mélange le tout. J'esquisse[9] un croquis pendant que je parle au téléphone; puis je le regarde plus tard et me dis qu'il vaut mieux garder celui-là. J'envie[10] les couturiers qui peuvent consciemment travailler dans les limites d'une page, dans le même style, avec tout en parfaite proportion.

DIANE RAFFERTY: Ce n'est pas votre méthode de travail.

CHRISTIAN LACROIX: Non, je gribouille[11] quelque chose au dos d'une enveloppe quand je me réveille ou sur une serviette dans un restaurant. Je ne peux pas voir une feuille vierge[12] sans vouloir dessiner dessus. Je sais exactement ce que je veux dire mais l'équipe de l'atelier[13] a du mal à déchiffrer mes gribouillages. Je lui donne cette première ébauche parce que l'attitude et l'ambiance sont là. C'est encore frais. Je ne travaille pas en drapant le tissu sur un mannequin.[14] Je suis plus proche du caricaturiste que du tailleur.[15] Je ne pars pas d'une coupe révolutionnaire, je préfère jouer à distance avec l'aspect superficiel.

DIANE RAFFERTY: Pourtant, la coupe est l'un de vos points forts.

CHRISTIAN LACROIX: J'ai beau admirer les couturiers qui mettent l'accent sur la coupe, je trouve leur travail un peu trop cérébral. Je veux plus de sensualité, une qualité plus tactile. Une femme, ce n'est pas de l'architecture; elle est en chair. De nos jours, les femmes ont acquis la liberté: elles sont présidentes, chefs d'entreprise; elles gagnent beaucoup d'argent et s'habillent comme cela leur chante. Elles n'ont plus rien à prouver. Porter une robe ou un bustier fait partie intégrante de leur liberté. En outre, le but de la mode n'a jamais été le confort.

DIANE RAFFERTY: Autrement, on porterait des pyjamas.[16]

CHRISTIAN LACROIX: Exactement! On veut que je sois "portable,"[17] mais quand je le suis, on se plaint que "ce n'est pas du Lacroix."

DIANE RAFFERTY: Vous avez dit un jour que la haute couture était un laboratoire d'idées.

CHRISTIAN LACROIX: Beaucoup plus qu'un laboratoire. C'est un musée destiné à conserver l'expérience des gens qui travaillent dans la couture; les premières, les couturières, les brodeuses. . . . Nous, les couturiers, nous sommes comme des écologistes qui protègent une espèce en voie d'extinction.[18] Ce que nous appelons la haute couture n'existe qu'en France. Nous avons les meilleures brodeuses. Il est de notre devoir de sauvegarder cette expertise.

DIANE RAFFERTY: Avez-vous la même attitude envers vos collections prêt-à-porter qu'envers la haute couture?

CHRISTIAN LACROIX: En essence, c'est la même chose. La femme qui s'habille dans le prêt-à-porter n'est pas différente de celle qui porte la haute couture. C'est la même femme à des moments différents. Pour le prêt-à-porter, je tiens compte davantage de la rue. La haute couture est le rêve d'une sorte d'élégance. J'adore jouer avec les conventions classiques de la mode . . . le marine et le blanc, les fleurs et les broderies.

174

Je joue avec tout ce qui est à ma disposition, d'une manière à la fois respectueuse et originale. Mais ma collection couture est purement égoïste. C'est la trame d'une histoire que je veux raconter moi-même.

FASHION, ALWAYS FASHION

Christian Lacroix, one of the top French couturiers, has injected new life into French couture, with his lavish pleats, huge collars, bouffant skirts, and unapologetic nostalgia for romantic femininity. For him, elegance is not always synonymous with simplicity.

DIANE RAFFERTY: What inspired your spring collections?

CHRISTIAN LACROIX: I didn't want to impose too precise a theme. That's so commercial. Instead, I felt like experimenting with form, color, fabric, and prints. But in trying to work as instinctively as possible, I found that what kept cropping up in my sketches was nostalgia for the carefree spirit of my happy student days. At the same time, I wanted to reconcile that nostalgia with the way people dress today. Ready-to-wear is a sublimation of the street. I must admit, I like to mix cultures, too.

DIANE RAFFERTY: In your ready-to-wear collection, the influence of English fashion of the 70s is striking.

CHRISTIAN LACROIX: That's right, but don't forget that the 1970s in London were nostalgic for the 1930s and 1940s. Fashion is like those Russian dolls: you open one up and another is inside, then another and another . . . It would be pretentious to say that a collection is like a novel, but it is rather like a photo album, with holiday mementos of my mother and sister in Arles. This kind of creation is just as modern as anything around today that people call modern.

DIANE RAFFERTY: Do you draw first in color?

CHRISTIAN LACROIX: No, black and white. Always. First, I ask myself what colors I want. I do everything separately: colors, fabrics. Afterward, I mix them all up. I make a little drawing while I am on the phone; then later I look at it and decide that it's better to keep that one. I envy designers who can consciously work on a single page, in the same style, with everything in perfect proportion.

DIANE RAFFERTY: It is not your way of working.

CHRISTIAN LACROIX: No, I scribble something on the back of an envelope when I wake up or on a napkin in a restaurant. I can't see a blank piece of paper without wanting to draw on it. I know exactly what I mean but it is hard for the team in the atelier to decipher my scribbles. I give them that first sketch because the look and mood are there. It's still fresh. I don't work by draping at all. I'm more of a cartoonist than a tailor. I don't start with a revolutionary cut. I prefer to play from a distance with the superficial side.

DIANE RAFFERTY: Yet I find that cut is one of your strong points.

CHRISTIAN LACROIX: Although I admire those designers who focus on cut, I find their work a little too cerebral. I want more sensuality, a more tactile quality. A woman is not architecture. She is flesh. Nowadays, women have won their freedom. They are presidents, company directors; they make lots of money and dress as they wish. They have nothing to prove. It's part of their freedom to put on a short skirt, a bustier. Comfort has never been the purpose of fashion.

DIANE RAFFERTY: Otherwise we'd all wear pajamas.

CHRISTIAN LACROIX: Exactly! People want me to be wearable, but when I am, they complain that "it doesn't look like Lacroix."

DIANE RAFFERTY: You once said that haute couture is a laboratory of ideas.

CHRISTIAN LACROIX: More than a laboratory. It's a museum for conserving the technical know-how of people who work in couture: the *premières,* the seamstresses, embroiderers . . . We, couturiers, are like ecologists protecting an endangered species. What they call haute couture exists only in France. We have the best embroiderers. It is our duty to safeguard this expertise.

DIANE RAFFERTY: Do you feel differently toward your ready-to-wear lines than about haute couture?

CHRISTIAN LACROIX: The essential is the same. The woman who wears ready-to-wear is no different from the one who wears haute couture. It's the same woman at different times. For ready-to-wear, I take the street more into consideration. Haute couture is a dream of a sort of elegance. I love playing with the classic conventions of fashion . . . navy and white, flowers, embroidery. I play with everything at my disposal in a way that is both respectful and original. But my couture line is purely selfish. It's the working of a story I want to tell myself.*

B. EN BREF

1. The word *mode* changes meaning, according to gender. *Il faut suivre le mode d'emploi.* (You have to follow the instructions.) *Le mode subjonctif est très utilisé en français.* (The subjunctive mood is used a lot in French.) *Que pensez-vous de cette nouvelle mode?* (What do you think about this new trend?) *Le Salon de la Mode aura lieu en septembre.* (The fashion trade show will take place in September.)

* Reprinted from the article "The Art of Sensuality," written by Diane Rafferty and published in *Connoisseur* magazine in June 1990.

2. Born in Arles in the early 1950s, Christian Lacroix began his career as a design assistant at Hermès, where he learned the techniques of fashion design. He refined his sense of design in Japan and received the coveted Golden Thistle in 1986. Frustrated by the conservatism of the fashion world and eager to create cheaper ready-to-wear clothing, he established his own company in Paris.

3. The names of traditional male professions remain masculine regardless of the gender of the person: *elle est médecin, elle est professeur.* The masculine is also used to show the degree of importance of the job. Compare: *Coco Chanel fut un grand couturier.* (Coco Chanel was a great designer.) *J'ai demandé à la couturière de raccourcir ma jupe.* (I asked my seamstress to shorten my skirt.)

4. Paris has maintained its status as the center of fashion for more than 140 years, transforming clothing from costume to fashion for a select clientele from all over the world. From Poiret's poufs of 1885 to the ageless silhouettes of Coco Chanel's suits, to the shorter hemlines by courageous Courrèges in 1965, new designers continue to stretch the imagination and push the limits of acceptability. Top French designers include: Pierre Cardin, Chanel, Christian Dior, Givenchy, Christian Lacroix, Lanvin, Ted Lapidus, Guy Laroche, Nina Ricci, Yves Saint-Laurent, Claude Montana, Karl Lagerfeld, and Jean-Paul Gaultier. The *haute couture* status was created in 1945. To qualify, designers must present two collections with fifty designs a year and have at least ten employees in their studios. A suit generally requires between 40 and 60 hours of work, and a long embroidered dress between 150 and 200.

5. Fashion shows are organized twice a year (during the last weeks of January and July) by the *Chambre syndicale,* which sends invitations to the who's who of society and two thousand journalists and photographers. They often take place in posh hotels and sometimes in a museum or theater. Fashion shows more and more are becoming high-tech, multimedia performances. At the end, the *couturier* traditionally appears on the runway with a model dressed in a wedding gown (known as the designer's bride) and surrounded by all the other models.

6. Shortly after the 1929 economic crash, the fashion houses were once again on their feet. However, because of exorbitant tariffs (up to 100 percent) on imports and the onset of World War II, scarce special fabrics and material had to be replaced by cheaper and more readily available ones, e.g., nylon for silk. After the war, changes in lifestyle and production techniques sparked the rise of ready-to-wear garments. Innovative companies copied *couturiers'* designs at a fraction of the cost, making fashion affordable for the masses. In 1972, Lanvin launched a ready-to-wear line for men, and many top designers followed suit, as the *haute couture* clientele started to decline.

7. Arles, a charming city steeped in history, was established as a Roman port and trading post on the banks of the Rhône around 100 B.C. Its growth was such that in A.D. 400 the Roman emperor Honorius made Arles the capital of what is today France, Spain, and Britain. The Roman ruins, the medieval cathedral, and the museums are a must-see.

8. When modified, *qualifier* is followed by *de* plus the adjective. *Elle l'a qualifié de menteur.* (She called him a liar.) *C'est une collection que l'on peut qualifier de très réussie.* (It's a collection we can call very successful.) *Ils ont qualifié son attitude d'exemplaire.* (They called his attitude exemplary.)

9. Note the different translations of "to sketch." *Le peintre a jeté le tableau qu'il avait à peine ébauché.* (The painter destroyed the painting he had barely sketched out.) *L'artiste a croqué un paysage.* (The artist sketched a landscape.) *L'écrivain a esquissé/ébauché les personnages de son nouveau roman.* (The writer sketched out the characters of his new novel.)

10. Compare the use of *envier* (to envy), *avoir envie de* (to feel like), and *une envie* (a craving). *Le jeune couturier envie le talent de Givenchy.* (The young designer envies Givenchy's talent.) *De quoi as-tu envie?* (What do you feel like having?) *J'ai envie d'acheter cette robe du soir.* (I feel like buying this evening gown.) *Elle a une envie de chocolat.* (She has a craving for chocolate.)

11. *Gribouiller* and *griffonner* are interchangeable. *Il a gribouillé ses commentaires dans la marge.* (He scribbled his comments in the margin.) *Elle a griffonné un mot puis elle est partie.* (She scribbled a note, then she left.)

12. The word *vierge* (virgin) has many figurative applications. *C'est une pellicule vierge.* (This is an unexposed film.) *Les pionniers sont arrivés sur une terre vierge.* (The pioneers arrived on virgin land.) *Donne-moi une feuille de papier vierge.* (Give me a blank piece of paper.) *Ce pull est en laine vierge.* (This sweater is made of virgin wool.)

13. *Le sculpteur travaille dans son atelier.* (The sculptor works in his studio.) *Pierre vient d'acheter un atelier aménagé près de la Bastille.* (Pierre has just bought a converted workshop near the Bastille.) *Les ateliers de l'usine ont été rénovés.* (The workshops in the factory have been renovated.) *Les couturières de l'atelier Chanel préparent une nouvelle collection.* (The Chanel house seamstresses are preparing a new collection.)

14. The term *mannequin* can have three different meanings in English. *La couturière a épinglé la robe sur le mannequin.* (The seamstress pinned the dress on the cloth dummy.) *Cette saison, les mannequins des vitrines des Galeries Lafayette ont tous les cheveux roux.* (This season, all the mannequins in the Galeries Lafayette windows have red hair.) *Caroline est mannequin chez Ricci.* (Caroline is a model at Ricci's.)

15. The translation of "suit" varies in French, depending on whether it is a man's or a woman's suit. Men wear *un costume* or *un complet* while women wear *un tailleur* (skirt with jacket) or *un ensemble* (dress or pants with jacket).

16. *Un pantalon* (pants) and *un pyjama* (pyjamas) remain singular in French, unless you are referring to several pairs.

17. The word *portable* has two different meanings. *Ces tenues démodées ne sont plus portables.* (These old-fashioned outfits are no longer wearable.) *Il vient d'acheter un téléviseur portable.* (He has just bought a portable television set.)

18. *En voie de* is a very handy expression, denoting an action in progress. *Cette maison de couture est en voie de réorganisation.* (This fashion house is undergoing reorganization.) *Le patient est en voie de guérison.* (The patient is getting better.) *Elle est en voie de perdre sa situation.* (She's heading for dismissal.) *Les loups sont une espèce en voie d'extinction.* (Wolves are an endangered species.)

C. GRAMMAIRE ET USAGE

1. *LE CONDITIONNEL PRÉSENT* (THE PRESENT CONDITIONAL)

The present conditional is formed by adding the following endings to the future stem of a verb: *-ais, -ais, -ait, -ions, -iez, -aient*. Note that these are the same endings as in the imperfect tense.

	PORTER	PRENDRE	CHOISIR
je	porterais	prendrais	choisirais
tu	porterais	prendrais	choisirais
il/elle/on	porterait	prendrait	choisirait
nous	porterions	prendrions	choisirions
vous	porteriez	prendriez	choisiriez
ils/elles	porteraient	prendraient	choisiraient

The present conditional is used:

a. to make a statement or a request more polite.

Auriez-vous la bonté de m'aider à boutonner ma robe?
Would you be so kind as to help me button my dress?

Voudriez-vous une veste droite ou croisée?
Would you like a single- or a double-breasted jacket?

b. with *si* clauses. When the *si* clause is in the imperfect, the main clause is in the present conditional.

Elle ferait une robe en dentelle si elle savait coudre.
She would make a lace dress if she knew how to sew.

Le couturier dessinerait toute la journée si son horaire le lui permettait.
The designer would draw all day long if his schedule permitted it.

c. with conditions introduced by *à* + an infinitive.

À t'entendre décrire sa nouvelle collection, on dirait qu'il a perdu la tête!
If people heard you describe his new collection, they'd think he's lost his mind.

À te voir habillée de cette manière, Jacques croirait que tu vas à un bal masqué.
If he saw you dressed like that, Jacques would think you're going to a masquerade party.

d. with conditions introduced by *en* + a present participle.

En boycottant le défilé de mode, ce jeune couturier risquerait de froisser sa clientèle.
If he were to boycott (By boycotting) the fashion show, this young designer would run the risk of offending his clientele.

En vendant du prêt-à-porter, son image serait ternie.
If he were to sell (By selling) ready-to-wear, his image would be tarnished.

e. with conditions introduced by *quand bien même*. This structure is used to achieve a more emphatic or dramatic effect.

Quand bien même il serait l'homme le plus riche du monde, je ne pourrais jamais l'aimer!
Even if he were the richest man in the world, I would never be able to love him.

Quand bien même elle me ferait cadeau de cette robe brodée de paillettes de Givenchy, je ne la porterais jamais.
Even if she gave me this sequined dress by Givenchy, I'd never wear it.

f. in more formal French, where the verb *savoir* in the present conditional is equivalent to *pouvoir* in the present indicative.

On ne saurait se passer du prêt-à-porter de nos jours.
Nowadays, one can't do without ready-to-wear.

Je ne saurais vous expliquer ce qui pousse les gens à porter ces tenues.
I can't explain to you what drives people to wear these outfits.

g. in reported speech, when the main verb is in the past tense and is referring to something that will happen in the future.

Amélie a annoncé qu'elle présenterait sa nouvelle collection en juin.
Amélie announced that she would introduce her new collection in June.

Vous a-t-elle dit que les demoiselles d'honneur seraient en noir?
Did she tell you that the maids of honor would be wearing black?

h. to express unconfirmed or alleged information. This usage is often referred to as the journalistic conditional.

Karl Lagerfeld présenterait sa prochaine collection sur la plage de La Baule.
Karl Lagerfeld is said to be presenting his next collection on La Baule beach.

Les ourlets seraient au-dessous du genou l'été prochain.
Hemlines are supposed to be below the knee next summer.

Le président serait amoureux d'une photographe de mode.
The president is reportedly in love with a fashion photographer.

2. *COMMENT DIRE* COULD, WOULD, *ET* SHOULD (HOW TO SAY "COULD," "WOULD," AND "SHOULD")

"Could," "would," and "should" have many different meanings in English and can therefore be translated into French in several ways. Every time you have to translate one of these verbs, be sure to analyze its meaning.

a. Would.

Je ne lui ai pas dit que je porterais cette robe très décolletée.
I didn't tell him I would wear this very low-cut dress.

Voulez-vous m'accompagner au Salon de la Mode?
Would you go with me to the fashion trade show?

Voudriez-vous lui faire savoir que son tailleur est prêt?
Would you let her know that her suit is ready?

S'il n'avait pas de papier, il dessinerait sur la nappe.
If he did not have paper, he would draw on a tablecloth.

Je lui ai demandé de rallonger cette jupe; il a refusé.
I asked him to lower the hem of this skirt; he wouldn't do it.

Note: "Would" is also used to translate the imperfect when it refers to repeated actions in the past.

Quand il vivait à Arles, il passait des journées entières à faire des croquis.
When he lived in Arles, he would spend days making sketches.

b. Could.

Pourriez-vous me dire où vous avez trouvé ce patron?
Could you tell me where you found this pattern?

Si la dentellière n'était pas si débordée, elle pourrait vous faire un col.
If the lacemaker were not so overworked, she could make you a collar.

Le mannequin n'a pas pu venir à la séance photo ce matin parce qu'elle a la grippe.
The model could not come to the photo session because she has the flu.

À cette époque-là, on ne pouvait pas découvrir les chevilles.
At that time, you couldn't let your ankles show.

c. Should.
"Should" is generally translated by *devoir* in the conditional.

On devrait sauvegarder ces techniques traditionnelles.
One should preserve these traditional techniques.

Elle ne devrait pas s'habiller si court!
She shouldn't wear such short skirts.

When "should" refers to a hypothetical situation, the French verb is in the imperfect.

Si vous aviez besoin de plus de tissu, n'hésitez pas à m'appeler.
If you should need more fabric, please don't hesitate to call me.

3. *EXPRESSIONS DE CONCESSION* (EXPRESSIONS OF CONCESSION)

Following are some expressions that will help you connect and organize your thoughts.

pourtant	however	*du moins*	at least
cependant	however	*au lieu de*	instead of
néanmoins	nevertheless	*sauf*	except
toutefois	nonetheless, however	*à défaut de*	for lack of
au contraire	on the contrary	*malgré*	despite
en revanche	on the other hand	*tandis que*	whereas

Vous devez le faire, sinon pour le plaisir, du moins pour le respect.
You have to do it, if not for pleasure, at least out of respect.

Personne ne l'a cru, cependant, il disait la vérité.
No one believed him; however, he was telling the truth.

Il est très arrogant. En revanche son frère est des plus courtois.
He is very arrogant. On the other hand, his brother is most pleasant.

Ce problème, si ridicule soit-il, doit être abordé.
This problem, however absurd it may be, must be addressed.

D. JEU DE MOTS

Something that will always come in handy is *l'argent*. Let's take a look at its many different uses.

Il en a pour son argent.
He got his money's worth.

Elle l'a accusé de jeter l'argent par les fenêtres.
She accused him of throwing money out the window.

L'argent n'a pas d'odeur.
Money has no smell.

Le temps, c'est de l'argent.
Time is money.

La parole est d'argent; le silence est d'or.
Words are silver, silence is gold.

L'argent ne fait pas le bonheur.
Money can't buy happiness.

L'argent est bon serviteur mais mauvais maître.
Money is a good servant but a bad master.

Il a mis de l'argent à gauche.
He put some money aside.

Ils veulent le beurre et l'argent du beurre.
They want to have their cake and eat it too.

L'argent lui fond dans les mains.
Money burns a hole in his pocket.

E. LE COIN DES AFFAIRES

LA CORRESPONDANCE (BUSINESS CORRESPONDENCE)

The height of French formality is reflected in letter writing. Even if you've established a close relationship with a business associate, his or her letters will remain formal. Your response should, likewise, be fairly formal, be addressed to *Monsieur* or *Madame*, and close with a polite phrase. Remember that, while French closings may sound a little pompous or overdone, they are really only set formulas that mean no more than "Sincerely yours" or "Cordially." Following are some standard phrases used in business correspondence.

Asking for information:

Pourriez-nous nous faire parvenir votre catalogue dans les plus brefs délais?
Could you please send us your catalogue as soon as possible?

Nous vous serions obligés de nous faire connaître votre décision par retour de courrier.
We would appreciate it if you could inform us about your decision immediately upon receipt of this letter.

Offering a service:

J'ai le plaisir de vous annoncer . . .
I have the pleasure to announce . . .

Nous avons l'honneur de vous informer . . .
We're delighted to inform you . . .

Placing an order:

Pourriez-vous nous expédier . . . le plus tôt possible?
Could you send us . . . as soon as possible?

Fulfilling an order:

Conformément à votre demande du 15 janvier, nous vous expédirons votre commande avant la fin de la semaine.
As per your request of January 15th, we'll ship your order by the end of the week.

En réponse/Suite à votre lettre, j'ai le plaisir de vous informer que nous sommes en mesure de vous fournir . . .
In response to your letter, I am pleased to inform you that we will be able to supply . . .

Apologizing:

Nous avons le regret de ne pouvoir donner une suite favorable à votre demande.
We regret that we won't be able to fulfill your request.

Malheureusement, nous nous voyons dans l'obligation de décliner votre offre . . .
Unfortunately, we have to decline your offer . . .

Nous regrettons qu'une erreur se soit glissée dans la facture du 12 avril.
We apologize for an inadvertent error in your bill dated April 12.

Requesting payment:

Notre comptable nous fait remarquer que votre facture du 3 mai n'a pas encore été réglée.
According to our records, you have an outstanding balance on your May 3 bill.

Concluding:

En attendant le plaisir de vous lire, veuillez croire, Madame, à l'assurance de mes sentiments.
Looking forward to hearing from you, sincerely.

Dans l'espoir que vous accepterez ces conditions, je vous prie d'agréer mes salutations distinguées.
Hoping you will accept our terms, I remain sincerely yours.

Following are several samples that may be useful as you compose your own correspondence.

Suite à notre conversation téléphonique du 10 octobre, nous souhaiterions commander 1000 imprimantes, ref. 348 A. Nous vous serions obligés de nous les faire parvenir dans les plus brefs délais.

Following our telephone conversation of October 10th, we would like to order 1000 printers, ref. 348 A. We would appreciate it if you could send them as soon as possible.

———————

Nous vous remercions de votre demande de renseignements concernant nos fournitures de bureau. Vous trouverez ci-joint notre catalogue ainsi que notre tarif de vente et nous avons le plaisir de confirmer que nous sommes en mesure d'effectuer une livraison avant la fin du mois.

Thank you for requesting information on our office supplies. Please find enclosed our price list. We are happy to confirm that we will be able to make a delivery before the end of the month.

———————

Nous avons le regret de vous faire savoir qu'il nous est impossible d'accepter votre livraison des cinquante cendriers en cristal qui ont subi des dégâts lors du transport.
Nous vous les réexpédions à vos frais aujourd'hui même en espérant obtenir satisfaction dès que possible. Au cas où vous ne pourriez pas satisfaire notre demande avant du 15 novembre, veuillez nous contacter immédiatement.

We are sorry to inform you that we cannot accept your shipment of fifty crystal ashtrays, which were damaged in transport.
We are returning them today at your expense, in the hopes of receiving a new shipment by November 15th. In the event that you cannot deliver by said date, please contact us immediately.

You may follow this sample business letter for format.

IPCO Injection Plastique Centre Ouest

SITAC SA
Direction Achats
25, boulevard de l'Industrie
92000 Nanterre

Nazelles/Amboise, le 17 octobre 1995

Messieurs,

Vous développez de nouveaux produits! Vous modifiez un produit existant! Vous cherchez un nouveau fournisseur! Notre société industrielle, IPCO, spécialisée dans la transformation des plastiques, effectue toute étude concernant la réalisation et le décor de pièces en plastique.

Notre vocation:
- l'étude, la mise en production de pièces en thermoplastique injecté.
- le moulage de paroi mince à haute cadence.
- la décoration (marquage à chaud, sérigraphie, tampographie de 1 à 4 couleurs).
- l'assemblage (soudure par ultra-son), montage, perçage.

Nos moyens:
Une unité de production, en 3 x 8, composée d'une équipe de professionels de la plasturgie et d'un matériel (Boy, Netstal, Klöckner à microprocesseurs) récent.

Notre situation géographique:
Près de Tours, à la conjonction des axes de communication Nord-Sud et Est-Ouest.

Nos secteurs d'activité:
- emballage: alimentaire, pharmaceutique . . .
- sous-traitance industrielle: automobile, aéronautique, connectique, électronique, micromécanique,
  bâtiment, mobilier, sanitaire, médical . . .
- produits standards: coupelle de conditionnement sous skinpack et rétractable, obturateur, ventouse, boîte, bouchon, cape de surbouchage, poignée, pince-à-papier.

Restant à votre disposition pour toute information complémentaire, ainsi que pour vous rendre visite, nous vous prions d'agréer, Messieurs, l'expression de nos sentiments distingués.

La direction commerciale
Brigitte HUARD

P.J. 1 documentation

**Z.I. Les Sables - 6, impasse des Sables F-37530
Nazelles/Amboise FRANCE
Tel. 33 (16) 47 23 14 66   FAX 33 (16) 47 30 42 94**

A. *Mettre les verbes entre parenthèses au conditionnel.*

1. *Elle (vouloir) ajouter une touche romantique à sa nouvelle collection.*
2. *Cette tenue (être) trop extravagante.*
3. *Lacroix (gribouiller) ses croquis sur n'importe quoi.*
4. *Nous (pouvoir) assister au défilé de mode de Givenchy cet automne.*
5. *Vous (devoir) mettre l'accent sur la coupe.*
6. *Ce chapeau des années 30 lui (aller) très bien.*
7. *(Savoir) vous la vérité?*
8. *Gaultier (finir) son défilé sur une note humoristique.*
9. *Qu'est-ce qu'il (falloir) faire pour recréer le style des années 40?*
10. *Christian (s'apercevoir) de la mauvaise qualité de cette soie.*

B. *Conjuguer les verbes entre parenthèses au conditionnel présent et à l'imparfait.*

1. *Elle (suivre) un cours à l'Institut de la Mode si ses moyens le lui (permettre).*
2. *Ce jeune couturier (vendre) sa collection prêt-à-porter à un prix plus modeste s'il le (pouvoir).*
3. *Il (être) en pyjama toute la journée s'il (travailler) chez lui.*
4. *La collection d'automne lui (plaire) beaucoup plus s'il n'y (avoir) pas tant de tissus à pois.*
5. *Les femmes (porter) toujours d'énormes épaulettes si elles ne pas (être) démodées.*
6. *Elle (essayer) la veste en laine rouge de Chanel si elle ne pas (devoir) être à son bureau à 14 heures.*
7. *Nous (aller) à ce défilé de mode si nous (connaître) le couturier.*
8. *Elle (mettre) une mini-jupe et un bustier si elle (être) plus mince.*
9. *Ma soeur me (faire) une robe en dentelle si elle (savoir) coudre.*
10. *Il (acheter) un nouveau costume s'il (decider) de se remarier.*

C. *Traduire.*

1. Could you please shorten this pair of pants?
2. She would take a course at a fashion institute in Paris if she had more money.
3. We should protect the French fashion industry.
4. If you should be late for his fashion show, he would be angry.
5. Claude could not finish her wedding gown before March 15th.
6. Would you wear this lavish low-cut dress to the theater?
7. The agent asked the designer to hire this model; he wouldn't do it.
8. If he were not so pretentious, he would do a ready-to-wear line.
9. Would she go to Asia if she needed exotic fabric?
10. Could you make another navy blue double-breasted jacket?

LEÇON 13

A. DIALOGUE

LA PRÉVENTION MÉDICALE.

Élodie et Matthew attendent[1] un enfant. Ils ont pris rendez-vous avec une sage-femme[2] d'une PMI[3] qui passe en revue le calendrier vaccinal.[4]

LA SAGE-FEMME: Élodie, vous avez une mine resplendissante. La grossesse[5] vous va à merveille.

ÉLODIE: Je me sens vraiment très bien.[6]

MATTHEW: Et encore mieux depuis que tu es en congé de maternité.[7]

ÉLODIE: C'est vrai, j'aurais dû m'arrêter un peu plus tôt mais je me sentais en pleine forme.

LA SAGE-FEMME: Très bien . . . Alors, aujourd'hui, vous aimeriez que je vous parle des vaccins?

MATTHEW: Oui, parce que ça a l'air plutôt compliqué. Le bébé a-t-il vraiment besoin de tous ces vaccins?

LA SAGE-FEMME: Vous savez, la vaccination contre les maladies infectieuses est l'un des plus grands succès de la médecine moderne.[8] Un nourrisson a un système immunitaire fragile qui a du mal à fabriquer des anti-corps et il ne faut donc pas prendre le calendrier vaccinal à la légère.

ÉLODIE: Par quoi faut-il commencer?

LA SAGE-FEMME: Dès le premier mois, vous pouvez faire vacciner votre enfant contre le B.C.G. Ce vaccin antituberculeux est obligatoire pour les enfants de moins de six ans[9] fréquentant toute collectivité: pouponnière, crèche,[10] école maternelle etc.

MATTHEW: À un mois! Pauvre petit! Ça va le rendre malade!

ÉLODIE: Matthew, tout le monde n'est pas si douillet[11] que toi!

LA SAGE-FEMME: Comme tout[12] médicament, les vaccins ont parfois des effets secondaires, mais ils sont insignifiants et cela vaut la peine.

MATTHEW: Par exemple?

LA SAGE-FEMME: Un brin de fièvre,[13] un bras endolori, une sensation de malaise, une perte d'appétit temporaire.

ÉLODIE: Rien de très grave.

LA SAGE-FEMME: Non, ce dont vous devez vous préoccuper, c'est de suivre de près les périodes charnières du développement de votre enfant afin de dépister tout problème éventuel.

ÉLODIE: Et quels sont les autres vaccins?

LA SAGE-FEMME: La vaccination associée DT (diphtérie, tétanos) est obligatoire avant l'âge de dix-huit mois, conseillée dès le troisième mois. Pratiquée en trois injections à un mois d'intervalle—avec rappel obligatoire un an après la première injection—elle est fréquemment combinée à la vaccination antipoliomyélitique.

MATTHEW: La coqueluche, la rougeole . . . notre bébé sera certainement plus susceptible[14] à ces maladies infantiles qu'à la diphtérie en plein cœur de Clermont-Ferrand.[15]

LA SAGE-FEMME: Détrompez-vous! Certaines maladies que l'on croyait avoir enrayées, sévissent[16] toujours comme le Saturnisme[17] et la méningite.[18]

ÉLODIE: Vous recommandez donc d'autres vaccins?

LA SAGE-FEMME: C'est un sujet auquel vous devriez réfléchir.

ÉLODIE: Ce n'est pas si compliqué; il s'agit de suivre ce calendrier à la lettre.

LA SAGE-FEMME: Et de tout inscrire dans votre carnet de santé.[19]

ÉLODIE: Au fait, est-ce qu'il y a des vaccins antitabac? Matthew m'avait promis de cesser de fumer pendant ma grossesse mais . . .

MATTHEW: Vous savez, avec Élodie, le bébé . . . je suis trop anxieux en ce moment . . .

LA SAGE-FEMME: Les progrès accomplis en vaccinologie suscitent les plus grands espoirs, mais on n'a pas encore mis au point de vaccin antitabac.

MATTHEW: Est-ce que les patchs sont efficaces à votre avis?

LA SAGE-FEMME: Les résultats sont prometteurs. Si cela vous intéresse, nous avons ici même un service spécialisé dans les patchs pour le mal de transports, la ménopause, le tabac, etc. Ça ne coute rien de vous renseigner. Et si vous vous inscrivez au programme, on vous donnera un carnet de santé, à vous[20] aussi . . .

MEDICAL PREVENTION.

Élodie and Matthew are expecting a child. They have made an appointment with a PMI midwife, who is reviewing the vaccination calendar.

MIDWIFE: Élodie, you look wonderful! Pregnancy suits you perfectly.

ÉLODIE: I feel really great.

MATTHEW: And even better since you're on maternity leave.

ÉLODIE: It's true. I should have stopped working a bit earlier, but I felt in terrific shape.

MIDWIFE: Good . . . So today, you'd like me to discuss vaccines?

MATTHEW: Yes, because it seems rather complicated. Does the baby really need all these vaccines?

MIDWIFE: You know, vaccination against infectious diseases is one of modern medicine's greatest triumphs. An infant has a fragile immune system that has difficulty producing antibodies, so vaccination should not be taken lightly.

ÉLODIE: Where do we start?

MIDWIFE: From the very first month, it's possible to have your child vaccinated for D.P.T. This vaccine against tuberculosis is mandatory for children under six years old attending any school: nursery, daycare, kindergarten, etc.

MATTHEW: At one month old! Poor little thing! It's going to make the baby sick!

ÉLODIE: Matthew, everybody is not as overly sensitive as you!

MIDWIFE: Like any medicine, vaccines may have side effects, but these are insignificant, and the protection is worth it.

MATTHEW: For instance?

MIDWIFE: A touch of fever, a sore arm, a feeling of discomfort, a temporary loss of appetite.

ÉLODIE: Nothing serious.

MIDWIFE: No, what you have to be concerned about is closely following the key periods in your child's development in order to detect any potential problems.

ÉLODIE: What are the other vaccines?

MIDWIFE: The combined DT (diphtheria, tetanus) vaccine is mandatory before the age of eighteen months but is recommended as early as the third month. Administered in three injections, one month apart, with a mandatory booster a year after the first injection, it is often combined with the polio vaccine.

MATTHEW: Whooping cough, measles . . . our baby will be more likely to catch these infant diseases than diphtheria in the heart of Clermont-Ferrand.

MIDWIFE: You're mistaken. Some diseases we thought we had under control are still rampant, like lead poisoning and meningitis.

ÉLODIE: Do you recommend other vaccines, then?

MIDWIFE: You should give it some thought.

ÉLODIE: It's not that difficult; all you have to do is follow this calendar to the letter.

MIDWIFE: And write everything down in your health record book.

ÉLODIE: By the way, are there any anti-smoking vaccines? Matthew had promised he would stop smoking during my pregnancy, but . . .

MATTHEW: You know, with Élodie, the baby . . . I am too anxious right now.

MIDWIFE: The advances in vaccination bring about the greatest of hopes, but we have not yet come up with an anti-smoking vaccine.

MATTHEW: In your opinion, are patches effective?

MIDWIFE: The results are promising. If you are interested, we have, right here, a department specializing in patches for motion sickness, menopause, smoking, etc. Asking for information won't cost you anything. And if you sign up for the program, we'll also give you a health record book of your very own.

B. EN BREF

1. "To expect" can be translated into French in several ways, depending on the context: *Qu'est-ce que tu veux, il est si incompétent!* (What do you expect—he is so incompetent!) *Elle attend des jumeaux.* (She is expecting twins.) *Nous ne savons pas à quoi nous attendre.* (We don't know what to expect.) *Je l'attends demain.* (I am expecting her tomorrow.) *Je veux que vous soyez à l'heure à la réunion.* (I expect you to be on time at the meeting.)

2. Midwives can work with private clients, in a private maternity, in a hospital, or in a PMI. They are in charge of prenatal care and family planning and also perform deliveries. They make home visits to women whose pregnancies are complicated.

3. PMI stands for *Protection Maternelle et Infantile* (Mother and Child Protection). This government agency was created in 1945 to fight infant mortality, which was very high after World War II. Today, its role is to promote good physical, mental, and social health for the entire family. It is open to everyone and free of charge. The staff is composed of internists, gynecologists, pediatricians, midwives, pedi-

atric nurses, psychologists, physical therapists, marriage counselors, and others who work as a team.

4. France's health care requirements for pregnant women and newborns are generally much more strict than in the United States. For example, pregnant women are required to make seven visits to their physician or midwife in order to receive the *allocation jeune enfant* (financial assistance provided for every woman from her fourth month of pregnancy until the baby is three months old. It may be extended based on financial need.). In addition, twenty medical exams are required by law for all children between birth and six years of age.

5. Some useful terms about pregnancy: *Ma sœur est enceinte.* (My sister is pregnant.) *Sa grossesse se passe très bien.* (Her pregnancy is going very well.) *Elle doit accoucher le 7 mars.* (She is due March 7th.) *Cette maternité a un programme d'accouchement sans douleur.* (This birth center has a program for the Lamaze method.)

6. The French never say *merci* when given a compliment about their physical appearance. Rather, they tell a little story about the item in question (for example, how old or inexpensive it is) or just smile!

7. Any working mother is entitled to a sixteen-week maternity leave: six weeks before and ten weeks after delivery.

8. France has one of the lowest infant mortality rates among developed countries and the lowest rate of any country with a population above 50 million. The United States, which leads the world in technology, is ranked twenty-second. France has extremely few incidences of low birth weight and a very high rate of immunization, as well as one of the lowest rates of teenage pregnancy.

9. In France, school is mandatory and free between the ages of six and sixteen.

10. Government-subsidized daycare centers are numerous in France.

11. Some French words do not have an exact equivalent in English. *Mon frère est très douillet.* (My brother is sensitive to pain/a cry-baby.) *Ma mère est très frileuse.* (My mother is sensitive to cold temperature.)

12. When used in the singular form and followed by a noun without an article, *tout* means "any."

13. The word *brin* has several translations, but, in general, it implies "a little bit." *Un brin d'herbe.* (A blade of grass.) *Un brin de paille.* (A wisp of straw.) *Un brin de mimosa.* (A spray of mimosa.) *Un brin de persil.* (A sprig of parsley.) *Un brin de causette.* (A bit of a chat.) *Un brin de vent.* (A breath of wind.) *Un brin de toilette.* (A quick wash and brush.) *Un brin de méchanceté.* (A touch of malice.)

14. *Susceptible* changes meaning based on context. *Fais attention à ce que tu dis, il est très susceptible.* (Be careful of what you say; he is very sensitive.) *Ce nouveau vaccin est susceptible de vous intéresser.* (This new vaccine is likely to interest you.)

15. Clermont-Ferrand, the capital of Auvergne, is famous for its lava cathedral. At an altitude of 1,200 feet, it is surrounded by volcanic buttes. The most famous is the *Puy de Dôme.* Clermont-Ferrand remains an important industrial center, well known for the manufacture of heavy rubber goods.

16. *Sévir* has several usages: *Les autorités ont décidé de sévir contre la fraude fiscale.* (The authorities have decided to crack down on tax evasion.) *Une épidémie de méningite sévit dans cette région.* (A meningitis epidemic is rampant in that region.) *Une bande de voyous sévit dans ce quartier de la ville.* (A group of hooligans is on a rampage in this neighborhood.) *S'il continue à faire des siennes, je vais devoir sévir.* (If he keeps acting up, I'll have to resort to harsh measures.)

17. *Saturnisme,* caused by lead poisoning, affects the nervous system and may result in serious brain disorders, even death. Infants living in old, ill-kept buildings (with ancient plumbing and peeling paint) are likely to be affected. In 1992, more than 2,000 cases were reported in Paris.

18. Meningitis afflicts about 1,000 children a year between their sixth and eighteenth months.

19. A *carnet de santé,* or a health record book, is issued by the Health Department to parents, who are then required to keep a record of their child's development. Any visit or intervention is entered into the book. It is essential to present a *carnet* to obtain any social benefits.

20. The *vous* appears twice to emphasize the object. Here, the midwife is teasing Matthew, telling him that he'll get a book just like his baby's.

C. GRAMMAIRE ET USAGE

1. *LE CONDITIONNEL PASSÉ* (THE PAST CONDITIONAL)

The past conditional is formed with the present conditional of *avoir* or *être* and the past participle of the main verb.

	SUIVRE	SE RENSEGNER
je	aurais suivi	me serais renseigné(e)
tu	aurais suivi	te serais renseigné(e)
il/elle/on	aurait suivi	se serait renseigné(e)
nous	aurions suivi	nous serions renseigné(e)s
vous	auriez suivi	vous seriez renseigné(e)(s)
ils/elles	auraient suivi	se seraient renseigné(e)s

Its usage is similar to that of the present conditional but, in general, it refers to past events. It is used:

a. in the main clause when the *si* clause is in the past perfect.

Elle aurait pris des précautions si on l'avait avertie.
She would have taken precautions if she had been warned.

Il se serait fait vacciner si une épidémie s'était déclarée.
He would have had a shot if an epidemic had broken out.

b. in journalistic style, to make a statement about a past event, not confirmed by authorities.

Le choléra aurait fait 1000 morts.
Cholera reportedly killed 1,000 people.

Les chercheurs auraient mis au point un nouveau vaccin.
The researchers reportedly came up with a new vaccine.

c. to indicate an action that occurred prior to an action described in the present conditional.

La sage-femme m'a promis qu'elle viendrait me voir quand elle aurait fini sa garde.
The midwife promised she would visit me after finishing her shift.

2. *COMMENT DIRE* WOULD HAVE, COULD HAVE *ET* SHOULD HAVE (HOW TO SAY "WOULD HAVE," "COULD HAVE," AND "SHOULD HAVE")

Élodie aurait consulté un médecin si elle avait eu de la fièvre.
Élodie would have consulted a doctor if she had had a fever.

Ils auraient pu faire des recherches s'ils avaient eu un laboratoire.
They could have done research if they had had a lab.

Est-ce qu'elle aurait pu prendre des antibiotiques?
Could she have taken antibiotics?

L'infirmière aurait dû prendre votre pouls.
The nurse should have taken your pulse.

Le radiologue aurait dû envoyer les radios.
The radiologist should have sent you the X-rays.

3. *LOCUTIONS ADVERBIALES* (ADVERBIAL LOCUTIONS)

French is not as rich as English in adverbs. Therefore, whole phrases are often used in French where a single word is enough in English. These adverbial phrases can be formed with:

a. a preposition + a noun.

L'infirmière parlait avec sagesse.
The nurse spoke wisely.

Il a lutté contre le cancer avec courage.
He fought against cancer courageously.

Il a agi sans scrupules.
He acted unscrupulously.

Ils s'entendent à merveille.
They get along marvelously.

b. *d'un air* + adjective.

Les sages-femmes ont répondu à nos questions d'un air content.
The midwives happily answered our questions.

"Je veux accoucher dans votre maternité," a-t-elle dit d'un air ravi.
"I want to have my baby in your birth center," she said delightedly.

c. *à la* + adjective, as in *filer à l'anglaise* (to take French leave), *à la légère* (lightly), *à l'européenne* (European style), *à la va-vite* (hastily).

Ce diagnostic a été fait à la va-vite.
This diagnosis was done hastily.

d. common adverbial expressions, such as: *en catimini* (on the sly), *en douce* (in secret), *à plat ventre* (flat on one's face), *à contre cœur* (unwillingly), *au fur et à mesure* (as), *à la sauvette* (hastily), *à la noix de coco* (worthlessly), *d'emblée* (straight off), *au dépourvu* (off guard).

Il faut inscrire les vaccinations dans le carnet au fur et à mesure.
You must write the vaccinations down in the booklet as you get them.

Il t'a encore donné des excuses à la noix de coco.
He has once again given you worthless excuses.

e. A past participle used as an adjective or a verb in more formal speech.

Résignée, elle accepta.
She accepted resignedly.

f. Some English adverbs placed in front of adjectives must often be translated into French with a noun plus an adjective.

Leur personnel médical est d'une intelligence remarquable.
Their medical staff is remarkably intelligent.

Cette clinique est d'une propreté impeccable.
This clinic is impeccably clean.

Les dents de cet enfant sont d'une blancheur étincellante.
This child's teeth are dazzlingly white.

4. *RENDRE + ADJECTIF* (*RENDRE* + AN ADJECTIVE)

When expressing the effect something or someone has (as in "to make someone happy"), be sure to use *rendre*, not *faire*.

La pénicilline l'a rendue malade.
The penicillin made her sick.

Les résultats de son examen l'ont rendu heureux.
The results of his test made him happy.

D. JEU DE MOTS

As in English, body imagery is popular in French idioms.

tête à tête—in private, alone

Nous avons eu une conversation en tête à tête.
We had a private talk.

nez à nez—face to face

Nos bateaux se sont retrouvés nez à nez.
Our boats ended up face to face.

côte à côte—side by side

Elles étaient assises côte à côte.
They were sitting side by side.

dos à dos—back to back

Il nous a placés dos à dos.
He had us sit back to back.

coude à coude—shoulder to shoulder

Les ouvrières travaillaient coude à coude dans l'atelier.
The workers worked shoulder to shoulder in the workshop.

face à face—face to face

Le juge a mis les deux témoins face à face.
The judge confronted the two witnesses face to face.

corps à corps—hand to hand

Ils ont lutté corps à corps.
They fought hand to hand.

bras dessus, bras dessous—arm in arm

Nous avons marché dans le Bois de Vincennes bras dessus, bras dessous.
We walked arm in arm in the *Bois de Vincennes*.

main dans la main—hand in hand

Les amants sont montés en haut de la Tour Eiffel main dans la main.
The lovers walked all the way up the Eiffel Tower hand in hand.

E. LE COIN DES AFFAIRES

LA MÉDECINE (MEDICINE)

Health care in France is generally as high in quality as in the United States. The French *Sécurité sociale* (Social Security) provides partial coverage for most medical expenses (such as medical, dental, eye care, and drugs), and only a small fraction of the population does not have coverage. Due to the rising cost of coverage, however, people have to participate more and more in the cost of treatment. It is not unusual to have *une mutuelle,* a secondary, private insurance policy much like those in the United States, to cover expenses not reimbursed by Social Security. Eligibility for a secondary policy is determined by a person's line of work, i.e., which *régime* (group) he or she may fall into. Typical *régimes* include *le régime des artisans et commerçants* (Craftspeople and Merchants' Group) and *le régime des exploitants agricoles* (Farmers' Group).

The green crosses all over France mark pharmacies. Pharmacies are strictly controlled, and it is difficult to find imported products (except in a few elite stores near the *Champs-Élysées* in Paris). If you will be taking prescribed medication during your stay in France, it is advisable to bring it along with you. To have medication shipped from the United States, special permission from the Secretary of Health may be required. Pharmacists in France are qualified to do more than dispense prescription drugs. They can provide basic diagnostic (blood and urine tests) and treatment services and are able to offer many drugs over the counter that could only be obtained with *une ordonnance* (a prescription) in the United States. For minor ailments, you may want to consult a pharmacist, who will provide immediate treatment or may be willing to recommend a good doctor.

French doctors like to prescribe a lot of medicinal products. It is not therefore surprising that France is one of the greatest consumers of prescription drugs in the world and that the pharmaceutical industry is one of the fastest growing. Don't be surprised if you come out of the pharmacy with a bag full of drugs to treat a bad cold. Your doctor will probably have prescribed some *sirop pour la toux* (cough syrup), *des gouttes* (drops), *des comprimés* (tablets), *des pastilles pour la gorge* (throat lozenges), and even *une boîte de suppositoires* (a box of suppositories).

Drug research is extensive and carefully monitored by the government. Many new products (to treat ulcers and heart and respiratory ailments, for example) are regularly released on the market. France is also at the cutting edge of *sida* (AIDS) research and is very open to *homéopathie* (homeopathy) and *médecine préventive* (preventive medicine). Spas have always enjoyed great popularity among the French, who consider their *cure thermale* (thermal therapy) to be a superior form of preventive medicine. The number of spas is on the rise throughout the country, and the state pays for a good portion of the treatment (minimum stay of twenty-one days), as long as it is prescribed by a physician (which is usually a simple formality).

The French have, in general, become more health conscious and can be found working out in gyms, much like in the United States. Smoking remains very popular, though it is on the decline. The government, which receives over 32 billion francs a year in revenues from the tobacco industry, has finally embarked on an anti-smoking campaign, having realized that medical costs related to smoking were soaring.

Foreign nationals employed in France are generally covered by the French *Sécurité sociale*. It is advisable to check the terms of the insurance provided by your company and to ask if your U.S. insurance covers you while you are traveling or working abroad. A list of English-speaking doctors is available at the American consulate. The American Hospital on the outskirts of Paris, with its English-speaking staff, is one of the best hospitals in the capital.

In case of a medical emergency, each town has its own SAMU *(Service d'Aide Médicale d'Urgence),* whose number is listed in the local telephone directory. Paris's SAMU number is 45.67.50.50. In addition, there is a 24-hour visiting doctor service, which can be reached at 47.07.77.77. If you have problems with the language, you can reach an English-speaking operator by dialing 19, waiting for a tone, then dialing 3313, and saying *Passez-moi le bureau anglais.* For other emergencies, dial 17 for the police and 18 for the fire department.

France imports a good majority of its medical instruments and supplies, as well as its analytical and scientific instrumentation, providing a window of opportunity for American firms. Indeed, the United States supplies approximately one third of France's imports of medical equipment and is the leading supplier of its scientific equipment. For restrictions on exporting electronic medical equipment to France, contact the U.S. Chamber of Commerce.

EXERCICES

A. *Mettre les verbes suivants au conditionnel passé.*

1. *Je (devoir)*
2. *Ils (savoir)*
3. *Vous (se faire vacciner)*
4. *Nous (dépister)*
5. *Cela (susciter)*
6. *Je (faire)*
7. *Elle (rentrer)*
8. *Tu (vouloir)*
9. *Vous (aller)*
10. *Elles (se renseigner)*

B. *Mettre les verbes entre parenthèses au conditionnel passé et au plus-que-parfait selon le sens.*

1. *Nous (se faire vacciner) si nous (voyager) en Afrique.*
2. *Elle (se préoccuper) de sa santé si elle (avoir) des symptômes.*
3. *La crèche (accepter) l'enfant s'il (être) plus âgé.*
4. *Si Mathilde (attraper) la rougeole, elle (rester) à la maison.*
5. *La sage-femme vous (donner) des conseils si vous le lui (demander).*
6. *Si Marc (avoir besoin) d'un rappel, je le (emmener) chez le médecin.*
7. *Nous (prendre) plus de précautions si on nous (prévenir).*
8. *Tu (s'inquiéter) si je (arriver) en retard.*
9. *Si nous (se retrouver) nez à nez, je lui (dire) ce que je pense de lui.*
10. *Ils (ne pas tomber) malades s'ils (faire) plus attention à leur régime.*

C. *Traduire.*

1. The vaccine made him sick for two days.
2. Midwives will give you advice during your pregnancy.
3. He fell flat on his face and broke his left arm.
4. I saw them walking arm in arm down the Champs-Élysées.
5. Their request caught us off guard.
6. What does the doctor think about your X-rays?
7. If your baby has a fever, call me immediately.
8. About a hundred children reportedly caught meningitis last year.
9. You should have asked her if there were any side effects.
10. Poverty is rampant in this region.
11. He accepted right away.
12. She is five months pregnant.
13. How long will she be on maternity leave?
14. It's our first child, so we don't know what to expect.
15. The researchers would have come up with a vaccine if they had had more money and a bigger laboratory.

LEÇON 14

A. DIALOGUE

COMMENT VOUS APPELEZ-VOUS?

Élodie et Matthew n'ont toujours pas arrêté[1] leur choix sur le prénom de leur futur bébé au grand désespoir de Florence, la mère d'Élodie. Un petit incident remet la question sur le tapis[2] . . . et le feu aux poudres!

MATTHEW: **Élodie, quelqu'un a téléphoné pendant que tu étais sortie.**

ÉLODIE: **Qui c'était?**

MATTHEW: **Un type[3] qui m'a dit qu'il s'appelait Camille . . .**

ÉLODIE: **Ah oui, c'est Camille Boissard, un consultant d'une nouvelle entreprise pour laquelle nous travaillons.**

MATTHEW: **Camille? Comme Camille Claudel?[4] C'est une blague? Camille, c'est un nom de femme!**

FLORENCE: **Ah, ah!** *(sarcasme)* **Si vous vous étiez penché[5] un peu plus sur la question, vous sauriez que Camille, comme Dominique et Claude, sont des noms androgynes.[6]**

ÉLODIE: **Maman, sois gentille . . . tous ces prénoms sont difficiles![7]**

MATTHEW: **Et si on l'appelait Dominique ou . . . Napoléone?[8]**

ÉLODIE: **Quelle horreur!**

FLORENCE: **À trois semaines de l'accouchement, je n'arrive pas à croire que vous ne vous soyez pas souciés de trouver un prénom pour ma future petite-fille!**

ÉLODIE: **Ne t'inquiète pas, on la fera baptiser,[9] ta petite-fille . . .**

FLORENCE: **De mon temps, c'étaient le parrain et la marraine qui choisissaient le prénom. Il y a quand même assez de saints sur le calendrier![10]**

ÉLODIE: **Maman, c'est dépassé tout ça. Tu sais, un prénom, ça colle à la peau pour toute la vie et c'est parfois dur à porter.**

FLORENCE: **Qu'est-ce que tu veux dire par là? Tu n'aimes pas ton prénom? Ton arrière-grand-mère s'appelait Élodie, tu devrais en être fière!**

ÉLODIE: **C'était un choix excellent dont tu peux te féliciter. Et Matthew et moi, nous essayons de trouver le nom parfait pour notre bébé.**

FLORENCE *(elle s'est radoucie):* **Matthew, vous n'avez pas de préférence?**

MATTHEW: **Florence, c'est assez joli.**

FLORENCE: **Mais non, c'est tellement commun.[11] Dans ma classe, on était cinq Florence[12] et tout le monde sait mon âge aujourd'hui!**

MATTHEW: **Alors Sabrina!**

FLORENCE: **Ah ça non! Monsieur Porchet,[13] le carreleur qui a saboté ma salle de bain a appelé sa fille Sabrina.[14]**

MATTHEW: **Alors, Margaux![15]**

FLORENCE: **Margaux Renna! Mais où avez-vous la tête? Tout le monde la surnommerait "Margarine" à l'école.**

ÉLODIE: **Moi, j'aime beaucoup Océanie . . . Ça rappelle les parfums des îles exotiques . . . et ça rime avec Élodie!**

FLORENCE: **L'état civil ne l'acceptera jamais.[16] Dieu merci!**

MATTHEW: **De toute façon, si son nom ne lui plaît pas, elle pourra toujours en changer plus tard . . .**

FLORENCE: **Vous vous croyez en Amérique où vous changez de nom comme de chemise! C'est extrêmement difficile de changer de nom de famille et pratiquement impossible de changer de prénom![17]**

ÉLODIE: **Alors, on lui en donnera une demi-douzaine et elle pourra choisir![18]**

MATTHEW: **Si jamais on retourne aux États-Unis . . . on devrait choisir un nom qui marche aussi en anglais.[19]**

FLORENCE: **Vous n'allez pas lui donner un prénom américain comme tout le monde ces temps-ci!**

MATTHEW: **Alors, nous allons l'appeler Joséphine . . .**

FLORENCE: **Oh! Matthew! C'est un si joli nom . . . et c'était le nom de ma grand-tante.**

MATTHEW: **C'est aussi le nom d'une impératrice.[20]**

ÉLODIE: **Et selon les prédictions des experts, Joséphine sera très à la mode en l'an 2025.**

MATTHEW: **Vive Joséphine!**

WHAT'S YOUR NAME?

Élodie and Matthew have not yet decided what to name their future baby, to the great despair of Florence, Élodie's mother. A small incident brings the topic up and lights the powder keg!

MATTHEW: Élodie, someone called while you were out.

ÉLODIE: Who was it?

MATTHEW: A guy who told me his name was Camille . . .

ÉLODIE: Ah, yes. Camille Boissard, a consultant for a new firm we're working for.

MATTHEW: Camille? Like Camille Claudel? Is this a joke? Camille is a woman's name!

FLORENCE (sarcastic): Ah! Ah! If you had done a little more homework, you'd know that Camille, along with Dominique and Claude, are androgynous names.

ÉLODIE: Mother, please be nice . . . all these names are difficult!

MATTHEW: What about calling her Dominique or . . . Napoléone?

ÉLODIE: How awful!

FLORENCE: At three weeks before you're due, I can't believe you still haven't come up with a name for my future granddaughter!

ÉLODIE: Don't worry, your granddaughter will get a name . . .

FLORENCE: In my time, the godfather and the godmother chose the first name. Don't tell me there aren't enough saints on the calendar!

ÉLODIE: All this is out of fashion. You know, a first name stays with you for the rest of your life, and it's sometimes hard to bear.

FLORENCE: What do you mean by that? Don't you like your first name? Your great grandmother was named Élodie; you should be proud of it!

ÉLODIE: It was an excellent choice you can be proud of. And Matthew and I are trying to find the perfect name for our baby.

FLORENCE (mellower): Matthew, don't you have a preference?

MATTHEW: Florence is a rather pretty name.

FLORENCE: No, it's so ordinary. In my class, there were five Florences, and everybody knows how old I am now!

MATTHEW: So, let's call her Sabrina!

FLORENCE: Absolutely not! Mr. Porchet, the tiler who wrecked my bathroom, named his daughter Sabrina.

MATTHEW: So, let's call her Margaux!

FLORENCE: Margaux Renna! Have you lost your mind? Everyone would nickname her "Margarine" at school.

ÉLODIE: I love Océanie . . . It reminds me of the fragrance of exotic islands . . . and it rhymes with Élodie!

FLORENCE: The clerk at City Hall will never accept it! Thank God!

MATTHEW: Anyway, if she doesn't like her name, she can always change it later on . . .

FLORENCE: You think you're in America where you change your name so easily! It's extremely difficult to change your family name and almost impossible to change your first name.

ÉLODIE: So, we'll give her half a dozen names, and she'll take her pick!

MATTHEW: And if one day we move back to the States . . . we should pick a name that also works in English.

FLORENCE: You're not going to give her an American name like everybody else these days!

MATTHEW: So, we're going to call her Joséphine . . .

FLORENCE: Oh. Matthew! That's such a pretty name . . . it was my great-aunt's name.

MATTHEW: It's also the name of an empress . . .

ÉLODIE: And according to the forecasters, Joséphine will be very much in fashion in 2025.

MATTHEW: Long live Joséphine!

B. EN BREF

1. The verb *arrêter* has several different meanings: *La police a arrêté une bande de jeunes.* (The police arrested a gang of young people.) *Arrêtez-moi devant la mairie.* (Drop me off in front of the city hall.) *Nous avons arrêté le jour du rendez-vous.* (We fixed the day of our appointment.) *Il a arrêté ses soupçons sur cet homme.* (He fixed his suspicions on this man.) *Le Sénat a arrêté des dispositions générales pour la prochaine session.* (The Senate laid down the general rules for the next session.)

2. The word *tapis* is used in many idiomatic expressions: *Le boxeur est allé au tapis.* (The boxer was knocked down.) *Il a envoyé son adversaire au tapis par ses remarques cinglantes.* (He floored his opponent with his scathing remarks.) *Le choix des prénoms revient toujours sur le tapis.* (The choice of a first name always comes back up for discussion.) *J'ai pris les bagages sur le tapis roulant.* (I picked up the luggage from the conveyor belt.)

3. Some colloquial words used to describe men may have derogatory meanings depending on the context. *Quel sale type!* (What a horrible guy!) *C'est un drôle de gars!* (That's a strange guy!) *C'est un individu sans scrupules.* (This guy has no scruples.) *Ce mec nous a joué un sale tour.* (This guy played a nasty trick on us.)

4. *Camille, Claude,* and *Dominique* are both male and female first names. Camille Claudel (1864–1943) was an accomplished sculptor whose talent was not fully recognized until the 1970s. She was the sister of the famous writer Paul Claudel and was Auguste Rodin's companion and model.

5. In France, it is still common for in-laws to use the formal *vous* form across class lines.

6. The sex of names has changed over time. Before the seventeenth century, Anne and Philippe could be either a boy or a girl. Today, many first names are still androgynous by sound: Pascal(e), André(e), René(e), Frédéric(que), Joël(le), Michel(èle).

7. An obstacle for foreigners doing business in Europe is the unfamiliarity of people's names. Whether on the phone or in person, you may not catch the person's name right away, which often leads to misunderstandings or mistaken identities. For example, don't call monsieur Pacard, monsieur Placard ("Mr. Closet") in error. It's not a bad idea to offer a business card in the hope of getting one in return.

8. Names with historical connotations are often dangerous because of revisionism. For example, *Adolphe,* which was very popular at one time, would have become popular again if it were not for Hitler.

9. Although the majority of French people who consider themselves Catholics do not attend mass on a regular basis, they do continue the rituals and traditions of the church. Social imperatives also play a great part; christenings, confirmations, and church weddings are still prevalent. The major religious groups in France are Catholics (75%), Muslims (5%), Jews (2%), and Protestants (2%). The French insist on the separation of church and state. Some bitter feuds still take place between supporters and adversaries of the clergy, especially on the issue of governmental subsidies for private schools.

10. Traditionally, names were picked from the list of saints on the calendar. The most popular saints' names in order of preference are: *Marie, Jeanne, Anne, Marguerite, Madeleine, Lucie,* and *Élizabeth* for girls; and *Jean, Pierre, Paul, François, Jacques, Antoine, André, Alexandre,* and *Étienne* for boys.

11. As in the United States, names experience upswings as well as downward trends in their popularity. For example, *Alison, Anaïs, Aude, Camille, Charlotte,* and *Anne-Sophie* for girls and *Alexis, Antoine, Emeri, Gaétan,* and *Quentin* for boys are currently in vogue. However, *Arlette, Christiane, Claudette, Georgette, Ghislaine,* and *Ginette* for girls and *Gaston, Gilbert,* and *Guy,* as well as the compound names beginning with *Jean,* have been out of fashion for a long time, but *Pierre-Jean* is very much in favor. The name *Brigitte,* which became famous in the 1960s with Brigitte Bardot, has experienced a free fall.

12. There are more female names because male names can be easily feminized *(Florent → Florence; Laurent → Laurence).* Note also that proper first and last names are not pluralized. *Il y avait trois Suzanne à table.* (There were three Suzannes at the table.) *Les Clément ont appelé leur fils Xavier.* (The Cléments named their son Xavier.)

13. Family (last) names appeared around the eleventh century. They were usually based on the name of a hamlet or a village (De L'Isle, Duplessis), physical aspect (Legrand, Leroux), profession (Boucher, Forgeron), or kinship (Cousin, Neveu). The most common family names in France are Martin, Bernard, Moreau, Durand, Petit, Dubois, Michel, Laurent, Simon, and Dupont.

14. Class still plays a key role in many facets of French society. Karl Marx may not have thought about it, but class struggle *(la lutte des classes)* is also reflected in the choice of names where a pyramidal effect can be noticed. A name favored by the upper class will be adopted by the middle class, then eventually picked up by the working class until it finally becomes altogether unpopular.

15. Henri IV's wife was named Margot, a derivative of Marguerite, a popular name throughout history. Also, Ernest Hemingway named his granddaughter Margaux to pay tribute to the great vintage wine of the Médoc region.

16. Many facets of French life are governed by a regulation of one sort or another. Although it may seem absurd, the laws pertaining to names are necessary to protect children from overly imaginative parents. When parents register the child at City Hall, his or her name must be accepted by the official in charge. If the official feels that the first name is contrary to the child's best interests, he or she is required to inform the public prosecutor. The latter will hand the case over to a family affairs judge, who will then approve the name or order its removal. If the public prosecutor turns down your request, you can go to a higher court, but in the meantime, your child is nameless, and you run the risk of losing your *allocations familiales* and other social benefits.

17. If you want to change your family name, you must send a request to the Keeper of the Seals, then to the State Council. A six-month waiting period can be expected and the whole process can be costly.

18. Children have to be registered at the town hall of the town where the delivery took place, no more than three days after birth, by the father, doctor, midwife, or anyone who witnessed the event. The *livret de famille* (family book) must be shown with the doctor's or midwife's certificate. It is recommended that parents pick three names from different registers (religious, ancestral, trendy) in hopes that the child will like one of them and adopt it, thus avoiding an official change with *l'état civil*.

19. Anglo-Saxon names based on mini-series are a big hit all over Europe. Don't be surprised to meet Jimmy, Steve, Jonathan, Lindsay, Jessica, Rebecca, Alicia, or Tiffany . . . DUBOIS! But the French are very good at changing the spelling and or gender of American names: for example, Djonatane for Jonathan.

20. Napoléon's first wife was Joséphine de Beauharnais.

C. GRAMMAIRE ET USAGE

1. *VERBE + PRÉPOSITION + INFINITIF* (VERB + PREPOSITION + INFINITIVE)

When followed by an infinitive, some French verbs take a preposition and others don't. There is no rule governing this, and the verbs must simply be memorized or acquired through use.

a. Some of the most common verbs that are not followed by a preposition are *aimer* (to like, to love), *désirer* (to wish), *espérer* (to hope), *préférer* (to prefer), *savoir* (to know), *sentir* (to feel), *voir* (to see), *oser* (to dare), *devoir* (to have to), and *avouer* (to admit).

Matthew adore taquiner sa belle-mère.
Matthew loves to tease his mother-in-law.

Ils ont avoué ne pas encore avoir rempli tous les formulaires.
They admitted that they hadn't filled out all the forms.

Elle n'a pas osé lui poser la question.
She did not dare ask him/her the question.

b. Many verbs are followed by the preposition *à* before an infinitive: *aider à* (to help), *apprendre à* (to learn), *arriver à* (to succeed), *autoriser à* (to authorize), *encourager à* (to encourage), *préparer à* (to prepare), *parvenir à* (to manage), *s'habituer à* (to get used to), *se plaire à* (to enjoy), and *renoncer à* (to give up the idea).

Ils ont renoncé à lui donner un prénom étranger.
They gave up the idea of giving her a foreign name.

Elle s'est habituée à faire des compromis avec son gendre.
She got used to making compromises with her son-in-law.

Ils ont réussi à décrocher le contrat.
They managed to get the contract.

c. Some verbs are followed by the preposition *de* when they precede an infinitive: *accepter de* (to accept), *accuser de* (to accuse), *cesser de* (to stop), *conseiller de* (to advise), *craindre de* (to fear), *empêcher de* (to prevent), *oublier de* (to forget), *remercier de* (to thank), *se dépêcher de* (to hurry), and *s'occuper de* (to take care).

Dépêchez-vous de choisir un nom!
Hurry up and choose a name!

Son parrain oublie toujours de lui souhaiter son anniversaire.
His godfather always forgets to wish him a happy birthday.

Ma filleule m'a remercié(e) de l'avoir aidée.
My goddaughter thanked me for having helped her.

d. Some verbs change meaning depending on the preposition that follows:

commencer:

M. Boissard commencera à travailler pour nous le 15 juin.
Mr. Boissard will start working for us on June 15th.
(the beginning of an action)

Commencer par lire ce livre sur les prénoms à la mode.
Start by reading this book on trendy first names.
(the beginning of a sequence)

décider:

Ils ont décidé de faire baptiser leur fils à l'église Saint-Eustache.
They decided to have their child baptized at the Saint-Eustache church.
(simply to make a decision)

Après des années d'hésitation, ils se sont décidés à avoir un enfant.
After years of hesitation, they finally decided to have a child.
(resolution, after reflection)

210

demander:

Ils ont demandé au prêtre de les aider à choisir un nom.
They asked the priest to help them choose a name. (simple request)

Elle a demandé à quitter la maternité un jour plus tôt.
She asked to leave the birth center a day earlier. (permission)

2. *"DONT" VERSUS "LEQUEL"* (*DONT* VERSUS *LEQUEL*)

a. *Dont* is used to replace nouns introduced by the preposition *de*. It is invariable and can be used for a person or a thing.

C'est le livre; j'ai parlé du livre.
C'est le livre dont je vous ai parlé.
It's the book I told you about. (lit.: It's the book about which I spoke to you.)

Il a choisi un prénom; j'ai horreur de ce prénom.
Il a choisi un prénom dont j'ai horreur.
He chose a first name I hate.

Elle ne peut pas vous prêter ce dont elle se sert.
She can't lend you what she is using.

When there is no antecedent, *ce* precedes *dont*. (See *Leçon* 4.)

Ce dont il se vante est ridicule.
What he is boasting about is absurd.

b. *Lequel, laquelle, lesquels, lesquelles* are used after all prepositions except *de*. If the antecedent is a person, it is more common to use *qui*, although *lequel* is acceptable.

Le consultant avec qui Élodie travaille s'appelle M. Boissard.
Le consultant avec lequel Élodie travaille s'appelle M. Boissard.
The consultant with whom Élodie is working is Mr. Boissard.

However, with *parmi* and *entre*, only *lequel* can be used.

Ce sont des personnes parmi lesquelles Matthew est mal à l'aise.
These are people among whom Matthew feels uncomfortable.

Les deux dames entre lesquelles elle est assise sont très bavardes.
The two ladies between whom she is sitting are very chatty.

If the antecedent is inanimate, *lequel* must be used.

Les noms auxquels Élodie pensent ne figurent pas sur la liste de l'état civil.
The names Élodie is thinking about are not on the official list.

La raison pour laquelle ils se sont disputés est absurde.
The reason why (for which) they argued is absurd.

Les critères sur lesquelles Florence se base sont dépassés.
The criteria on which Florence bases her argument are old-fashioned.

D. JEU DE MOTS

French has always had the reputation of being a "fiery" language . . .

Il est en train de jouer avec le feu.
He's playing with fire.

Elle fait feu de tout bois.
She makes the most of all her opportunities.

L'enfant a mis le feu aux rideaux en jouant avec des allumettes.
The child set fire to the curtains while playing with matches.

Après avoir mangé le plat épicé, il avait la bouche en feu.
After eating the spicy dish, his mouth was burning.

Il n'y a pas le feu.
There's no rush.

Il n'y a pas de fumée sans feu.
Where there's smoke there's fire.

Vous avez du feu?
Do you have a light?

Il a fait cette remarque dans le feu de sa colère.
He made this remark in the heat of anger.

J'en mettrais ma main au feu.
I would swear to it.

Cet homme est toujours sous le feu des projecteurs.
He is always in the limelight.

Cette mission était un baptême du feu.
This mission was a baptism of fire.

Nous nous sommes arrêtés aux feux.
We stopped at the traffic lights.

Il était entre deux feux.
He was caught between a rock and a hard place.

E. LE COIN DES AFFAIRES

L'ÉDUCATION (EDUCATION)

France has one of the highest percentages in the world of young people enrolled full-time in both public and private institutions. School is mandatory for children aged six to sixteen, and public schools are free of charge, with books provided by local communities until the end of junior high school. Most private schools are Catholic and are heavily subsidized by the state. The subsidies are opposed by many who insist on the separation of church and state, and the debate seems unlikely to be permanently resolved.

School curriculum is established on a national, rather than a local, level by the Ministry of National Education. Children normally attend elementary and secondary school until the age of sixteen, when many decide to enter the work force or proceed to specialized technical schools. Academically oriented students attend a *lycée* and must pass the rigorous *Baccalauréat* exam in their final year in order to proceed to college. There are also *lycées techniques,* which are geared to prepare students for a *bac technique* and many skilled blue-collar jobs.

Institutions of higher education in France include general universities as well as more specialized institutions. The oldest and most widely known French university is the Sorbonne, which was established by Richelieu in the seventeenth century and is named for Robert de Sorbon, who founded a theological seminary on the premises in 1253. The French counterparts to American Ivy League colleges are called the *Grandes Écoles,* and it is here that most of the future French leaders are groomed. Attendance at one of the *Grandes Écoles* is a virtual guarantee of a successful future.

The *École Nationale d'Administration (ÉNA)* trains students for public service and is a prerequisite for most politicians, whatever their tendencies. Without a degree from *ÉNA,* those who wish to take part in government must work their way slowly through the ranks and seldom, if ever, reach the higher echelons. Students coming out of *Polytechnique* generally work in the upper ranks of many large state and private industrial firms, and many businesses hire graduates of the *École des Hautes Études Commerciales (HEC).*

Because the number of expatriates is expanding rapidly, Paris and other major cities are eager to satisfy their needs. The European Council of International Schools currently lists sixteen international schools in France, offering a wide spectrum of curricula, including the American system. In Paris there are three private American schools—the American School of Paris, the International School of Paris, and Marymount International—as well as several bilingual schools, including *L'École active bilingue* and *Lycée international de St Germain en Laye.* In addition, many adult programs are available throughout France, in Aix-en-Provence, Montpellier, Tours, Grenoble, and Nice, among others.

EXERCICES

A. *Compléter les phrases suivantes en ajoutant une préposition si nécessaire.*

1. *Ils désirent (faire baptiser) leur enfant.*
2. *Elle a renoncé (essayer) de convaincre son beau-père.*
3. *Nous espérons (passer) une semaine en Normandie.*
4. *Le responsable de l'état civil refuse (aider) ce couple.*
5. *Je préfère (savoir) la réponse tout de suite.*
6. *Ils se sont habitués (vivre) en banlieue.*
7. *Bertrand se plaît (taquiner) sa sœur.*
8. *Vous a-t-il autorisé (révéler) cette histoire.*
9. *J'ai complètement oublié (téléphoner) à Sabrine.*
10. *Il faut l'empêcher (faire) cette bêtise.*

B. *Compléter en utilisant un pronom relatif.*

1. *Les documents sur _____ nous nous basons, sont incomplets.*
2. *_____ elle est fière, c'est de sa petite-fille.*
3. *L'agence pour _____ il travaille est au bord de la faillite.*
4. *Voici les vidéocassettes _____ je vous avais parlé.*
5. *L'homme avec _____ ils discutent, m'a joué un sale tour l'an passé.*
6. *Peux-tu me prêter les brochures _____ tu n'as plus besoin?*
7. *_____ elle a horreur, c'est de l'hypocrisie!*
8. *Les diplomates parmi _____ ils se trouvaient sont tous australiens.*
9. *La chaise sur _____ il est assis, n'est pas en très bon état.*
10. *Le style de vie _____ il s'est habitué est vraiment absurde.*

C. *Traduire.*

1. The person with whom she is talking is Florent's godmother.
2. What kind of name did they choose for their company?
3. This always comes back up for discussion.
4. He helped us make a decision.
5. They won't find what they need.
6. They'll never get used to getting up so early.
7. He didn't stop at the traffic lights.
8. She thanked us for having given some good advice.
9. Don't forget to congratulate her.
10. This name is old-fashioned.

LEÇON 15

A. DIALOGUE

TRAVAILLER OU NE PAS TRAVAILLER LE DIMANCHE...

Dimanche midi à Paris: Maud et Alex s'apprêtent à sortir. Mathieu, le frère de Maud, passe à l'improviste avant d'aller à une manifestation en faveur du repos dominical.[1] Les trois expriment leurs opinions sur le sujet.

MATHIEU: **Comme j'étais dans le quartier, j'ai décidé de passer vous dire bonjour. Je ne vous dérange pas, hein?**

MAUD: **Non, non . . . Mais qu'est ce que tu fais de si bon matin, place de la Nation?**

MATHIEU: **Il y a une manif[2] à 14 heures.**

MAUD: **Ah! Encore cette histoire de repos dominical!**

MATHIEU: **Pour moi, le dimanche c'est sacré![3]**

MAUD: **Ça se voit que ce n'est pas toi qui fais les courses! Les hypermarchés[4] sont toujours bondés le samedi!**

MATHIEU: **Qu'est-ce que tu as besoin d'acheter le dimanche? À mon avis, tout ça, c'est une question d'organisation.**

MAUD: **Et qu'est-ce que tu fais le dimanche matin quand tu t'aperçois qu'il ne te reste plus un gramme de beurre?**

MATHIEU: **Y a[5] toujours monsieur Lambert, l'épicier du coin.**

MAUD: **Ah, je vois . . . deux poids, deux mesures. Si je suis[6] ton raisonnement, ton épicier, lui, n'a pas le droit à[7] son dimanche!**

MATHIEU: **Ça n'a rien à voir![8] Les petits commerçants ne peuvent pas baisser le rideau[9] le dimanche car c'est ce jour-là qu'ils font de bonnes affaires.**

MAUD: **Alors pourquoi ne pas autoriser l'ouverture des hypermarchés? Ça donnerait un petit coup de pouce à l'économie, non? Qu'est-ce que tu en penses, Alex?**

ALEX: **Vous êtes là en présence d'une situation paradoxale.**

MATHIEU: **Il faut toujours que tu nous fasses un sermon!**

MAUD: **Mais laisse-le donc[10] parler!**

ALEX: **D'une part, l'Hexagone[11] se prive d'emplois en interdisant l'ouverture dominicale de certains établissements; ce qui est regrettable dans la conjoncture actuelle.**

MAUD: **Car cela permettrait de créer des emplois.**

MATHIEU: Tu sais combien ils gagnent, les employés des hypermarchés?

MAUD: Il faudrait veiller à ce qu'ils touchent [12] un salaire double et à ce qu'ils aient deux jours de repos consécutifs.

MATHIEU: Tu rêves! Ça permettrait au patronat d'exercer un véritable chantage à l'emploi.

MAUD: Qu'est-ce que tu entends par là?

MATHIEU: "Mademoiselle Maud, quoique vous ayez les qualifications requises, comme vous n'êtes pas en mesure de travailler le dimanche, nous nous trouvons dans l'impossibilité de vous embaucher . . ."

MAUD: Tu dramatises toujours! Laisse donc Alex finir son explication!

MATHIEU: Alex, nous sommes tout ouïe.

ALEX: D'autre part, ces nouveaux emplois risquent de supprimer le gagne-pain [13] des petits commerçants qui misent sur le dimanche pour lutter contre la concurrence des grandes surfaces.

MATHIEU: Tout compte fait, d'un point de vue économique, ça ne servirait à rien?

ALEX: Il est fort possible que les effets soient neutres. En outre, si les petits commerçants disparaissaient, bon nombre de consommateurs de ton genre se plaindraient de ne pas pouvoir acheter leur camembert en allant chercher leur journal dominical.

MATHIEU: Quoi qu'il en soit, tu ne crois pas que les Français aient mieux à faire le dimanche que de pousser un caddie? [14] Quel jour est-on censé profiter de la vie de famille?

MAUD: Maman n'en croirait pas ses oreilles!

ALEX: Mathieu n'a pas tout à fait tort. La plupart des structures d'accueil (pouponnières, crèches, etc.) étant fermées le dimanche, les enfants risquent de se retrouver tout seuls devant la télé.

MAUD: Oui, mais mon cher Mathieu, c'est une question d'organisation, si je peux me permettre de te citer!

MATHIEU: Qu'est-ce que tu veux dire par là?

MAUD: Si l'on veut être concurrentiel sur le marché international, il faut peut-être faire quelques sacrifices, débloquer des crédits et mettre en place des infrastructures qui faciliteront le travail dominical.

216

MATHIEU: **Tu rigoles ou quoi?**

ALEX: **Ce n'est pas la peine de monter sur vos grands chevaux! Le chapitre du travail dominical ne sera pas clos de sitôt!**

MATHIEU: **Je t'assure que Paris serait transformé en un champ de barricades, si tout le monde était obligé de travailler le dimanche.**

MAUD: **Et si tu ne pouvais plus faire la grasse matinée . . .**

MATHIEU: **Maud, tu pourrais me faire un café avant que je m'en aille?**

MAUD: **Oh! C'est pas vrai!**[6] **Il ne me reste plus un seul grain de café!**

ALEX: **Du café! Du café! Du café! Ah ça ira, ça ira, ça ira . . .**

To Work or Not to Work on Sundays . . .

On a Sunday morning in Paris, Maud and Alex are getting ready to go out. Mathieu, Maud's brother, comes by unexpectedly before going to a demonstration in favor of "Sundays off." The three express their opinions on the subject.

MATHIEU: Since I was in the neighborhood, I decided to stop by to say hello. I'm not bothering you, am I?

MAUD: No, no . . . But what are you doing on *Place de la Nation* so early in the morning?

MATHIEU: There's a rally at two o'clock.

MAUD: Oh! This "Sundays off" business again!

MATHIEU: For me, Sunday is sacred!

MAUD: It's obvious that *you* don't do the shopping! The supermarkets are jam-packed on Saturdays!

MATHIEU: What do you need to buy on Sundays? In my opinion, it's all a matter of organization!

MAUD: And what do you do on a Sunday morning when you notice that you don't have a speck of butter left?

MATHIEU: There is always Mr. Lambert, the grocer on the corner.

MAUD: I see . . . double standards. If I follow your reasoning, *your* grocer is not entitled to his Sunday!

MATHIEU: That has nothing to do with it! Small shopkeepers cannot shut their doors on Sundays because that's the day they do the most business.

MAUD: Then why not allow the supermarkets to open? That would give a little boost to the economy, wouldn't it? What do you think, Alex?

ALEX: You are faced with a paradoxical situation here.

MATHIEU: You always have to give us a lecture!

MAUD: Come on, let him talk!

ALEX: On the one hand, France is depriving itself of jobs by prohibiting the opening of some establishments on Sundays, which is a pity in the present circumstances.

MAUD: Because that would lead to the creation of new jobs.

MATHIEU: Do you know how much supermarket employees make?

MAUD: We would have to make sure they get double-time and two days off in a row.

MATHIEU: You're dreaming! That would enable employers to resort to blackmail with their employees.

MAUD: What do you mean by that?

MATHIEU: "Miss Maud, although you have the required skills, since you aren't willing to work Sundays, we find it impossible to hire you . . ."

MAUD: You always have to dramatize! Let Alex finish his explanation!

MATHIEU: Alex, we're all ears.

ALEX: On the other hand, these new employment opportunities may eliminate the jobs of small shopkeepers who count on Sundays to fight against the supermarket competition.

MATHIEU: All things considered, from an economic point of view, it would be useless?

ALEX: The effects may very well be neutral. Besides, if small shopkeepers were to disappear, many consumers of your kind would complain about not being able to buy their camembert while going to pick up their Sunday paper.

MATHIEU: Whatever the case may be, don't you think that the French have better things to do on Sundays than push a shopping cart? On which day are we supposed to enjoy family life?

MAUD: Mom wouldn't believe her ears!

ALEX: Mathieu has a point there. Since most childcare institutions (nurseries, daycare, etc.) are closed on Sundays, children may end up alone in front of the TV.

MAUD: Yes, but my dear Mathieu, it's all a question of organization, if I may quote you!

MATHIEU: What do you mean by that?

MAUD: If you want to be competitive on the international market, we may need to make some sacrifices, release some funds, and set up some infrastructures in order to make it easy to work on Sundays.

MATHIEU: You've got to be kidding!

ALEX: Get off your high horses! The "Sundays off" issue will not be resolved for a long time!

MATHIEU: I assure you that Paris would be transformed into a sea of barricades if everyone had to work on Sundays.

MAUD: And if you couldn't sleep late . . .

MATHIEU: Maud, could you make me a cup of coffee before I go?

MAUD: Oh, no! I can't believe it! I don't have a single coffee bean left!

ALEX: We want coffee! We want coffee! We want coffee! . . .

B. EN BREF

1. According to French law, employees may not work on Sundays, though stores are not forced to close. In other words, small store owners can remain open, as they can work alone, but larger stores must close. Exceptions to this law are jobs that cannot be interrupted due to public need or safety requirements. These include nuclear plants, hospitals, tourist facilities, emergency services, and leisure and cultural institutions. One French worker out of five works on Sundays. The law also makes some seemingly arbitrary distinctions; for example, cut flowers may be sold on Sundays, but potted plants may not. The British company Virgin drew much attention (and free advertising) over this issue by refusing to close its Paris store on Sundays even at the cost of paying hefty fines each week. Adding fuel to the fire is the fact of a British company daring to try to challenge the French *Code du Travail*. The European Union Court ruled that only governments can authorize Sunday hours depending on socio-cultural, national, or regional specificities.

2. As in English, French words are often shortened. For example: *la télé* for *la télévision, le resto* for *le restaurant, le ciné* for *le cinéma, le labo* for *le laboratoire.*

3. *Sacré* has a very different meaning depending on whether it precedes or follows a noun: *Elle a eu une sacrée chance!* (She was damn lucky!) *Nous avons écouté de la musique sacrée dans le monastère.* (We listened to sacred music in the monastery.)

4. *Hypermarchés* are mega-supermarkets where you can buy anything from food to appliances to carpets.

5. In colloquial language, it is not uncommon to drop parts of certain expressions, as in *y a* for *il y a, y a pas* for *il n'y a pas,* or *sais pas* for *je ne sais pas.*

6. Remember that *être* and *suivre* have the same present indicative form in the first person singular. *Je suis votre pensée.* (I'm following your thought.) *Je suis à votre disposition.* (I'm at your disposal.)

7. Be sure to distinguish between *avoir le droit de,* which is used with a verb, and *avoir droit à,* which is used with a noun. *Il a le droit de manifester.* (He has the right to demonstrate.) *Nous avons droit à nos idées.* (We're entitled to our ideas.)

8. Note the idiomatic usage of *voir* here. *Cette manifestation n'a rien à voir avec notre lutte.* (This demonstration has nothing to do with our struggle.) *Qu'est-ce que ça a à voir avec ce que je te demande?* (What does that have to do with what I'm asking?)

9. *Un rideau de fer* (a metal shutter). *Un rideau d'arbres* (a screen of trees). *Un rideau de feu* (a fire curtain). *Il a tiré le rideau sur le passé.* (He drew a veil on the past.) *Elle a acheté des doubles rideaux.* (She bought some drapes.)

10. Remember that *donc* is used to stress interrogative and exclamatory sentences. *Que faisais-tu donc?* (What the heck were you doing?) *Viens donc!* (Come on!)

11. *L'Hexagone* is another way of referring to France, which has a hexagonal shape. *Les ministres ont parlé de l'économie hexagonale.* (The ministers talked about the French economy.)

12. The verb *toucher* can take on different meanings, depending on the context. *Je voudrais toucher ce chèque.* (I'd like to cash this check.) *Elle touchera une prime à la fin du mois.* (She'll get a bonus by the end of the month.) *Son geste m'a beaucoup touché.* (I was deeply touched by her gesture.) *La balle l'a touché en plein cœur.* (He was hit by a bullet in the heart.) *L'Hexagone n'a pas été touché par cette récession.* (France was not affected by that recession.)

13. When you earn a living, you can *gagner votre vie, gagner votre pain, gagner votre croûte* or *gagner votre bifteck.* There are also many words for work, including *la tâche* (task), *la besogne* (work), *le labeur* (hard work), *le boulot* (job, colloquial).

14. In a supermarket, you push either *un caddie* or *un chariot* (cart).

C. GRAMMAIRE ET USAGE

1. *LE PRÉSENT DU SUBJONCTIF* (THE PRESENT SUBJUNCTIVE)

The mood of a verb determines how one views a fact or an event. The subjunctive is the mood of subjectivity. It may refer to the speaker's personal opinion or deal with a hypothetical action.

The present subjunctive of regular verbs is formed by adding the subjunctive endings *(-e, -es, -e, ions, iez, ent)* to the subjunctive stem. The stem for *je, tu, il, elle, ils* and *elles* is found by dropping *-ent* from the third-person-plural present indicative form *(autoriser: ils autorisent → autoris → j'autorise)*. For *nous* and *vous,* the stem is found by dropping the *-ons* from the first-person-plural present indicative form *(recevoir: nous recevons → recev → nous recevions)*. Note that the *nous* and *vous* subjunctive forms are the same as the imperfect indicative forms.

	RISQUER	*APERCEVOIR*	*PRENDRE*
je	*risque*	*aperçoive*	*prenne*
tu	*risques*	*aperçoives*	*prennes*
il/elle/on	*risque*	*aperçoive*	*prenne*
nous	*risquions*	*apercevions*	*prenions*
vous	*risquiez*	*aperceviez*	*preniez*
ils/elles	*risquent*	*aperçoivent*	*prennent*

Je doute qu'ils l'autorisent à prendre ses vacances en mai.
  I doubt they'll allow her to take her vacation in May.

Il faut que vous lui disiez ce que vous pensez.
  You have to tell him what you think.

The stems of irregular verbs[1] in the present subjunctive need to be memorized. The endings, however, remain the same.

Je suis ravie que tu puisses faire la grasse matinée le dimanche.
  I am delighted you can sleep late on Sundays.

Tu veux que je te fasse une tasse de café?
  Do you want me to make you a cup of coffee?

---

[1] For the conjugation of irregular verbs, see Appendix I, page 347.

Some verbs have irregular subjunctive stems in all but the first- and second-person plural forms.

Il se peut que j'aille à Paris ce week-end.
I may go to Paris this weekend.

Il se peut que nous allions à la manifestation.
We may go to the demonstration.

Qu'il le veuille ou non, il devra signer cette pétition!
Whether he wants to or not, he'll have to sign this petition!

Il est ravi que vous vouliez nous joindre à lui.
He is delighted that you want to join him.

While the indicative mood is used to express fact or certainty, the subjunctive mood is used to express personal opinion, moods, and hopes as well as to describe hypothetical events. It is generally used:

a. with expressions of wish, emotion, and doubt.

Son patron voudrait qu'il fasse des heures supplémentaires le dimanche.
His boss would like him to do overtime on Sundays.

Mathieu tient à ce que tu l'appelles avant midi.
Mathieu insists that you call him before noon.

Je crains que l'épicerie ne² soit déjà fermée.
I'm afraid the grocery store is already closed.

Elle doute que ce programme permette la création d'emplois.
She doubts this program will help create jobs.

Keep in mind that where English often uses an infinitive or *-ing* form of a verb, French requires a separate clause introduced by *que* when the subjects of the two clauses are different.

Mathieu veut que Marie aille à la manifestation avec lui.
Mathieu wants Marie to go to the demonstration with him.

Alex tient à ce que vous parliez au représentant syndical.
Alex insists on you talking to the union representative.

When the subject of the main clause and the dependent clause is the same, however, the infinitive introduced by *de* is used instead of the subjunctive.

Il est content de pouvoir faire les courses chez l'épicier le dimanche.
He is glad he can shop at the grocer's on Sundays.

---

² The expletive *ne* is used after *avoir peur, craindre, à moins que, de peur que, de crainte que*. It is not a negation and is not translated.

Elle n'est pas sûre d'avoir une réponse avant la fin du mois.
She is not sure she'll have an answer by the end of the month.

Ils ont peur d'être licenciés.
They are afraid of being laid off.

    b. after certain impersonal expressions.[3] Some of the most common include: *il est bien, il est bon, il est nécessaire, il est juste, il est naturel,* and *il est étonnant.*

Il est important que vous revendiquiez vos droits.
It is important that you claim your rights.

Il est possible que nous adhérions à ce syndicat.
We may (It is possible that we will) join this union.

Il vaut mieux que tu sois à l'heure au rendez-vous.
You'd better (It is better that you) be on time for your appointment.

    c. after certain conjunctions: *afin/pour que* (so that, in order to), *quoique/bien que* (although), *à moins que* (unless), *pourvu que* (provided that), *jusqu'à ce que* (until), *avant que* (before), and *sans que* (without).

Pourvu qu'ils s'aperçoivent de leur erreur à temps.
Let's hope they realize their mistake in time!

Quoiqu'il soit compétent, il est extrêmement paresseux.
Although he is competent, he is extremely lazy.

A useful way to avoid using the subjunctive when the conjunction *sans que* is followed by the verb *savoir* is with the expression *à l'insu de.*

Il a pris un rendez-vous à la clinique sans que je le sache.
Il a pris un rendez-vous à la clinique à mon insu.
He made an appointment at the clinic without my knowing.

Elle s'est fait faire un lifting sans que nous le sachions.
Elle s'est fait faire un lifting à notre insu.
She had a face lift without our knowing it.

    d. when asking or forbidding a person or thing to do something.

Qu'elle quitte cette salle immédiatement!
Have her leave the room immediately!

Qu'il aille au diable!
Let him go to hell!

---

[3] Some common impersonal expressions that do *not* require the subjunctive include: *il est probable, il est vrai, il me semble, il est exact, il est clair, il est sûr.* For more on the usage of the subjunctive with impersonal expressions, see *Leçon 16.*

Que la lumière soit!
Let there be light!

The *que* is omitted in certain idiomatic expressions:

Sauve qui peut!
Everyone for himself!

Certain special cases also require the subjunctive:

a. dependent clauses that begin with *que*.

Que ce problème soit de nature politique, il n'y a pas l'ombre d'un doute.
There is no doubt that this problem is of a political nature.

Qu'il ait refusé de se joindre à la manifestation, cela va sans dire.
The fact that he refused to join the demonstration goes without saying.

b. the expressions *non . . . que, ce n'est pas que, non pas que.*

Ce n'est pas qu'il soit stupide mais il est paresseux.
It is not that he's stupid, but he's lazy.

c. *il s'agit . . . que,* when stating something to be accomplished.

Il ne s'agit pas que vous vous lanciez seul dans cette aventure.
It is out of the question that you undertake this venture alone.

Il s'agit que nous prenions des décisions de concert.
We have to make decisions together (in harmony).

When stating a fact, the indicative is used:

Il s'agit qu'il n'a pas un grain de bon sens.
It's a matter of his not having any common sense.

d. *il suffit que* (unless referring to a fact).

Il suffit que vous le disiez pour que l'on vous croie.
You just have to say it to be believed.

Il suffit que vous leur souriez pour qu'ils signent le contrat.
All you have to do is smile, and they'll sign the contract.

e. *le fait que.*

Le fait qu'elle soit compétente explique son succès.
The fact that she is competent explains her success.

2. *LE SUBJONCTIF PASSÉ* (THE PAST SUBJUNCTIVE)

The past subjunctive is used under the same circumstances as the present subjunctive. However, the action in the subordinate clause must have taken place before the action in the main clause. The past subjunctive is formed with the present subjunctive of *avoir* or *être* and the past participle of the main verb.

	EXPRIMER	*PARTIR*
je	*aie exprimé*	*sois parti(e)*
tu	*aies exprimé*	*sois parti(e)*
il/elle/on	*ait exprimé*	*soit parti(e)*
nous	*ayons exprimé*	*soyons parti(e)s*
vous	*ayez exprimé*	*soyez parti(e)(s)*
ils/elles	*aient exprimé*	*soient parti(e)s*

Je doute qu'Alex soit allé à la manifestation.
I doubt Alex went to the demonstration.

Nous sommes désolés que vous n'ayez pas pu vous joindre à nous.
We're sorry you couldn't join us.

D. JEU DE MOTS

When doing business in France, you'll come across different expressions with the verb *travailler*.

Est-ce qu'il travaille au noir?
Is he working off the books?

Ils ont travaillé d'arrache-pied pour finir le projet.
They worked very hard to finish the product.

Elle travaille pour la gloire.
She works for love.

Il travaille pour le roi de Prusse.
He works for peanuts.

Il travaillait comme une bête de somme.
He used to work like a horse.

Il travaille du chapeau.
He talks through his hat.

Elle doit souvent travailler sans filet.
She often has to work without a safety net.

Il travaille la pâte.
He kneads the dough.

Elle travaille son violon.
She practices her violin.

Cette idée la travaille.
That idea is constantly on her mind.

E. LE COIN DES AFFAIRES

LES SYNDICATS (LABOR UNIONS)

One of France's greatest resources is its highly skilled workforce, which is rewarded not only with relatively high wages but also with an extensive social net. Due to the recession in the mid-1990s, however, labor has suffered quite a bit, and unemployment became one of France's most urgent problems. Despite government efforts to stem layoffs, the unemployment rate continued to rise.

The majority of the French labor force is employed in the service sector, followed by industry and construction, and only six percent in agriculture. In November 1993, France passed a five-year employment law intended to reorganize work, reduce the overall costs on low-wage employees, and create jobs in the service sector. Great emphasis was placed on job training programs and subsidized public-sector employment.

The French work week is limited to 39 hours, and overtime is permitted only in certain professions and only with prior approval by a labor inspector. French employees generally receive at least five weeks paid vacation per year.

The labor force in France can influence management on three levels: labor unions *(syndicats)*, personal representatives *(délégués du personnel)*, and works committees *(comités d'entreprise)*. Labor unions are local units and may be created in any company, regardless of the number of employees. Local units are often linked to regional organizations and one of five national confederations, which are recognized by government as "representative" and can negotiate anywhere. Despite dropping membership, the influence of trade unions in France is much greater than that of their U.S. counterparts. Unions participate in directing the unemployment and retirement systems and medical insurance.

Personnel representatives, required in every enterprise of more than ten employees, are elected by their fellow employees for one-year terms and may be re-elected indefinitely. They serve as liaisons between labor and management. Companies with more than fifty employees must provide for the formation of a works committee whose members are elected by the employees and meet at least once a month. Management must consult the committee on all questions related to the general affairs of the company and must report the company's financial, commercial, and employment situation to the committee.

EXERCICES

A. *Mettre les verbes entre parenthèses au subjonctif présent.*

1. *Nous craignons que ces mesures (aboutir) dans une impasse.*
2. *Il se peut que le patronat (faire) quelques concessions.*
3. *Pensez-vous qu'ils (pouvoir) faire face à la concurrence?*
4. *Quoiqu'ils (avoir) peur des répercussions, ils manifestent.*
5. *Ce n'est pas que vous (être) incompétent mais vous êtes trop lent.*
6. *Nous tenons à ce que les hypermarchés (respecter) la loi.*
7. *Alex est ravi que Mathieu (aller) à la manifestation.*
8. *Il faut que vous (exprimer) vos idées sur le sujet.*
9. *Il est rare que les employés (être) d'accord avec les patrons.*
10. *Pourvu qu'il (vouloir) bien nous aider!*

B. *Mettre les verbes entre parenthèses à l'indicatif ou au subjonctif.*

1. *Il me semble que Maud (être) d'accord avec Alex.*
2. *Les commerçants ont peur qu'un hypermarché (s'ouvrir) juste à côte.*
3. *Ils manifestent pour que le repos dominical (être) respecté.*
4. *Il vaut mieux que tu (faire) les courses dans le courant de la semaine.*
5. *Il est probable qu'elle (recevoir) une augmentation de salaire.*
6. *Il est possible qu'elle (s'apercevoir) des erreurs dans le texte.*
7. *Qu'elle (prendre) la décision qui lui semble la plus raisonnable!*
8. *Il est certain que le patron (se plaindre) demain à la réunion.*
9. *Nous nous attendons à ce que vous (savoir) ce qui se passe.*
10. *Je doute que vous (toucher) des heures supplémentaires.*

C. *Traduire.*

1. Although he is entitled to open on Sundays, he prefers to rest.
2. We are glad that you were able to spend a month in Europe.
3. It is not that his job is difficult, but it is boring.
4. I doubt this measure could boost the economy.
5. They'll demonstrate until they get what they want.
6. Do you want me to go with you to Maud's?
7. Unless we complain, the boss won't give us a raise.
8. They are sorry this day care center is not open on Sundays.
9. He was sad he had to work all week.
10. How long have they been fighting against foreign competition?

LECTURE

LES TÉLÉDIFFUSEURS PARTICIPENT À L'ESSOR DE L'INDUSTRIE*

Les grands mouvements qui bouleversent¹ aujourd'hui l'échiquier² télévisuel mondial ont depuis plusieurs années façonné cette industrie au Québec: l'éclatement³ du monopole des télévisions publiques, la croissance⁴ des chaînes commerciales, la consolidation d'une industrie de la production indépendante, la progression de la câblodistribution et la multiplication des canaux spécialisés.

Aujourd'hui, le Québec possède une télévision des plus développées et diversifiées . . . En plus des quatre chaînes généralistes francophones, deux autres diffusent⁵ en anglais. Le Québec offre également des chaînes en provenance des États-Unis, des canaux spécialisés, des services de télévision payante et hors programmation de même que la télévision communautaire. Le téléspectateur a donc le choix de regarder entre 25 et 35 canaux . . . Les télédiffuseurs publics travaillent de plus en plus étroitement⁶ avec l'entreprise privée, qu'il s'agisse de l'achat d'émissions ou de coproductions. Selon Claude Bédart, directeur des communications à Radio-Canada, la société d'État prévoit que 50% des émissions à l'affiche seront à moyen terme produites par l'entreprise indépendante . . .

Les canaux spécialisés du Québec ont une longueur d'avance sur leurs équivalents en Europe. Musique Plus a contribué à bâtir⁷ au Québec une véritable industrie du videoclip. Innovatrice et audacieuse, la télé musicale québécoise entretient⁸ depuis quelques années des liens avec les projets européens du genre. Pour sa part, le Réseau des sports concrétisait,⁹ il y a deux ans, une entente d'échanges de programmes avec la chaîne française TV Sport. Quant à Canal Famille, qui fait partie du groupe Astral Communications et ne possède pas d'infrastructure de production, il est présent sur la scène internationale en investissant dans la coproduction d'émissions pour enfants.

Météomédia est reconnu comme l'un des services de télévision spécialisée les plus innovateurs du monde. De Montréal, ce réseau¹⁰ diffuse des nouvelles météorologiques à l'ensemble du Canada. Ses installations sophistiquées lui permettent d'offrir à chaque région des informations et des cartes adaptées à ses conditions climatiques particulières. C'est Northern Telecom qui fabrique ce système d'adressabilité haut de gamme¹¹ conçu chez Météomedia et dont près de 5 000 appareils ont déjà été vendus au Weather Channel des États-Unis.

Depuis sa création en Europe en 1984, TV5, la chaîne "satellite" internationale de la francophonie connaît une croissance soutenue dans le monde. Le Québec s'y est joint . . . et créait deux ans plus tard son propre service, TV5 Québec Canada, administré par un consortium de diffuseurs et de téléviseurs et de producteurs des secteurs public et privé.

* Reprinted from *Magazine Québec international.*

Accessible à cinq millions de foyers[12] *canadiens par l'entreprise de plus de 110 réseaux de câble, TV5 Québec Canada offre aux francophones et aux francophiles du pays une programmation diversifiée en provenance de toute la francophonie. Réciproquement, TV5 Europe diffuse une programmation qui met les émissions québécoises en évidence auprès d'un auditoire de 24 millions de foyers dans 50 pays. TV5 Québec Canada est aussi diffusée aux États-Unis auprès de 40 000 abonnés*[13] *de la communauté francophone louisianaise, par l'intermédiaire du câblodistributeur CTA. Depuis 1990, International Channel, un canal spécialisé multilingue américain, accessible à trois millions d'abonnés du câble, propose quant à*[14] *lui des blocs de programmation en français offerts par TV5 Québec Canada.*

VOCABULAIRE

1.	*bouleverser*	to upset, disrupt
2.	*l'échiquier*	chessboard
3.	*l'éclatement*	explosion, burst
4.	*la croissance*	growth
5.	*diffuser*	to broadcast
6.	*étroitement*	strictly, closely
7.	*bâtir*	to build
8.	*entretenir*	to maintain, keep
9.	*concrétiser*	to materialize, solidify
10.	*le réseau*	network
11.	*haut de gamme*	top of the line
12.	*le foyer*	home
13.	*l'abonné*	subscriber
14.	*quant à*	as for

LEÇON 16

A. DIALOGUE

LES AUTOROUTES DE L'INFORMATION.

Laure et Pascal passent la journée au Salon de l'informatique à Québec.[1]

EXPOSANT 1: Ça vous intrigue?

LAURE: À quoi ça sert?

EXPOSANT 1: Ce dispositif[2] permet de sauvegarder[3] vos données[4] sur un disque dur de grande capacité et vous assure une sécurité totale.

PASCAL: Toi qui as[5] tant de mésaventures avec tes disquettes,[6] ce ne serait peut-être pas un mauvais investissement . . .

EXPOSANT 1: Il est bien connu que chaque jour, des milliers d'utilisateurs perdent leurs données en une fraction de seconde.

PASCAL: Il n'y a donc pas que ton ordinateur qui fait des siennes.

LAURE: Tu parles d'une consolation!

EXPOSANT 1: Si vous commandez ce dispositif au Salon, nous vous offrirons n'importe quel logiciel de notre gamme. C'est une promotion spéciale, profitez-en.

LAURE: C'est très gentil, mais pour le moment, il est plus important que j'investisse dans un nouveau portable plus performant.

EXPOSANT 1: Vous comptez vous en servir pour les affaires?

LAURE: Il se peut que j'en aie besoin pour une série de conférences en Asie.

EXPOSANT 1: J'ai ce qu'il vous faut: un portable doté d'un écran[7] au design unique qui se décroche puis se retourne pour se dresser face à votre auditoire.

LAURE: C'est formidable!

PASCAL: Et quelle est son autonomie?[8]

EXPOSANT 1: Il a plus de dix heures d'autonomie et il pèse environ 2,5 kilos.

PASCAL: Le mien pèse à peine deux kilos, ce qui est un atout considérable.

LAURE: Pas de souris?

EXPOSANT 1: **Une boule de commande à l'avant du clavier en guise de**[9] **souris.**

PASCAL: **D'autres gadgets?**[10]

EXPOSANT 1: **Il dispose d'un microphone intégré; vous pouvez également enregistrer vos messages téléphoniques, recevoir des télécopies, et accéder au Minitel.**[11]

LAURE: **Tout cela est fascinant. Vous avez une brochure, s'il vous plaît?**

EXPOSANT 1: **Voilà.**

LAURE: **Nous allons faire un petit tour et nous repasserons tout à l'heure.**

PASCAL: **Regarde Laure, avec ce CD-ROM, tu peux simuler la navigation pour les courses de voilier.**

EXPOSANT 2: **C'est l'outil parfait pour affiner ses stratégies et affûter ses entraînements.**

LAURE: **Comment ça marche?**

EXPOSANT 2: **Le programme vous donne tout changement de direction du vent, des conditions météorologiques et des courants marins.**[12]

LAURE: **De quoi épater Newton . . .**

PASCAL: **La victoire programmée ou presque . . .**

LAURE: **Et si on allait jeter un coup d'œil aux dictionnaires?**

EXPOSANT 3: **Au cas où vous auriez le moindre doute sur l'orthographe d'un mot, ce correcteur orthographique vous fournira la réponse appropriée.**

PASCAL: **Et si j'ai besoin d'une citation de Charles de Gaulle**[13] **au Québec?**[14]

EXPOSANT 3: **En cliquant sur l'icône "citations," vous effectuerez des recherches à partir du nom de l'auteur, du titre de l'ouvrage ou encore du mot clef. Outre la liste des citations, vous pourrez consulter le dictionnaire des analogies, des homonymes, des synonymes, des mots dérivés et de la phonétique.**

PASCAL: **Mon ami Jim de Calgary qui écorche**[15] **notre langue en aurait bien besoin.**

LAURE: **Regarde . . .**

PASCAL: **Si tu mets ce casque de vision stéréoscopique et ce gant à capteurs sensoriels, tu vas t'immerger dans un monde virtuel. Allez, essaie!**

EXPOSANT 3: **Je vous propose les récifs de corail australiens, une mer d'huile, un véritable paradis sous-marin qui vous envoûtera.**

PASCAL: **Je t'accompagne?**

LAURE: **Non, j'ai rendez-vous avec les dauphins.**[16] **Au revoir.**

THE INFORMATION HIGHWAY.

Laure and Pascal are spending the day at the computer trade show in Québec.

EXHIBITOR 1: Intriguing?

LAURE: What is it used for?

EXHIBITOR 1: This device allows you to save your data on a high capacity hard disk and ensures total safety.

PASCAL: For you who have so many mishaps with your disk, it might not be a bad investment . . .

EXHIBITOR 1: It's well known that, every day, thousands of users lose their data within a fraction of a second.

PASCAL: Your computer is not the only one acting up, then.

LAURE: What a consolation!

EXHIBITOR 1: If you order this device at the trade show, we'll give you any software in our line. It's a special promotion; take advantage of it.

LAURE: That's very nice, but for the time being, it's more important for me to invest in a new and more efficient laptop.

EXHIBITOR 1: Do you plan to use it for business?

LAURE: I may need it for a series of conferences in Asia.

EXHIBITOR 1: I have just what you need: a portable equipped with a specially designed screen that can be pulled off and flipped back to face your audience.

LAURE: That's wonderful!

PASCAL: How self-sufficient is it?

EXHIBITOR 1: It runs on batteries for more than ten hours and weighs about 5.5 pounds.

PASCAL: Mine weighs hardly 4 pounds, which is a definite plus.

LAURE: No mouse?

EXHIBITOR 1: A ball in front of the keyboard is used instead of a mouse.

PASCAL: Other gadgets?

EXHIBITOR 1: It is equipped with a built-in microphone; you can also record your phone messages, receive faxes, and access the Minitel.

LAURE: All this is fascinating. Do you have a brochure, please?

EXHIBITOR 1: Here you go.

LAURE: We're going to walk around for a bit, and we'll be back a little later.

PASCAL: Laure, take a look . . . with this CD-ROM, you can simulate navigation for sailboat races.

LAURE: How does it work?

EXHIBITOR 2: The program indicates any change of wind direction or weather conditions and underwater currents.

LAURE: Newton would be impressed!

PASCAL: Programmed victory, almost . . .

LAURE: How about looking at the dictionaries?

EXHIBITOR 3: In case you have the slightest doubt about the spelling of a word, this spell check will provide you with the appropriate answer.

PASCAL: And if I need a quotation by Charles de Gaulle when he was in Québec?

EXHIBITOR 3: By clicking on the "quotation" icon you'll be able to do your research with the author's name, the title of the work, or even the key word. Besides the list of quotations, you'll be able to consult the dictionary of analogies, homonyms, synonyms, and derived words, and phonetics.

PASCAL: My friend Jim from Calgary, who butchers our language, could use something like that.

LAURE: Look . . .

PASCAL: If you put on this stereoscopic vision helmet and this glove with sensors, you'll immerse yourself in a virtual world. Come on, try it on . . .

EXHIBITOR 3: I suggest the Australian coral reefs, a calm sea, a true underwater paradise that will enchant you.

PASCAL: Can I go with you?

LAURE: No, I have a date with the dolphins. Bye.

B. EN BREF

1. Québec, the capital of the province of Québec, is second in size only to Montréal. The old city has retained its charm and French character.

2. The word *dispositif* (device, system) may come in very handy. *Le ministère de la défense a mis en place un nouveau dispositif d'attaque.* (The defense ministry has set up a new plan of attack.) *Un dispositif a été établi pour enrayer l'épidémie.* (A complete plan of action was set up to stop the epidemic.) *Leur entreprise a installé un dispositif de sécurité très performant.* (Their company has installed a very effective security system.) *Cet ordinateur est doté d'un dispositif de contrôle.* (This computer is equipped with a control system.) *Ce dispositif de fermeture ne marche plus.* (This locking device does not work any more.)

3. There are many ways to translate the word "save." *Ce chirurgien lui a sauvé la vie.* (This surgeon saved his/her life.) *Je t'ai gardé un morceau de gâteau au chocolat.* (I saved you a piece of chocolate cake.) *Ton soutien m'a épargné de nombreux ennuis.* (Your support saved me a lot of trouble.) *Tu économiseras au moins mille francs.* (You'll save at least a thousand francs!) *Elle met de l'argent de côté pour ses vacances.* (She is saving for her vacation.) *Il se ménage pour le marathon.* (He is saving his strength for the marathon.) *Vive le roi!* (God save the King!)

4. In computer science, the word *donnée* is often used to refer to different kinds of information: *le traitement des données* (data processing), *la base de données* (data base), *la banque de données* (data bank), *le fichier des données* (data file).

5. Note that *avoir* agrees with *tu* and not *qui*.

6. *Sa collection de disques des années 50 vaut une fortune.* (His collection of records from the fifties is worth a lot of money.) *Cette disquette n'est pas compatible avec mon ordinateur.* (This disk is not compatible with my computer.) *Son hernie discale le fait beaucoup souffrir.* (His slipped disk gives him a lot of pain.)

7. The word "screen" can be translated in different ways: *L'écran de ce portable est trop petit.* (The screen on this laptop is too small.) *La propriété était bordée d'un rideau de peupliers.* (The property was lined with a screen of poplars.) *Un paravent japonais serait idéal pour son atelier.* (A Japanese screen would be ideal for his/her artist's studio.) *Il faut acheter une moustiquaire pour cette fenêtre.* (You must buy a screen for this window.)

8. Note the different usages of the word *autonomie. Certains Corses réclament leur autonomie.* (Some people from Corsica want to be self-governed.) *Son autonomie, c'est ce qui lui manque le plus.* (Most of all he misses being self-sufficient.) *Ma caméra a deux heures d'autonomie.* (My camera can run on batteries for two hours.)

9. The word *guise* has several meanings. *Elle n'en fait qu'à sa guise.* (She does as she pleases.) *À votre guise!* (As you wish!) *Il portait un foulard en guise de cravate.* (He wore a scarf instead of a tie.) *Le clown portait une casserole en guise de chapeau.* (The clown wore a pan as a hat.)

10. The use of Americanisms in French is a topic of heated debate, but things aren't always what they seem. The word "gadget," seemingly an anglicism, is indeed a nineteenth-century English word used by sailors to refer to any small device. However, originally it was borrowed from the French word *gâchette* (trigger), and now the French have simply borrowed it back!

11. In the 1980s, France established an electronic system connected to the phone and managed by *France Telecom.* From the privacy of your home, you can look up a phone number, place an order in a store, reserve a train or plane ticket, buy stock at the *Bourse,* check tomorrow's weather. An electronic mailbox allows subscribers to exchange ideas and even see each other on the screen.

12. There are many *courants* in French: *Attention! le courant de cette rivière est très rapide.* (Be careful! This river's current is very fast.) *Il se plaint toujours des courants d'air.* (He always complains about drafts.) *Débranchez votre ordinateur en cas de panne de courant.* (Unplug your computer if there is a power failure.) *Nous vous enverrons un nouveau clavier dans le courant de la semaine.* (We'll send you a new keyboard during the course of the week.) *Cette agence analyse les courants de l'opinion publique.* (This agency analyzes the trends of public opinion.) *Tenez-nous au courant!* (Keep us posted!)

13. In 1967, Charles de Gaulle's moving speech in favor of the independence of the province of Québec ended with the famous words: *"Vive le Québec libre!"*

14. Québec, the largest province in Canada, is three times the size of France. With a population of about seven million, it represents some twenty-five percent of the total population of Canada. French is the mother tongue of eighty percent of all Québecois. It is a young, pluralistic society that has retained its French origins.

15. *Écorcher* has various usages: *Elle s'est écorché les genoux en tombant.* (She scratched her knees falling.) *Ce col m'écorche la peau.* (This collar is chafing my skin.) *Il a écorché la sonate de Chopin.* (He murdered Chopin's sonata.) *Ce son m'écorche les oreilles.* (This sound is grating on my ears.) *Ce boucher écorche ses clients.* (This butcher fleeces his clients.)

16. In French, *un dauphin* is a dolphin but also the heir apparent to the throne. You won't hear the difference, but you'll see that *le Dauphin de Louis XIV* is capitalized.

C. GRAMMAIRE ET USAGE

1. *LE SUBJONCTIF APRÈS LES EXPRESSIONS IMPERSONNELLES* (THE SUBJUNCTIVE AFTER IMPERSONAL EXPRESSIONS)

The subjunctive is used after certain impersonal expressions. Some common ones include: *il est possible* (it is possible), *il semble* (it seems), *il faut* (it is necessary), *il est dommage* (it is a shame), *il vaut mieux* (it would be better), *il est inutile* (it is useless), *il est temps* (it is time), and *comment se fait-il* (how come).

Il faut que nous soyons reliés par satellite.
We have to be connected by satellite.

Comment se fait-il que vous n'ayez pas sauvegardé votre dossier?
How come you didn't save your file?

Il est dommage que tu ne puisses pas venir avec nous au salon.
It's a shame you can't come with us to the trade show.

Other impersonal expressions are followed by the indicative because they indicate certainty. Some of the most common are: *il est certain* (it is sure), *il est évident* (it is obvious), *il est exact* (it is accurate), *il est clair* (it is clear), *il est prévu* (it is planned), *il est probable* (it is likely), *il est sûr* (it is sure), *il me semble* (it seems to me), *il est vrai* (it is true), *il est prouvé* (it is proven).

Il est évident que ce musicien travaille dans un studio piloté par un ordinateur.
It's obvious that this musician works in a computerized studio.

Il me semble que ton CD-ROM est un outil de travail indispensable.
It seems that your CD-ROM is an indispensable work tool.

Il est vrai que la technologie est en constante évolution.
It is true that technology is in constant evolution.

When negated, some of these expressions convey uncertainty, and thus require the subjunctive. Compare.

Il est certain que nous adopterons ce nouveau système numérique.
It's certain that we'll adopt this new numeric system.

Il n'est pas certain que nous adoptions ce nouveau système numérique.
It's not sure that we'll adopt this new numeric system.

Il est probable qu'elle choisira cette imprimante.
She will probably choose this printer.

Il est peu probable qu'elle choisisse cette imprimante.
It is unlikely that she'll choose this printer.

In questions, the subjunctive can be used after impersonal expressions that do not require it, in order to underscore the speaker's doubts.

Est-il vrai qu'ils soient coupables?
Is it true that they are guilty? (The speaker is uncertain about the guilt.)

Est-il vrai qu'ils sont coupables?
Is it true that they are guilty? (The speaker, who thinks they are guilty, is asking for confirmation.)

2. *LES PRONOMS POSSESSIFS* (POSSESSIVE PRONOUNS)

Possessive pronouns replace possessive adjectives and the nouns to which they refer. They agree in gender and number with those nouns.

MASCULINE SINGULAR	FEMININE SINGULAR	MASCULINE PLURAL	FEMININE PLURAL
le mien	la mienne	les miens	les miennes
le tien	la tienne	les tiens	les tiennes
le sien	la sienne	les siens	les siennes
le nôtre	la nôtre	les nôtres	les nôtres
le vôtre	la vôtre	les vôtres	les vôtres
le leur	la leur	les leurs	les leurs

J'utilise mes logiciels, elle utilise les siens.
I use my software, she uses hers.

Son scanner marche bien mais pas le mien.
His/her scanner works well, mine does not.

When a possessive follows the verb "to be," a stressed pronoun introduced by the preposition *à* is generally used.

Cette souris sans fil est à moi.
This wireless mouse is mine.

À qui sont ces logiciels? Ils sont à nous.
   Whose software is this? It's ours.

   When possessive pronouns are used instead in this context, strong
   emphasis is placed on the notion of ownership.

Ce n'est pas le vôtre, c'est le mien!
   It's not yours, it's mine!

   English speakers often have difficulty translating expressions such as: "a
   cousin of mine, a book of mine," as French does not use the possessive
   pronoun but the possessive adjective.

Un de mes amis vous appelera la semaine prochaine.
   A friend of mine will call you next week.

   Some common idiomatic expressions are also formed with possessive
   pronouns:

   a. *les miens, les tiens, les siens:* one's family, one's group.

*Cet informaticien parle d'une façon bizarre et même les siens ne le comprennent
pas.*
   This computer scientist talks in a strange way and even his family can't
   understand him.

Elle a été déshéritée par les siens.
   She was disowned by her own people.

Serez-vous des nôtres ce soir?
   Will you join us tonight?

   b. *y mettre du sien:* to try hard, to make an effort.

Si tu veux réussir, il faut y mettre du tien.
   If you want to succeed, you have to contribute your share.

   c. *faire des siennes:* to act up.

Il a encore fait des siennes.
   He's acting up again.

   d. *à la tienne, à la vôtre:* cheers.

À la vôtre!
   Cheers!

D. JEU DE MOTS

After spending some time in France, you'll realize that *l'huile* is not meant only for salad dressing. Take a look at some idioms.

Ils naviguaient sur une mer d'huile.
They were sailing on a calm sea.

Les mécanismes de cette institution sont bien huilés.
The workings of this institution are running smoothly.

Sa remarque n'a fait qu'ajouter de l'huile sur le feu.
Her remark only added fuel to the fire.

Les huiles de la compagnie d'informatique sont passées ce matin.
The top brass of the company stopped by this morning.

C'est une huile du parti socialiste.
He is one of the big shots of the Socialist party.

Ça n'a fait que verser de l'huile sur les plaies.
That only served to pour oil on troubled waters.

Ça a fait tache d'huile.
It spread like wildfire.

Ça baigne dans l'huile.
Everything is going smoothly.

Il lui faudra de l'huile de coude pour accomplir cette tâche.
He'll need a lot of elbow grease to accomplish this job.

N'oublie pas ton huile solaire si tu vas à la plage.
Don't forget your suntan lotion if you go to the beach.

Elle préfère l'huile à l'aquarelle.
She prefers oil paintings to watercolors.

E. LE COIN DES AFFAIRES

LES ORDINATEURS (COMPUTERS)

France is technologically very advanced, and the use of computers is as widespread as in the United States. The French market is the fourth largest in the world, and the United States supplies most of its hardware *(le matériel)*. With greater and greater emphasis placed on personal computers and software *(le logiciel)*, this market is one of the best commercial prospects for U.S. export and investment in France. France itself is at the cutting edge of software development, though U.S. firms control the packaged software market with programs such as Microsoft Word, WordPerfect, and Lotus 123.

One of the most difficult aspects of using a computer or discussing applications in France is the plethora of new vocabulary you'll need to learn. The following diagram might help you familiarize yourself with some of the most common computer terminology.

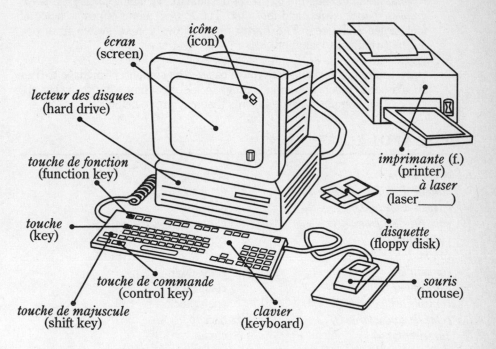

Once you begin using the computer, you may be familiar with the layout of the screen, but you'll again need to get used to entirely new terms. To open a file *(ouvrir un fichier),* go to the menu bar *(la barre de menus),* click *(cliquer)* the File *(Fichier)* menu, and drag the mouse *(faire glisser la souris)* to "open" *(Ouvrir).* Other options commonly found under the *Fichier* menu include: *Nouveau* (New), *Fermer* (Close), *Enregistrer* (Save), *Enregistrer sous* (Save As), *Rechercher* (Find), *Résumé* (Summary Info.), *Imprimer* (Print), and *Quitter* (Quit).

La barre de menus will probably also feature some of the following menus: *Édition* (Edit), *Affiche* (View or Layout), *Insère* (Insert), *Format* (Format), *Polices* (Font), *Outils* (Tools), and *Écran* (Window). The *Édition* menu allows you to copy, cut, and paste *(faire des recopies, effacements et déplacements),* and to find and replace text *(faire la recherche et le remplacement de texte).*

The *Affiche* menu controls how your document will be displayed—*le mode page* (page layout) or *le mode plan* (outline)—and lets you view embedded elements of your document, such as *En-têtes et pieds de page* (Headers and

Footers) and *Notes de bas de page* (Footnotes). The *Insère* menu enables you to create *Tableaux* (Tables) and *Notes de bas de page*, as well as to insert the current date, symbols, and *fichiers externes* (outside files), including *graphes* (pictures) and *feuilles de calcul* (spreadsheets). The *Format* menu defines the format of documents, including *caractères, paragraphes, pages, styles,* and *tableaux*. The *Polices* menu offers a choice of font styles and sizes. The *Écran* menu allows you to switch from one *fenêtre* (window) to another.

Once you're comfortable with these basics, the computer-language barrier should seem much less intimidating. In the meantime, the following are some other computer-related terms that may prove helpful.

VOCABULAIRE

balayage (m)	scanning
banque de données (f)	databank
base de données (f)	database
capacité de mémoire (f)	memory capacity
commande (f)	command
commutateur (m)	switch
compatible	compatible
conducteur (m)	conductor
contrôle orthographique (m)	spell check
copie de sauvegarde (f)	backup
curseur (m)	cursor
en ligne	on-line
fil (m)	wire
formater	format (v)
haut-parleur (m)	speaker
imprimante (f)	printer
imprimante à laser (f)	laser printer
informatique (f)	computer science
installer	install (v)
interrupteur (m)	switch
mettre à jour	update (v)
mémoire principale (f)	main memory
mise en mémoire (f)	storage
modem (m)	modem
numérique	digital
octet (m)	byte
onde (f)	wave
pagination (f)	paging
portable, portatif (m)	laptop

processeur (m)	processor
programmer	program (v)
puce (f)	chip
raccorder	connect (v)
réseau (m)	network
son (m)	sound
tonalité (f)	tone
traitement de données (m)	data processing
traitement de texte (m)	word processing
trier	sort (v)
unité binaire (f)	bit
vider	empty trash (v)
virus (m)	virus

EXERCICES

A. *Mettre les verbes entre parenthèses au subjonctif présent.*

1. *Il se peut que nous (assister) à la conférence le 15 mai.*
2. *Il est possible que ce scanner ne pas (être) en état de marche.*
3. *Il est essentiel que vous lui (montrer) les statistiques.*
4. *Il suffit que vous (savoir) faire marcher cet ordinateur.*
5. *Il est regrettable que vous ne pas (avoir) une autre imprimante.*
6. *Il est inconcevable que le patron (recevoir) ce représentant.*
7. *Il faut que vous (faire) la présentation avec ce CD-ROM.*
8. *Il est rare qu'ils (aller) au Salon de l'informatique.*
9. *Il serait préférable que nous (être) reliés par satellite.*
10. *Il faut que vous (sauvegarder) ces données.*

B. *Mettre les verbes entre parenthèses à l'indicatif ou au subjonctif selon le cas.*

1. *Il me semble que cet ordinateur (être) en panne.*
2. *Il est étrange que votre société ne pas (pouvoir) adopter ce système.*
3. *Est-il commun que les écoles élémentaires (avoir) tant d'ordinateurs?*
4. *Il est surprenant que ce logiciel ne pas (avoir) de dictionnaire français.*
5. *Est-il vrai que ce CD-ROM (être) un atout considérable?*
6. *Comment se fait-il que vous ne (utiliser) plus de ce clavier?*
7. *Il est probable que d'ici peu tous les PDG (avoir) leur portatif.*
8. *Il est évident que l'autonomie de cet ordinateur (battre) tous les records.*
9. *Il est exact que cet ordinateur (être doté) d'un écran au contraste excellent.*
10. *Cela ne vaut pas la peine que vous (commander) ce dispositif.*

C. *Compléter les phrases suivantes avec le pronom possessif.*

1. *Ce n'est pas le mien, c'est* (his).
2. *J'emporte mon ordinateur portatif en voyage. Emportez-vous* (yours)?
3. *Mon ordinateur est muni d'un correcteur orthographique.* (Theirs) *aussi.*
4. *Ce sont mes disquettes. Où sont* (yours)?
5. *L'informaticien a ses idées sur la réalité virtuelle et elle a* (hers).
6. *Prêtez-moi vos logiciels et je vous prêterai* (mine).
7. *Ils s'intéressent à nos ordinateurs et nous nous intéressons à* (theirs).
8. *Il faut que Pascal fasse réparer sa souris et que tu fasses réparer* (yours).
9. *Elle montre cet écran en couleur à son patron et Laure le montre à* (hers).
10. *Ils s'étonnent de nos résultats mais pas de* (yours).

LEÇON 17

A. DIALOGUE

UN TOUR D'HORIZON.

Trois jeunes architectes, Érica, une Hollandaise, Ishi, un Japonais, et Douglas, un Américain, sont en voyage d'études à Paris. Après avoir passé une semaine à sillonner la capitale, ils partagent leurs opinions sur l'urbanisme parisien à la terrasse de la Closerie des Lilas.[1]

DOUGLAS: Je n'étais pas revenu à Paris depuis mon enfance. C'est une métamorphose totale!

ÉRICA: Pas toujours pour le mieux! La Tour Montparnasse, par exemple, est vraiment hideuse.[2]

ISHI: Malgré tout, Paris est un paradis pour les amateurs d'architecture! Moi, je pense que la France a réussi à merveille à harmoniser l'ancien et le moderne même quand il s'agit de bâtiments administratifs.[3]

DOUGLAS: Au fait, vous avez vu le ministère de l'économie et des finances?[4]

ISHI: Non, pas encore.

DOUGLAS: C'est une construction phénoménale. La partie frontale est en forme de viaduc dont une pile a les pieds dans la Seine.

ÉRICA: De toute évidence, ce bâtiment montre la volonté des urbanistes de prendre en compte la Seine dans les aménagements de la ville. Et le Palais Omnisport,[5] juste à côté, est très impressionnant avec ses façades de gazon.

ISHI: À propos de verdure, je n'aurais jamais pensé qu'il y en avait tant à Paris: des bois,[6] des jardins,[7] des parcs,[8] des squares . . .[9]

ÉRICA: Et aussi des vignes! Je suis allée voir les vignes de Montmartre.[10]

DOUGLAS: Tu plaisantes?

ÉRICA: Non, chaque année, on produit trois cents litres de vin en plein cœur de Montmartre.

ISHI: Ce qui est formidable aussi, ce sont les fontaines.[11] Elles ajoutent une qualité unique à la ville, un sens d'éternité.

DOUGLAS: Que d'eau, que d'eau . . . Vous savez que je m'intéresse en particulier à la reconversion des anciens quartiers.

ÉRICA: Dans ce domaine, vous avez vraiment fait des miracles aux États-Unis: Boston, Philadelphie, Baltimore . . .

DOUGLAS: C'est pour cette raison que je suis allé voir la reconversion d'un lavoir[12] du dix-neuvième siècle qui a été racheté par ses futurs habitants.

ISHI: Et alors?

DOUGLAS: C'est fascinant! Les logements, tous différents, s'organisent comme des maisons individuelles.[13] La diversité des couleurs et des matériaux donnent un cachet indéniable à cet ancien lavoir qui vit toujours en plein Paris.

ISHI: Il est si difficile de privilégier les besoins de la vie moderne sans sacrifier l'ancien. Et c'est essentiel pour la qualité de la vie . . .

ÉRICA: Telle est notre mission d'architecte.

ISHI: On a fait la même chose dans le dix-neuvième arrondissement. Au lieu de détruire les anciens entrepôts, on a tiré parti des architectures industrielles et artisanales pour faire des logements.

DOUGLAS: Et en général, on a gardé l'immense verrière qui éclaire la galerie intérieure.

ISHI: Exactement. D'ailleurs, sur le plan social, c'est idéal car on rejoint les visions utopiques de vie communautaire.

DOUGLAS: Dans quel sens?

ISHI: Grâce aux escaliers intérieurs qui desservent[14] les appartements, on assiste à une meilleure socialisation des résidents qui peuvent flâner dans la galerie . . .

ÉRICA: . . . et rejoindre l'autre bout de la rue sans se mouiller quand il pleut!

DOUGLAS: À Paris, c'est parfois utile . . . Après mon lavoir, j'ai fait une pause aux Buttes de Chaumont, puis j'ai traversé le Canal St-Martin[15] et longé le boulevard[16] de la Chapelle pour aller à la Goutte d'Or.[17]

ISHI: La Goutte d'Or . . . Sur les traces de Gervaise.[18]

DOUGLAS: Ça a bien changé depuis l'époque de Zola.

ÉRICA: Au fait, vous êtes allés à la Géode?[19]

ISHI: Non, pas encore. Mais je compte bien explorer le quartier de la Villette[20] ce week-end.

ÉRICA: La Géode est une forme pure par excellence: une sphère réfléchissante en métal poli posée sur un plan d'eau.

DOUGLAS: **C'est pourquoi on a l'impression qu'elle flotte.**

ÉRICA: **Exactement. Et le Zénith[21] est un véritable tour de force!**

ISHI: **C'est ce que tout le monde dit. J'ai d'ailleurs acheté des billets pour un concert de musique antillaise car j'ai hâte de voir comment ils ont aménagé l'intérieur.**

ÉRICA: **Tu verras, c'est super. On peut le classer à mi-chemin entre le chapiteau et le monument high tech. Ce temple de la musique se monte et se démonte en un clin d'œil.**

ISHI: **Érica, tu veux m'accompagner?**

ÉRICA: **Euh . . .**

DOUGLAS: **Ne vous en faites pas pour moi. Carmen[22] m'attend à la Bastille.[23]**

SURVEYING PARIS.

Three young architects—Érica, a Dutch woman, Ishi, a Japanese man, and Douglas, an American man—are on a study trip in Paris. After spending a week crisscrossing the capital, they share their opinions on urban planning in Paris on the terrace of the *Closerie des Lilas*.

DOUGLAS: I have not been back to Paris since my youth. It's a total metamorphosis!

ÉRICA: Not always for the best! The *Montparnasse* Tower, for instance, is really hideous.

ISHI: Despite everything, Paris is a paradise for architecture lovers! I think France has managed to maintain harmony between the old and the modern very well, even with administrative buildings.

DOUGLAS: By the way, did you see the Ministry of Economy and Finance?

ISHI: No, not yet.

DOUGLAS: It's a phenomenal construction. The front has the shape of a viaduct with one column in the Seine.

ÉRICA: Obviously, that building reflects the intention to take the Seine into account in urban planning. And the *Palais Omnisport* next door is quite impressive with its grassy facades.

ISHI: Speaking of green spaces, I would never have thought that there were so many in Paris: woods, parks, small public gardens.

ÉRICA: And vines, too! I visited the *Montmartre* vineyard.

DOUGLAS: You're joking!

ÉRICA: No, every year, three hundred liters of wine are produced in the heart of Montmartre.

ISHI: The fountains are also wonderful. They add a unique quality to the city, a sense of eternity.

DOUGLAS: Water, water . . . You know that I am especially interested in the rehabilitation of old neighborhoods.

ÉRICA: In that domain, you've certainly performed miracles in the United States: Boston, Philadelphia, Baltimore.

DOUGLAS: That's why I went to see the conversion, by its future tenants, of a nineteenth-century wash-house.

ISHI: And?

DOUGLAS: It's fascinating! The apartments are all different and are set up like individual homes. The diversity of colors and material gives an indisputable charm to this wash-house still in use in the center of Paris.

ISHI: It's so hard to favor the needs of modern life without sacrificing the old, which is essential for the quality of life . . .

ÉRICA: Such is our mission as architects.

ISHI: They did the same thing in the nineteenth *arrondissement*. Instead of destroying the old warehouses, they transformed industrial buildings and workshops to make homes.

DOUGLAS: And, in general, they've kept the huge glass roofs which allow light into the indoor galleries.

ISHI: Exactly. Besides, from a social point of view, it's ideal because we meet the utopian visions of communal life again.

DOUGLAS: In what sense?

ISHI: The indoor staircases that service the apartments promote better social interaction between the residents, who can wander around in the galleries . . .

ÉRICA: . . . and reach the other side of the street without getting wet when it rains!

DOUGLAS: In Paris, that can be useful. After the wash-house, I stopped at the *Buttes de Chaumont*. Then I crossed the St. Martin Canal and walked along the *boulevard de la Chapelle* to go to the *Goutte d'Or* section.

ISHI: The *Goutte d'Or,* on Gervaise's tracks.

DOUGLAS: Things have really changed since Zola's time.

ÉRICA: By the way, did you go to the *Géode?*

ISHI: No, not yet. I'm planning to explore the *Villette* section this weekend.

ÉRICA: The *Géode* is the purest expression of form: a reflected sphere of polished metal built on a water basin.

DOUGLAS: That's why it looks as if it's floating.

ÉRICA: Exactly. The *Zénith* is also a tour de force.

ISHI: That's what everybody says. So I bought tickets for a concert of Caribbean music, because I'm eager to see what they did inside.

ÉRICA: You'll see, it's great! It can be classified halfway between a circus tent and a high-tech structure. This temple of music can be put up and down in a wink.

ISHI: Érica, do you want to come with me?

ÉRICA: Uh . . .

DOUGLAS: Don't worry about me. Carmen is waiting for me at the Bastille Opera.

B. EN BREF

1. *La Closerie des Lilas, Boulevard Montparnasse,* is one of Paris's best known restaurants. Its celebrity dates back to the nineteenth century, when it served as "headquarters" for Baudelaire, Verlaine, and many other Symbolist poets.

2. The *Tour Montparnasse,* with fifty-eight floors, was built in 1973 in the southern part of Paris to accommodate offices. It was the first modern structure erected in Paris and was the subject of great controversy. Today, the Parisian Wall Street, with its many high-rises, is right outside of Paris in a section called *la Défense.*

3. The construction of buildings in Paris is strictly regulated. Tall buildings are not allowed in the downtown area and many hearings are required before the erection of any modern structure can be approved, in order to ensure that it will not clash with the *monuments historiques.*

4. For about 100 years, the Richelieu wing of the Louvre was the home of the ministry of the economy and finance. In 1994, the Richelieu wing became part of the museum again, and the ministry painfully gave up its Louis XVI furniture and decor to move its 6,300 civil servants to an ultramodern office in Bercy in the southeast corner of the capital.

5. The *Palais Omnisport* is located at the *Quai de Bercy.* This multipurpose arena, designed to accommodate all kinds of sporting, cultural, and artistic events, can be altered accordingly.

6. The two main *bois* just at the periphery of Paris are the *Bois de Vincennes* and the *Bois de Boulogne.*

7. For a stroll in Paris, try *le Jardin du Luxembourg, le Jardin des Tuileries, le Jardin des Plantes, le Jardin de la Villette, le Jardin des Cinq Sens, le Jardin du Musée Rodin, le Jardin d'Albert Kahn,* and *le Jardin Shakespeare.*

8. *Le Parc de Bagatelle* and *le Parc floral de Paris* are two famous Parisian parks.

9. Paris has a multitude of small parks called *squares* where Parisians can stroll, play with their children, or have a rendezvous.

10. The *Butte de Montmartre* is the highest hill of the city. In the past, Montmartre, with its numerous cafés and clubs, was the center of bohemian life. Although most of the artists are gone, you can still have your portrait sketched on the *place du Tertre.* Every year about 500 bottles of red *"Clos Montmartre"* are produced on the two-acre vineyard.

11. If, after Versailles, you still want to see more fountains, you can go to *la fontaine des Innocents, la fontaine du Châtelet, la fontaine Molière, la fontaine de l'Archevêché, la fontaine Saint-Sulpice, la fontaine des Quatre Saisons, la fontaine Médicis* or the impressive *fontaine des Quatre Parties du Monde, avenue de l'Observatoire.*

12. This *lavoir* is located at *11 rue du Buisson-St-Louis,* 10th *arrondissement,* Belleville. It was bought by a self-managed group whose main idea was to set up living quarters inside the wooden structure of the laundry on either side of a pedestrian way linking the *rue du Buisson St-Louis* with the *rue du Faubourg du Temple.*

13. The French still prefer to live in individual houses. One out of every two inhabitants owns his or her home.

14. *Le village est desservi par deux autobus chaque jour.* (There is bus service twice a day.) *Cette région est très bien desservie.* (The town is well served by public transportation.)

15. Under Louis XIV, the provosts of Paris made plans to create the *Canal St-Martin* to provide the capital with water, but construction did not begin until the period of Napoléon I. It was completed in 1823. Only six barges pass along the canal every day. It was almost covered by a road but was saved by Parisians who rallied to keep the canal intact.

16. Napoléon III ordered the prefect of the Seine, the Baron Haussman (1809–1891), to execute major public works to transform the capital. At that time, Paris streets were narrow, winding, and dirty. Haussman created wide arteries in the city to improve the quality of life and also to enable the army to place its cannons there to fight any rebellion. He redesigned the *place de l'Étoile*, enlarged the *parvis* in front of *Notre-Dame* (the zero point from which all road distances in France are measured), created the Opera and Republic squares, and built ten new bridges over the Seine. He also put in the sewer system, built water reservoirs, and created numerous gardens throughout the city.

17. The *Goutte d'Or*, a working-class section located in the eighteenth *arrondissement*, has undergone major renovations. Low-income housing has been either built or renovated to accommodate the working-class population.

18. Gervaise, the heroine of Zola's *l'Assommoir*, is the symbol of all the *blanchisseuses* (laundresses). The story, which takes place in the *Goutte d'Or*, is a valuable portrait of Paris in the nineteenth century and more specifically of the decline of a hardworking woman lost to alcohol.

19. The *Géode*, an omnimax movie theater, accommodates 357 viewers who sit in the center of a 100-square-meter hemispheric screen.

20. After the old *abattoirs de la Villette* (slaughterhouses) closed in 1977, President Valéry Giscard d'Estaing appointed an architect to conceive *la Cité des Sciences et de l'Industrie*. It has now become the center for science, education, artistic creation, and folk art.

21. The *Zénith*, located in the *Parc de la Villette*, is an impressive concert hall with multimedia technology.

22. Carmen, the main character of an opera by the French composer Georges Bizet (1838–1875), is a masterpiece of lyric drama.

23. Designed by Canadian Carlos Ott, the *Bastille* opera house opened on July 14, 1989.

C. GRAMMAIRE ET USAGE

1. *CONJONCTIONS CORRÉLATIVES* (CORRELATIVE CONJUNCTIONS)

A big stumbling block for non-native French speakers are the expressions used to smoothly connect one idea to the next. Following are some of the more common ones:

a. *Expressions de conséquence: alors* (so, then), *ainsi* (thus), *donc* (therefore), *par conséquent* (consequently), *si bien que* (so that), *aussi* (therefore, also), *à tel point que* (so . . . that), *tellement . . . que* (so much . . . that), *c'est pourquoi* (that's why), *de sorte . . . que* (so . . . that), *ce qui explique* (which explains).

Ainsi, rien n'a changé depuis ta dernière visite?
So, nothing has changed since your last visit?

On craignait des inondations, c'est pourquoi on a évacué les habitants.
They were worried about floods, that's why the residents were evacuated.

C'était si grave qu'on a dû faire venir le médecin.
It was so serious that the doctor had to be sent for.

b. *Expressions d'hypothèse: en cas de* + noun (in case), *au cas où* + clause (in case), *peut-être* (maybe), *dans l'hypothèse* (in case).

Au cas où vous seriez disponible ce soir, appelez-moi.
In case you're free tonight, call me.

En cas de besoin, vous pouvez toujours joindre Pierre au bureau.
If need be, you can always reach Pierre at his office.

c. *Expressions de justification et de dépendance: par exemple* (for example), *c'est-à-dire* (that is to say), *comme* (like, as), *d'ailleurs* (besides), *en effet* (yes, indeed), *surtout* (especially), *en particulier* (in particular), *notamment* (notably), *selon* (according to), *en fonction de* (according to).

Sa réussite est en fonction de son travail.
His success is a result of his work.

Érica n'a pas vu le Trocadéro, moi non plus d'ailleurs.
Érica has not seen the *Trocadéro;* neither have I, for that matter.

Ils s'intéressent surtout à l'architecture moderne.
They are interested above all in modern architecture.

2. *COMMENT FAIRE PASSER LE MESSAGE* (HOW TO GET YOUR MESSAGE ACROSS)

The French language doesn't employ vocal stress as much as English. To compensate, one must resort to other means: adding pronouns, adjectives, adverbs, etc. In French you can make your point by:

a. repeating the pronoun.

Moi, je connais Paris comme ma poche.
I know Paris like the back of my hand.

L'architecte lui-même nous a présenté le plan de conversion.
The architect himself presented the conversion plan to us.

Les projets en cours de rénovation, je les connais tous.
I know all the present renovation projects.

b. adding *c'est.*

c'est + noun

La pyramide du Louvre, c'est une merveille!
The Louvre pyramid is wonderful!

c'est + adjective

La socialisation des habitants, c'est essentiel!
The socialization of the residents is essential!

c'est . . . + a relative pronoun

Depuis trois ans, c'est son cousin qui dirige notre usine.
For the past three years, his cousin has been running our factory.

Ce sont des dépenses auxquelles il ne pourra jamais faire face.
He will never be able to deal with these expenses.

c. using *c'est que* + subjunctive.

Ma crainte, c'est qu'ils se perdent dans ces ruelles.
My fear is that they'll get lost in these small streets.

d. stressing the noun.

C'est de ce bâtiment dont je vous parlais hier.
It's this building I was telling you about yesterday.

C'est à une transformation de ce genre que je pensais.
This is the kind of conversion I was thinking about.

e. repeating the negation.

Bien que le dollar soit faible en ce moment, il ne faut pas non plus dramatiser.
Although the dollar is weak these days, we must *not* overreact.

f. by switching the phrase order.

Pour mettre en valeur ce bâtiment, l'architecte a construit une aile en verre.
To make this building stand out, the architect constructed a glass wing.

3. *COMMENT EXPRIMER SES IDÉES* (HOW TO EXPRESS YOUR IDEAS)

The French language has many different ways and nuances for expressing the same thing. To avoid repeating the same verbs *(il pense, il a dit),* you must familiarize yourself with synonyms.

a. Variations of the verb "to want": *vouloir* (to want), *demander* (to ask), *exiger* (to demand), *proposer* (to suggest), *souhaiter* (to wish), *tenir à* (to insist), *désirer* (to wish), *avoir l'intention* (to intend), *avoir envie* (to feel like), *aspirer* (to aspire).

Désirez-vous parler à l'architecte?
Do you want to speak to the architect?

Je tiens à lui parler immédiatement.
I insist on talking to him immediately.

b. Variations of the verb "to say": *dire* (to say), *indiquer* (to indicate), *préciser* (to specify), *déclarer* (to state), *raconter* (to tell), *expliquer* (to explain), *montrer* (to show), *exprimer* (to express), *relater* (to tell), *affirmer* (to assert), *prétendre* (to claim).

Il a du mal à exprimer ses pensées.
He has trouble saying what he thinks.

Ils prétendent que les travaux seront finis le 15 octobre.
They claim that the construction will be finished by October 15th.

c. Variations of the verb "to think": *penser* (to think), *croire* (to think, to believe), *trouver* (to find), *estimer* (to think, to consider), *considérer* (to consider), *avoir l'impression* (to have the feeling), *imaginer* (to figure out), *présumer* (to assume), *supposer* (to suppose), *soupçonner* (to suspect), *concevoir* (to conceive), *envisager* (to contemplate).

Ils envisagent de s'installer à Paris.
They are thinking about settling in Paris.

J'ai l'impression que ces plans d'aménagements ne plairont pas aux Parisiens.
I have a feeling that the Parisians won't like these urban planning projects.

D. JEU DE MOTS

The expression *en plein* is very popular in French.

À Paris, il y a encore de nombreux marchés en plein air.
In Paris, there are still many outdoor markets.

Il est arrivé en plein milieu de la réunion.
He arrived right in the middle of the meeting.

Il est dangereux de rester en plein soleil.
It's dangerous to stay in the heat of the sun.

Leur entreprise est en plein essor.
Their company is expanding.

Il a été tué en pleine jeunesse.
He was killed in the bloom of youth.

Il l'a poignardé en pleine poitrine.
He stabbed him right in the chest.

Il faut visiter ce quartier en plein jour.
You have to visit this neighborhood in broad daylight.

Leur maison est en pleine campagne.
Their house is in the middle of the country.

Ne la dérangez pas, elle est en plein travail.
Don't disturb her; she's in the midst of her work.

Quand vous serez en pleine mer, vous verrez des requins.
When you are out at sea, you'll see some sharks.

En plein dans le mille!
You hit the bull's-eye!

E. LE COIN DES AFFAIRES

PARLONS POLITIQUE
(LET'S TALK POLITICS)

As you know, the French are great conversationalists, and discussing politics is one of their favorite pastimes. To participate in such discussions, you should have a basic understanding of the workings of the French government.

France is a republic, run by a president, a prime minister, and two houses of parliament. Its present-day constitution was created by Charles de Gaulle in 1958. The president *(le président de la République),* who is the head of state, is elected by direct suffrage and can serve up to two seven-year terms. *Le président* is the commander in chief of the armed forces, appoints the prime minister *(le premier ministre),* appoints and presides over the Council of Ministers *(le Conseil des ministres),* signs orders and decrees set forth by the council, submits draft laws to the parliament for referendum, and negotiates and ratifies treaties. As guardian of the constitution, he has the right to pardon and to propose revisions to the constitution. The president also has the power to dissolve the National Assembly *(Assemblée nationale)* and call for new elections, as well as to institute dictatorial rule in times of national crisis.

Le premier ministre directs the operation of the government, ensures the execution of the laws, initiates legislation, and is responsible to the National Assembly and to the president. He suggests appointments for and works closely with the Council of Ministers, which is similar to the U.S. Cabinet. Traditionally, the president deals primarily with questions of defense and foreign policy, while the prime minister, along with the government, is more concerned with domestic and economic affairs.

The parliament consists of the lower house—the directly elected National Assembly—and the upper house, the indirectly elected Senate *(le Sénat).* The 577 members of the National Assembly serve five-year terms and are elected by double ballot (i.e., in the first round, all but the two top candidates are eliminated; then one of the two is elected in the second). The 321 members of the Senate are indirectly elected by local councillors and serve nine-year terms, with elections held every three years for one-third of the Senate seats. The Assembly has more power than the Senate. The Senate may attempt to change or turn down a bill, but its motion may be denied by the Assembly. Nevertheless, bills generally pass through each house several times before they are adopted or rejected. A bill may be introduced by the government or a private member, but larger issues are rarely resolved with bills introduced by an individual.

The French government is more centralized than the United States government, though the modern trend is decentralization. Local government is run on three levels: *régions,* which elect their own assemblies and executives (much like U.S. states); *départements,* which have an elected council; and *communes,* which have an elected council and a mayor. A *commune* can vary in size from a small village to a large city.

EXERCICES

A. *Compléter en utilisant une des expressions suivantes: donc, c'est pourquoi, tellement . . . que, au cas où, en cas de, c'est-à-dire, selon, surtout.*

1. *Téléphonez-moi _____ d'urgence.*
2. *Ils ont _____ marché dans les rues de Paris _____ ils sont épuisés.*
3. *C'est un maharajah, _____ un prince de l'Inde.*
4. *_____ vous auriez besoin de quelque chose, n'hésitez pas à nous appeler.*
5. *Je pense _____ je suis.*
6. *Il aime le sport, _____ le football.*
7. *_____ cet architecte, nous devrions aller faire un tour dans ce quartier.*
8. *Leur appartement leur a coûté une fortune, _____ ils sont sans un sou.*

B. *Reformuler les phrases en commençant par "c'est . . . que" pour accentuer le sens.* (Rephrase the sentences, beginning with *c'est . . . que* for emphasis.)

EXEMPLE: *Nous parlons de lui.*
  C'est de lui que nous parlons.

1. *Il présente son projet.*
2. *Ils ont choisi le plus beau bâtiment.*
3. *Tu te moques de moi.*
4. *Ils pensent au projet de rénovation.*
5. *Elle parle de son prochain voyage à Paris.*
6. *Nous pensons à cette solution.*
7. *Il me confie tous ses secrets.*
8. *Elle compte sur toi.*
9. *Vous détestez ce quartier.*
10. *Nous avons peur de sa réaction.*

C. *Traduire.*

1. After spending a week in Paris, they decided to buy an apartment in the 15th *arrondissement*.
2. By the way, have you seen Érica today?
3. Instead of demolishing the old building, they decided to renovate it.
4. I never would have thought there were so many gardens in Paris.
5. He claims there are hundreds of barges on the St. Martin Canal.
6. I have a feeling Douglas will be late.
7. Despite all the problems, they'll have a house built in this neighborhood.
8. You don't have a watch; that's why you're always late.
9. I insist on talking to the architect at the end of the meeting.
10. The sun brightens the whole apartment.

LEÇON 18

A. DIALOGUE

ET SI ON ACHETAIT UNE MAISON DE CAMPAGNE?

Cassandre et Gregory ont décidé d'acheter une résidence secondaire[1] dans le Limousin.[2] Un agent immobilier leur fait visiter un vieux moulin[3] aménagé.

L'AGENT: Attention! Baissez la tête!

GREGORY: Ces maisons ne sont vraiment pas faites pour des Américains de ma taille.

CASSANDRE: Tu sais, au dix-huitième siècle, les Français étaient un peu moins grands qu'aujourd'hui. Tu dois quand même avouer que ce moulin a beaucoup de cachet.[4]

GREGORY: Du cachet, ça c'est indéniable . . .

L'AGENT: Ce moulin a appartenu au Comte de Paris.[5]

GREGORY: Mais tu te rends compte[6] des travaux qu'il va falloir faire?

L'AGENT: La charpente est en parfait état, la toiture[7] et les gouttières[8] ont été entièrement refaites il y a quelques années. C'est un véritable bijou.

GREGORY: À qui le dites-vous! On nous a dit qu'il faudrait respecter les normes des Beaux-Arts[9] si on veut toucher à quoi que ce soit dans la région.

L'AGENT: C'est exact. Votre architecte[10] pourra vous conseiller.

CASSANDRE: Qu'est-ce que tu inspectes dans ce placard?

GREGORY: L'humidité . . . Toi qui es si frileuse, ça ne t'inquiète pas de vivre dans une demeure si ancienne?

L'AGENT: L'isolation[11] du toit et des murs est excellente et ces doubles vitrages sont une garantie contre les courants d'air.

CASSANDRE: Et la chaudière est presque neuve, si j'ai bonne mémoire.

L'AGENT: La chaudière et la cuve[12] à mazout ont deux ans maximum. Et si vous souhaitez jeter un coup d'œil aux factures de mazout et d'électricité, je vous les montrerai bien volontiers.

GREGORY: Avec plaisir, Euh . . . il me semble qu'il n'y a pas beaucoup de prises électriques[13] dans ce moulin . . .

Pendant que Gregory gratte une poutre avec un canif pour détecter la présence de vermine, Cassandre glisse un mot à l'oreille de l'agent. Elle avance à tâtons vers l'agent.

CASSANDRE: **Je vous avais bien dit que ce ne serait pas simple . . . Je rêve de vivre dans un moulin depuis mon enfance. Il faut absolument qu'on réussisse à le convaincre.**

L'AGENT *(à Cassandre):* **Attendez, on va l'emmener au salon . . .**

L'AGENT: **Ce qu'il y a d'exceptionnel dans ce moulin, c'est la distribution des pièces et la recherche du détail. Passons donc au salon.**

GREGORY: **Oh! Quelle merveille! Une cheminée!** [14]

L'AGENT: **Les chenets et le soufflet sont d'époque . . .**

GREGORY: **Ils font partie de la maison?** [15]

L'AGENT: **Ils sont à vous.**

CASSANDRE: **Vous savez, Gregory a un faible pour les cheminées . . .**

GREGORY: **On n'achète pas une maison sur un coup de tête parce que la cheminée vous plaît.**

CASSANDRE: **Bien sûr, mais ce moulin est idéal pour nous et les dépendances** [16] **sont très appréciables.**

GREGORY: **J'ai peur qu'on soit un peu loin de tout.**

CASSANDRE: **C'est la raison pour laquelle on veut être à la campagne!**

L'AGENT: **Et le hameau est très bien desservi; le boulanger passe tous les jours** [17] **et le boucher, au moins trois fois par semaine.**

GREGORY: **Quels sont les projets d'aménagement de la région?**

L'AGENT: **Autant que je sache, rien n'est prévu dans la région mais vous pouvez consulter le cadastre** [18] **et le plan d'occupation des sols à la mairie.**

GREGORY: **Et les impôts?** [19]

L'AGENT: **Les impôts fonciers, bien sûr, et une taxe d'habitation qui est minime. Quelle que soit votre décision, je dois vous dire que j'ai montré le moulin à un couple hollandais à la retraite qui semblait s'y intéresser énormément.**

CASSANDRE: **Je crois qu'il est temps de passer chez le notaire.** [20]

WHAT ABOUT BUYING A COUNTRY HOME?

Cassandre and Gregory have decided to buy a country home in the Limousin region. A real estate agent shows them an old converted mill.

AGENT: Watch out ! Lower your head!

GREGORY: These houses are not really made for Americans my size.

CASSANDRE: You know, in the eighteenth century, the French were a little shorter than today. You have to admit, though, that this mill has a lot of charm.

GREGORY: Charm! No one can deny that.

AGENT: This mill belonged to the Count of Paris.

GREGORY: But do you realize the amount of work that has to be done here?

AGENT: The framework is in perfect shape; the roofing and gutters were completely redone a few years ago. It's a real jewel.

GREGORY: You're telling me . . . We've been told that we'll have to conform to the Beaux-Arts standards if we want to do the slightest alteration to any building in the region.

AGENT: That's correct. Your architect will be able to advise you.

CASSANDRE: What are you examining in this closet?

GREGORY: Dampness. You who are so sensitive to the cold, don't you worry about living in such an old dwelling?

AGENT: The roof and wall insulation is excellent, and these double-paned windows are a guarantee against drafts.

CASSANDRE: And the boiler is almost new, if I remember correctly.

AGENT: The boiler and the oil tank are two years old at the most. And if you want to have a look at the oil and electricity bills, I'll gladly show them to you.

GREGORY: With pleasure. Uh . . . it seems that there are not too many outlets in this mill.

While Gregory scratches a beam with a pocketknife to check for any vermin, Cassandre whispers a word to the agent. She tiptoes toward the agent.

CASSANDRE: I told you it wouldn't be easy . . . I've dreamt of living in a mill since I was a child. We absolutely have to find a way to convince him.

AGENT (to Cassandre): Wait, we're going to take him to the living room.

AGENT: What is exceptional about this mill is the layout of the rooms and the special attention to detail. Let's go into the living room.

GREGORY: Oh! How wonderful! A fireplace!

AGENT: The andirons and the bellows are period pieces.

GREGORY: Do they come with the house?

AGENT: They're all yours.

CASSANDRE: You know, Gregory has a weakness for fireplaces . . .

GREGORY: You don't buy a house impulsively because you like the fireplace.

CASSANDRE: Of course not, but this mill is ideal for us, and the annexes are a plus.

GREGORY: I'm afraid we'll be far from everything.

CASSANDRE: That's why we want to be in the country!

AGENT: And the hamlet has a lot of amenities. The baker comes by every day and the butcher at least three times a week.

GREGORY: What are the development plans in the area?

AGENT: As far as I know, nothing is planned in the area, but you can check the survey and the zoning plans at the town hall.

GREGORY: What about taxes?

AGENT: A property tax, of course, and a communal tax which is very small. Whatever your decision, I must tell you that I showed it to a retired Dutch couple who seemed very interested.

CASSANDRE: I think it's time to go see our lawyer.

B. EN BREF

1. If you plan on buying a country home in France, you can choose *une bergerie* (converted sheep pen), *un chalet* (chalet), *une chartreuse* (country cottage), *un château* (castle), *une ferme* (farm), *une gentilhommière* (small manor house), *une grange* (barn), *un manoir* (manor house), *un mas* (farmhouse in the South of France), *une métairie* (old share-cropping farm), *un moulin* (mill), or *une villa* (villa).

2. Limoges, the capital of the Limousin region in the center of France, is famous for its thirteenth-century cathedral in the center of the old town and the *Musée Adrien Boucher,* which hosts an extensive collection of porcelain, Limoges's main industry. In the Middle Ages, Limoges was already known as the center for goldsmiths' work and the minting of coins.

3. There is more than one kind of *moulin: un moulin à farine* (flour mill), *un moulin à vent* (windmill), *un moulin à eau* (water-mill), *moulin à café* (coffee mill), *moulin à poivre* (pepper mill), *moulin à prières* (prayer wheel). And if the agent talks too much, he or she is *un moulin à paroles* (a chatterbox).

4. The word *cachet* has different meanings: *Il a pris un cachet d'aspirine.* (He took an aspirin tablet.) *J'ai vérifié le cachet de la poste.* (I checked the postmark.) *Le porcelainier a mis son cachet sur la soupière.* (The porcelain manufacturer put his trademark on the soup terrine.) *Cette chapelle a beaucoup de cachet.* (This chapel is quite charming.) *Le cachet de ce chanteur est de 100 000 francs.* (This singer's fee is 100,000 francs.)

5. The *Comte de Paris* still lives in Paris. If the monarchy were reinstated, he would be king!

6. A lot of words sound the same, although they have different meanings: *un comte* (count), *un compte* (account), *un conte* (tale).

7. A roof can be covered with *tuiles* (tile), *ardoise* (slate), or *chaume* (thatch).

8. The English word "gutter" can be translated into French in two different ways. *À l'automne, les gouttières sont parfois bouchées à cause des feuilles mortes.* (In the fall, gutters are often clogged because of the dead leaves.) *Il a jeté sa cigarette dans le caniveau.* (He threw his cigarette in the gutter.)

9. In many regions old buildings may be subject to very strict guidelines for renovation. Stones, tiles, beams, and other features must match the original style. Raising a house or adding a window has to be approved. In some villages, you cannot add a window if it will infringe on your neighbor's privacy.

10. For renovations of old homes and special construction permits, you have to consult one of the fifty government-approved architects.

11. Be careful with words that sound almost the same: *Cet isolement est insupportable.* (This solitude is unbearable.) *Ce manoir a une très bonne isolation thermique.* (This mansion has good thermal insulation.) *Il a attrapé une insolation.* (He got sunstroke.)

12. *Une cuve* (vat), *une cuve à mazout* (oil tank), *une cuve de réacteur* (reactor vessel), *une cuve de développement de photographe* (photo developing tank).

13. The word *prise* refers to both an outlet and a socket.

14. The word *cheminée* has different meanings: *Nous étions assis près de la cheminée.* (We were sitting by the fireplace.) *La cheminée a failli s'écrouler.* (The chimney almost collapsed.) *Les cheminées de l'usine s'élèvent à l'horizon.* (Chimney stacks rise in the horizon.) *Nous avons besoin d'autres cheminées d'aération.* (We need other air shafts.)

15. If you buy a house with fixtures included, make a list of them before the owner moves out; otherwise, you may be unpleasantly surprised when you find *la poignée de porte* (door handle), *le chambranle* (mantelpiece), *la baignoire* (tub), *le lavabo* (bathroom sink), or *les boiseries* (wood panelling) missing.

16. Among the *dépendances: le garage* (garage), *la cabane à outils* (toolshed), *l'annexe* (annex), *le pigeonnier* (pigeon house), *le bélvédère* (gazebo).

17. If you have no shops in your village, a van will come by during the week to deliver fresh goods, newspapers, and, once in a while, even to sharpen your knives.

18. The *cadastre* is the town registry where properties (acreage, value) are listed.

19. The *taxe d'habitation* (community tax) covers services rendered by the town with a contribution for regional expenses. *L'impôt foncier* (property tax) is payable by the property's owner. It is calculated based on the estimated local rental value of the property. Both taxes are due on January 1st.

20. A *notaire* is a government official who oversees all the documents involved in the purchase of a house. There is a limited number of *notaires* in France (about 8,000). Their training is similar to a lawyer's and they play an important role in legal transactions from loans to leases to inheritances. They often act on behalf of the seller and the buyer, who both pay notarial fees.

C. GRAMMAIRE ET USAGE

1. *LES SONS ET LES GENRES* (SOUND AND GENDER)

When learning a new language, you encounter many foreign sounds. Sometimes you think you understand them, but you can very easily be sidetracked and misled by words that do not mean what you think they mean. (This often lends itself to funny jokes. *"J'avais le mousse dans les cheveux."* I had the cabin boy in my hair.) In that respect, gender plays a key role.

a. Some words sound the same but have no common root history (i.e., they do not share the same etymology).

book	*le livre*	*la livre*	pound
cabin boy	*le mousse*	*la mousse*	moss, foam
walk, turn, trick	*le tour*	*la tour*	tower
page boy	*le page*	*la page*	page
stove	*le poêle*	*la poêle*	frying pan
vase	*le vase*	*la vase*	slime

Le mousse a grimpé en haut du mât.
  The cabin boy climbed all the way up the mast.

Le sol était couvert de mousse.
  The ground was covered with moss.

b. Some are homonyms with a common ancestor.

crêpe	*le crêpe*	*la crêpe*	pancake
critic (person)	*le critique*	*la critique*	criticism, review
handle	*le manche*	*la manche*	sleeve
report/thesis	*le mémoire*	*la mémoire*	memory
clerk's office	*le greffe*	*la greffe*	transplant, graft
physique	*le physique*	*la physique*	physics
balance	*le solde*	*la solde*	sale
veil	*le voile*	*la voile*	sail

Sa grand-mère faisait les meilleures crêpes du monde.
  Her/his grandmother used to make the best crêpes in the world.

Hier soir, elle portait une élégante robe de crêpe.
  Last night, she wore an elegant dress made of crêpe.

c. Another category, homophones (words that sound the same but are spelled differently), may create quite a bit of confusion.

| liver | *le foie* | *la fois* | time | *la foi* | faith |
| mayor | *le maire* | *la mer* | ocean | *la mère* | mother |

Les parents de Marc étaient tristes quand ils ont appris qu'il avait perdu la foi.
Marc's parents were sad when they found he had lost his faith.

Elle a donné un morceau de foie à son chat.
She gave her cat a piece of liver.

Il était une fois dans la ville de Foix, une marchande de foie qui a dit: "c'est la première et la dernière fois que je vends du foie dans la ville de Foix."
Once upon a time in the town of Foix, there was a woman who sold liver who said: "By God, this is the first and the last time that I sell liver in the town of Foix."

2. *VERBES + PRÉPOSITIONS* (VERBS + PREPOSITIONS)

In some cases, a French verb does not need a preposition (while you may need one in English).

Il est entré.
He walked in.

Ils ont abandonné leurs recherches.
They gave up on their research.

But in many instances, English verbs used with a preposition cannot be translated into French with only one verb. For example, the expression "to run across the street" consists of two ideas: crossing the street and running. To formulate the sentence in French, you must translate the preposition with a verb, then add the gerund or a complement to describe the English verb. It takes a lot of time to acquire the reflex of switching from preposition to verb and vice versa, so be sure to practice as much as possible.

Il a traversé la rue en courant.
He ran across the street.

Elles sont sorties de la pièce en sautillant (à cloche-pied).
They hopped out of the room.

Cassandre est entrée dans le salon en boitant.
Cassandre limped into the living room.

Il a ouvert la porte brusquement.
He burst open the door.

Elle l'a frôlé en passant puis a disparu.
    She brushed by him and disappeared.

Une feuille est tombée en tourbillonnant.
    A leaf came fluttering down.

Le livre s'est refermé en tombant.
    The book fell shut.

Le chat a nettoyé son bol d'un coup de langue.
    The cat licked its plate clean.

Another important aspect of understanding the difference in the use of prepositions in English and French is that some French verbs take an indirect object, while their English counterparts take a direct object, and vice versa.

répondre à quelqu'un	to answer someone
obéir à quelqu'un	to obey someone
téléphoner à quelqu'un	to call someone
demander à quelqu'un	to ask someone
regarder quelqu'un	to look at someone
écouter quelqu'un	to listen to someone
chercher quelque chose	to look for something

L'agent immobilier a téléphoné à un de ses clients.
    The real estate agent called one of his/her clients.

Nous cherchons une maison de campagne en Normandie.
    We are looking for a country home in Normandy.

3. *COMMENT DIRE* WHATEVER (HOW TO SAY "WHATEVER")

"Whatever" can be translated into French in different ways, depending on whether it's followed by a verb or a noun.

a. whatever + verb:
If whatever is followed by a verb, the neutral *quoi que* is used.

Quoi que vous fassiez, parlez-en d'abord avec votre notaire.
    Whatever you do, tell your lawyer first.

Quoi qu'en dise l'architecte, ces poutres sont très abimées.
    Whatever the architect may say, these beams are badly damaged.

b. whatever + noun:
When followed by a noun, use *quel que, quels que, quelle que* or *quelles que,* according to the gender of the noun.

Quelle que soit la hauteur des fenêtres, installez des moustiquaires.
Whatever the height of the windows, put up some screens.

Quelles que soient les raisons, ne vous disputez pas avec vos voisins.
Whatever the reasons, don't argue with your neighbors.

D. JEU DE MOTS

Keep your ears open for the word *oreille,* which appears in many French expressions.

Il nous casse les oreilles avec ses histoires.
He is boring us stiff with his stories.

Vous pouvez dormir sur vos deux oreilles.
You can sleep soundly.

Ça m'a mis la puce à l'oreille.
That made me suspicious.

Il m'a dit cela dans le creux de l'oreille.
He whispered that into my ear.

Ils commencent à m'échauffer les oreilles!
They're starting to get on my nerves!

Je crois qu'il n'a écouté que d'une oreille.
I think he only listened with one ear.

Ça entre par une oreille et ça sort par l'autre.
It goes in one ear and out the other.

Le maire a fait la sourde oreille à notre demande.
The mayor turned a deaf ear to our request.

Les oreilles ont dû lui siffler.
Her ears must have been burning.

Les murs ont des oreilles.
The walls have ears.

Le chat a dressé l'oreille.
The cat pricked up its ears.

Ce n'est pas tombé dans l'oreille d'un sourd.
It didn't fall on deaf ears.

Ventre affamé n'a pas d'oreilles.
There is no reasoning with a hungry man.

E. LE COIN DES AFFAIRES

LE PLACEMENT (INVESTMENT)

With its location at the heart of a dynamic and unified European market, its excellent infrastructure, its institutional stability, its productive work force, and its high standard of living, France is one of the most attractive locations for U.S. direct foreign investment. By the end of 1992, U.S. direct investment in France totaled $23.3 billion, making the United States the single largest foreign investor in France.

A high rate of unemployment is France's most prominent economic problem, and the government sees direct foreign investment as one of the best possible sources of new jobs. Therefore, French policy is to welcome and stimulate foreign investors by offering a wide range of financial and fiscal incentives. These incentives include subsidies for job creation, backed by European grants, French government grants, regional cash grants, and subsidies from major industrial groups. Foreign investors also receive subsidies and tax credits for job training and obtain real estate exemption and local subsidies for land and industrial plants. General fiscal incentives include tax exemptions and tax credits.

Foreign investments are responsible for approximately 25 percent of industrial output and 35 percent of exports. Still, foreign firms do not receive the same treatment as French or EU investors and occasionally face interference from government officials. These investors must receive the approval of the Ministry of Economics when buying an existing French business. To qualify as an "established" EU-controlled firm, a business must have annual sales of more than 1 billion French francs and must have been in business for at least three years. This interference is due to privatization measures designed to reduce the government deficit in France. As part of these measures, the French government reserves the right to retain a "golden share" in those firms deemed essential to the national interest, allowing the government to block the sale of assets as well as screen potential investors. Initial equity purchases by non-EU investors may not exceed 20 percent in any single firm to be privatized.

Nevertheless, France still provides promising markets for American manufacturers, many of whom have reported excellent results from their participation in French trade fairs and exhibitions. Some of the best commercial prospects include: franchising, computer hardware and software, plastics and resins, scientific laboratory instruments, telecommunication equipment, industrial chemicals, medical equipment, security and safety equipment, and the aviation/aerospace sector. U.S. investors should be aware, however, that structural rigidities, high social security costs, and relatively high wages and benefits result in high manufacturing costs as compared to the United States.

U.S. government programs assist and encourage U.S. companies to export to France by providing market data, analyzing France's viable commercial prospects, identifying agents and distributors, organizing trade missions, and providing turn-key facilities at major French trade exhibitions. Counseling facilities as well as market research services are also available at the U.S. embassy and at U.S. Department of Commerce offices throughout the United States.

EXERCICES

A. *Compléter en utilisant l'article défini ou indéfini approprié.*

1. *Gregory adore _____ poêle à bois dans la cuisine.*
2. *Il manque _____ page trois du dossier que le notaire nous a remis.*
3. *Il espère que _____ mémoire qu'il écrit sera un jour publié.*
4. *As-tu lu _____ critique du nouveau film de Tavernier ce matin dans le journal?*
5. *Elle nous a offert _____ vase en cristal.*
6. *Je voudrais savoir _____ solde de mon compte.*
7. *Il a cassé _____ manche du couteau.*
8. *Dans certains pays les femmes portent _____ voile.*
9. *Voulez-vous faire _____ tour avec moi cet après-midi?*
10. *Il a _____ foie fragile.*

B. *Compléter en utilisant une préposition si nécessaire.*

1. *Elle a répondu _____ l'annonce dans le journal.*
2. *Gregory regarde _____ l'état de la cheminée.*
3. *Elle a eu raison d'écouter _____ les conseils du notaire.*
4. *L'enfant obéi _____ ses parents.*
5. *Nous cherchons _____ une villa au bord de la mer.*

C. *Traduire.*

1. He ran out of the room.
2. Whatever you decide, I'll be happy for you.
3. Whatever her age, this child is very bright.
4. She hopped across the street.
5. They would like to live in this medieval tower.
6. He slammed the door shut.
7. Cassandre put the flowers in a vase.
8. Whatever you think, this house doesn't have enough outlets.
9. This house has very good insulation.
10. Who cleaned the gutters?

LEÇON 19

A. DIALOGUE

LES VIGNOBLES DE FRANCE.

Jeremy, auteur américain, a décidé d'écrire un roman policier[1] avec, pour toile de fond, la région de Bordeaux.[2] Son amie Isabelle l'emmène faire un tour quelque peu spécial des vignobles[3] de Sauternes.[4]

JEREMY: Isabelle, j'ai les reins[5] en compote!

ISABELLE: Qui est-ce qui t'as appris cette expression?

JEREMY: C'est Saint-Vincent![6] Il se demande bien pourquoi tu me fais faire les vendanges à la fin octobre![7]

ISABELLE: L'apprentissage sur le tas! Tu voulais, je cite, "t'imprégner du monde mystérieux de la viniculture." Mais si tu es si crevé, va donc bavarder un moment avec notre ami le vigneron.

Jeremy, tout courbaturé, ne se le fait pas dire deux fois. Il pose son sécateur et se dirige tant bien que mal vers le bout du rang où le vigneron fait une pause-café.

M. GALLET: Alors Jeremy, vos recherches, ça avance?

JEREMY: Douloureusement, très douloureusement . . . Encore une chance qu'il ne pleuve pas!

M. GALLET: De la pluie? Ne parlez pas de malheur![8] Il faut cueillir le raisin quand il est sec. À la moindre averse,[9] on est obligés d'interrompre les vendanges.

JEREMY: Combien de vendangeurs avez-vous?

M. GALLET: Une quarantaine. Ils reviennent fidèlement dans la région chaque année, souvent avec leur famille.

JEREMY: Ah, je vois . . . Au fait, monsieur Gallet, en arrivant de Paris hier, j'ai remarqué qu'il n'y avait plus une seule grappe de raisin sur les vignes dans les autres régions. Pourquoi est-ce que vous, vous vendangez si tard?

M. GALLET: Ah! la pourriture noble, mon jeune ami, la pourriture noble![10]

JEREMY: La pourriture?

M. GALLET: Je vous expliquerai ça en détail un peu plus tard. Je dois retourner au chai,[11] vous voulez m'accompagner?

JEREMY: Euh . . . Isabelle est . . .

M. GALLET: Je vous ferai goûter quelque chose qui vous donnera de l'inspiration pour votre roman. Isabelle m'a parlé d'une histoire de meurtre plutôt sombre et je vous jure qu'il n'y a pas plus sombre que ma cave. Allez, venez.

Jeremy abandonne Isabelle à son triste sort pour suivre M. Gallet dans sa cave.

JEREMY: Brrr!!! Qu'il fait frais!

M. GALLET: Le vin doit être conservé à une température constante d'environ dix degrés, dans la pénombre et la plus grande tranquillité.[12]

JEREMY: Dans quel ordre est-ce que vous procédez?

M. GALLET: Les raisins sont égrappés, pressés, puis le moût est fermenté pour faire du vin. Ensuite il est placé dans un fût de chêne ou une cuve inoxydable pendant environ deux ans avant la mise en bouteille.[13]

JEREMY: Ça représente combien de bouteilles par an?

M. GALLET: Ça dépend des années. Le rendement maximum est vingt-cinq hectolitres par hectare.[14] Si on dépasse, on risque d'avoir la Brigade des fraudes sur le dos,[15] mais ça, c'est une autre histoire.

Isabelle fait irruption dans la cave.

ISABELLE: Je savais bien où j'allais vous trouver.

M. GALLET: Ah! Isabelle! Vous arrivez à point pour la dégustation . . .

ISABELLE: Je n'allais pas vous laisser boire tous seuls.

M. GALLET: Passez-moi trois verres,[16] s'il vous plaît.

ISABELLE: Oh! Quelle couleur magnifique!

M. GALLET: Vous devez admirer cette belle robe ambrée aux reflets émeraude.[17]

ISABELLE: Ce Sauternes est si brillant et si limpide.[18] Et quel arôme!

M. GALLET: Allez-y Jeremy, il faut humer lentement pour vous imprégner du parfum.

JEREMY: Ça sent le miel.

M. GALLET: Le miel, l'acacia et un soupçon de pêche.

JEREMY: C'est un vin de dessert?

ISABELLE: C'est le vin par excellence pour accompagner le foie gras.

M. GALLET: **Mais c'est aussi irrésistible avec le roquefort.**

JEREMY: **Est-ce que je pourrais en rapporter quelques bouteilles aux États-Unis?**

ISABELLE: **Autant que je sache, c'est aussi économique de les acheter là-bas à moins que tu n'en commandes un camion-citerne!**

JEREMY: **Citerne, citerne . . . Ah mais bien sûr . . . c'est là que le meurtrier avait caché les cadavres . . .**[19]

ISABELLE: **Qu'est-ce que tu racontes?**

JEREMY: **Ça y est, j'ai la clé de mon roman . . .**

M. GALLET: **Alors, on arrose ça. À la vôtre!**

The Vineyards of France.

Jeremy, an American writer, has decided to write a detective novel with the Bordeaux region as the setting. His friend Isabelle takes him on a somewhat special tour of the Sauternes vineyards.

JEREMY: Isabelle, my back is killing me.

ISABELLE: Who taught you that expression?

JEREMY: Saint Vincent. He is really wondering why you're making me harvest at the end of October.

ISABELLE: Learning on the job! You wanted, and I quote, "to immerse yourself in the mysterious world of wine-making." But if you are so exhausted, go chat for a moment with our friend, the wine maker.

Jeremy, stiff all over, doesn't need to be told twice. He puts down his pruning shears and heads, as well as he can, toward the end of the row where the wine maker is taking a coffee break.

MR. GALLET: So, Jeremy, how is your research coming along?

JEREMY: Painfully, very painfully . . . We're lucky it's not raining.

MR. GALLET: Raining! God forbid! The grapes have to be picked dry. Any downpour and we'd have to interrupt the harvest.

JEREMY: How many grape pickers do you have?

MR. GALLET: About forty. They come back faithfully every year, often with their families.

JEREMY: Oh, I see . . . As a matter of fact, Mr. Gallet, coming from Paris yesterday, I noticed that there wasn't a single bunch of grapes on the vines in the other regions anymore. Why do you harvest so late?

MR. GALLET: Oh! The "noble rot," my young friend, the "noble rot."

JEREMY: The rot?

MR. GALLET: I'll explain that to you in detail a little later. I have to return to the cellar. Do you want to join me?

JEREMY: Eh . . . Isabelle is . . .

MR. GALLET: I'll let you taste something that will give you inspiration for your novel. Isabelle told me about a rather somber murder story, and I assure you that there is nothing more somber than my wine cellar. Let's go, come on.

Jeremy leaves Isabelle to her sad fate and follows Mr. Gallet into his cellar.

JEREMY: Brrr! It's so cold!

MR. GALLET: Wine must be kept at a constant temperature of about ten degrees, in the dark, and in complete tranquillity.

JEREMY: In what order do you proceed?

MR. GALLET: The grapes are stalked and pressed, then the must is fermented to make wine. Then it is placed into an oak barrel or a stainless-steel vat for about two years before bottling.

JEREMY: How many bottles does it add up to per year?

MR. GALLET: That depends on the year. The maximum yield is 25 hectoliters per hectare.[1] If you go over that, you risk having the fraud inspectors on your back, but that's another story.

Isabelle enters the cellar.

ISABELLE: I knew exactly where I would find you.

MR. GALLET: Oh! Isabelle! You're right on time for the tasting.

ISABELLE: I wasn't going to let you drink alone.

MR. GALLET: Hand me three glasses, please.

ISABELLE: Oh! What a magnificent color!

MR. GALLET: You must admire this beautiful amber color with its glimmers of emerald green.

ISABELLE: This Sauternes is so bright and so clear. And what an aroma!

MR. GALLET: Come on, Jeremy, you have to sniff slowly in order to soak up the fragrance.

JEREMY: It smells like honey.

MR. GALLET: Honey, acacia, and a hint of peach.

---

[1] 1 hectoliter = 2,000 liters; 1 hectare = 2.47 acres.

JEREMY: It's a dessert wine?

ISABELLE: It's the perfect wine to accompany foie gras.

MR. GALLET: But it's also irresistible with Roquefort cheese.

JEREMY: Could I take some bottles back to the States?

ISABELLE: As far as I know, it's just as cheap to buy them over there unless you are ordering a tanker.

JEREMY: A tanker, a tanker . . . Ah! yes, of course . . . that's where the murderer hid the corpses . . .

ISABELLE: What are you talking about?

JEREMY: That's it, I've got the key to my novel . . .

MR. GALLET: So, let's drink to that! Cheers!

B. EN BREF

1. You can read different kinds of novels: *un roman d'amour* (a love story), *un roman policier* (a detective novel), *un roman d'aventures* (an adventure story), *un roman de mœurs* (a social novel), *un roman-feuilleton* (a serial), *un roman historique* (a historical novel), or *un roman de série noire* (a thriller).

2. Built on the Garonne River, Bordeaux is a large harbor that accommodates about forty cruise ships every year.

3. Other French vineyards in the Bordeaux region are located in the *communes* of St-Émilion, Pomerol, Graves, and Médoc. Vineyards are found throughout France in Bourgogne, Côtes du Rhône, Côtes de Provence, Languedoc-Roussillon, Vallée de la Loire, Beaujolais, Alsace, Corse, and Champagne.

4. The Sauternes district, about 30 miles south of Bordeaux, stretches over 6,400 acres of land on the left bank of the Garonne River. The prestigious A.O.C. *(Appellation d'Origine Contrôlée)* applies only to five *communes,* Sauternes, Barsac, Bommes, Preignac, and Fargues. Thanks to its microclimate (morning mist and afternoon sun) and a gravelly soil covering a base of limestone and clay, the Sauternes region produces luscious, sweet wines that are among the most unusual in the world.

5. Be careful with the pronunciation and meaning of the following words: *rien* (nothing), *le rein* (kidney), *la reine* (queen), *le renne* (reindeer), *les rênes* (reins).

6. Saint Vincent, the winemakers' patron saint, is honored every year on January 22. In some regions, St. Vincent's Day is still the most important event on the wine-making calendar.

7. In practice, much of the Sauternes region is harvested in only two or three pickings during late September or early October. The best estates have their pickers on the vineyards up to six times over a period of three months.

8. The word *malheur* appears in many idiomatic expressions usually evoking a negative, but sometimes a positive, idea: *En cas de malheur, appelez-nous.* (Should an accident happen, call us.) *Il a eu le malheur d'avoir affaire à eux.* (He was unfortunate enough to have to deal with them.) *Cet enfant a fait le malheur de ses parents.* (This child brought sorrow upon his parents.) *Un malheur n'arrive jamais seul.* (When it rains, it pours.) *Le malheur des uns fait le bonheur des autres.* (One man's joy is another man's sorrow.) *C'était le grand malheur de sa vie.* (It was the great tragedy of his life.) *Son groupe de rock favori a fait un malheur au Zénith.* (Her favorite rock group was a big hit at the Zénith.)

9. *La pluie* (rain), *la grêle* (hail), and *le gel* (frost) can have catastrophic effects on the harvest.

10. The morning fog that rises from the Ciron Valley provides the moisture necessary for *la pourriture noble,* the "noble rot," to appear. Grapes become covered with a fungus *(botrytis Cinerea),* take on a plum color, and gradually shrivel up. As water evaporates from the grape pulp, the concentration of sugar reduces the acidity and increases the alcohol content (to approximately 20 percent). The grape is then "overripe" and can be harvested. This means not only one picking but several to ensure that all the grapes have been fully affected by the *pourriture noble.*

11. *Le chai* is the place where the wine is stored.

12. Wine must be kept away from any source of heat or vibrations. (Vineyards were a major preoccupation for engineers who designed the TGV express train route.) Bottles must lie horizontally to keep the cork wet.

13. Bottles come in different sizes: half-bottle (375 ml), bottle (750 ml), magnum (1.5 liter), double magnum (3 liters), Marie-Jeanne (3.2 liters), Jeroboam (4.5 liters), Impériale (6 liters), Salmanazar (9 liters), Balthazar (12 liters), Nabuchodonozor (15 liters).

14. The average is from 15 to 20 hectoliters per hectare. *Château d'Yquem,* one of the most famous vineyards in the world, is passionately committed to quality and boasts that it produces only one glass per vine.

15. The *Brigade de répression des fraudes* (similar to the FBI) and the *Institut national des appellations d'origine* oversee various aspects of the French wine laws, such as those controlling wine making, assuring that no beet sugar is added to boost the alcohol content of a wine.

16. A wine glass must be of clear color and fairly thin. Its tulip shape is designed to capture the wine's aromas, and its long stem allows tasters to hold the glass without warming it.

17. The adjective *émeraude* does not agree in gender and number with the noun it qualifies.

18. Wine has its own complex language. Here are a few adjectives you can use to talk about wine: *charnu* (fleshy), *gouleyant* (smooth), *soyeux* (silky), *tendre* (delicate), *charpenté* (robust), *moelleux* (mellow), *âpre* (harsh), *rond* (round), *souple* (supple), *épicé* (spicy), *corsé* (full-bodied), *cuivré* (coppery), *doré* (golden), *liquoreux* (syrupy), *savoureux* (luscious).

19. The word *cadavre* (corpse) can be used in a figurative way: *C'est un cadavre ambulant.* (He is a walking corpse.) *Ce n'était plus que le cadavre d'une belle ville.* (It was only the shadow of a great city.) *Après la soirée, j'ai ramassé une douzaine de cadavres.* (After the party, I picked up a dozen empty bottles.)

C. GRAMMAIRE ET USAGE

Tant, autant, tant de, tant . . . que, etc. are difficult to learn, as they look and often sound the same. First, let's see how *autant* is used in French.

1. L'USAGE D' "AUTANT" (USAGE OF *AUTANT*)

Autant can be used:

a. in comparisons with adverbs, nouns, and adjectives.

Ils produisent autant que nous.
They produce as much as we do.

Ils n'embauchent pas autant de vendangeurs que vous.
They do not hire as many grape pickers as you do.

Ce viticulteur est autant modeste que compétent.
This wine maker is as modest as he is skillful.

  b. alone.

Vous avez eu de la chance cette année, je ne peux pas en dire autant.
You were lucky this year; I cannot say as much for myself.

  c. in comparisons of a parallel structure.

Autant le premier jour de vendanges était amusant, autant les autres étaient pénibles pour Jéremy.
As much as the first day of harvest was fun, the other ones were painful for Jeremy.

Autant vous l'aimez, autant elle vous hait.
She hates you as much as you love her.

  d. as a conjunction.

Autant que je sache, ils visiteront la région des vignobles avec nous.
As far as I know, they'll visit the vineyard region with us.

Autant que je puisse m'en souvenir, leurs vins sont exquis.
To the best of my recollection, their wines are exquisite.

Autant que je voudrais t'aider, cela m'est absolument impossible.
However much I would like to help you, it's quite impossible.

  e. preceding an infinitive.

Autant finir le projet maintenant que de le repousser au mois prochain.
Better to finish the project now than to postpone it until next month.

Autant ne rien faire du tout.
We might as well do nothing.

  f. as an adverb of intensity.

Son départ est d'autant plus regrettable qu'il était estimé de tous.
His departure is all the more regrettable because he was liked by everyone.

  And let's not forget:

Autant en emporte le vent.
Gone with the wind.

2. *L'USAGE DE "TANT"* (USAGE OF *TANT*)

Tant can be used:

a. as an adverb of intensity.

Jeremy a tant travaillé qu'il est tout courbaturé.
   Jeremy worked so much that he is sore all over.

Inutile de tant vous presser.
   No use rushing so much.

b. as a quantity adverb: *tant de* + noun.

Nous avons goûté tant de vins que nous étions un peu gris.
   We tasted so many wines that we were a little tipsy.

M. Gallet nous a raconté tant d'histoires drôles que nous ne nous sommes pas ennuyés.
   Mr. Gallet told us so many funny stories that we didn't get bored.

c. with an adjective or past participle.

Ils ont interrompu les vendanges tant le ciel était menaçant.
   They interrupted the harvest because the sky looked so threatening.

Et le moment tant attendu finalement arriva.
   The long-awaited moment finally arrived.

d. as a conjunction.
When *tant que* precedes or follows a main clause in the future tense, the *tant que* clause is also in the future tense. Otherwise it follows the same tense pattern as in English.

Tant qu'ils produiront du vin mousseux, nous leur en achèterons.
   As long as they make sparkling wine, we'll buy from them.

Il fera les vendanges tant qu'il n'aura pas mal aux reins.
   He'll pick grapes as long as he doesn't have any back pain.

Nous restons à la plage tant qu'il fait beau.
   We stay on the beach as long as the weather is nice.

e. in idiomatic expressions.

S'il est tant soit peu honnête, il ne vous vendra pas de piquette.
   If he is at all honest, he won't sell you vinegary wine.

S'il vient, tant mieux; sinon, tant pis!
   If he comes, great; if not, too bad!

Tant qu'à faire, je vais déboucher un bon Bourgogne.
   While we're at it, I'm going to open a good bottle of Burgundy.

Nous avons trouvé notre chemin tant bien que mal.
   We found our way somehow or other.

Vous m'en direz tant!
   Now I understand!

En tant que connaisseur, je vous recommande ce vin.
   As a connoisseur, I recommend this wine.

3. *INTERJECTIONS* (INTERJECTIONS)

French is rich in colorful exclamations that alone express what a hundred words cannot. Some interjections are designed to attract a person's attention, or to communicate a message or greeting directly to a specific individual.

Adieu!	Farewell!	*Hep!*	Hey!
Allô!	Hello!	*Hourra!*	Hurrah!
À quoi bon?	What's the point?	*Chut!*	Shh!
Au secours!	Help!	*Gare!*	Watch out!
Au feu!	Fire!	*Motus!*	Not a word!
Bravo!	Bravo!	*Pouce!*	Truce!
Bis!	Encore!	*Psitt!*	Psst!
Chiche!	I dare you! I bet you're wrong!		

Qui sait si on se reverra? Adieu!
   Who knows if we'll see each other again? Farewell!

Tu n'es pas capable de le faire. —Chiche!
   You're not capable of doing it. —I bet you I am!

Psitt! Viens par ici!
   Psst! Come this way.

Other interjections clearly express the speaker's opinion about or reaction to something. The reaction may be one of:

a. pain.

Aïe!	Ouch!
Ouille!	Ouch!
Hélas!	Alas!

b. surprise.

Hein!	What?
Eh bien!	Well!
Tiens, tiens!	Well, well!
Ça par exemple!	Well, I'll be . . . !
Zut!	Darn!

c. elation.

Chic!	Terrific!
Miam-miam!	Yum-yum!
Hourra!	Hurray!

d. indifference.

Bof!	No big deal.
Bah!	Pooh!

e. disgust.

Pouah!	Ugh!
Peuh!	Bah! Pooh!

f. relief.

Ouf!	Whew!

Some interjections are simply onomatopoeic noise expressions:

Boum!	Bang!	*Pan! Pan!*	Bang! Bang!
Couic!	Squeak!	*Toc toc toc!*	Knock! Knock!
Crac!	Crack!	*Tic-tac!*	Tick-tock!
Paf!	Bam!		

Aïe! Tu me fais mal!
    Ouch! You're hurting me!

Toc toc toc! Il y a quelqu'un?
    Knock! Knock! Anybody home?

Ouf! On a enfin terminé!
    What a relief! We're finally done!

D. JEU DE MOTS

France, a country of many wines, has quite a few expressions relating to wine and drinking.

La vérité est dans le vin.
  In vino veritas.

Ce sont les tonneaux vides qui font le plus de bruit.
  Empty barrels make the most noise.

Quand le vin est tiré, il faut le boire.
  You've made your bed, now lie in it.

Qui a bu boira.
  Once a drunk, always a drunk.

Le bon vin fait parler latin.
  Good wine unties the tongue.

Il a le vin triste/gai.
  He's a sad/happy drunk.

Il a dû mettre de l'eau dans son vin.
  He had to moderate his pretensions.

Il est en train de cuver son vin.
  He's sleeping it off.

Mieux vaut dire d'un verre qu'il est à moitié plein qu'à moitié vide.
  It's better to say the glass is half full than half empty.

Il est toujours entre deux vins.
  He is always drunk.

Il tient bien le vin.
  He holds his wine well.

E. LE COIN DU VIN

Charles-François Panard (1694–1765) a enfermé dans une bouteille ventrue ces vers admiratifs dédiés au vin.

Que mon
F l a c o n
Me semble bon;
Sans lui
L'ennui
Me nuit;
Me suit;
Je sens
Mes sens
Mourants
P e s a n t s
Quand je le tiens
Dieu que je suis bien!
Que son aspect est agréable!
Que je fais cas de ces divers présents!
C'est de son sein fécond et de ses heureux flancs
Que coule ce nectar si doux, si délectable,
Qui rend dans les esprits tous les cœurs satisfaits,
Cher objet de mes vœux, tu fais toute ma gloire,
Tant que mon cœur vivra de tes charmants bienfaits
Il saura conserver la fidèle mémoire,
Ma muse à te louer se consacre à jamais,
Tantôt dans un caveau et tantôt sous ma treille
Répétera cent fois cette aimable chanson;
Règne sans fin ma charmante bouteille
Règne sans fin, mon cher flacon.

F. LE COIN DES AFFAIRES

L'AGRICULTURE (AGRICULTURE)

Agriculture has played a major role in the French economy since World War II, when France, along with its European neighbors, suffered great food shortages and set out to produce as much food as possible to feed the nation. By the 1970s, the country had become self-sufficient and began exporting to other European nations. Thanks to ever-improving technology, the dramatic increase in productivity continued throughout the 1980s, making France a true agricultural giant, second only to the United States in agricultural exports. This mass production eventually resulted in a drop in prices, and EU price regulations led to harsh competition for French farmers. Small farmers were hardest hit and became heavily indebted despite government subsidies. Many were forced to leave their farms in what has come to be known as *l'exode rural* (the rural exodus). As a result, the agricultural labor force dropped sharply, from 20 percent of the working population in 1962 to 6 percent in 1994.

The farmers who remain, angry with the government's handling of the agriculture crisis and determined to hold on to their livelihood, organized demonstrations with shock tactics such as bringing pigs to the *Préfecture*, pouring thousands of liters of wine or milk on the highways, and dumping tons of potatoes on the doorsteps of government offices.

While the agricultural labor force has sharply declined, French agricultural production has tripled. Some of the most successful and productive farms in the world are located in the northern region of the country, where mainly cereal crops are cultivated: oats *(l'avoine)*, corn *(le maïs)*, barley *(l'orge)*, and wheat *(le blé)*. The sugar-beet industry is also important in the Picardy region, as beets are not only one of the country's top commodities, but are also used to feed the nation's cattle. Normandy and Brittany are renowned for apples, which are used for cider and Calvados. Brittany also produces much of the country's potatoes, cauliflower, and artichokes. Other areas of the country, such as the Loire Valley, Provence, and Languedoc-Roussillon, provide France with its fruits and vegetables.

Livestock, which constitutes more than one third of total farm produce, has also experienced significant changes with the advent of modern technology. Genetic advances, especially artificial insemination, have greatly improved the quality of cattle. The main regions for raising livestock in France are: Normandy and Charolais for beef; the Pyrénées, the Massif Central, Provence, Normandy, and Corsica for sheep; and Brittany for pigs. Britain is France's main competitor for lamb, and Denmark and Holland for pork.

Dairy products represent another large portion of the agricultural market. France produces more than 350 kinds of cheese from cow's, goat's, and sheep's milk, with Brie (from east of Paris), Camembert (from Normandy), and Roquefort (from the Massif Central) among the most famous. Normandy and the Charentes region are known for their rich, high-quality butter. France ranks second in the world, after the United States, in cheese production.

France's primary agricultural export is wine, with sugar and dairy products following. France's agricultural products are among the best in the world. The *Appellation d'Origine Contrôlée (AOC)*, which has been in existence since 1935 and attests to a product's authenticity and high quality, now plays an important role in revitalizing the agricultural economy. The emphasis on quality rather than quantity, embodied in products such as Beaufort cheese, is designed to cater to the elite gourmet market and has enabled small farmers to earn a living, instead of relying on subsidies. To qualify for the *AOC,* products must have a strong regional identity in addition to being of the highest quality.

Another new weapon in French farmers' fight for survival is rural tourism. With its age-old reputation as a great agricultural nation, France is beginning to capitalize on the romantic and nostalgic image of its countryside and attract more and more tourists, weary of the chaos of modern living.

The United States is the largest non-EU exporter of food and agricultural products to France. These exports include raw cotton, wood, wool, and hides. Other U.S. agricultural exports to France include fresh fruits (particularly tropical and exotic fruits), fruit juices, frozen foods, snack foods and products with a distinctive flavor (such as Tex-Mex), nuts, breakfast cereals, and pet foods. U.S. exporters will find it easier to export to France if their products come from hormone-free animals slaughtered at EU-approved facilities in the United States. Very high import duties make it almost impossible to export dairy products, especially cheeses, to France.

EXERCICES

A. *Mettre les verbes entre parenthèses au temps qui convient.*

1. *Tant qu'il ne pas (avoir) trop de courbatures, il continuera à vendanger.*
2. *Tant qu'il (pleuvoir), les vendangeurs restent à la maison.*
3. *Cet homme reviendra chaque année tant que le vigneron le (embaucher).*
4. *Tant qu'il y (avoir) des dégustations, les touristes visiteront cette cave.*
5. *Tant que vous y (être), achetez une caisse de Bourgogne.*
6. *Jeremy restera en France tant qu'il (faire) des recherches pour son roman.*
7. *Isabelle aidera Jeremy tant qu'elle (avoir) le temps.*
8. *Tant qu'il (faire) beau, le vigneron ne s'inquiète pas pour sa récolte.*
9. *Le vigneron sera heureux tant que son rendement (être) suffisant.*
10. *Tant que le vin (sentir) le miel et l'acacia, c'est un vin de dessert.*

B. *Traduire.*

1. This champagne is good, but I can't say the same for this sparkling wine.
2. There are as many vineyards here as on the other side of the hill.
3. I had never seen him drink as much.
4. As much as he was charming with you, he was unpleasant with me.
5. As far as I know, Jeremy's novel is a thriller.
6. This wine maker produces as much as his neighbor.
7. Mr. Gallet told us so many funny stories that we forgot about the time.
8. The grape pickers had worked so much that they were exhausted.
9. However much I would like to visit your cellar, I'm afraid of the dark.
10. We might as well open another bottle.

C. *Traduire les mots entre parenthèses.*

1. *Il va se plaindre au patron?* (What's the point?)
2. (Terrific!) *On va fêter l'anniversaire d'Isabelle ce soir!*
3. (Ouch!) *Je me suis coupé le doigt avec mon sécateur.*
4. (Fire! Fire!) *la maison brûle!*
5. (Knock, knock), *y a quelqu'un?*
6. (Shh!) *taisez-vous!*
7. (Not a word!) *tu me le promets?*
8. (Hurray!) *La récolte est terminée.*
9. *T'es pas capable d'embrasser Jeremy?* (Bet you I will!)
10. *M. Gallet, nous allons vous quitter.* (Farewell!)

LEÇON 20

A. DIALOGUE

A LA MARTINIQUE.

Céline, metteur en scène, vient d'achever le tournage d'un film en Martinique. [1]
Elle invite Charles, le cadreur, Hughes, le directeur de la photographie, et
Justine, la costumière pour un dîner d'adieu.

CÉLINE: Je tiens à vous remercier. Vous avez tous été vraiment formidables! Le dynamisme de l'équipe toute entière, sa capacité d'écoute et son imagination débordante m'ont permis de réaliser un excellent travail.

HUGHES: Apportez les couronnes de laurier . . .

CÉLINE: Non, je ne blague pas . . . Votre équipe a fait preuve d'une maturité d'esprit qui est rare ces temps-ci.

HUGHES: Je sens qu'on va avoir une prime . . .[2]

CÉLINE: Hughes! . . . Ce que je veux dire, c'est que vous avez tous parfaitement collaboré avec l'équipe locale, ce qui m'a facilité la tâche,[3] et je vous en suis fort reconnaissante.

HUGHES: Ça, c'est surtout grâce à[4] Charles.

CÉLINE: C'est vrai. Charles, vous avez fait un travail hors pair et je ne sais[5] comment vous remercier de tous vos efforts.

CHARLES: C'était un véritable plaisir de vous accueillir à Saint-Pierre[6] et de participer à votre projet.

CÉLINE: Vraiment, je vous tire mon chapeau parce que ce n'est pas facile de se joindre aux membres d'un groupe si soudé.[7]

JUSTINE: Ça, c'est parce que Charles a très bon caractère . . . Il a toujours l'air d'excellente humeur et il a un bon sens de l'humour.

HUGHES: Ce qui n'est pas vrai pour tout le monde . . .

JUSTINE: Qu'est-ce que tu entends par là?

CÉLINE: C'est bien la peine de vous faire des compliments . . . Je retire ce que j'ai dit sur la maturité si vous commencez à vous chamailler.

CHARLES: Hughes ne peut pas s'empêcher de taquiner Justine . . .

CÉLINE: À quel sujet?

CHARLES: Le costume de Joséphine[8] a un peu souffert pendant la scène tournée sur la Montagne Pelée . . .

287

CÉLINE: Hughes, vous êtes insupportable! . . . Justine, je dois vous féliciter car malgré les conditions parfois difficiles, vous avez réalisé l'impossible.

JUSTINE: Merci, Céline. C'était une expérience enrichissante. Comme d'habitude, tout en nous guidant, vous nous laissez énormément de liberté. De plus, cette île est un véritable paradis . . .

CHARLES: Céline, maintenant que tout est bouclé, puis-je me permettre de vous offrir cette bouteille de rhum vieux[9] et de vous poser[10] une question?

CÉLINE: Allez-y, je vous en prie . . .

CHARLES: Pourquoi avez-vous choisi la Martinique, plutôt qu'une autre île des Antilles?[11] Vous auriez pu tourner la scène avec Joséphine sur n'importe quelle autre île?

SERVEUR: Pardon messieurs-dames, votre table là-bas, près des cocotiers, sera prête dans quelques minutes.

CÉLINE: Comme vous savez, j'avais besoin du Parc floral[12] et aussi du Musée des poupées[13] qui est unique en son genre.

CHARLES: J'en suis ravi! C'est parfait pour moi et pour l'économie de la Martinique![14]

CÉLINE: Je dois vous avouer qu'il y a une autre raison. J'ai découvert l'île il y a une vingtaine d'années et c'était le coup de foudre! C'est pareil à un tableau de Gauguin[15]—un festival éternel de couleurs et de parfums.

HUGHES: En parlant de festival, j'ai décidé de revenir pour le carnaval.[16]

CÉLINE: Quelle bonne idée! Et vous Justine?

JUSTINE: Euh . . .

CHARLES: Comme j'ai quelques jours de libre, je vais en profiter pour emmener Justine au Rocher du Diamant.[17] On ira faire de la plongée sous-marine[18] ou pêcher le barracuda.

Le serveur vient les chercher pour les faire asseoir à l'ombre des cocotiers.

CÉLINE (*murmure à Hughes*): Alors, mon vieux, tu t'es encore fait avoir! Une autre partie de pêche qui t'est passée sous le nez.[19]

HUGHES (*à Céline*): Ben oui, qu'est-ce que tu veux que je te dises. . . . Y a ceux qui pêchent le barracuda et y a les autres qui rentrent bredouilles!

————

In Martinique.

Céline, a film director, has just finished shooting a film in Martinique. She invites Charles, the cameraman, Hughes, the director of photography, and Justine, the costume designer, to a farewell dinner.

CÉLINE: I must thank you, you've all been really great! The energy of the whole team, your ability to listen, and your bubbling imagination have enabled me to do a wonderful job.

HUGHES: Bring on the laurels!

CÉLINE: No, I'm not kidding . . . Your team showed a maturity of spirit that is rare these days.

HUGHES: I have the feeling that we're going to get a bonus . . .

CÉLINE: Hughes! . . . What I want to say is that you all cooperated perfectly with the local team, which made my life easy, and I'm really grateful.

HUGHES: That is, above all, thanks to Charles.

CÉLINE: That's true. Charles, your work has been outstanding, and I don't know how to thank you for all your efforts.

CHARLES: It was a real pleasure to welcome you to Saint-Pierre and to be part of your project.

CÉLINE: Really, I take my hat off to you because it's not so easy to join a group that's so tight.

JUSTINE: That's because Charles is very good-natured . . . He's always in an excellent mood, and he has a great sense of humor.

HUGHES: Which can't be said for everyone . . .

JUSTINE: What do you mean by that?

CÉLINE: Why bother giving you compliments? I'll take back what I said about maturity if you start squabbling.

CHARLES: Hughes can't keep from teasing Justine . . .

CÉLINE: About what?

CHARLES: Josephine's costume suffered a little during the scene on *Mont Pelée*.

CÉLINE: Hughes, you are impossible! . . . Justine, I must congratulate you because, in spite of the sometimes difficult conditions, you managed very well.

JUSTINE: Thank you, Céline. It's really been an enriching experience. As usual, while giving us guidance, you also gave us a great deal of freedom. What's more, this island is a real paradise . . .

CHARLES: Céline, now that everything is wrapped up, I'd like to give you this bottle of old rum and ask you a question.

CÉLINE: Please do.

CHARLES: Why did you choose Martinique over another island in the Caribbean? Couldn't you have shot the scene with Josephine on any other island?

WAITER: Excuse me, ladies and gentlemen, your table will be ready in a few minutes.

CÉLINE: As you know, I needed the Floral Park as well as the Doll Museum, which is unique.

CHARLES: I'm delighted! It's perfect for me and for the economy of Martinique!

CÉLINE: I have to admit that there's another reason . . . I discovered the island about twenty years ago, and it was love at first sight! It's just like a Gauguin painting—an eternal celebration of color and fragrance.

HUGHES: Talking about celebrations, I've decided to come back for the carnival.

CÉLINE: What a good idea! And you Justine?

JUSTINE: Uh . . .

CHARLES: As I have a few days off, I'm going to take advantage of them to take Justine to the Diamond Rock. We'll go scuba diving or barracuda fishing.

The waiter comes over to seat them under the shade of the coconut trees.

CÉLINE (whispers to Hughes): Well, my friend, you blew it again . . . You let the boat sail without you!

HUGHES (to Céline): Well, yes, what can I say . . . There are those who fish for barracuda, and then there are those who go home alone.

B. EN BREF

1. The Caribbean island of Martinique, whose capital is Fort-de-France, is characterized by its lush vegetation, extensive tropical rain forest, and fertile soil covered by banana and pineapple plantations and fields of sugar cane. The island was originally inhabited by the Arawaks, who were exterminated by the Carib Indians. French settlers arrived in the seventeenth century, wiped out the Caribs, and brought African slaves to cultivate sugar cane. The success of Martinique's sugar cane industry attracted the British, who fought the French for control of the island until 1815, when it was finally restored to France. Today, Martinique is considered a French *Région* (much like a U.S. state) and is governed by a prefect, appointed by the French minister of the interior. Martinique enjoys one of the highest standards of living among the Caribbean islands. Martinicans speak Créole, an altered form of old French spoken during the time of Louis XIII. Even if you speak fluent French you may sometimes have trouble understanding this very colorful language.

2. The word *prime* can take on several meanings. *L'entreprise leur a promis une prime de rendement.* (The company promised them a productivity bonus.) *Le gouvernement nous a proposé une prime à l'exportation.* (The government offered us an export premium.) *Ils ont donné un porte-clés en prime.* (They gave away a key chain as a free gift.)

3. Be aware of the homonyms *tâche* and *tache: Le patron nous a assigné une tâche difficile.* (The boss gave us a hard job to do.) *Elle a fait une tache sur sa veste.* (She stained her jacket.)

4. Be sure to differentiate between *grâce à,* which is followed by a noun, and *parce que,* which is followed by a verb. *Nous avons passé un séjour merveilleux grâce à vous.* (We had a wonderful stay thanks to you.) *Vous devez restez quelques jours de plus parce que vous n'avez pas tout vu.* (You must stay a few more days because you haven't seen everything.)

5. *Pas* is optional with the verbs *oser, cesser, pouvoir,* and *savoir. Elle ne cesse de parler.* (She does not stop talking.) *Je n'ose vous le promettre.* (I dare not promise you.)

6. Once called the "Paris of the West Indies," Saint-Pierre was totally destroyed and its 30,000 inhabitants calcified when *Mont Pelée* erupted in 1902. A drunkard named Siparis, who was thrown into a jail cell for the night, was the sole survivor. The *Musée vulcanologique* holds objects excavated from the eruption, including household items, charred by the extreme heat, and distorted clocks that all stopped at the same time.

7. *Souder* literally means "to solder," or to join firmly, but its figurative usage comes in handy as well. *Ils prévoient de souder ces deux organismes.* (They are planning to fuse these two *companies of organizations*.) *Il devra souder ces deux pièces d'acier.* (He'll have to solder these two steel pieces.) *La coque est complètement soudée.* (The hull is welded throughout.) *Ses os ne se souderont pas très vite.* (His bones won't knit very fast.)

8. Joséphine, born Marie-Josèphe Tascher de la Pagerie, was married (by arrangement) to Alexandre de Beauharnais in 1779, at the age of sixteen. She became Napoléon's first wife in 1796 but was repudiated in 1809 because of their childless marriage (although she had two children from her first marriage). She died near Paris in 1814. A museum dedicated to Joséphine shows mementos belonging to the empress, including passionate letters from Napoléon.

9. Remember that *vieux* usually means "old" not "former," when placed before the noun. This case is an exception.

10. Be sure not to confuse *poser* (used when asking a question) and *demander* (used in all other cases). *Je pose une question.* (I'm asking a question.) *Il m'a demandé un service.* (He asked me a favor.)

11. The French Antilles encompass Martinique, Guadeloupe, St-Barthélemy, and St-Martin.

12. *Le Parc floral et culturel* features a wide variety of exotic flowers and an aquarium. The name Martinique is derived from the Arawak word "Madinia," which means *l'île des fleurs* (island of flowers).

13. *Le Musée des poupées végétales* features a collection of exotic doll sculptures made from plants and tree branches.

14. Martinique's economy is agricultural; it exports sugar, rum, bananas, and pineapples. However, the sugar industry is in a state of crisis, as its sugar cane is unable to compete with the cheaper beet sugar. There is some light industry but most manufactured goods and many staples are imported. Tourism plays an ever-increasing role in the economy. Unemployment remains at above 30 percent.

15. *Le Musée Gauguin* has on display letters, documents, sketches, and reproductions of some of the artist's paintings, produced while he was on the island.

16. The festivals are one of Martinique's main attractions. For *Carnaval,* which takes place in February, the whole island spends five days dancing and singing in the streets. All businesses come to a halt, and the streets spill over with parties and parades, culminating in the election of the *Reine du Carnaval* (Carnival Queen).

17. *Le Diamant* is a friendly village with an idyllic beach stretching for a couple of miles and dominated by the famous *Rocher du Diamant.*

18. Some water sports you can enjoy in Martinique include: *la voile* (sailing), *la planche à voile* (windsurfing), *la plongée sous-marine* (diving), and *le ski nautique* (water skiing).

19. Notice the switch from *vous* to *tu* when the conversation becomes private. See *Le coin des affaires* in *Leçon* 7 for more on business etiquette.

C. GRAMMAIRE ET USAGE

1. *LES FAUX-AMIS* (FALSE COGNATES)

Faux-amis are one of the major stumbling blocks in acquiring a foreign language. Following are some that you are most likely to encounter.

Abus is commonly used to mean "excess, overindulgence" and usually not "abuse."

L'abus des sucreries nuit à la santé.
Overindulgence in sweets is harmful to one's health.

Les sévices exercés sur les enfants sont en hausse.
Child abuse is increasing.

Disposer should not be confused with "to dispose of," which is *jeter* or *se débarrasser de.*

Vous disposerez d'une voiture.
You'll have a car at your disposal.

Elle a disposé les assiettes sur la table.
She arranged the plates on the table.

Vous pouvez disposer.
You may leave now.

Une injure is an insult, not an injury *(une blessure).*

Il leur a adressé des injures.
He insulted them.

Actuel and *actuellement* mean "current" and "currently" and should not be confused with their *faux-amis* "actual" *(vrai, réel)* and "actually" *(vraiment, à vrai dire).*

La programmation actuelle risque de changer en automne.
The current programming may change in the fall.

Ils sont actuellement à Paris.
They are presently in Paris.

Avertissement does not mean "advertisement" (which is *une publicité* or *une réclame);* rather it is a warning or a small preface in a book.

Le patron lui a donné un avertissement.
The boss gave her a warning.

Je n'aime pas leur nouvelle publicité/réclame pour Orangina.
I don't like their new advertisment for Orangina.

Une recette is a recipe, not a receipt *(un reçu).*

C'est une recette facile à faire.
It's a very easy recipe to make.

Il a oublié de me donner un reçu.
He forgot to give me a receipt.

Fournitures does not refer to furniture *(les meubles),* but to supplies.

Il faut commander des fournitures de bureau.
We must order some office supplies.

Ces meubles sont en mauvais état.
This furniture is in bad condition.

Original is used in the sense of "new, innovative" while *originel* refers to origins.

Une œuvre originale.
An original work.

Le péché originel.
Original sin.

Do not confuse *les préservatifs* (condoms) with *les conserves* (preserves).

Les préservatifs servent à lutter contre le sida.
  Condoms are used in the fight against AIDS.

  Le bail is not "bail" but a rental agreement.

Ils ont un bail de dix ans.
  They have a ten-year lease.

Il a été mis en liberté sous caution.
  He was freed on bail.

  Répondre is not always translated as "to respond," and vice versa.

Ça ne répond pas à mes espérances.
  It falls short of my expectations.

Comment a-t-il réagi?
  How did he respond?

  Humeur (mood) should not be confused with *humour* (sense of humor).
  Keep in mind, too, that these two words are pronounced differently.

Il est de bonne/mauvaise humeur.
  He is in a good/bad mood.

Elle a beaucoup d'humour.
  She has a great sense of humor.

  Formel is generally used to mean "strict," not "formal."

Le patron a donné l'ordre formel de ne pas partir avant son retour.
  The boss gave strict orders not to leave before his return.

Je suis invitée à un dîner officiel au consulat.
  I'm invited to a formal dinner at the consulate.

Elle est très guindée/à cheval sur les convenances.
  She is very formal.

2. *LES NOMS ET LEUR NOMBRE* (NOUNS AND THEIR NUMBER)

a. Some nouns are used in the plural only, either because of their Latin origin or their collective sense. These include: *les archives* (archives), *les environs* (surroundings), *les frais* (expenses), *les mœurs* (mores), *les vivres* (provisions), *les fiançailles* (engagement), *les funérailles* (funeral), *les honoraires* (fees), *les arrhes* (deposit), *les préparatifs* (preparation), *les pincettes* (tongs).

Ils viennent d'annoncer leurs fiançailles.
They just announced their engagement.

Les funérailles auront lieu à la cathédrale de Sainte-Catherine.
The funeral will take place at Saint Catherine's Cathedral.

Some mountain ranges and archipelagoes are also always plural: *Les Pyrénées* (Pyrenees), *les Alpes* (Alps), *les Vosges* (Vosges), *les Cévennes* (Cevennes), *les Antilles* (Caribbean), *les Baléares* (Baleares).

Nous avons fait de la randonnée dans les Alpes cet été.
We went hiking in the Alps this summer.

b. Some nouns have different meanings when singular and when plural. Compare: *le ciseau* (chisel) and *les ciseaux* (scissors); *la vacance* (vacancy) and *les vacances* (vacation); *la lunette* (telescope lens) and *les lunettes* (eyeglasses); *la menotte* (hand) and *les menottes* (handcuffs); and *la nouille* (idiot) and *les nouilles* (noodles).

Il y a une vacance dans ce bâtiment.
There's a vacancy in this building.

c. When referring to personal attributes (parts of the body, clothing, demeanor), French uses the singular, while English uses the plural form.

Ses collègues sont entrés dans la salle de bal avec leur mari.
Her colleagues walked into the ballroom with their husbands.

If *mari* were plural, it would mean that each wife had more than one husband.

Les invités ont ôté leur imperméable et leur chapeau avant de s'asseoir.
The guests took off their raincoats and hats before sitting down.

Le chirurgien leur a sauvé la vie.
The surgeon saved their lives.

3. *L'ARGOT* (SLANG)

An examination of the French language would not be complete without some notion of slang. While much of slang relies on idiomatic expressions that must simply be memorized or acquired over time, there are a few rules that will help you speak more like a native.

a. Word abbreviations.
One way of speaking a more colloquial French is by using abbreviations.

le propriétaire	*proprio*	owner
l'apéritif	*apéro*	a drink before dinner
le dictionnaire	*dico*	dictionary
l'automobile	*auto*	car
le laboratoire	*labo*	laboratory
le cinéma	*ciné*	cinema
la photographie	*photo*	photography
le microphone	*micro*	microphone
la faculté	*fac*	college
la diapositive	*diapo*	slide
la publicité	*pub*	advertising
la manifestation	*manif*	demonstration
sympathique	*sympa*	friendly
sensationnel	*sensas*	terrific

Toute l'équipe a pris l'apéro sur la terrasse.
The whole crew had a drink before dinner on the balcony.

La nouvelle pub sur la Martinique est sensas.
The new ad on Martinique is terrific.

b. Nicknames.
Family members are often given "creative" titles, such as *mes vieux* for *mes parents, ma vieille* for *ma mère, mon vieux* for *mon père, ma frangine* for *ma sœur, mon frangin* for *mon frère, ma belle-frangine* for *ma belle-sœur,* and *mon beauf* for *mon beau-frère.*

Sa frangine est très sympa.
His/her sister is very nice.

Mes vieux sont à la Martinique—venez tous bouffer à la maison samedi soir?
My folks are in Martinique—why don't you all come over for dinner Saturday night?

D. JEU DE MOTS

Table appears in many French idiomatic expressions.

On l'a acheté avec un dessous-de-table.
They bought him with a bribe.

Ils ont fait table rase du passé.
They made a clean sweep of the past.

Pierre a mis la table et sa sœur l'a débarrassée.
Pierre set the table, and his sister cleared it.

Son mari arrive à la maison et met les pieds sous la table.
Her husband arrives home and expects to be served his dinner.

Ils avaient tellement bu qu'ils ont roulé sous la table.
They drank themselves under the table.

Mettez-vous à table, s'il vous plaît.
Sit down at the table, please.

Il s'est finalement mis à table.
He finally confessed.

Leurs concurrents ont mis leurs cartes sur la table.
The competition put their cards on the table.

Ils aiment beaucoup les plaisirs de la table.
They really enjoy eating.

Elle a mis son collier sur la table de nuit.
She put her necklace on her nightstand.

E. LE COIN DES AFFAIRES

QUEL CADEAU OFFRIR?
(WHICH GIFT TO GIVE?)

The occasions for gift-giving in France are very similar to those in the United States. It is appropriate to give gifts to new business partners in order to establish good rapport, to thank someone for their help or reward them for a job well done, and to wish them a happy New Year. The nature of the gifts, however, may differ. Following are some general guidelines to keep in mind as you consider a possible purchase.

First of all, gifts should never be too costly, as they may be considered a bribe. Do not be surprised or offended if an expensive gift is returned accompanied by a note saying: *Je vous remercie d'avoir pensé à moi, cependant, je ne suis pas à même d'accepter un cadeau d'une telle valeur.* (Thank you for thinking of me; however, I am not in a position to accept such a valuable gift.)

A gift from the United States or one symbolic of the two countries (such as a reproduction of a painting or a print of Lafayette during the war, or a compact disc set of New Orleans jazz) will always be more appreciated than one bought in France. American gadgets and electronic devices are especially popular, but be sure to include a transformer, if it is required. If your associate knows English well, a book on American business or politics would also be appropriate.

If you will be working with a team of French colleagues, T-shirts, sweatshirts, and baseball caps with logos of American sports teams or universities are always well received. For higher-level executives, a more personalized gift should be given, if possible. You may want to consult a secretary or assistant about their superior's special interests or hobbies. Gifts such as a subscription to a specialized magazine, a rare stamp, a book on cars or planes, or a Steuben crystal miniature are sure to be cherished. If a secretary has been especially helpful in the course of your dealings with his or her supervisor, a gift certificate to a nearby department store or a box of chocolates would be a nice gesture of appreciation.

Avoid giving sharp objects, such as scissors or knives (with the exception of letter openers), as they symbolize cutting the bonds of friendship. If you do opt to bring a special type of knife (such as an antique), be sure to ask for a symbolic "payment" (usually a few centimes) to counteract the superstitions associated with giving sharp objects.

Traditional and always popular gifts include: pen and pencil sets (with refills), fine stationery, calendars, calculators, key chains, ashtrays, picture frames, electronic address books, bookends, and diaries. If your gift features your company's logo, it should not be too prominent, as the gift will then be considered more of an advertisement than a gift. If you are invited to a business associate's home, it is customary to take a bottle of liqueur, or brandied fruit, as well as a nice bouquet of flowers. Flowers are always given in odd numbers and should be delivered the morning of or the morning after the dinner party. Chrysanthemums and carnations should be avoided, as the former are associated with death, and the latter are said to have an "evil eye." An appropriate phrase for the card accompanying your bouquet would be: *Avec tous mes/nos remerciements.* (With all my/our thanks.) Do not take wine, unless it's an exceptionally good vintage, as wine is a French staple and will not be considered a special gift.

If you are one of few guests at a partner's home (i.e., were invited to dinner as opposed to a cocktail party), you may want to consider taking gifts for the children. These include American memorabilia (T-shirts, caps), toys that are the current fad in the States, or items of popular culture (TV shows, rock groups) for teenagers. Music cassettes or compact discs are a good idea, as well, but U.S. videocassettes will not work in France, as they use a different system. Presents are strongly suggested for newborns, along with token gifts (such as chocolates) for any other siblings. Remember never to give gifts before the birth of a child, as it is considered to bring bad luck. As a result, baby showers are not given in France, nor are bridal showers.

The French reaction to receiving a gift is more understated than that of most Americans. In other words, don't expect someone to react too emotionally. In fact, they may not even open the gift immediately. After offering a gift with: *Je vous ai apporté ce petit souvenir des États-Unis* (I brought you this small souvenir from the United States) or *Permettez-moi de vous offrir ce petit cadeau* (Please accept this small gift. —more formal), you might hear a slightly embarrassed: *Merci, c'est très gentil de votre part* (Thank you; that's very nice of you) or *Vous n'auriez pas dû* (You shouldn't have) in response.

EXERCICES

A. *Remplacer les mots soulignés par une expression d'argot.*

1. *J'ai acheté un nouveau <u>dictionnaire</u>.*
2. *À quelle heure commence la <u>manifestation</u>?*
3. *On m'a dit que Jacques était très <u>sympathique</u>.*
4. *Elle a rendez-vous avec Pierre à midi à la <u>faculté</u>.*
5. *Viens prendre l'<u>apéritif</u> chez nous ce soir.*
6. *Est-ce qu'elle t'a montré ses <u>diapositives</u>?*
7. *Le chanteur a laissé tomber le <u>microphone</u>.*
8. *Comment s'appelle ton <u>propriétaire</u>.*
9. *J'ai rencontré son <u>frère</u> chez Marc.*
10. *As-tu vu la dernière <u>publicité</u> de L'Oréal?*

B. *Traduire.*

1. She arranged the Creole dishes on the table.
2. The owner gave them a ten-year lease.
3. It's not a serious injury.
4. The boss will talk to us about the present situation.
5. When I arrived in the office, there was a warning on the door.
6. Her secretary has lost all the receipts.
7. We don't have any more office supplies.
8. How did they respond to the news?
9. I like to work with her because she's always in a good mood.
10. The police arrested him for accepting bribes.

DEUXIÈME RÉVISION

A. *Mettre les verbes entre parenthèses au subjonctif.*

1. *Il se peut que cette entreprise (faire) faillite.*
2. *On craint que le taux de chômage ne (être) plus élevé que l'an passé.*
3. *Je suis ravi que vous (pouvoir) vous joindre à nous.*
4. *Il faut que vous (signer) ce contrat.*
5. *Il est possible que nous (acheter) cette maison de campagne en Vendée.*
6. *Il voudrait que vous lui (apporter) une bouteille de Sauternes.*
7. *Je doute que vous (avoir) le droit d'agir ainsi.*
8. *Je ne crois pas que ce (être) une bonne idée.*
9. *Il acceptera leur offre quoiqu'il (vouloir) travailler au Japon.*
10. *Ils viendront ce week-end à moins que le bébé (être) encore malade.*

B. *Mettre les verbes entre parenthèses au conditionnel.*

1. *Ce rapport (être) plus clair s'il y avait des statistiques.*
2. *Nous (acheter) des actions si leur entreprise était plus stable.*
3. *Cette collection me (plaire) si les couleurs étaient moins sombres.*
4. *Nous nous (s'inscrire) à un cours si nous avions plus de temps libre.*
5. *Est-ce que vous (aller) en Europe si vous aviez des vacances cet hiver?*
6. *Les consommateurs (se plaindre) moins si la qualité était meilleure.*
7. *Nous (faire) de bonnes affaires si nous allions au marché aux puces.*
8. *Est-ce que vous (pouvoir) me donner un renseignement?*
9. *Elle (prendre) rendez-vous chez le dentiste si elle avait mal aux dents.*
10. *Nous (déboucher) une bonne bouteille de vin si vous veniez nous voir.*

C. *Mettre les verbes au conditionnel passé et au plus-que-parfait selon le sens.*

1. *J'irais à la campagne si j'avais le temps.*
2. *Nous louerions une maison en Italie si vous veniez avec nous.*
3. *Nous dégusterions de bons vins si nous visitions une cave.*
4. *Il accepterait cet emploi si le salaire était plus élevé.*
5. *Elle investirait dans cette compagnie si elle pouvait.*
6. *Notre agence vous aiderait si vous le vouliez.*
7. *Mon couturier vous ferait une robe si vous en aviez besoin.*
8. *Il prendrait du sirop s'il toussait.*
9. *Le vin serait meilleur cette année s'il faisait beau.*
10. *Ils embaucheraient plus d'ouvriers si leurs commandes augmentaient.*

D. *Traduire.*

1. She made her fortune by investing in this company.
2. Their house is surrounded by a white fence.
3. I spent hours trying to explain the situation to them.
4. This new pharmaceutical product is likely to interest you.
5. They should have been more careful.
6. You should not take their advice lightly.

7. I'm afraid the pharmacy is already closed.
8. Although there is no fireplace, they will buy this house.
9. They didn't hire as many grape pickers this year as last year.
10. The insulation of this house has to be redone.

LECTURE

LE CHAMP DES RÊVES*

Illusion romantique? Mythe historique? Orgueil[1] gaulois? Dans une certaine mesure, l'attitude de la France à l'égard de son patrimoine rural est nourrie de tous ces éléments. On ne comprend pas grand-chose à la France actuelle ou à celle d'antan si on oublie le lien[2] étroit qui existe entre la campagne et ses agriculteurs. Car la France—nation riche en haute technologie, industries de pointe et innovations scientifiques—est consciente que ses racines rurales remontent à près de 2000 ans.

Les agriculteurs constituent une des classes qui, à un moment donné de l'histoire, ont incarné les mouvements économiques et philosophiques de la France. Les artisans, les canuts, les mineurs ont transformé la France contemporaine avant d'être sacrifiés à l'autel du changement technologique et économique. C'est cette destinée qui, de nos jours, est rejetée non seulement par les 6% des agriculteurs qui demeurent mais par les 94% des non-agriculteurs qui sont soudés[3] à la France rurale par chaque fibre de leur être.

Si cette vieille terre de France perdait ses agriculteurs et ses bergers, elle perdrait ses racines. Il n'est pas un Français qui ne se sente lié à quelque région rurale, bien que ce lien soit souvent de nature mythique. C'est une histoire d'amour. L'amour d'un paysage[4] façonné par des siècles de labeur.[5] L'amour des images anciennes qui ont disparu: la charrue et le sillon,[6] le meuglement[7] des vaches[8] qu'on emmène à l'abattoir, les troupeaux[9] de moutons[10] qui paissent dans les prairies des Alpes. L'amour des odeurs de fumier[11] et de foin[12] fraîchement coupé, depuis longtemps disparues. Les Français revivent ces sensations par leurs souvenirs et par la littérature, le cinéma et la peinture. Peu importe que cette image corresponde à la réalité ou qu'il y ait un décalage par rapport au monde rural d'aujourd'hui.

L'angoisse[13] de la France rurale face aux défis économiques actuels est tout aussi importante chez les citadins pour qui la défense de l'environnement est synonyme de protection des agriculteurs. Qu'adviendra-t-il des paysages des Alpes et des Pyrénées lorsque les cultures auront disparu? Des sentiers[14] envahis par les broussailles, des chemins dévastés par l'érosion. Les villages, eux aussi, disparaîtront faute de commerces et d'écoles qui doivent leur survie[15] aux agriculteurs.

Cette perspective d'un avenir sombre n'est pas rare parmi ceux qui défendent un style de vie qui, de toute évidence, n'est plus rentable.[16] C'est cette France agonisante—un paysage rural dont les citadins en quête[17] de leurs racines[18] ont rêvé—qui engendre une solidarité inconditionnelle du reste du pays. C'est un

* Reprinted courtesy of *France* magazine (Winter 1992/93).

style de vie évoqué de façon si passionnée dans notre art et notre littérature que
nous avons l'impression de l'avoir vécu nous-mêmes.

VOCABULAIRE

1.	*l'orgueil*	pride, conceit
2.	*le lien*	link
3.	*souder*	to solder, to weld
4.	*le paysage*	countryside
5.	*le labeur*	labor, hard work
6.	*le sillon*	furrow
7.	*le meuglement*	mooing
8.	*la vache*	cow
9.	*le troupeau*	herd
10.	*le mouton*	sheep
11.	*le fumier*	manure
12.	*le foin*	hay
13.	*l'angoisse*	anguish
14.	*le sentier*	path
15.	*la survie*	survival
16.	*rentable*	profitable
17.	*la quête*	quest
18.	*la racine*	root

CORRIGÉ DES EXERCISES (ANSWER KEY)

LEÇON 1

A. 1. *répondez*   2. *pleut*   3. *finissons*   4. *écoutent*   5. *sais*   6. *sors*
7. *prends*   8. *choisit*   9. *faites*   10. *sommes*

B. 1. *Comprenez-vous l'explication?* 2. *Veulent-ils signer le contrat?*
3. *Emmène-t-elle ses enfants en Europe?* 4. *Est-ce que je choisis une bonne bouteille de vin pour notre table?* 5. *Êtes-vous à court d'idées?* 6. *Arrivons-nous à midi?* 7. *Va-t-il prendre une importante décision?* 8. *Risquent-elles d'obtenir l'autorisation à la dernière minute?* 9. *Y a-t-il toujours des embouteillages dans ce quartier?* 10. *Faites-vous un voyage en Europe chaque année?*

C. 1. *Il ne dort jamais en avion.* 2. *Un collègue m'attend à l'aéroport.*
3. *Combien coûte cette carte routière?* 4. *Apportez-moi un thé citron, s'il vous plaît.* 5. *Ils finissent toujours avant nous.* 6. *Venez-vous avec nous? Est-ce que vous venez avec nous? Vous venez avec nous?* 7. *Nous acceptons votre invitation.* 8. *Je ne peux pas vous donner une réponse.* 9. *Ils louent une voiture à l'aéroport.* 10. *Nous avons beaucoup de chance!*

LEÇON 2

A. 1. *se plaignent-ils*   2. *nous disons*   3. *s'aperçoit*   4. *se disputent*   5. *se mange*

B. 1. *s'occupe de*   2. *souvenez-vous*   3. *s'amuse*   4. *nous promenons*
5. *s'inquiète*

C. 1. *Ils se reposent dans le jardin.* 2. *Ne t'inquiète pas, Jennifer aimera sa chambre.* 3. *Les Français s'embrassent toujours pour dire bonjour.*
4. *Patrick se lave les mains avant de manger le gâteau.* 5. *Vous souvenez-vous s'il y a un magnétoscope dans la chambre?*

D. 1. *17 h 25*   2. *22 h 45*   3. *14 h 20*   4. *19 h 35*   5. *20 h 10*

LEÇON 3

A. 1. *Julia lui téléphone d'une cabine.* 2. *Elle me l'envoie.* 3. *Ils ne l'acceptent pas.* 4. *Vous lui donnez des renseignements.* 5. *Elle le feuillette.* 6. *Caroline lui donne le paquet.* 7. *Nous l'avons oublié.* 8. *Je ne vais pas la reconnaître.*

B. 1. *Nous le lui demandons.* 2. *Mathilde le lui a-t-elle envoyé?* 3. *Le lui sert-elle?* 4. *Mathilde la lui envoie.* 5. *Mme Sabatier le lui a donné.* 6. *Nous la leur annonçons.* 7. *Je la lui donne.* 8. *Tu les leur expliques.*

C. 1. *va faire*   2. *va téléphoner*   3. *allons déjeuner*   4. *va recevoir*   5. *vais lui offrir*

D. 1. *venais de*   2. *vient d'acheter*   3. *venaient d'entrer*   4. *vient d'arriver*
5. *venait de*

A. 1. *Les débats sont plus intéressants que les feuilletons.* 2. *Le présentateur de la 2 est moins séduisant que le présentateur de la 5.* 3. *Cet acteur est moins bon que cette actrice.* 4. *Les films doublés sont plus agaçants que les films sous-titrés.* 5. *Leur publicité est moins originale que la vôtre.*

B. 1. *C'est le festival le plus renommé du pays.* 2. *C'est le film policier le plus populaire de l'année.* 3. *C'est le présentateur le moins amusant de cette chaîne.* 4. *C'est l'actrice la plus belle du festival.* 5. *C'est le magazine hebdomadaire le moins regardé de toutes les chaînes.*

C. 1. *que* 2. *à laquelle* 3. *lequel* 4. *dont* 5. *qui* 6. *lesquelles* 7. *Ce qui* 8. *à quoi/à qui* 9. *Ce dont* 10. *Quoi*

D. 1. *Plus j'étudie, plus j'apprends.* 2. *Ce dont j'ai besoin, c'est d'une télévision avec un plus grand écran.* 3. *Je ne me souviens pas du film dont vous parlez.* 4. *Quand diffusera-t-on le documentaire? Je n'en ai pas la moindre idée.* 5. *Ils sont richissimes.* 6. *C'est le pire feuilleton que j'aie jamais vu.* 7. *Ce que je déteste, c'est la publicité.* 8. *Catherine est ma sœur cadette.* 9. *Pouvez-vous deviner de quoi il s'agit?* 10. *Cette émission hebdomadaire fait un tabac.*

LEÇON 5

A. 1. *Cette* 2. *Ces* 3. *cet* 4. *Cette* 5. *ces* 6. *ces* 7. *ce* 8. *cette* 9. *ces* 10. *Cet*

B. 1. *celle-ci ou celle-là* 2. *celles-ci ou celles-là* 3. *celui-ci ou celui-là* 4. *ceux-ci ou ceux-là* 5. *celui-ci ou celui-là*

C. 1. *des tissus bleu pâle* 2. *des étoffes vermillon et or* 3. *ces tableaux néo-réalistes* 4. *Ces peintures vert foncé* 5. *Ces housses de couette bleu ciel*

D. 1. *Quitte à trop dépenser, elle a engagé deux décorateurs célèbres.* 2. *Ils ont choisi le canapé rouge vif quitte à choquer leurs amis.* 3. *Ils passeront plus de temps dans l'appartement de Joan quitte à être en retard pour leur prochain rendez-vous.* 4. *Joan veut aller au marché aux puces quitte à devoir se lever de bonne heure.* 5. *Quitte à le regretter plus tard, elle a peint la cuisine en orange vif.*

LEÇON 6

A. 1. *Elle a dû poser sa candidature avant le 15 mai.* 2. *Ils ont répondu à une annonce dans le journal.* 3. *Il n'a pas pris ces décisions.* 4. *Julien ne s'est pas assis dans son bureau.* 5. *Êtes-vous retourné en Aquitaine?*

B. 1. *travaillait* 2. *était* 3. *habitions* 4. *envisageaient* 5. *suiviez*

C. 1. *avais* 2. *a passé* 3. *ont exploré* 4. *a sonné* 5. *avait* 6. *habitions* 7. *a offert* 8. *parlait* 9. *étaient/a apporté* 10. *ont fini*

D. 1. *Si on posait notre candidature pour ce poste?* 2. *Si on invitait le directeur commercial à déjeuner avec nous?* 3. *Si on explorait davantage le marché chinois? 4. Si on célébrait les succès de cette décennie? 5. Si on prenait rendez-vous avec le vice-président?*

LEÇON 7

A. 1. *a passé* 2. *suis rentré* 3. *a sorti* 4. *a rentré* 5. *sont passés* 6. *a démonté* 7. *sont sortis* 8. *ont descendu* 9. *as retourné* 10. *êtes-vous descendu(e)(s)*
B. 1. *Il travaille chez Renault depuis trois mois.* 2. *Patrick habite à Toulouse depuis deux ans.* 3. *L'entreprise utilise ces machines depuis une vingtaine d'années.* 4. *Mon père est contremaître depuis trente ans.* 5. *Nous fabriquons ces produits depuis dix ans.*
C. 1. *Elle a cessé de fumer il y a dix ans.* 2. *Notre syndicat a lutté contre des pause-café plus courtes pendant des semaines.* 3. *Ces bénéfices n'existaient pas il y a vingt ans.* 4. *Notre équipe se plaignait de ce mécanicien depuis des semaines quand la direction l'a renvoyé (l'a mis à la porte).* 5. *Elle n'a pas reçu d'augmentation depuis deux ans.* 6. *La direction a mis sur pied un nouveau programme de formation il y a un an.* 7. *L'entreprise n'a pas changé ses procédés de fabrication depuis longtemps.* 8. *Il se servait de cette machine depuis des mois quand soudain elle est tombée en panne.* 9. *Les mécaniciens menacent de se mettre en grève depuis un mois.* 10. *Airbus l'a embauché la semaine dernière.*

LEÇON 8

A. 1. *fera* 2. *connaîtra* 3. *frissonnera* 4. *sera* 5. *enverra* 6. *mettrez* 7. *auras* 8. *pourrons* 9. *préviendrez* 10. *partira*
B. 1. *sera* 2. *viendront* 3. *pourra* 4. *devra* 5. *feront*
C. 1. *toi* 2. *eux* 3. *Lui non plus.* 4. *nous* 5. *elle*
D. 1. *Connaissez-vous Émilie, la nouvelle remplaçante?* 2. *Savez-vous si Carole jouera le rôle de Phèdre?* 3. *L'éclairagiste créera une ambiance romantique.* 4. *Les acteurs savent leur rôle par cœur.* 5. *La costumière ne sait pas si Phèdre aimera sa robe.* 6. *La pièce fera un tabac (aura beaucoup de succès) aux États-Unis.* 7. *Les jeunes acteurs connaissent la pauvreté au début de leur carrière.* 8. *Est-ce que tous les acteurs savent chanter?*

LEÇON 9

A. 1. *broyer* 2. *râpe* 3. *éplucher* 4. *démoule* 5. *pétrit* 6. *égoutter* 7. *bouillir* 8. *bat* 9. *hacher* 10. *mariner*
B. 1. *a réussi à* 2. *suivre* 3. *permet de* 4. *s'est décidée à* 5. *m'a aidé à* 6. *projette d'* 7. *as osé* 8. *nous attendons à* 9. *s'intéresse à* 10. *avons décidé de*
C. 1. *Michael s'amuse à apprendre à faire une mousse au chocolat.* 2. *Ajouter*

une gousse d'ail et faire cuire pendant une heure. 3. Pour éviter de brûler la
sauce, il faut la remuer lentement. 4. Il a épluché les pommes de terre et les
a mises dans la poêle. 5. Elle a fait fondre le beurre avant de le verser dans
la casserole.

LEÇON 10

A. 1. *quoi* 2. *Qui* 3. *Lequel* 4. *laquelle* 5. *Que* 6. *Qui* 7. *quoi*
8. *lesquelles* 9. *Que* 10. *quoi*

B. 1. *Qui est-ce qui a sillonné la France à la recherche de plantes rares?*
2. *Qu'est-ce qu'il faut faire pour reproduire les mêmes senteurs? 3. À qui*
est-ce qu'il pensait en créant ce nouveau parfum? 4. Qu'est-ce qu'ils
faisaient au Moyen-Age? 5. Pour qui est-ce qu'il travaille?

C. 1. *Scrupuleusement* 2. *Récemment* 3. *Doucement* 4. *Passivement*
5. *Lentement* 6. *Profondément* 7. *Suffisamment* 8. *Mollement*
9. *Vivement* 10. *Gentiment*

PREMIÈRE RÉVISION

A. 1. *a expliqué* 2. *est sortie* 3. *a bavardé* 4. *s'est débrouillé* 5. *a protégé*
6. *a choisi* 7. *avons procuré* 8. *ont attendu* 9. *êtes-vous souvenu(e)(s)*
10. *sont passés*

B. 1. *servira* 2. *mélangeront* 3. *iront* 4. *saura* 5. *fondra* 6. *pourrons*
7. *devront* 8. *recevra* 9. *voudra* 10. *luttera.*

C. 1. *Ont-ils rendez-vous à Paris avec le PDG de Peugeot? 2. Pense-t-elle que*
les ouvriers se mettront en grève demain? 3. Les chanteurs voulaient-ils des
chambres non-fumeur? 4. Connais-tu Fontainebleau comme ta poche?
5. *Est-ce que je jette un coup d'œil aux gâteaux toutes les quinze minutes?*
6. *Scarlett a-t-elle fouetté le cheval fatigué? 7. Devez-vous utiliser ces*
centrifugeuses? 8. A-t-il raccroché parce que la discussion devenait
enflammée? 9. Diffuserez-vous un feuilleton à vingt heures? 10. Emmènera-
t-elle Hervé dans un café très branché?

D. 1. *L'objectif est de les promouvoir. 2. Michael s'y inscrit. 3. Nos jardiniers*
en plantent. 4. Karen l'a envoyée. 5. Jeremy va au théâtre pour y assister.
6. *Les voyageurs l'ont rattrapé. 7. Ils veulent les leur vendre. 8. Brice les*
emmènera au marché aux puces. 9. Le médecin lui parlera du tabagisme.
10. *Elle l'a remerciée.*

E. 1. *Nous sommes censés arriver à midi. 2. Ne vous en faites pas, le*
rédacteur (la rédactrice) sera ici dans cinq minutes. 3. Il a démissioné hier.
4. *Où achetez-vous vos matières premières? 5. Il a versé les ingrédients*
secrets dans la cuve. 6. Je ne suis pas à même de vous aider. 7. Cette
chaise-ci est plus confortable que celle-là. 8. Elle a acheté une table en
acajou pour son salon. 9. Apportez-moi les contrats que vous venez de leur
envoyer. 10. Permettez-moi de vous présenter ma mère, Madame
Fontenelle.

LEÇON 11

A. 1. *La rubrique économique est présentée par Hervé et Corinne.* 2. *La conférence de presse a été annulée par le ministre de l'économie.* 3. *Une baisse du dollar sera annoncée par les experts financiers.* 4. *Les taux d'intérêt ont été augmentés par la Réserve fédérale.* 5. *Les villages du Club Med au Mexique sont fréquentés par les Canadiens.*

B. 1. *Julie présente les tendances hebdomadaires.* 2. *Leur manque de compétence nous a déçus.* 3. *Eurotunnel remportera sans doute la Palme.* 4. *Le président a fait ces déclarations.* 5. *Les téléspectateurs aiment ce gourou financier.* 6. *La reprise se confirme.* 7. *Une montagne de dossiers couvre le bureau du présentateur.* 8. *Le Japon reçoit chaque jour cette rubrique financière.* 9. *L'état de l'économie allemande influence la valeur des devises.* 10. *Notre équipe rédigera le rapport annuel avant la fin du mois.*

C. 1. *Les consommateurs respectent cet expert financier.* 2. *Les deux journalistes ont écrit ce rapport.* 3. *On achète souvent les actions par téléphone.* 4. *Les lingots d'or se vendent bien en période de récession.* 5. *On ne leur a pas permis de publier ces chiffres.* 6. *Ça ne se dit pas en anglais.* 7. *À la conférence économique de Genève, on parle au moins quatre langues.* 8. *Un cambiste m'a donné ces conseils.* 9. *Elle s'est laissé influencer par son agent de change.* 10. *La Bourse était remplie d'investisseurs.*

D. 1. *Sachant qu'il n'avait pas beaucoup d'argent, il a investi avec prudence.* 2. *Il écoutait la radio en rédigeant son rapport.* 3. *Fatiguant tout le monde, l'analyste a recommencé sa présentation.* 4. *Tout en étant en colère contre son secrétaire, le PDG ne l'a pas renvoyé.* 5. *Leur compagnie a fait fortune en fabriquant des pièces en plastique.* 6. *En rejetant cette mesure, le président risque de perdre les élections.* 7. *Le cambiste ira directement à la Bourse en arrivant à Paris.* 8. *Il s'est rendu compte de ses erreurs en finissant son rapport.* 9. *Tout en étant très strict, le PDG était estimé de ses employés.* 10. *Profitant du marché favorable, il a acheté de nombreuses actions.*

LEÇON 12

A. 1. *voudrait* 2. *serait* 3. *gribouillerait* 4. *pourrions* 5. *devriez* 6. *irait* 7. *Sauriez* 8. *finirait* 9. *faudrait* 10. *s'apercevrait*

B. 1. *suivrait/permettaient* 2. *vendrait/pouvait* 3. *serait/travaillait* 4. *plairait/avait* 5. *porteraient/étaient* 6. *essaierait/devait* 7. *irions/ connaissions* 8. *mettrait/était* 9. *ferait/savait* 10. *achèterait/décidait*

C. 1. *Pourriez-vous raccourcir ce pantalon, s'il vous plaît?* 2. *Elle suivrait un cours dans un institut de mode à Paris si elle avait plus d'argent.* 3. *Nous devrions protéger l'industrie de la mode française.* 4. *Si vous étiez en retard pour son défilé de mode, il serait en colère.* 5. *Claude n'a pas pu finir sa robe de mariage avant le 15 mars.* 6. *Porteriez-vous cette somptueuse robe décolletée au théâtre?* 7. *L'agent a demandé au couturier d'engager ce mannequin; il a refusé. 8. S'il n'était pas si prétentieux, il ferait une collection prêt-à-porter. 9. Irait-elle en Asie si elle avait besoin de tissu exotique? 10. Pourriez-vous faire une autre veste croisée bleu marine?*

LEÇON 13

A. 1. *J'aurais dû.* 2. *Ils auraient su.* 3. *Vous vous seriez fait vacciner.* 4. *Nous aurions dépisté.* 5. *Cela aurait suscité.* 6. *J'aurais fait.* 7. *Elle serait rentrée.* 8. *Tu aurais voulu.* 9. *Vous seriez allé.* 10. *Elles se seraient renseignées.*

B. 1. *Nous nous serions fait vacciner si nous avions voyagé en Afrique.* 2. *Elle se serait préoccupée de sa santé si elle avait eu des symptômes.* 3. *La crèche aurait accepté l'enfant s'il avait été plus âgé.* 4. *Si Mathilde avait attrapé la rougeole, elle serait restée à la maison.* 5. *La sage-femme vous aurait donné des conseils si vous le lui aviez demandé.* 6. *Si Marc avait eu besoin d'un rappel, je l'aurais emmené chez le médecin.* 7. *Nous aurions pris plus de précautions si nous avions été prévenus.* 8. *Tu te serais inquiété si j'étais arrivé en retard.* 9. *Si nous nous étions retrouvés nez à nez, je lui aurais dit ce que je pense de lui.* 10. *Ils ne seraient pas tombés malades s'ils avaient fait plus attention à leur régime.*

C. 1. *Le vaccin l'a rendu malade pendant deux jours.* 2. *Les sages-femmes vous donneront des conseils pendant votre grossesse.* 3. *Il est tombé à plat ventre et s'est cassé le bras gauche.* 4 *Je les ai vus descendre les Champs-Elysées bras dessus, bras dessous.* 5. *Leur demande nous a pris au dépourvu.* 6. *Qu'est-ce que votre médecin pense de vos radios?* 7. *Si votre bébé a de la fièvre, appelez-moi immédiatement.* 8. *Une centaine d'enfants auraient attrapé la méningite l'année dernière.* 9. *Vous auriez dû lui demander s'il y a des effets secondaires.* 10. *La pauvreté sévit dans cette région.* 11. *Il a accepté d'emblée.* 12. *Elle est enceinte de cinq mois.* 13. *Combien de temps sera-t-elle en congé de maternité?* 14. *C'est notre premier enfant, nous ne savons pas à quoi nous attendre.* 15. *Les chercheurs auraient mis au point un vaccin s'ils avaient eu plus d'argent et un plus grand laboratoire.*

LEÇON 14

A. 1. *Ils désirent faire baptiser leur enfant.* 2. *Elle a renoncé à essayer de convaincre son beau-père.* 3. *Nous espérons passer une semaine en Normandie.* 4. *Le responsable de l'état civil refuse d'aider ce couple.* 5. *Je préfère savoir la réponse tout de suite.* 6. *Ils se sont habitués à vivre en banlieue.* 7. *Bertrand se plaît à taquiner sa sœur.* 8. *Vous a-t-il autorisé à révéler cette histoire.* 9. *J'ai complètement oublié de téléphoner à Sabrine.* 10. *Il faut l'empêcher de faire cette bêtise.*

B. 1. *lesquels* 2. *Ce dont* 3. *laquelle* 4. *dont* 5. *qui/lequel* 6. *dont* 7. *Ce dont* 8. *lesquels* 9. *laquelle* 10. *auquel*

C. 1. *La personne avec qui (laquelle) elle parle est la marraine de Florent.*

2. *Quel genre de nom ont-ils choisi pour leur entreprise?* 3. *Ça revient toujours sur le tapis.* 4. *Ils nous a aidés à prendre une décision.* 5. *Ils ne trouveront pas ce dont ils ont besoin.* 6. *Ils ne s'habitueront jamais à se lever tôt.* 7. *Il ne s'est pas arrêté aux feux.* 8. *Elle nous a remercié de lui avoir donné de bons conseils.* 9. *N'oublie pas de la féliciter.* 10. *Ce nom est démodé.*

LEÇON 15

A. 1. *aboutissent* 2. *fasse* 3. *puissent* 4. *aient* 5. *soyez* 6. *respectent* 7. *aille* 8. *exprimiez* 9. *soient* 10. *veuille*

B. 1. *est* 2. *s'ouvre* 3. *soit* 4. *fasses* 5. *recevra* 6. *s'aperçoive* 7. *prenne* 8. *se plaindra* 9. *sachiez* 10. *touchiez*

C. 1. *Quoiqu'il ait le droit d'ouvrir le dimanche, il préfère se reposer.* 2. *Nous sommes contents que vous ayez pu passer un mois en Europe.* 3. *Ce n'est pas que son travail soit difficile mais c'est ennuyeux.* 4. *Je doute que cette mesure puisse donner un coup de pouce à l'économie.* 5. *Ils manifesteront jusqu'à ce qu'ils obtiennent ce qu'ils veulent.* 6. *Voulez-vous que j'aille avec vous chez Maud?* 7. *À moins que nous nous plaignions, le patron ne nous donnera pas d'augmentation.* 8. *Ils regrettent que cette crèche ne soit pas ouverte le dimanche.* 9. *Il était triste de devoir travailler toute la semaine.* 10. *Depuis combien de temps luttent-ils contre la concurrence étrangère?*

LEÇON 16

A. 1. *assistions* 2. *ne soit pas* 3. *montriez* 4. *sachiez* 5. *n'ayez pas* 6. *reçoive* 7. *fassiez* 8. *aillent* 9. *soyons* 10. *sauvegardiez*

B. 1. *est* 2. *ne puisse pas* 3. *aient* 4. *n'ait pas* 5. *soit* 6. *utilisiez* 7. *auront* 8. *bat* 9. *est doté* 10. *commandiez*

C. 1. *le sien* 2. *le vôtre* 3. *Le leur* 4. *les vôtres* 5. *les siennes* 6. *les miens* 7. *aux leurs* 8. *la tienne* 9. *au sien* 10. *des vôtres*

LEÇON 17

A. 1. *en cas d'urgence* 2. *tellement . . . que* 3. *c'est-à-dire* 4. *Au cas où* 5. *donc* 6. *surtout* 7. *Selon* 8. *c'est pourquoi*

B. 1. *C'est son projet qu'il présente.* 2. *C'est le plus beau bâtiment qu'ils ont choisi.* 3. *C'est de moi dont tu te moques.* 4. *C'est le projet de rénovation auquel ils pensent.* 5. *C'est de son prochain voyage à Paris dont elle parle.* 6. *C'est la solution à laquelle nous pensons.* 7. *C'est à moi qu'il confie tous ses secrets.* 8. *C'est sur toi qu'elle compte.* 9. *C'est ce quartier que vous détestez.* 10. *C'est de sa réaction dont nous avons peur.*

C. 1. *Après avoir passé une semaine à Paris, ils ont décidé d'acheter un appartement dans le 15ème arrondissement.* 2. *Au fait, est-ce que vous avez vu Érica aujourd'hui?* 3. *Au lieu de démolir le vieux bâtiment, ils ont décidé de le rénover. 4. Je n'aurais jamais pensé qu'il y avait tant de jardins à Paris. 5. Il prétend qu'il y a des centaines de péniches sur le Canal St-Martin. 6. J'ai l'impression que Douglas sera en retard. 7. Malgré tous les problèmes, ils feront construire une maison dans ce quartier. 8. Vous n'avez pas de montre, c'est pourquoi vous êtes toujours en retard. 9. Je tiens à parler à l'architecte à la fin de la réunion. 10. Le soleil éclaire tout l'appartement.*

LEÇON 18

A. 1. *le* 2. *la* 3. *le* 4. *la* 5. *un* 6. *le* 7. *le* 8. *le* 9. *un* 10. *le*
B. 1. *à* 2. none 3. none 4. *à* 5. none
C. 1. *Il est sorti de la pièce en courant.* 2. *Quoi que vous décidiez, je serai heureux(se) pour vous.* 3. *Quel que soit son âge, cette enfant est très intelligente.* 4. *Elle a traversé la rue en sautillant.* 5. *Ils voudraient habiter dans cette tour médiévale.* 6. *Il a fermé la porte brusquement.* 7. *Cassandre a mis les fleurs dans un vase.* 8. *Quoi que vous pensiez, cette maison n'a pas assez de prises.* 9. *Cette maison a une très bonne isolation.* 10. *Qui a nettoyé les gouttières?*

LEÇON 19

A. 1. *n'aura pas* 2. *pleut* 3. *l'embauchera* 4. *aura* 5. *êtes* 6. *fera* 7. *aura* 8. *fait* 9. *sera* 10. *sent*
B. 1. *Ce champagne est bon mais je ne peux pas en dire autant de ce mousseux.* 2. *Il y a autant de vignobles ici que de l'autre côté de la colline.* 3. *Je ne l'avais jamais vu boire autant.* 4. *Autant il était charmant avec vous, autant il était désagréable avec moi.* 5. *Autant que je sache, le roman de Jeremy est un policier.* 6. *Ce vigneron produit autant que son voisin.* 7. *M. Gallet nous a raconté tant d'histoires drôles que nous avons oublié l'heure.* 8. *Les vignerons avaient tant travaillé qu'ils étaient épuisés.* 9. *Autant que je voudrais visiter votre cave, j'ai peur du noir.* 10. *Autant déboucher une autre bouteille!*
C. 1. *À quoi bon?* 2. *Chic!* 3. *Aïe! Ouille!* 4. *Au feu! Au feu!* 5. *Toc, toc, toc,* 6. *Chut!* 7. *Motus!* 8. *Hourra!* 9. *Chiche!* 10. *Adieu!*

LEÇON 20

A. 1. *dico* 2. *manif* 3. *sympa* 4. *fac* 5. *apéro* 6. *diapos* 7. *micro* 8. *proprio* 9. *frangin* 10. *pub*
B. 1. *Elle a disposé les plats créoles sur la table.* 2. *Le propriétaire leur a donné un bail de dix ans.* 3. *Ce n'est pas une blessure grave.* 4. *Le patron nous parlera de la situation actuelle.* 5. *Quand je suis arrivé(e) au bureau, il y avait un avertissement sur la porte.* 6. *Sa secrétaire a perdu tous ses reçus.* 7. *Nous n'avons plus de fournitures de bureau.* 8. *Comment ont-ils*

réagi à la nouvelle? 9. J'aime travailler avec elle parce qu'elle est toujours de bonne humeur. 10. La police l'a arrêté pour avoir accepté des dessous-de-table.

DEUXIÈME RÉVISION

A. 1. *fasse* 2. *soit* 3. *puissiez* 4. *signiez* 5. *achetions* 6. *apportiez* 7. *ayez* 8. *soit* 9. *veuille* 10. *soit*

B. 1. *serait* 2. *achèterions* 3. *plairait* 4. *inscririons* 5. *iriez* 6. *se plaindraient* 7. *ferions* 8. *pourriez* 9. *prendrait* 10. *déboucherions*

C. 1. *Je serais allé à la campagne si j'avais eu le temps. 2. Nous aurions loué une maison en Italie si vous étiez venus avec nous. 3. Nous aurions dégusté de bons vins si nous avions visité une cave. 4. Il aurait accepté cet emploi si le salaire avait été plus élevé. 5. Elle aurait investi dans cette compagnie si elle avait pu. 6. Notre agence vous aurait aidé si vous l'aviez voulu. 7. Mon couturier vous aurait fait une robe si vous en aviez eu besoin. 8. Il aurait pris du sirop s'il avait toussé. 9. Le vin aurait été meilleur cette année s'il avait fait beau. 10. Ils auraient embauché plus d'ouvriers si leurs commandes avaient augmenté.*

D. 1. *Elle a fait fortune en investissant dans cette entreprise. 2. Leur maison est entourée d'une clôture blanche. 3. J'ai passé des heures à essayer de leur expliquer la situation. 4. Ce nouveau produit pharmaceutique est susceptible de vous intéresser. 5. Ils auraient dû être plus prudents. 6. Vous ne devriez pas prendre leurs conseils à la légère. 7. J'ai peur que la pharmacie ne soit déjà fermée. 8. Bien qu'il n'y ait pas de cheminée, ils achèteront cette maison.*
9. *Ils n'ont pas embauché autant de vendangeurs cette année que l'année dernière. 10. Il faut refaire l'isolation de cette maison.*

APPENDIXES

A. PRONUNCIATION CHART

This chart will serve as a quick reference guide to French sounds.

CONSONANTS

French Spelling	Approximate Sound	Example
b, d, k, l, m, n, p, s, t, v, z	same as in English	
c (before e, i, y)	s	cinéma
c (before a, o, u)	k	cave
ç (appears only before a, o, u)	s	français
ch	sh	chaud
g (before e, i, y)	s (as in measure)	âge
g (before a, o, u)	g in game	gâteau
gn	ni in onion	agneau
h	always silent	homme
j	s in measure	Jacques
qu, final q	k	qui
r	pronounced in back of mouth, rolled like light gargling sound	Paris
ss	s	tasse
s (beginning of word or before consonant)	s	salle / disque
s (between vowels)	z in Zelda	maison
th	t	thé
x	x in exact	exact
x	x in excellent	excellent
ll	y in yes	volaille
ll	as in ill	elle

French Spelling	Approximate Sound	Example
a, à, â	<u>a</u> in father	*la*
é, er, ez (end of word)	<u>ay</u> in lay	*thé*
		parler
		allez
e plus final pronounced consonant	<u>e</u> in met	*belle* (l is the final pronounced consonant)
è, ai, aî	<u>e</u> in met	*père*
		chaîne
e, eu	<u>u</u> in put	*le*
i	<u>ee</u> in beet	*ici*
i plus vowel	<u>y</u> in yesterday	*lion*
o, au, eau, ô	<u>o</u> in both	*mot*
		chaud
		beau
		hôte
ou	<u>oo</u> in toot	*vous*
oi, oy	<u>wa</u> in watt	*moi*
u	no equivalent in English —say <u>ee</u>, then round your lips	*tu* *fumeurs*
ui	<u>wee</u> as in week	*lui*
euille	no equivalent in English —say <u>uh</u> and follow it with y	*feuille*
eille	<u>ay</u> as in hay	*merveilleux*

Nasal vowels are sounds produced when air is expelled from both the mouth and the nose. In French, a consonant that follows a nasal vowel is not fully pronounced. For example, the French word *on:* pronounce the nasal vowel *o* through the mouth and nose, but we do not sound the following consonant *n* or *m*. That is, do not touch the roof of your mouth with the tip of the tongue.

French Spelling	Approximate Sound	Example
an, en	vowel in balm	*France*
em	vowel in balm	*emmener*
in, ain, ein	vowel in man	*fin*
im, aim	vowel in man	*faim*
ien	y̲ + vowel in men	*bien*
ion	y̲ + vowel in song	*station*
oin	w̲ + vowel in man	*loin*
on	vowel in song	*bon*
om	vowel in song	*tomber*
un	vowel in lung	*un*

B. DAYS, MONTHS, AND SEASONS

1. THE DAYS OF THE WEEK

lundi	Monday
mardi	Tuesday
mercredi	Wednesday
jeudi	Thursday
vendredi	Friday
samedi	Saturday
dimanche	Sunday

2. THE MONTHS OF THE YEAR

janvier	January
février	February
mars	March
avril	April
mai	May
juin	June
juillet	July
août	August
septembre	September
octobre	October
novembre	November
décembre	December

3. THE SEASONS OF THE YEAR

printemps	spring
été	summer
automne	fall
hiver	winter

C. IMPERSONAL EXPRESSIONS THAT REQUIRE THE SUBJUNCTIVE

cela ne sert à rien	it is pointless
cela vaut la peine	it is worth the trouble
comment se fait-il	how come
il arrive	it happens
il est acceptable	it is acceptable
il est anormal	it is abnormal
il est bon	it is good
il est commun	it is common
il est concevable	it is conceivable
il est courant	it is usual
il est dommage	it is a shame
il est essentiel	it is essential
il est étrange	it is strange
il est fâcheux	it is unfortunate
il est honteux	it is a shame
il est impensable	it is unthinkable
il est impératif	it is imperative
il est impossible	it is impossible
il est inadmissible	it is inadmissible
il est inconcevable	it is inconceivable
il est inutile	it is useless
il est inutile d'espérer	it is hopeless
il est juste	it is just
il est naturel	it is natural
il est nécessaire	it is necessary
il est normal	it is normal
il est possible	it is possible
il est préférable	it is preferable
il est rare	it is rare
il est rassurant	it is comforting
il est regrettable	it is regrettable
il est surprenant	it is surprising
il est temps	it is time
il faut	one must
il se peut	it may be
il semble	it seems
il suffit	it is enough
il vaut mieux	it is better

D. ADVERBS WITH
SPELLING IRREGULARITIES

absolument	absolutely
aveuglément	blindly
énormément	enormously
éperdûment	frantically, madly
expressément	expressly
gentiment	nicely
grièvement	seriously
immensément	immensely
poliment	politely
précisément	precisely
profondément	deeply
profusément	profusely
résolument	resolutely
uniformément	uniformly

E. SUBJECTIVE PRONOMINAL VERBS

s'en aller	to go away
s'apercevoir	to realize
s'écrouler	to collapse
s'enfuir	to flee
s'evanouir	to faint
se moquer	to make fun
se plaindre	to complain
se souvenir	to remember
se taire	to keep quiet

F. LETTER WRITING

1. FORMAL INVITATIONS AND ACCEPTANCES

FORMAL INVITATIONS

Monsieur et madame de Montour vous prient de leur faire l'honneur d'assister à un bal, donné en l'honneur de leur fille Marie-José, le dimanche huit avril à neuf heures du soir.

> *M. et Mme de Montour*
> *35 avenue Hoche*
> *75016 Paris*

R.S.V.P.

Mr. and Mrs. de Montour request the pleasure of your presence at a ball given in honor of their daughter, Marie-José, on Sunday evening, April eighth, at nine o'clock.

> Mr. and Mrs. de Montour
> 35 avenue Hoche
> 75016 Paris

R.S.V.P.

R.S.V.P. stands for *Répondez s'il vous plaît.* Please answer.

NOTE OF ACCEPTANCE

Monsieur et madame du Panier vous remercient de votre aimable invitation à laquelle ils se feront un plaisir de se rendre.

Mr. and Mrs. du Panier thank you for your kind invitation and will be delighted to come.

2. THANK-YOU NOTES

le 14 mars 1993

Chère Madame,

Je tiens à vous remercier de l'aimable attention que vous avez eue en m'envoyant le charmant présent que j'ai reçu. Ce tableau me fait d'autant plus plaisir qu'il est ravissant dans le cadre de mon studio.
Je vous prie de croire à l'expression de mes sentiments de sincère amitié.

> *Renée Beaujoly*

322

March 14, 1993

Dear Mrs. Duparc,

   I should like to thank you for the delightful present you sent me. The picture was all the more welcome because it fits in so beautifully with the other things in my studio.
   Thank you ever so much.

Sincerely yours,
Renée Beaujoly

3. INFORMAL LETTERS

le 5 mars 1994

Mon cher Jacques,

   Ta dernière lettre m'a fait grand plaisir.
   Tout d'abord laisse-moi t'annoncer une bonne nouvelle: je compte venir passer une quinzaine de jours à Paris au commencement d'avril et je me réjouis à l'avance à l'idée de te revoir ainsi que les tiens qui je l'espère, se portent bien.
   Colette vient avec moi et se fait une grande joie à l'idée de connaître enfin ta femme. Les affaires marchent bien en ce moment, espérons que ça continuera. Tâche de ne pas avoir trop de malades au mois d'avril, enfin il est vrai que ces choses-là ne se commandent pas.
   Toute ma famille se porte bien, heureusement.
   J'ai pris l'apéritif avec Dumont l'autre jour, qui m'a demandé de tes nouvelles. Son affaire marche très bien.
   J'allais presque oublier le plus important, peux-tu me réserver une chambre au Grand Hôtel pour le cinq avril, je t'en saurais fort gré.
   J'espère avoir le plaisir de te lire très bientôt.
   Mes meilleurs respects à ta femme.

En toute amitié,
André

Dear Jack,

I was very happy to receive your last letter.

First of all, I've some good news for you. I expect to spend two weeks in Paris at the beginning of April and I'm looking forward to the prospect of seeing you and your family, all of whom I hope are well.

Colette's coming with me; she's delighted to be able at last to meet your wife. Business is pretty good right now. Let's hope it will keep up. Try not to get too many patients during the month of April, though I suppose that's a little difficult to arrange.

Fortunately, my family is doing well.

I had cocktails with Dumont the other day and he asked about you. His business is going well.

I almost forgot the most important thing. Can you reserve a room for me at the Grand Hotel for April the fifth? You'll be doing me a great favor.

I hope to hear from you soon. My best regards to your wife.

> Your friend,
> Andrew

Paris, le 3 avril 1993

Ma Chérie,

J'ai bien reçu ta lettre du trente et je suis heureuse de savoir que ta fille est tout à fait remise.

Rien de bien nouveau ici, sauf que Pierre me donne beaucoup de mal, enfin toi aussi tu as un fils de cet âge-là, et tu sais ce que je veux dire!

Nous avons vu ton mari l'autre soir, il est venu dîner à la maison; il se porte bien et voudrait bien te voir de retour.

Tu as bien de la veine d'être à la montagne pour encore un mois. Que fais-tu de beau toute la journée à Chamonix? Y a-t-il encore beaucoup de monde là-bas? Il paraît que les de Villneque sont là. A Paris tout le monde parle des prochaines fiançailles de leur fille.

Nous sommes allés à une soirée l'autre soir chez les Clergeaud, cette femme ne sait pas recevoir, je m'y suis ennuyée à mourir.

Voilà à peu près tous les derniers potins de Paris, tu vois que je te tiens bien au courant, tâche d'en faire autant.

Embrasse bien Françoise pour moi.

> *Meilleurs baisers de ton amie,*
> *Monique*

Paris, April 3, 1993

Darling,

I received your letter of the thirtieth and I'm happy to learn that your daughter has completely recovered.

Nothing new here, except that Pierre is giving me a lot of trouble. You have a son of the same age, so you know what I mean.

We saw your husband the other night—he had dinner at our house. He's well and is looking forward to your coming home.

You're lucky to be staying in the mountains for another month! What do you do all day long in Chamonix? Is it still very crowded? It seems that the de Villneques are there. In Paris, the future engagement of their daughter is the talk of the town.

The other evening we went to a party given by the Clergeauds. She doesn't know how to entertain and I was bored to death.

That's about all of the latest Paris gossip. You see how well I keep you posted—try to do the same.

Give my love to Françoise.

Love,
Monique

4. FORMS OF SALUTATIONS AND COMPLIMENTARY CLOSINGS

SALUTATIONS
FORMAL

Monsieur l'Abbé,	Dear Reverend:
Monsieur le Député,	Dear Congressman:
Madame le Député,	Dear Congresswoman:
Monsieur le Maire,	Dear Mayor (Smith):
Madame le Maire,	Dear Mayor (Smith): (f)
Cher Professeur,	Dear Professor (Smith):
Cher/Chère Maître (Mon cher Maître),	Dear Mr./Mrs. (Smith): (Lawyers are addressed as "Maître" in France.)
Monsieur,	Dear Sir:
Messieurs,	Gentlemen:
Cher Monsieur Varnoux,	My dear Mr. Varnoux:
Chère Madame Gignoux,	My dear Mrs. Gignoux:

INFORMAL

Mon Cher Roger	Dear Roger
Ma Chère Denise,	Dear Denise,
Chéri,	Darling *(m)*,
Chérie,	Darling *(f.)*,
Mon Chéri,	My darling (m.),
Ma Chérie,	My darling *(f.)*,

325

1. *Agréez, je vous prie, l'expression de mes salutations les plus distinguées.*
("Please accept the expression of my most distinguished greetings.") Very truly yours.
2. *Veuillez agréer l'expression de mes salutations distinguées.*
("Will you please accept the expression of my distinguished greetings.") Very truly yours.
3. *Veuillez agréer, Monsieur, mes salutations empressées.*
("Sir, please accept my eager greetings.") Yours truly.
4. *Veuillez agréer, Monsieur, mes sincères salutations.*
("Sir, please accept my sincere greetings.") Yours truly.
5. *Agréez, Monsieur, mes salutations distinguées.*
("Sir, accept my distinguished greetings.") Yours truly.
6. *Votre tout dévoué.*
("Your very devoted.") Yours truly.

INFORMAL

1. *Je vous prie de croire à l'expression de mes sentiments de sincère amitié.*
("Please believe in my feelings of sincere friendship.") Very sincerely.
2. *Meilleures amitiés.*
("Best regards.") Sincerely yours.
3. *Amicalement.*
("Kindly.") Sincerely yours.
4. *Mes pensées affectueuses* (or *amicales*).
("My affectionate *or* friendly thoughts.") Sincerely.
5. *En toute amitié.*
("In all friendship.") Your friend.
6. *Amitiés.*
Regards.
7. *Affectueusement.*
Affectionately.
8. *Très affectueusement.*
("Very affectionately.") Affectionately yours.
9. *Je vous prie de bien vouloir transmettre mes respects à Madame votre mère.*
Please give my regards to your mother.
10. *Transmets mes respects à ta famille.*
Give my regards to your family.
11. *Rappelle-moi au bon souvenir de ta famille.*
Remember me to your family.
12. *Embrasse tout le monde pour moi.*
("Kiss everybody for me.") Give my love to everybody.
13. *Je t'embrasse bien fort.* ⎫ Love.
Mille baisers. ⎭
14. *A bientôt.*
See you soon.
15. *Grosses bises.*
Kisses.
16. *Mille baisers.*
A thousand kisses.
17. *Tu me manques.*
I miss you.

5. FORM OF THE ENVELOPE

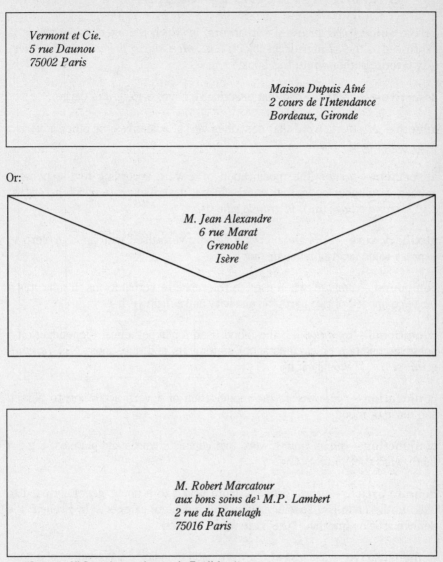

Vermont et Cie.
5 rue Daunou
75002 Paris

Maison Dupuis Aîné
2 cours de l'Intendance
Bordeaux, Gironde

Or:

M. Jean Alexandre
6 rue Marat
Grenoble
Isère

M. Robert Marcatour
aux bons soins de[1] *M.P. Lambert*
2 rue du Ranelagh
75016 Paris

---

[1] *"In care of." Sometimes written as in English: c/o.*

G. DICTIONARY OF
GRAMMATICAL TERMS

active voice—*voix active:* a verbal form in which the agent of an action is expressed as the grammatical subject; e.g., *Mon auteur préféré a écrit ce livre.* (My favorite author wrote this book.)

adjective—*adjectif:* a word that describes a noun; e.g., *grand* (large).

adverb—*adverbe:* a word that describes verbs, adjectives, or other adverbs; e.g., *rapidement* (quickly).

agreement—*accord:* the modification of a word according to the person, gender, or number of another word which it describes or to which it relates; e.g. *le grand village* (m.), *la grande ville* (f.)

auxiliary verb—*verbe auxiliaire:* a helping verb used with another verb to express some facet of tense or mood.

compound—*composé:* when used in reference to verbal forms, it indicates a tense composed of two parts: an auxiliary and a main verb.

conditional—*conditionnel:* the mood used for hypothetical (depending on a possible condition or circumstance) statements and questions; e.g. *Je mangerais si . . .* (I would eat if . . .)

conjugation—*conjugaison:* the modification of a verb according to person and tense or mood.

conjunction—*conjonction:* a word that connects words and phrases; e.g., *et* (and), *mais* (but), etc.

definite article—*article défini:* a word linked to a noun; generally used to indicate the noun is a specific instance of a general category. In French, the definite articles (meaning "the") are *le, la,* and *les.*

demonstrative—*démonstratif:* a word used to indicate the position of a noun in relation to the speaker. Demonstrative adjectives are used together with a noun (*J'aime cette ville.* I like this city.); demonstrative pronouns replace the noun (*J'aime celui-ci.* I like this one.).

direct object—*complément d'objet direct:* the person or thing undergoing the action of a verb. For example, in the sentence "I wrote a letter to John," the direct object is "a letter."

ending—*terminaison:* the suffixes added to the stem that indicate gender, number, tense, mood, or part of speech.

gender—*genre:* grammatical categories for nouns, generally unrelated to physical gender and often determined by word ending. French has two genders —masculine and feminine—which refer to both animate and inanimate nouns; e.g., *le village* (m.), *la ville* (f.).

imperative—*imperatif:* the command form; e.g., *Donnez moi le livre.* (Give me the book.).

imperfect—*imparfait:* the past tense used to describe ongoing or habitual actions or states without a specified time frame; often referred to as the descriptive past tense.

impersonal verb—*verbe impersonnel:* a verb for which the subject is the impersonal pronoun *il* and for which there is no real subject. Impersonal verbs are often used to indicate natural phenomena, such as weather, climate, or time (*Il fait froid en hiver.* It's cold in the winter.), as well as in various set expressions such as *il y a* (there is/are), *il faut que* (it is necessary that), etc.

indefinite article—*article indéfini:* a word linked to a noun; used when referring to a noun or class of nouns in a general way. In French the indefinite articles (meaning "a, an") are *un, une,* and *des.*

indicative—*indicatif:* the mood used for factual or objective statements and questions.

indirect object—*complément d'objet indirect:* the ultimate recipient of the action of a verb, often introduced by a preposition. For example, in the sentence "I wrote a letter to John," the indirect object is "John."

infinitive—*infinitif:* the basic, uninflected form of a verb found in the dictionary, i.e. before the person, number, tense, or mood have been specified; e.g., *parler* (to speak).

intransitive—*intransitif:* a verb which may not take a direct object.

inversion—*inversion:* reversing the order of subject and verb, often used in question formation.

mood—*mode:* a reflection of the speaker's attitude toward what is expressed by the verb. The major moods in French are the indicative, subjunctive, and imperative.

noun—*nom:* a word referring to a person, place, thing, or abstract idea; e.g., *ville* (city), *amour* (love), etc.

number—*nombre:* the distinction between singular and plural.

participle—*participe:* a verbal form that often has the function of an adjective or adverb but may have the verbal features of tense and voice, often used in the formation of compound tenses; e.g., present and past participles: *mangeant/mangé* (eating/eaten).

passive voice—*voix passive:* a verbal form in which the recipient of the action is expressed as the grammatical subject; e.g., *Ce livre a été écrit par mon auteur préféré.* (This book was written by my favorite author.).

person—*personne:* the grammatical category that distinguishes between the speaker (first person—I, we), the person spoken to (second person—you), and the people and things spoken about (third person—he, she, it, they). It is often used in reference to pronouns and verbs.

pluperfect—*plus-que-parfait:* the past perfect.

possessive—*possessif:* indicating ownership; e.g., *mon* (my) is a possessive adjective.

predicate—*attribut:* the part of a clause that expresses the state of the subject; it usually contains the verb with or without objects and complements.

preposition—*préposition:* a word used to express spatial, temporal, or other relationships; e.g., *à* (to), *sur* (on), etc.

present perfect—*passé composé:* the past tense used to describe actions that began and were completed in the past, usually at a single moment or during a specific period, useful for narration of events.

pronominal verb—*verbe pronominal:* a verb conjugated with a pronoun in addition to the subject. The two major groups of pronominal verbs are reflexive (where the action reflects back on the subject:—*se laver* (to wash oneself); and reciprocal, where the subjects, always plural, act upon each other—*se rencontrer* (to meet each other).

pronoun—*pronom:* a word that replaces a noun; e.g., *je* (I), *le* (him/it), *cela* (this).

reciprocal—*reciproque:* see **pronominal**

reflexive—*réfléchi:* see **pronominal.**

simple—*simple:* one-word verbal forms conjugated by adding endings to a stem.

stem—*radical:* in conjugation, the part of a verb used as the base to which endings are added. The stem used to form most simple tenses of French regular verbs is derived by simply dropping the infinitive endings (*-er, -ir,* or *-re*); e.g., *parler → parl- → je parle.*

subject—*sujet:* the agent of an action or the entity experiencing the state described by a verb. For example, in the sentence "I wrote a letter to John," the subject is "I."

subjunctive—*subjonctif:* the mood used for nonfactual or subjective statements or questions.

tense—*temps:* the time of an action or state, i.e., past, present, future.

transitive—*transitif:* a verb which may take a direct object.

verb—*verbe:* a word expressing an action or state; e.g., *écrire* (to write).

H. GRAMMAR SUMMARY

1. SUBJECT PRONOUNS

	SINGULAR		PLURAL
je	I	*nous*	we
tu	you (fam.)	*vous*	you (pl. or polite sing.)
il, elle	he, she, it	*ils*	they (m. or m. + f.)
on	one	*elles*	they (f.)

2. STRESSED PRONOUNS

	SINGULAR		PLURAL
moi	me	*nous*	us
toi	you (fam.)	*vous*	you (pl. or polite sing.)
lui	him	*eux*	them (m. or m. + f.)
elle	her	*elles*	them (f.)

3. REFLEXIVE PRONOUNS

	SINGULAR		PLURAL
me	myself	*nous*	ourselves
te	yourself (fam.)	*vous*	yourself (polite)
se	him/her/it/oneself		yourselves
		se	themselves

4. DIRECT OBJECT PRONOUNS

	SINGULAR		PLURAL
me	me	*nous*	us
te	you (fam.)	*vous*	you (pl. or polite sing.)
le, l'	him, it	*les*	them
la, l'	her, it		

5. INDIRECT OBJECT PRONOUNS

SINGULAR		PLURAL	
me	to me	*nous*	to us
te	to you (fam.)	*vous*	to you (pl. or polite
lui	to him, to her		sing.)
	to it	*leur*	to them

6. DOUBLE OBJECT PRONOUNS— GENERAL PLACEMENT GUIDELINES

FIRST	SECOND	THIRD
me *te* *se* *nous* *vous*	*le* *la* *les*	*lui* *leur*

For example:

*Je **vous les** donne.*
*Elle **les leur** a envoyé(e)s.*

7. DEMONSTRATIVE PRONOUNS

	MASCULINE	FEMININE
SINGULAR	*celui*	*celle*
PLURAL	*ceux*	*celles*

8. POSSESSIVE PRONOUNS

	MASCULINE SINGULAR	MASCULINE PLURAL	FEMININE SINGULAR	FEMININE PLURAL
my	*le mein*	*les miens*	*la mienne*	*les miennes*
your (fam.)	*le tien*	*les tiens*	*la tienne*	*les tiennes*
his, her, its	*le sien*	*les siens*	*la sienne*	*les siennes*
your (polite)	*le vôtre*	*les vôtres*	*la vôtre*	*les vôtres*
our	*le nôtre*	*les nôtres*	*la nôtre*	*les nôtres*
your (pl.)	*le vôtre*	*les vôtres*	*la vôtre*	*les vôtres*
their	*le leur*	*les leurs*	*la leur*	*les leurs*

9. INTERROGATIVE PRONOUNS

	MASCULINE	FEMININE
SINGULAR	*lequel*	*laquelle*
PLURAL	*lesquels*	*lesquelles*

10. PREPOSITIONS + INTERROGATIVE PRONOUNS

PRONOUN	AFTER *DE*	AFTER *À*
lequel	*duquel*	*auquel*
laquelle	*de laquelle*	*à laquelle*
lesquels	*desquels*	*auxquels*
lesquelles	*desquelles*	*auxquelles*

11. PLURAL OF NOUNS—GENERAL GUIDELINES

SINGULAR ENDING	PLURAL ENDING	SINGULAR EXAMPLE	PLURAL EXAMPLE
Regular	-s	*le livre*	*les livres*
-s, -x, -z	no change	*le choix*	*les choix*
-al or -ail	-aux	*le cheval*	*les chevaux*
-au or -eu	-aux or -eux	*l'oiseau*	*les oiseaux*

12. ARTICLES

	DEFINITE	INDEFINITE
MASCULINE	*le*	*un*
FEMININE	*la*	*une*
MASCULINE or FEMININE before vowel or silent *h*	*l'*	*un / une*
PLURAL	*les*	*des*

13. PREPOSITIONS + DEFINITE ARTICLES

PREPOSITION	+ *LE*	+ *LA*	+ *LES*
de	*du*	*de la*	*des*
à	*au*	*à la*	*aux*

14. POSSESSIVE ADJECTIVES

	MASCULINE	FEMININE	PLURAL
my	*mon*	*ma*	*mes*
your	*ton*	*ta*	*tes*
his, her, its	*son*	*sa*	*ses*
our	*notre*	*notre*	*nos*
your	*votre*	*votre*	*vos*
their	*leur*	*leur*	*leurs*

15. INTERROGATIVE ADJECTIVES

	MASCULINE	FEMININE
SINGULAR	*quel*	*quelle*
PLURAL	*quels*	*quelles*

16. DEMONSTRATIVE ADJECTIVES

	MASCULINE	FEMININE
SINGULAR	ce, cet	cette
PLURAL	ces	ces

17. IRREGULAR ADJECTIVES

MASCULINE	MASCULINE before vowel or silent *h*	EXAMPLE
beau	bel	un bel hôtel
nouveau	nouvel	le nouvel ordinateur
vieux	vieil	un vieil homme
ce	cet	cet arbre

18. IRREGULAR COMPARATIVES AND SUPERLATIVES

POSITIVE	COMPARATIVE	SUPERLATIVE
bon	meilleur	le meilleur
mauvais	plus mauvais	le plus mauvais
	pire	le pire
petit	plus petit	le plus petit
	moindre	le moindre

I. VERB CHARTS

1. FORMS OF THE REGULAR VERBS

A. CLASSES I, II, III

INFINITIVE	PRES. & PAST PARTICIPLES	PRESENT INDICATIVE	PRESENT SUBJUNCTIVE†	CONVERSATIONAL PAST	PAST SUBJUNCTIVE	IMPERFECT INDICATIVE
-*er* ending *parler*	*parlant* *parlé*	*parl* + *e* *es* *e* *ons* *ez* *ent*	*parl* + *e* *es* *e* *ions* *iez* *ent*	*j'ai* *tu as* *il a* *nous avons* *vous avez* *ils ont* + *parlé*	*que j'aie* *que tu aies* *qu'il ait* *que nous ayons* *que vous ayez* *qu'ils aient* + *parlé*	*parl* + *ais* *ais* *ait* *ions* *iez* *aient*
-*ir* ending *finir*	*finissant* *fini*	*fin* + *is* *is* *it* *issons* *issez* *issent*	*finiss* + *e* *es* *e* *ions* *iez* *ent*	*j'ai* *tu as* *il a* *nous avons* *vous avez* *ils ont* + *fini*	*que j'aie* *que tu aies* *qu'il ait* *que nous ayons* *que vous ayez* *qu'ils aient* + *fini*	*finiss* + *ais* *ais* *ait* *ions* *iez* *aient*
-*re* ending *vendre*	*vendant* *vendu*	*vend* + *s* *s* — *ons* *ez* *ent*	*vend* + *e* *es* *e* *ions* *iez* *ent*	*j'ai* *tu as* *il a* *nous avons* *vous avez* *ils ont* + *vendu*	*que j'aie* *que tu aies* *qu'il ait* *que nous ayons* *que vous ayez* *qu'ils aient* + *vendu*	*vend* + *ais* *ais* *ait* *ions* *iez* *aient*

† Like the past subjunctive, the present subjunctive verb is always preceded by *que* or *qu'* + the appropriate pronoun, as in *"Il faut que je parle"* and *"Je veux qu'il quitte la maison."*

PAST PERFECT	FUTURE	FUTURE PERFECT	CONDITIONAL	CONDITIONAL PERFECT	IMPERATIVE
j'avais + parlé tu avais il avait nous avions vous aviez ils avaient	parler + ai as a ons ez ont	j'aurai + parlé tu auras il aura nous aurons vous aurez ils auront	parler + ais ais ait ions iez aient	j'aurais + parlé tu aurais il aurait nous aurions vous auriez ils auraient	parle parlons parlez
j'avais + fini tu avais il avait nous avions vous aviez ils avaient	finir + ai as a ons ez ont	j'aurai + fini tu auras il aura nous aurons vous aurez ils auront	finir + ais ais ait ions iez aient	j'aurais + fini tu aurais il aurait nous aurions vous auriez ils auraient	finis finissons finissez
j'avais + vendu tu avais il avait nous avions vous aviez ils avaient	vendr + ai as a ons ez ont	j'aurai + vendu tu auras il aura nous aurons vous aurez ils auront	vendr + ais ais ait ions iez aient	j'aurais + vendu tu aurais il aurait nous aurions vous auriez ils auraient	vends vendons vendez

B. VERBS ENDING IN -CER AND -GER

INFINITIVE	PRES. & PAST PARTICIPLES	PRESENT INDICATIVE	PRESENT SUBJUNCTIVE[†]	CONVERSATIONAL PAST	PAST SUBJUNCTIVE	IMPERFECT INDICATIVE
placer[1]	plaçant placé	place places place plaçons placez placent	place places place placions placiez placent	j'ai tu as il a + placé nous avons vous avez ils ont	que j'aie que tu aies qu'il ait + placé que nous ayons que vous ayez qu'ils aient	plaçais plaçais plaçait placions placiez plaçaient
manger[2]	mangeant mangé	mange manges mange mangeons mangez mangent	mange manges mange mangions mangiez mangent	j'ai tu as il a + mangé nous avons vous avez ils ont	que j'aie que tu aies qu'il ait + mangé que nous ayons que vous ayez qu'ils aient	mangeais mangeais mangeait mangions mangiez mangeaient

[1] Verbs like placer: commencer, lancer, etc.
[2] Verbs like manger: plonger, ranger, arranger, etc.

PAST PERFECT	FUTURE	FUTURE PERFECT	CONDITIONAL	CONDITIONAL PERFECT	IMPERATIVE
j'avais + *placé*	*placer* + *ai*	*j'aurai* + *placé*	*placer* + *ais*	*j'aurais* + *placé*	
tu avais	*as*	*tu auras*	*ais*	*tu aurais*	*place*
il avait	*a*	*il aura*	*ait*	*il aurait*	
nous avions	*ons*	*nous aurons*	*ions*	*nous aurions*	*plaçons*
vous aviez	*ez*	*vous aurez*	*iez*	*vous auriez*	*placez*
ils avaient	*ont*	*ils auront*	*aient*	*ils auraient*	
j'avais + *mangé*	*manger* + *ai*	*j'aurai* + *mangé*	*manger* + *ais*	*j'aurais* + *mangé*	
tu avais	*as*	*tu auras*	*ais*	*tu aurais*	*mange*
il avait	*a*	*il aura*	*ait*	*il aurait*	
nous avions	*ons*	*nous aurons*	*ions*	*nous aurions*	*mangeons*
vous aviez	*ez*	*vous aurez*	*iez*	*vous auriez*	*mangez*
ils avaient	*ont*	*ils auront*	*aient*	*ils auraient*	

C. VERBS ENDING IN -ER WITH CHANGES IN THE STEM

INFINITIVE	PRES. & PAST PARTICIPLES	PRESENT INDICATIVE	PRESENT SUBJUNCTIVE†	CONVERSATIONAL PAST	PAST SUBJUNCTIVE	IMPERFECT INDICATIVE
acheter[1]	*achetant* *acheté*	*achète* *achètes* *achète* *achetons* *achetez* *achètent*	*achète* *achètes* *achète* *achetions* *achetiez* *achètent*	*j'ai* + *acheté* *tu as* *il a* *nous avons* *vous avez* *ils ont*	*que j'aie* + *acheté* *que tu aies* *qu'il ait* *que nous ayons* *que vous ayez* *qu'ils aient*	*achet* + *ais* *ais* *ait* *ions* *iez* *aient*
appeler[2]	*appelant* *appelé*	*appelle* *appelles* *appelle* *appelons* *appelez* *appellent*	*appelle* *appelles* *appelle* *appelions* *appeliez* *appellent*	*j'ai* + *appelé* *tu as* *il a* *nous avons* *vous avez* *ils ont*	*que j'aie* + *appelé* *que tu aies* *qu'il ait* *que nous ayons* *que vous ayez* *qu'ils aient*	*appel* + *ais* *ais* *ait* *ions* *iez* *aient*
payer[3]*	*payant* *payé*	*paie/paye* *paies/payes* *paie/paye* *payons* *payez* *paient/payent*	*paie/paye* *paies/payes* *paie/paye* *payons* *payez* *paient/payent*	*j'ai* + *payé* *tu as* *il a* *nous avons* *vous avez* *ils ont*	*que j'aie* + *payé* *que tu aies* *qu'il ait* *que nous ayons* *que vous ayez* *qu'ils aient*	*pay* + *ais* *ais* *ait* *ions* *iez* *aient*
préférer[4]	*préférant* *préféré*	*préfère* *préfères* *préfère* *préférons* *préférez* *préfèrent*	*préfère* *préfères* *préfère* *préférions* *préfériez* *préfèrent*	*j'ai* + *préféré* *tu as* *il a* *nous avons* *vous avez* *ils ont*	*que j'aie* + *préféré* *que tu aies* *qu'il ait* *que nous ayons* *que vous ayez* *qu'ils aient*	*préfér* + *ais* *ais* *ait* *ions* *iez* *aient*

[1] Verbs like *acheter*: *mener, amener, emmener, se promener, lever, se lever, élever.*

[2] Verbs like *appeler*: *se rappeler, jeter.*

[3] Verbs like *payer*: *essayer, employer, ennuyer, essuyer, nettoyer.* (See note below.)

[4] Verbs like *préférer*: *expérer, répéter, célébrer, considérer, suggérer, protéger.*

* Verbs ending in *-oyer* may use *i* or *y* in the present (except for *nous* and *vous* forms), the future, and the conditional, as in *payer, essayer.* Verbs ending in *-oyer, -uyer* change *y* to *i* (as in *essayer, ennuyer, employer, nettoyer*). These changes are indicated by the use of italic.

	PAST PERFECT	FUTURE	FUTURE PERFECT	CONDITIONAL	CONDITIONAL PERFECT	IMPERATIVE
acheter	j'avais tu avais il avait nous avions vous aviez ils avaient + acheté	achèter + ai as a ons ez ont	j'aurai tu auras il aura nous aurons vous aurez ils auront + acheté	achèter + ais ais ait ions iez aient	j'aurais tu aurais il aurait nous aurions vous auriez ils auraient + acheté	achète achetons achetez
appeler	j'avais tu avais il avait nous avions vous aviez ils avaient + appelé	appeller + ai as a ons ez ont	j'aurai tu auras il aura nous aurons vous aurez ils auront + appelé	appeller + ais ais ait ions iez aient	j'aurais tu aurais il aurait nous aurions vous auriez ils auraient + appelé	appelle appelons appelez
payer	j'avais tu avais il avait nous avions vous aviez ils avaient + payé	paier or payer + ai as a ons ez ont	j'aurai tu auras il aura nous aurons vous aurez ils auront + payé	paier or payer + ais ais ait ions iez aient	j'aurais tu aurais il aurait nous aurions vous auriez ils auraient + payé	paie/paye payons payez
préférer	j'avais tu avais il avait nous avions vous aviez ils avaient + préféré	préférer + ai as a ons ez ont	j'aurai tu auras il aura nous aurons vous aurez ils auront + préféré	préférer + ais ais ait ions iez aient	j'aurais tu aurais il aurait nous aurions vous auriez ils auraient + préféré	préfère préférons préférez

D. VERBS ENDING IN -OIR

INFINITIVE	PRES. & PAST PARTICIPLES	PRESENT INDICATIVE	PRESENT SUBJUNCTIVE †	CONVERSATIONAL PAST	PAST SUBJUNCTIVE	IMPERFECT INDICATIVE
recevoir[1]	recevant	reçois	reçoive	j'ai	que j'aie	recev + ais
	reçu	reçois	reçoives	tu as	que tu aies	ais
		reçoit	reçoive	il a	qu'il ait	ait
		recevons	recevions	nous avons	que nous ayons	ions
		recevez	receviez	vous avez	que vous ayez	iez
		reçoivent	reçoivent	ils ont	qu'ils aient	aient
				+ reçu	+ reçu	

FUTURE	FUTURE PERFECT	CONDITIONAL	CONDITIONAL PERFECT	IMPERATIVE
recevr + ai	j'aurai	recevr + ais	j'aurais	reçois
as	tu auras	ais	tu aurais	recevons
a	il aura	ait	il aurait	recevez
ons	nous aurons	ions	nous aurions	
ez	vous aurez	iez	vous auriez	
ont	ils auront	aient	ils auraient	
	+ reçu		+ reçu	

PAST PERFECT
j'avais
tu avais
il avait
nous avions
vous aviez
ils avaient
+ reçu

[1] Verbs like recevoir: devoir (dois, doive, dû).

E. VERBS ENDING IN -NDRE

INFINITIVE	PRES. & PAST PARTICIPLES	PRESENT INDICATIVE	PRESENT SUBJUNCTIVE†	CONVERSATIONAL PAST	PAST SUBJUNCTIVE	IMPERFECT INDICATIVE
craindre¹	craignant craint	crains crains craint craignons craignez craignent	craigne craignes craigne craignions craigniez craignent	j'ai tu as il a + craint nous avons vous avez ils ont	que j'aie que tu aies qu'il ait + craint que nous ayons que vous ayez qu'ils aient	craign + ais ais ait ions iez aient
éteindre²	éteignant éteint	éteins éteins éteint éteignons éteignez éteignent	éteigne éteignes éteigne éteignions éteigniez éteignent	j'ai tu as il a + éteint nous avons vous avez ils ont	que j'aie que tu aies qu'il ait + éteint que nous ayons que vous ayez qu'ils aient	éteign + ais ais ait ions iez aient

¹ Verbs like *craindre*: *plaindre*, to pity. The reflexive form, *se plaindre*, means "to complain," and in the compound tenses is conjugated with *être*.
² Verbs like *éteindre*: *peindre*, to paint; *teindre*, to dye.

PAST PERFECT	FUTURE	FUTURE PERFECT	CONDITIONAL	CONDITIONAL PERFECT	IMPERATIVE
j'avais tu avais il avait + craint nous avions vous aviez ils avaient	craindr + ai as a ons ez ont	j'aurai tu auras il aura + craint nous aurons vous aurez ils auront	craindr + ais ais ait ions iez aient	j'aurais tu aurais il aurait + craint nous aurions vous auriez ils auraient	crains craignons craignez
j'avais tu avais il avait + éteint nous avions vous aviez ils avaient	éteindr + ai as a ons ez ont	j'aurai tu auras il aura + éteint nous aurons vous aurez ils auront	éteindr + ais ais ait ions iez aient	j'aurais tu aurais il aurait + éteint nous aurions vous auriez ils auraient	éteins éteignons éteignez

F. COMPOUND TENSES OF VERBS CONJUGATED WITH *ÊTRE*

CONVERSATIONAL PAST	PAST SUBJUNCTIVE	PAST PERFECT	FUTURE PERFECT	CONDITIONAL PERFECT
je suis allé(e)	que je sois allé(e)	j'étais allé(e)	je serai allé(e)	je serais allé(e)
tu es allé(e)	que tu sois allé(e)	tu étais allé(e)	tu seras allé(e)	tu serais allé(e)
il est allé	qu'il soit allé	il était allé	il sera allé	il serait allé
elle est allée	qu'elle soit allée	elle était allée	elle sera allée	elle serait allée
nous sommes allé(e)s	que nous soyons allé(e)s	nous étions allé(e)s	nous serons allé(e)s	nous serions allé(e)s
vous êtes allé(e)(s)	que vous soyez allé(e)(s)	vous étiez allé(e)(s)	vous serez allé(e)(s)	vous seriez allé(e)(s)
ils sont allés	qu'ils soient allés	ils étaient allés	ils seront allés	ils seraient allés
elles sont allées	qu'elles soient allées	elles étaient allées	elles seront allées	elles seraient allées

G. COMPOUND TENSES OF REFLEXIVE VERBS (ALL REFLEXIVE VERBS ARE CONJUGATED WITH *ÊTRE*)

CONVERSATIONAL PAST	PAST SUBJUNCTIVE	PAST PERFECT	FUTURE PERFECT	CONDITIONAL PERFECT
je me suis levé(e)	*que je me sois levé(e)*	*je m'étais levé(e)*	*je me serai levé(e)*	*je me serais levé(e)*
tu t'es levé(e)	*que tu te sois levé(e)*	*tu t'étais levé(e)*	*tu te seras levé(e)*	*tu te serais levé(e)*
il s'est levé	*qu'il se soit levé*	*il s'était levé*	*il se sera levé*	*il se serait levé*
elle s'est levée	*qu'elle se soit levée*	*elle s'était levée*	*elle se sera levée*	*elle se serait levée*
nous nous sommes levé(e)s	*que nous nous soyons levé(e)s*	*nous nous étions levé(e)s*	*nous nous serons levé(e)s*	*nous nous serions levé(e)s*
vous vous êtes levé(e)(s)	*que vous vous soyez levé(e)(s)*	*vous vous étiez levé(e)(s)*	*vous vous serez levé(e)(s)*	*vous vous seriez levé(e)(s)*
ils se sont levés	*qu'ils se soient levés*	*ils s'étaient levés*	*ils se seront levés*	*ils se seraient levés*
elles se sont levées	*qu'elles se soient levées*	*elles s'étaient levées*	*elles se seront levées*	*elles se seraient levées*

2. FREQUENTLY USED IRREGULAR VERBS

The correct auxiliary verb is indicated in parentheses below each verb. For compound tenses, use the appropriate form of the auxiliary verb + past participle.

INFINITIVE	PRES. & PAST PARTICIPLES	PRESENT INDICATIVE	PRESENT SUBJUNCTIVE	IMPERFECT INDICATIVE	FUTURE	CONDITIONAL	IMPERATIVE
aquérir to acquire (*avoir*)	*acquérant* *acquis*	*acquiers* *acquiers* *acquiert* *acquérons* *acquérez* *acquièrent*	*acquière* *acquières* *acquière* *acquiérions* *acquiériez* *acquièrent*	*acquér* + *ais* *ais* *ait* *ions* *iez* *aient*	*acquerr* + *ai* *as* *a* *ons* *ez* *ont*	*acquerr* + *ais* *ais* *ait* *ions* *iez* *aient*	*acquiers* *acquérons* *acquérez*
aller to go (*être*)	*allant* *allé(e)(s)*	*vais* *vas* *va* *allons* *allez* *vont*	*aille* *ailles* *aille* *allions* *alliez* *aillent*	*all* + *ais* *ais* *ait* *ions* *iez* *aient*	*ir* + *ai* *as* *a* *ons* *ez* *ont*	*ir* + *ais* *ais* *ait* *ions* *iez* *aient*	*va* *allons* *allez*
(*s'*)*asseoir*† to sit (down) (*être*)	*asseyant* *assis(e)(s)*	*assieds* *assieds* *assied* *asseyons* *asseyez* *asseyent*	*asseye* *asseyes* *asseye* *asseyions* *asseyiez* *asseyent*	*assey* + *ais* *ais* *ait* *ions* *iez* *aient*	*asseyer* + *ai* *as* or *assiér* + *a* *ons* or *assoir* + *ez* *ont*	*asseyer* + *ais* *ais* or *assiér* + *ait* *ions* or *assoir* + *iez* *aient*	*assieds-toi* *asseyons-nous* *asseyez-vous*

† There is a variant form of the conjugation of *s'asseoir* based on the present participle *assoyant* and first person singular *assois*, but this is rather archaic and is rarely used. There are also two variant forms for the future stem: *assiér-* and *assoir-*. *Assiér-* is frequently used.

INFINITIVE	PRES. & PAST PARTICIPLES	PRESENT INDICATIVE	PRESENT SUBJUNCTIVE	IMPERFECT INDICATIVE	FUTURE	CONDITIONAL	IMPERATIVE
avoir to have (*avoir*)	*ayant* *eu*	*ai* *as* *a* *avons* *avez* *ont*	*aie* *aies* *ait* *ayons* *ayez* *aient*	*av* + *ais* *ais* *ait* *ions* *iez* *aient*	*aur* + *ai* *as* *a* *ons* *ez* *ont*	*aur* + *ais* *ais* *ait* *ions* *iez* *aient*	*aie* *ayons* *ayez*
battre to beat (*avoir*)	*battant* *battu*	*bats* *bats* *bat* *battons* *battez* *battent*	*batte* *battes* *batte* *battions* *battiez* *battent*	*batt* + *ais* *ais* *ait* *ions* *iez* *aient*	*battr* + *ai* *as* *a* *ons* *ez* *ont*	*battr* + *ais* *ais* *ait* *ions* *iez* *aient*	*bats* *battons* *battez*
boire to drink (*avoir*)	*buvant* *bu*	*bois* *bois* *boit* *buvons* *buvez* *boivent*	*boive* *boives* *boive* *buvions* *buviez* *boivent*	*buv* + *ais* *ais* *ait* *ions* *iez* *aient*	*boir* + *ai* *as* *a* *ons* *ez* *ont*	*boir* + *ais* *ais* *ait* *ions* *iez* *aient*	*bois* *buvons* *buvez*
conclure to conclude (*avoir*)	*concluant* *conclu*	*conclus* *conclus* *conclut* *concluons* *concluez* *concluent*	*conclue* *conclues* *conclue* *concluions* *concluiez* *concluent*	*conclu* + *ais* *ais* *ait* *ions* *iez* *aient*	*conclur* + *ai* *as* *a* *ons* *ez* *ont*	*conclur* + *ais* *ais* *ait* *ions* *iez* *aient*	*conclus* *concluons* *concluez*

INFINITIVE	PRES. & PAST PARTICIPLES	PRESENT INDICATIVE	PRESENT SUBJUNCTIVE	IMPERFECT INDICATIVE	FUTURE	CONDITIONAL	IMPERATIVE
conduire to drive to lead (avoir)	conduisant conduit	conduis conduis conduit conduisons conduisez conduisent	conduise conduises conduise conduisions conduisiez conduisent	conduis + ais ais ait ions iez aient	conduir + ai as a ons ez ont	conduir + ais ais ait ions iez aient	conduis conduisons conduisez
connaître to know (avoir)	connaissant connu	connais connais connaît connaissons connaissez connaissent	connaisse connaisses connaisse connaissions connaissiez connaissent	connaiss + ais ais ait ions iez aient	connaîtr + ai as a ons ez ont	connaîtr + ais ais ait ions iez aient	connais connaissons connaissez
courir to run (avoir)	courant couru	cours cours court courons courez courent	coure coures coure courions couriez courent	cour + ais ais ait ions iez aient	courr + ai as a ons ez ont	courr + ais ais ait ions iez aient	cours courons courez

INFINITIVE	PRES. & PAST PARTICIPLES	PRESENT INDICATIVE	PRESENT SUBJUNCTIVE	IMPERFECT INDICATIVE	FUTURE	CONDITIONAL	IMPERATIVE
croire to believe (*avoir*)	*croyant* *cru*	*crois* *crois* *croit* *croyons* *croyez* *croient*	*croie* *croies* *croie* *croyions* *croyiez* *croient*	*croy* + *ais* *ais* *ait* *ions* *iez* *aient*	*croir* + *ai* *as* *a* *ons* *ez* *ont*	*croir* + *ais* *ais* *ait* *ions* *iez* *aient*	*crois* *croyons* *croyez*
cueillir to gather to pick (*avoir*)	*cueillant* *cueilli*	*cueille* *cueilles* *cueille* *cueillons* *cueillez* *cueillent*	*cueille* *cueilles* *cueille* *cueillions* *cueilliez* *cueillent*	*cueill* + *ais* *ais* *ait* *ions* *iez* *aient*	*cueiller* + *ai* *as* *a* *ons* *ez* *ont*	*cueiller* + *ais* *ais* *ait* *ions* *iez* *aient*	*cueille* *cueillons* *cueillez*
devoir must to owe to ought (*avoir*)	*devant* *dû*	*dois* *dois* *doit* *devons* *devez* *doivent*	*doive* *doives* *doive* *devions* *deviez* *doivent*	*dev* + *ais* *ais* *ait* *ions* *iez* *aient*	*devr* + *ai* *as* *a* *ons* *ez* *ont*	*devr* + *ais* *ais* *ait* *ions* *iez* *aient*	not used
dire to say to tell (*avoir*)	*disant* *dit*	*dis* *dis* *dit* *disons* *dites* *disent*	*dise* *dises* *dise* *disions* *disiez* *disent*	*dis* + *ais* *ais* *ait* *ions* *iez* *aient*	*dir* + *ai* *as* *a* *ons* *ez* *ont*	*dir* + *ais* *ais* *ait* *ions* *iez* *aient*	*dis* *disons* *dites*

INFINITIVE	PRES. & PAST PARTICIPLES	PRESENT INDICATIVE	PRESENT SUBJUNCTIVE	IMPERFECT INDICATIVE	FUTURE	CONDITIONAL	IMPERATIVE
dormir to sleep (*avoir*)	*dormant* *dormi*	*dors* *dors* *dort* *dormons* *dormez* *dorment*	*dorme* *dormes* *dorme* *dormions* *dormiez* *dorment*	*dorm* + *ais* *ais* *ait* *ions* *iez* *aient*	*dormir* + *ai* *as* *a* *ons* *ez* *ont*	*dormir* + *ais* *ais* *ait* *ions* *iez* *aient*	*dors* *dormons* *dormez*
écrire to write (*avoir*)	*écrivant* *écrit*	*écris* *écris* *écrit* *écrivons* *écrivez* *écrivent*	*écrive* *écrives* *écrive* *écrivions* *écriviez* *écrivent*	*écriv* + *ais* *ais* *ait* *ions* *iez* *aient*	*écrir* + *ai* *as* *a* *ons* *ez* *ont*	*écrir* + *ais* *ais* *ait* *ions* *iez* *aient*	*écris* *écrivons* *écrivez*
envoyer to send (*avoir*)	*envoyant* *envoyé*	*envoie* *envoies* *envoie* *envoyons* *envoyez* *envoient*	*envoie* *envoies* *envoie* *envoyions* *envoyiez* *envoient*	*envoy* + *ais* *ais* *ait* *ions* *iez* *aient*	*enverr* + *ai* *as* *a* *ons* *ez* *ont*	*enverr* + *ais* *ais* *ait* *ions* *iez* *aient*	*envoie* *envoyons* *envoyez*
être to be (*avoir*)	*étant* *été*	*suis* *es* *est* *sommes* *êtes* *sont*	*sois* *sois* *soit* *soyons* *soyez* *soient*	*ét* + *ais* *ais* *ait* *ions* *iez* *aient*	*ser* + *ai* *as* *a* *ons* *ez* *ont*	*ser* + *ais* *ais* *ait* *ions* *iez* *aient*	*sois* *soyons* *soyez*

INFINITIVE	PRES. & PAST PARTICIPLES	PRESENT INDICATIVE	PRESENT SUBJUNCTIVE	IMPERFECT INDICATIVE	FUTURE	CONDITIONAL	IMPERATIVE
faillir† to fail *(avoir)*	*faillant* *failli*	not used	not used	not used	*faillir* + *ai* *as* *a* *ons* *ez* *ont*	*faillir* + *ais* *ais* *ait* *ions* *iez* *aient*	not used
faire to do to make *(avoir)*	*faisant* *fait*	*fais* *fais* *fait* *faisons* *faites* *font*	*fasse* *fasses* *fasse* *fassions* *fassiez* *fassent*	*fais* + *ais* *ais* *ait* *ions* *iez* *aient*	*fer* + *ai* *as* *a* *ons* *ez* *ont*	*fer* + *ais* *ais* *ait* *ions* *iez* *aient*	*fais* *faisons* *faites*
falloir to be necessary, must (used only with *il*) *(avoir)*	no pres. part. *fallu*	*il faut*	*il faille*	*il fallait*	*il faudra*	*il faudrait*	not used
fuir to flee *(avoir)*	*fuyant* *fui*	*fuis* *fuis* *fuit* *fuyons* *fuyez* *fuient*	*fuie* *fuies* *fuie* *fuyions* *fuyiez* *fuient*	*fuy* + *ais* *ais* *ait* *ions* *iez* *aient*	*fuir* + *ai* *as* *a* *ons* *ez* *ont*	*fuir* + *ais* *ais* *ait* *ions* *iez* *aient*	*fuis* *fuyons* *fuyez*

† Used in expressions such as *Il a failli tomber.* He nearly fell (lit., he failed to fall).

INFINITIVE	PRES. & PAST PARTICIPLES	PRESENT INDICATIVE	PRESENT SUBJUNCTIVE	IMPERFECT INDICATIVE	FUTURE	CONDITIONAL	IMPERATIVE
haïr to hate (*avoir*)	*haïssant* *haï*	*hais* *hais* *hait* *haïssons* *haïssez* *haïssent*	*haïsse* *haïsses* *haïsse* *haïssions* *haïssiez* *haïssent*	*haïss* + *ais* *ais* *ait* *ions* *iez* *aient*	*haïr* + *ai* *as* *a* *ons* *ez* *ont*	*haïr* + *ais* *ais* *ait* *ions* *iez* *aient*	*hais* *haïssons* *haïssez*
lire to read (*avoir*)	*lisant* *lu*	*lis* *lis* *lit* *lisons* *lisez* *lisent*	*lise* *lises* *lise* *lisions* *lisiez* *lisent*	*lis* + *ais* *ais* *ait* *ions* *iez* *aient*	*lir* + *ai* *as* *a* *ons* *ez* *ont*	*lir* + *ais* *ais* *ait* *ions* *iez* *aient*	*lis* *lisons* *lisez*
mettre to put to place (*avoir*)	*mettant* *mis*	*mets* *mets* *met* *mettons* *mettez* *mettent*	*mette* *mettes* *mette* *mettions* *mettiez* *mettent*	*mett* + *ais* *ais* *ait* *ions* *iez* *aient*	*mettr* + *ai* *as* *a* *ons* *ez* *ont*	*mettr* + *ais* *ais* *ait* *ions* *iez* *aient*	*mets* *mettons* *mettez*

INFINITIVE	PRES. & PAST PARTICIPLES	PRESENT INDICATIVE	PRESENT SUBJUNCTIVE	IMPERFECT INDICATIVE	FUTURE	CONDITIONAL	IMPERATIVE
mourir to die (*être*)	*mourant* *mort(e)(s)*	*meurs* *meurs* *meurt* *mourons* *mourez* *meurent*	*meure* *meures* *meure* *mourions* *mouriez* *meurent*	*mour +* *ais ais ait ions iez aient*	*mourr +* *ai as a ons ez ont*	*mourr +* *ais ais ait ions iez aient*	*meurs* *mourons* *mourez*
mouvoir† to move (*avoir*)	*mouvant* *mû*	*meus* *meus* *meut* *mouvons* *mouvez* *meuvent*	*meuve* *meuves* *meuve* *mouvions* *mouviez* *meuvent*	*mouv +* *ais ais ait ions iez aient*	*mouvr +* *ai as a ons ez ont*	*mouvr +* *ais ais ait ions iez aient*	*meus* *mouvons* *mouvez*
naître to be born (*être*)	*naissant* *né(e)(s)*	*nais* *nais* *naît* *naissons* *naissez* *naissent*	*naisse* *naisses* *naisse* *naissions* *naissiez* *naissent*	*naiss +* *ais ais ait ions iez aient*	*naîtr +* *ai as a ons ez ont*	*naîtr +* *ais ais ait ions iez aient*	*nais* *naissons* *naissez*
ouvrir to open (*avoir*)	*ouvrant* *ouvert*	*ouvre* *ouvres* *ouvre* *ouvrons* *ouvrez* *ouvrent*	*ouvre* *ouvres* *ouvre* *ouvrions* *ouvriez* *ouvrent*	*ouvr +* *ais ais ait ions iez aient*	*ouvrir +* *ai as a ons ez ont*	*ouvrir +* *ais ais ait ions iez aient*	*ouvre* *ouvrons* *ouvrez*

† *Mouvoir* is seldom used except in compounds like *émouvoir*, to move (emotionally).

INFINITIVE	PRES. & PAST PARTICIPLES	PRESENT INDICATIVE	PRESENT SUBJUNCTIVE	IMPERFECT INDICATIVE	FUTURE	CONDITIONAL	IMPERATIVE
partir to leave to depart (*être*)	*partant* *parti(e)(s)*	*pars* *pars* *part* *partons* *partez* *partent*	*parte* *partes* *parte* *partions* *partiez* *partent*	*partir + ais* *ais* *ait* *ions* *iez* *aient*	*partir + ai* *as* *a* *ons* *ez* *ont*	*partir + ais* *ais* *ait* *ions* *iez* *aient*	*pars* *partons* *partez*
plaire to please (to be pleasing to) (*avoir*)	*plaisant* *plu*	*plais* *plais* *plaît* *plaisons* *plaisez* *plaisent*	*plaise* *plaises* *plaise* *plaisions* *plaisiez* *plaisent*	*plais + ais* *ais* *ait* *ions* *iez* *aient*	*plair + ai* *as* *a* *ons* *ez* *ont*	*plair + ais* *ais* *ait* *ions* *iez* *aient*	*plais* *plaisons* *plaisez*
pleuvoir to rain (used only with *il*) (*avoir*)	*pleuvant* *plu*	*il pleut*	*il pleuve*	*il pleuvait*	*il pleuvra*	*il pleuvrait*	not used
pouvoir† to be able, can (*avoir*)	*pouvant* *pu*	*peux (puis)*† *peux* *peut* *pouvons* *pouvez* *peuvent*	*puisse* *puisses* *puisse* *puissions* *puissiez* *puissent*	*pouv + ais* *ais* *ait* *ions* *iez* *aient*	*pourr + ai* *as* *a* *ons* *ez* *ont*	*pourr + ais* *ais* *ait* *ions* *iez* *aient*	not used
prendre to take (*avoir*)	*prenant* *pris*	*prends* *prends* *prend* *prenons* *prenez* *prennent*	*prenne* *prennes* *prenne* *prenions* *preniez* *prennent*	*pren + ais* *ais* *ait* *ions* *iez* *aient*	*prendr + ai* *as* *a* *ons* *ez* *ont*	*prendr + ais* *ais* *ait* *ions* *iez* *aient*	*prends* *prenons* *prenez*

† The interrogative of *pouvoir* in the first person singular is always *Puis-je?*

INFINITIVE	PRES. & PAST PARTICIPLES	PRESENT INDICATIVE	PRESENT SUBJUNCTIVE	IMPERFECT INDICATIVE	FUTURE	CONDITIONAL	IMPERATIVE
résoudre to resolve (*avoir*)	*résolvant* *résolu*	*résous* *résous* *résout* *résolvons* *résolvez* *résolvent*	*résolve* *résolves* *résolve* *résolvions* *résolviez* *résolvent*	*résolv* + *ais* *ais* *ait* *ions* *iez* *aient*	*résoudr* + *ai* *as* *a* *ons* *ez* *ont*	*résoudr* + *ais* *ais* *ait* *ions* *iez* *aient*	 *résous* *résolvons* *résolvez*
rire to laugh (*avoir*)	*riant* *ri*	*ris* *ris* *rit* *rions* *riez* *rient*	*rie* *ries* *rie* *riions* *riiez* *rient*	*ri* + *ais* *ais* *ait* *ions* *iez* *aient*	*rir* + *ai* *as* *a* *ons* *ez* *ont*	*rir* + *ais* *ais* *ait* *ions* *iez* *aient*	 *ris* *rions* *riez*
savoir to know (*avoir*)	*sachant* *su*	*sais* *sais* *sait* *savons* *savez* *savent*	*sache* *saches* *sache* *sachions* *sachiez* *sachent*	*sav* + *ais* *ais* *ait* *ions* *iez* *aient*	*saur* + *ai* *as* *a* *ons* *ez* *ont*	*saur* + *ais* *ais* *ait* *ions* *iez* *aient*	 *sache* *sachons* *sachez*
suffire to be enough, to suffice (*avoir*)	*suffisant* *suffi*	*suffis* *suffis* *suffit* *suffisons* *suffisez* *suffisent*	*suffise* *suffises* *suffise* *suffisions* *suffisiez* *suffisent*	*suffis* + *ais* *ais* *ait* *ions* *iez* *aient*	*suffir* + *ai* *as* *a* *ons* *ez* *ont*	*suffir* + *ais* *ais* *ait* *ions* *iez* *aient*	 *suffis* *suffisons* *suffisez*

INFINITIVE	PRES. & PAST PARTICIPLES	PRESENT INDICATIVE	PRESENT SUBJUNCTIVE	IMPERFECT INDICATIVE	FUTURE	CONDITIONAL	IMPERATIVE
suivre to follow (*avoir*)	*suivant* *suivi*	*suis* *suis* *suit* *suivons* *suivez* *suivent*	*suive* *suives* *suive* *suivions* *suiviez* *suivent*	*suiv* + *ais* *ais* *ait* *ions* *iez* *aient*	*suivr* + *ai* *as* *a* *ons* *ez* *ont*	*suivr* + *ais* *ais* *ait* *ions* *iez* *aient*	*suis* *suivons* *suivez*
(se)taire to be quiet, to say nothing (*être*)	*taisant* *tu(e)(s)*	*tais* *tais* *tait* *taisons* *taisez* *taisent*	*taise* *taises* *taise* *taisions* *taisiez* *taisent*	*tais* + *ais* *ais* *ait* *ions* *iez* *aient*	*tair* + *ai* *as* *a* *ons* *ez* *ont*	*tair* + *ais* *ais* *ait* *ions* *iez* *aient*	*tais-toi* *taisons-nous* *taisez-vous*
tenir to hold, to keep (*avoir*)	*tenant* *tenu*	*tiens* *tiens* *tient* *tenons* *tenez* *tiennent*	*tienne* *tiennes* *tienne* *tenions* *teniez* *tiennent*	*ten* + *ais* *ais* *ait* *ions* *iez* *aient*	*tiendr* + *ai* *as* *a* *ons* *ez* *ont*	*tiendr* + *ais* *ais* *ait* *ions* *iez* *aient*	*tiens* *tenons* *tenez*
vaincre to conquer (*avoir*)	*vainquant* *vaincu*	*vaincs* *vaincs* *vainc* *vainquons* *vainquez* *vainquent*	*vainque* *vainques* *vainque* *vainquions* *vainquiez* *vainquent*	*vainqu* + *ais* *ais* *ait* *ions* *iez* *aient*	*vaincr* + *ai* *as* *a* *ons* *ez* *ont*	*vaincr* + *ais* *ais* *ait* *ions* *iez* *aient*	*vaincs* *vainquons* *vainquez*

INFINITIVE	PRES. & PAST PARTICIPLES	PRESENT INDICATIVE	PRESENT SUBJUNCTIVE	IMPERFECT INDICATIVE	FUTURE	CONDITIONAL	IMPERATIVE
valoir to be worth *(avoir)*	*valant* *valu*	*vaux* *vaux* *vaut* *valons* *valez* *valent*	*vaille* *vailles* *vaille* *valions* *valiez* *vaillent*	*val + ais* *ais* *ait* *ions* *iez* *aient*	*vaudr + ai* *as* *a* *ons* *ez* *ont*	*vaudr + ais* *ais* *ait* *ions* *iez* *aient*	*vaux* † *valons* *valez*
venir to come *(être)*	*venant* *venu(e)(s)*	*viens* *viens* *vient* *venons* *venez* *viennent*	*vienne* *viennes* *vienne* *venions* *veniez* *viennent*	*ven + ais* *ais* *ait* *ions* *iez* *aient*	*viendr + ai* *as* *a* *ons* *ez* *ont*	*viendr + ais* *ais* *ait* *ions* *iez* *aient*	*viens* *venons* *venez*
vivre to live *(avoir)*	*vivant* *vécu*	*vis* *vis* *vit* *vivons* *vivez* *vivent*	*vive* *vives* *vive* *vivions* *viviez* *vivent*	*viv + ais* *ais* *ait* *ions* *iez* *aient*	*vivr + ai* *as* *a* *ons* *ez* *ont*	*vivr + ais* *ais* *ait* *ions* *iez* *aient*	*vis* *vivons* *vivez*
voir to see *(avoir)*	*voyant* *vu*	*vois* *vois* *voit* *voyons* *voyez* *voient*	*voie* *voies* *voie* *voyions* *voyiez* *voient*	*voy + ais* *ais* *ait* *ions* *iez* *aient*	*verr + ai* *as* *a* *ons* *ez* *ont*	*verr + ais* *ais* *ait* *ions* *iez* *aient*	*vois* *voyons* *voyez*

† The imperative of *valoir* is not often used.

GLOSSARY

FRENCH–ENGLISH

A

à *to, in, at*
  à bientôt *see you soon*
  à côté *next to*
  à droite *on the right*
  à fond *in depth*
  à gauche *on the left*
  à l'étranger *abroad*
  à l'improviste *unexpectedly*
  à la hausse *on the rise*
  à la légère *lightly*
  à la retraite *retired*
  à merveille *wonderfully*
  à peine *hardly*
  à pied *on foot*
  à vos/te souhaits *Bless you (after sneezing)*
  à votre disposition *at your disposal*
  au fait *by the way*
  au fond *in the back*
  au hasard *at random*
  au milieu *in the middle*
  au revoir *good-bye*
abat-jour *(m)* *lamp shade*
aborder *to approach*
acacia *(m)* *acacia*
acajou *(m)* *mahogany*
accouchement *(m)* *delivery (of a baby)*
accrocher *to hang*
accueil *(m)* *reception; welcome*
accuser *to accuse*
acheter *to buy*
achever *to finish; to complete*
acier *(m)* *steel*
action *(f)* *action; stock*
actualités *(f.pl.)* *news*
actuel *present*
actuellement *presently*
addition *(f)* *bill (in a restaurant)*
adieu *(m)* *farewell*
adorer *to love; to adore*
affaires *(f.pl.)* *business*
affiche *(f)* *poster*
afficher *to post*
affûter *to sharpen*
âge *(m)* *age*
agent immobilier *(m)* *real estate broker*
agneau *(m)* *lamb*
agréable *pleasant*
agrumes *(m.pl.)* *citrus fruits*
aider *to help*
ail *(m)* *garlic*
ailleurs *elsewhere*

aimer *to love*
alcootest *(m)* *breathalizer test*
algue *(f)* *seaweed*
aller *to go*
  aller et retour *round-trip (ticket)*
  aller simple *one-way (ticket)*
allergie *(f)* *allergy*
allergique *allergic*
allonger (se) *to lie down*
alors *then*
amateur *(m)* *amateur; lover of*
ambré *amber-colored*
amer *bitter*
américain *American*
ami(e) *(m.,f.)* *friend*
amour *(m)* *love*
amuser (se) *to enjoy oneself*
an *(m)* *year*
androgyne *androgynous*
anglais *English*
année *(f)* *year*
anniversaire *(m)* *birthday*
annoncer *to announce*
anticorps *(m.pl.)* *antibodies*
antillais *Caribbean*
antiquaire *(m)* *antique dealer*
antitabac *(m)* *anti-smoking*
août *August*
apercevoir (se) *to realize*
apercevoir *to notice*
appareil *(m)* *receiver*
appartement *(m)* *apartment*
appartenir *to belong to*
appeler *to call*
apporter *to bring*
apprendre *to learn*
apprentissage sur le tas *(m)* *on-the-job training*
approcher (se) *to come close*
après *after*
après-midi *(f)* *afternoon*
araignée *(f)* *spider*
arborer *to display*
architecte *(m)* *architect*
architecture *(f)* *architecture*
argent *(m)* *money*
argent liquide *(m)* *cash*
argenterie *(f)* *silverware*
armoire *(f)* *armoire*
arôme *(m)* *aroma*
arracher *to pull*
arrêter (se) *to stop*
arrhes *(m.pl.)* *deposit*

arrivée *(f)* *arrival*
arriver *to arrive*
arroser *to drink to, to toast*
artichaut *(m)* *artichoke*
article *(m)* *article*
artisan *(m)* *craftsman*
ascenseur *(m)* *elevator*
asperge *(f)* *asparagus*
asseoir (se) *to sit down*
assez *enough; fairly*
astreignant *demanding*
atelier *(m)* *workshop, studio*
atteindre *to attain, to reach*
attendre *to wait*
attendre un enfant *to expect a baby*
atterrir *to land*
aubergine *(f)* *eggplant*
audacieux *daring*
auditoire *(m)* *audience*
augmentation *(f)* *increase; raise*
augmenter *to increase*
aujourd'hui *today*
aussi *also*
autant *as much*
autobus *(m)* *bus (intra-city)*
autocar *(m)* *bus (inter-city)*
automne *(f)* *fall*
autonomie *(f)* *self-sufficient; battery-run*
autoroute *(f)* *highway*
autre *other*
autrefois *formerly*
avancer *to advance; to promote*
  avancer à tâtons *to tiptoe*
avant *before*
avec *with*
averse *(f)* *shower*
avis *(m)* *opinion, notice*
avoir *to have*
  avoir besoin *to need*
  avoir du mal *to have trouble*
  avoir envie *to feel like*
  avoir hâte *to be eager*
  avoir l'air *to seem, to appear*
  avoir l'intention *to intend*
  avoir l'occasion *to have the opportunity*
  avoir le chic *to have a knack*
  avoir lieu *to take place*
  avoir mal *to hurt*
  avoir peur *to fear*
  avoir tort *to be wrong*
avouer *to admit*
avril *April*

B

bagage *(m)* *luggage*
bail *(m)* *lease*
baisser *to lower*
bal *(m)* *ball*
baladeur *(m)* *Walkman*
balai *(m)* *broom*

balle de tennis *(f)* *tennis ball*
banlieue *(f)* *suburbs*
banque *(f)* *bank*
baptiser *to christen, baptize*
battre *to beat*
bavarder *to chat*
beau *beautiful*
beau-frère *(m)* *brother-in-law*
beau-père *(m)* *father-in-law*
beaucoup *much; a lot*
belle-mère *(f)* *mother-in-law*
belle-soeur *(f)* *sister-in-law*
besoin *(m)* *need*
beurre *(m)* *butter*
bien *well; good*
bien sûr *of course*
bientôt *soon*
bijou *(m)* *jewel*
billet *(m)* *ticket*
blague *(f)* *joke*
blaguer *to joke*
blanquette de veau *(f)* *veal stew*
blessure *(f)* *injury*
bleu *blue*
blond *blond*
bœuf *(m)* *beef*
boire *to drink*
boisson *beverage*
bon *good*
bondé *crowded*
bonjour *good morning*
bonne affaire *(f)* *good deal*
bouche *(f)* *mouth*
  bouche à oreille *(m)* *word of mouth*
bouger *to move*
bouillir *to boil*
boulot *(m)* *job*
bouquet *(m)* *bunch; bouquet*
bouteille *(f)* *bottle*
boutique *(f)* *shop*
branché *trendy*
bricolage *(m)* *odd jobs; tinkering*
broderie *(f)* *embroidery*
brodeuse *(f)* *embroideress*
bruit *(m)* *noise*
brûler *to burn*
bulle *(f)* *bubble*
bureau *(m)* *office*
  bureau de change *(m)* *exchange bureau*

C

C.V. *(m)* *résumé*
cela *this*
ça va? *how are you?*
cabine *(f)* *booth, cabin*
  cabine d'essayage *(f)* *dressing room*
cacher *to hide*
cachet *(m)* *charm*
cadastre *(m)* *survey*
cadavre *(m)* *corpse; empty bottle*

caddie *(m)* shopping cart
cadeau *(m)* gift
cadreur *(m)* cameraman
café *(m)* coffee
caisse *(f)* cash register
camion-citerne *(m)* tanker
campagne *(f)* country(side)
canapé *(m)* sofa
canif *(m)* pocketknife
capituler to surrender
car *(m)* bus (inter-city)
carnet *(m)* booklet
   carnet de santé *(m)* health record book
carré square
carreleur *(m)* tile installer
carrière *(f)* career
carte *(f)* card; menu
   carte de visite *(f)* business card
   carte routière *(f)* road map
casque *(m)* helmet
casse-croûte *(m)* snack
casser to break
cave *(f)* cave, cellar
celui this one
centrifugeuse *(f)* blending vat
cesser to cease, to stop
chaîne *(f)* channel
chair *(f)* flesh
chaire *(f)* chair, professorship
chaise *(f)* chair
chaleur *(f)* heat
chambre *(f)* room
champ *(m)* field
champignon *(m)* mushroom
chance *(f)* luck
changer to change
chantage *(m)* blackmail
chanteur *(m)* singer
chapeau *(m)* hat
charger to load
chariot *(m)* cart
charnière *(f)* pivot, turning point
charpente *(f)* woodwork
chat *(m)* cat
châtaignier *(m)* chestnut tree
château *(f)* castle
chaud hot
chaudière *(f)* boiler
chauffage *(m)* heating system
chef *(m)* chef
chef-d'oeuvre *(m)* masterpiece
cheminée *(f)* fireplace; chimney
chemise *(f)* shirt (man's)
chemisier *(m)* shirt (woman's)
chêne *(m)* oak
chenet *(m)* andiron
cher dear; expensive
chercher to look for
chéri darling
cheveux *(m.pl.)* hair
chiffre *(m)* figure (numeral)
chocolat *(m)* chocolate

choix *(m)* choice
chômage *(m)* unemployment
choquer to shock
chose *(f)* thing
cidre *(m)* cider
cimetière *(m)* cemetery
cinéma *(m)* cinema
circulation *(f)* traffic
cire d'abeille *(f)* beeswax
citer to quote
citron *(m)* lemon
clair light; clear
clavier *(m)* keyboard
cliquer to click
cloison *(f)* partition
clou *(m)* nail
cocotier *(m)* coconut tree
cœur *(m)* heart
coiffeuse *(f)* dressing table
col *(m)* collar
collègue *(m., f.)* colleague
coller to stick; to glue
combien how much, how many
commander to order
commencer to begin; to start
comment how
commerçant *(m)* shopkeeper
commode *(f)* dresser
commun common
compagnie *(f)* company
composer to dial
comprendre to understand
comprimé *(m)* pill
compter to count
concurrence *(f)* competition
concurrent *(m)* competitor
conduire to drive
confier (se) to confide
confortable comfortable
congé *(m)* holiday
   congé de maternité *(m)* maternity leave
   congé payé *(m)* paid vacation
connaissance *(f)* knowledge
connaître to know
consciemment consciously
conseil *(m)* advice
conseiller to advise
conservateur *(m)* curator
consigne *(f)* orders, instruction
consommation *(f)* consumption
construire to build
continuer to continue; to go on
contre against
contrefaçon *(f)* counterfeiting
contremaître *(m)* foreman
convaincre to convince
corail *(m)* coral
correspondance *(f)* correspondence
corsé tough
côte *(f)* coast
côte d'Azur *(f)* Riviera
coucher (se) to go to bed

361

couette *(f)* down quilt
couleur *(f)* color
coup *(m)* blow
  coup d'œil *(m)* glance
  coup de fil *(m)* phone call
  coup de foudre *(m)* love at first sight
  coup de peinture *(m)* paint job
  coup de pouce *(m)* boost
coupe *(f)* cut
couple *(m)* couple
cour *(f)* courtyard
couramment *fluently*
courant d'air *(m)* draft
coureur *(m)* runner
courir *to run*
couronne *(f)* crown
cours *(m)* course, class
court *short*
cousin(e) *(m.,f.)* cousin
coussin *(m)* cushion
coûter *to cost*
couturier *(m)* fashion designer
couturière *(f)* dressmaker, seamstress
craindre *to worry*
crainte *(f)* fear
crèche *(f)* daycare center
créer *to create*
crevé *exhausted*
crochet *(m)* hook
croire *to believe*
croissance *(f)* growth
croquis *(m)* sketch
crustacés *(m.pl.)* shellfish
cueillir *to gather; to pick*
cuir *(m)* leather
cuire *to cook*
cuisine *(f)* kitchen; cooking
cuisse *(f)* thigh
cuisson *(f)* cooking time
cuve *(f)* vat
  cuve à mazout *(f)* oil tank

D

de *of, from*
  d'accord *all right*
  d'ailleurs *besides*
dame *(f)* lady
dans *in*
danseur *(m)* dancer
date *(f)* date
dauphin *(m)* dolphin; eldest son of king
débat *(m)* debate
débloquer *to release*
déborder *to bubble over*
débouchés *(m.pl.)* prospects
débrouiller (se) *to get by*
décalage horaire *(m)* jet lag
décembre *December*
décennie *(f)* decade
déchiffrer *to decipher*

décider *to decide*
décision *(f)* decision
déclarer *to declare*
décor *(m)* decor
décorateur *(m)* interior designer
décorer *to decorate*
décrocher *to pick up*
dédouaner *to clear Customs*
déguster *to savor; to taste*
délabré *delapidated*
délicieux *delicious*
demain *tomorrow*
demander *to ask*
démarrer *to start (up)*
demeure *(f)* dwelling
demeurer *to remain*
demi *half*
démissionner *to resign*
dénicher *to discover, to unearth*
dénouement *(m)* conclusion
dent *(f)* tooth
dépasser *to pass*
dépense *(f)* expense
dépister *to detect; to screen*
déplacement *(m)* travel, movement
déposer *to drop off*
depuis *since*
déranger *to bother*
dernier *last*
descendre *to go down; to get off*
désirer *to desire; to wish*
désolé *sorry*
dessert *(m)* dessert
détester *to hate*
deux poids, deux mesures *double standard*
devant *in front of*
devenir *to become*
deviner *to guess*
devis *(m)* estimate
devises étrangères *(f.pl.)* foreign currency
dévoiler *to reveal*
devoir *must; to have to*
différent *different*
diffuser *to broadcast*
digne *worthy*
diluer *to dilute*
dîner *(m)* dinner
dîner *to have dinner*
diplôme *(m)* degree, diploma
dire *to say*
directeur *(m)* director
direction *(f)* direction; management
diriger *to run, to guide*
disponible *available*
dispositif *(m)* device
disposition *(f)* disposal
distraire (se) *to entertain (oneself)*
distribuer *to distribute*
divulguer *to reveal*
document *(m)* document
documentaire *(m)* documentary
doigt *(m)* finger

domaine *(m)* estate
donc *therefore; so*
donner rendez-vous *to make an appointment*
donner *to give*
dont *whose; of which*
dos *(m)* back
doter *to endow*
douane *(f)* Customs
double *double*
  double vitrage *(m)* double-paned
    window
  doubles rideaux *(m.pl.)* drapes
doubler *to pass (car); to dubb*
douillet(te) *sensitive to pain*
douleur *(f)* pain
douzaine *(f)* about twelve
drapeau *(m)* flag
droit *(m)* right
drôle *funny; strange*

E

eau *(f)* water
ébaucher *to sketch*
ébéniste *(m)* cabinetmaker
échantillon *(m)* sample
éclairagiste *(m)* lighting engineer
école maternelle *(f)* nursery school
écorcher *to peel*
écran (m) *screen*
écrire *to write*
effectuer *to carry out*
efficace *efficient*
également *also*
égoïste *selfish*
égrapper *to stalk*
élection *(f)* election
élégant *elegant*
éloigné *far*
embarquement *(m)* boarding
embarquer *to board*
embaucher *to hire*
embouteillages *(m.pl.)* traffic jam
embrasser *to kiss*
émission *(f)* program
emmener *to take (someone)*
empêcher *to prevent*
en *in, at, to; some*
  en bas *at the bottom; downstairs*
  en dépit *in spite*
  en direct *live*
  en face *across the street*
  en outre *besides*
  en plein essor *in full expansion*
  en quête *in quest*
  en solde *on sale*
  en tenue *in uniform*
  en tout cas *in any case*
  en vouloir à *to hold a grudge against*
enchanté *delighted*
encombré *crowded, congested*

endolori *sore*
enfance *(f)* youth
enfant *(m.,f.)* child
enflammé(e) *heated, inflamed*
ennui *(m)* boredom; problem
ennuyer (se) *to get bored*
enregistrer *to check; to record*
enseignement *(m)* teaching
enseigner *to teach*
ensuite *then*
entamer *to strike up, to start*
entendre *to hear*
entourer *to surround*
entraînement *(m)* training
entraîner (se) *to train*
entre *between*
entrée *(f)* entrance
entrepôt *(m)* warehouse
entreprise *(f)* company
entretien *(m)* interview
envahir *to invade*
environ *about*
envisager *to contemplate*
envoler (se) *to take off*
envoûter *to bewitch*
envoyer *to send*
épargne *(f)* savings
épargner *to save*
épatant *sensational*
épater *to amaze*
épicier *(m)* grocer
éplucher *to peel*
éponge *(f)* sponge
épouvantable *scary; awful*
épuiser *to exhaust*
équipe *(f)* team
équitation *(f)* horseback riding
érable *maple wood*
escalader *to climb*
escargot *(m)* snail
espèce *(f)* species
essayer *to try*
essence *(f)* gas
établir *to establish; to make*
étage *(m)* floor (of a building)
étagère *(f)* shelf
étanche *air-tight, waterproof*
étape *(f)* step, stage
état *(m)* state
États-Unis *(m.pl.)* United States
été *(m)* summer
étiqueter *to label*
étoffe *(f)* fabric
étranger *strange*
être *to be*
  être censé *to be supposed*
  être en retard *to be late*
  être muté *to be transferred*
  être obligé *to have to*
  être sur le point *to be on the verge*
étude *(f)* study
étudiant(e) *(m.,f.)* student

étudier *to study*
Europe *(f)* *Europe*
évidemment *obviously*
exactement *exactly*
exagérer *to exaggerate*
examen *(m)* *exam*
excellent *excellent*
exercice *(m)* *exercise*
expérience *(f)* *experiment*
explorer *to explore*
exposition *(f)* *exhibit*
exquis *exquisite*
exténuer *to exhaust*

F

fabriquer *to make; to manufacture*
facture *(f)* *bill*
facultatif *optional*
faible *weak*
faïence *(f)* *earthenware*
faille *(f)* *fault; flaw*
faillite *(f)* *bankruptcy*
faire *to do; to make*
 faire la cuisine *to cook*
 faire les courses *to shop*
 faire preuve *to show; to exhibit*
 faire un tabac *to be a big hit*
faire (s'en) *to worry*
faire à (se) *to get used to*
falloir *to have to*
famille *(f)* *family*
fantastique *fantastic*
faute *(f)* *error; mistake*
fauteuil *(m)* *armchair*
féerique *magical*
félicitations *(f.pl.)* *congratulations*
féliciter *to congratulate*
femme *(f)* *woman; wife*
fenêtre *(f)* *window*
fermer *to close*
fermeture *(f)* *closing*
festival *(m)* *festival*
fête *(f)* *party, celebration*
fêter *to celebrate*
feu *(m)* *fire*
feuilleton *(m)* *series*
feuilletter *to leaf through*
feux de circulation *(m.pl.)* *traffic lights*
février *February*
fidélité *(f)* *faithfulness*
fier (ère) *proud*
figure de proue *(f)* *figurehead*
film *(m)* *film*
finir *to finish; to end*
fiole *(f)* *vial*
fixer un rendez-vous *to make an appointment*
flacon *(m)* *bottle*
flâner *to stroll*
fleur *(f)* *flower*
flotter *to float*

foie *(m)* *liver*
 foie gras *(m)* *goose liver*
fois *(f)* *time*
foncé *dark*
force majeure *(f)* *act of God*
forme *(f)* *shape*
fou *crazy*
fouetter *to whip*
foule *(f)* *crowd*
four *(m)* *oven*
fournir *to supply*
fourniture *(f.pl.)* *supplies*
franc *(m)* *franc*
français *French*
franchement *frankly*
frangin *(m)* *brother* (fam.)
frangine *(f)* *sister* (fam.)
fréquenter *to attend*
frère *(m)* *brother*
frissonner *to shiver*
frite *(f)* *French fry*
froid *cold*
fumer *to smoke*
fumeur *smoker*
furieux *furious*
fût *(m)* *barrel*

G

gaffe *(f)* *blunder*
gagne-pain *(m)* *livelihood*
gagner *to earn; to win*
gamme *(f)* *scale, range*
garderie *(f)* *nursery*
gare *(f)* *train station*
gastronomie *(f)* *gastronomy*
gâteau *(m)* *cake*
gazon *(m)* *lawn*
gêner *to bother, to embarrass*
gens *(m.pl.)* *people*
gestion *(f)* *management*
glisser *to slip*
global *global*
gourou *(m)* *guru*
goût *(m)* *taste*
gouttière *(f)* *gutter*
gouvernement *(m)* *government*
grâce à *thanks to*
graisse *(f)* *fat*
grand *large, big*
 grand magasin *(m)* *department store*
grand-mère *(f)* *grandmother*
grand-père *(m)* *grandfather*
graphologie *(f)* *graphology, handwriting analysis*
grappe *(f)* *bunch (of grapes)*
gratter *to scratch*
grave *serious*
gravure *(f)* *etching*
grève *(f)* *strike*
gribouillage *(m)* *scribbling*
gribouiller *to scribble*

grippe (f)   flu
grossesse (f)   pregnancy
guichet (m)   window

H

habiller   to dress up
habiter   to live
habitude (f)   habit
hameau (m)   hamlet
harmoniser   to harmonize
hauteur (f)   height
hebdomadaire   weekly
hein?   eh?
hésiter   to hesitate
heure (f)   time
hideux   hideous
histoire (f)   story; history
hiver (m)   winter
homme (m)   man
horloge   clock
   horloge pointeuse (f)   time clock
hors-d'oeuvre (m.pl.)   appetizers
hortensia (m)   hydrangea
hôtel (m)   hotel
hôtesse (f)   flight attendant
housse (f)   cover
huile (f)   oil
humer   to sniff
humeur (f)   mood
humour (m)   humor
hypermarché (m)   large supermarket

I

ici   here
idée (f)   idea
il (m)   he; it
  il faut   one must, it's necessary
  il s'agit   it is about
  il vaut mieux   it is better
  il y a   here is; there are
île (f)   island
impossible   impossible
impôt (m)   tax
  impôt foncier (m)   property tax
imprégner (se)   to immerse; to soak up
impressionnant   impressive
incendie (m)   fire
indemnité (f)   allowance, compensation
indéniable   undeniable
indicatif numérique (m)   area code
indice (m)   indicator
indiquer   to indicate
inestimable   priceless
infirmier(ère)   nurse
informatique (f)   computer science
informatiser   to computerize
infortuné   ill-fated
injure (f)   insult

inoxydable   stainless steel
inquiéter (se)   to worry
inscrire (se)   to register; to sign up
insouciance (f)   carelessness
installer (se)   to settle
insuffler   to breathe life into
insupportable   unbearable
interdire   to prohibit
intéressant   interesting
intéresser à (se)   to be interested in
investir   to invest
invité (m)   guest
inviter   to invite
insolation (f)   sunstroke
isolation (f)   insulation
isolé   detached
italien   Italian
itinéraire (m)   itinerary
ivresse (f)   intoxication

J

jamais   never
jambe (f)   leg
jambon (m)   ham
janvier   January
jardin (m)   garden
jaune   yellow
jeter   to throw
jeu (m)   game
jeudi   Thursday
joindre   to meet; to join
jouer   to play
joueur (m)   player
jour (m)   day
  jour de repos (m)   day off
  jour férié (m)   holiday
juillet   July
juin   June
jupe (f)   skirt
jurer   to clash; to swear
jusqu'à   until

K

kilo (m)   kilo
kilomètre (m)   kilometer

L

laisse (f)   leash
laisser   to leave
laiton   brass
lancer   to throw
langage (m)   language
lavoir (m)   washhouse
léguer   to bequeath
lésiner   to skimp
lever (se)   to get up

liberté (f) freedom
libre free
limpide clear; limpid
lire to read
lit (m) bed
littérature (f) literature
livre (f) pound
livre (m) book
location (f) rental
logement (m) housing
logiciel (m) software
loin far
loisir (m) leisure
longer to border
lors during
louer to rent
loyer (m) rent
lumière (f) light
lunatique moody
lundi Monday
lutter to struggle

M

macérer to macerate
Madame Madam, Mrs.
Mademoiselle Miss
magnifique magnificent
mai May
main (f) hand
maintenant now
mairie (f) town hall
mais but
maison (f) house
maîtrise (f) Master's degree
maîtriser to bring under control, to master
malade sick
maladie (f) disease
malheureusement unfortunately
manche (f) sleeve
manchette (f) cuff
manger to eat
manifestant (m) demonstrator
manifestation (f) protest, rally
manifester to demonstrate
mannequin (m) model
manquer to miss
mansardé sloping ceiling
marchander to bargain
marché (m) market
  marché aux puces (m) flea market
marcher to walk
mardi Tuesday
marier (se) to get married
marraine (f) godmother
mars March
marteau (m) hammer
match (m) game
matière grise (f) gray matter
matin (m) morning
mauvais bad

mécanicien (m) mechanic
médecin (m) doctor
médecine (f) medicine (the science or profession)
médicament (m) medicine; pills
meilleur better
mélanger to mix
même same, even
mémoire (f) memory
menacer to threaten
merci thank you
mercredi Wednesday
mère (f) mother
merisier wild cherry
message (m) message
metteur en scène film director
mettre to put, to place
  mettre en relief to enhance
  mettre en valeur to enhance
  mettre le feu aux poudres to light the powder keg
meuble (m) furniture
meurtre (m) murder
meurtrier (m) murderer
midi noon
miel (m) honey
miette (f) crumb
mine (f) expression (facial)
miracle (m) miracle
miroir (m) mirror
mite (f) moth
mode (f) fashion
moelleux soft; fluffy
moins less
mois (m) month
moment (m) moment
monde (m) world
monnaie (f) change
monsieur sir
montagne (f) mountain
monter to go up
montrer to show
moquer de (se) to make fun
moteur (m) engine
mouiller (se) to get wet
moulin (m) mill
moulure (f) molding
mourir to die
moût (m) must
Moyen-Age (m) Middle Ages
muguet (m) lily-of-the-valley
munir to provide
mur (m) wall
muscle (m) muscle
musée (m) museum
musique (f) music

N

nager to swim
naissance (f) birth

nappe *(f)* tablecloth
néanmoins *nonetheless*
négocier *to negotiate*
neige *(f)* snow
nettoyage à sec *(m)* dry cleaning
nez *(m)* nose
nom *(m)* name
nombre *(m)* number
non *no*
nord *(m)* north
notaire *(m)* lawyer
note *(f)* bill
notion *(f)* notion
nourrisson *(m)* infant
nouveau *new*
nouvelle *(f)* a piece of news
novembre *November*
noyer *(m)* walnut tree
nuage *(m)* cloud

O

objet *(m)* object
obligatoire *compulsory*
occasion *(f)* opportunity
occupé *busy*
occuper (se) *to take care*
octobre *October*
odeur *(f)* smell
œil *(m)* eye
œuvre *(f)* work
offre *(f)* offer
offrir *to offer*
oncle *(m)* uncle
opéra *(m)* opera
opprimer *to oppress*
or *(m)* gold
ordinateur *(m)* computer
ordonnance *(f)* prescription
oreillons *(m.pl.)* mumps
organiser *to organize*
orgue *(m)* organ
orthographe *(f)* spelling
oser *to dare*
ou *or*
où *where*
oublier *to forget*
ouïr *to hear*
outil *(m)* tool
ouverture *(f)* opening
ouvrir *to open*

P

page *(f)* page
palais *(m)* palace; palate (medical
    term)
pâle *pale, light*
pantalon *(m)* pants
papier peint *(m)* wallpaper

paquet *(m)* package
par *by; through*
    par cœur *by heart*
paraître *to seem*
parc *(m)* park
pareil *similar*
parent *(m)* relative
parents *(m.pl.)* parents
paresseux *lazy*
parfait *perfect*
parler *to speak*
parrain *(m)* godfather
partager *to share*
parti *(m)* political party
participer *to participate*
partir *to leave*
passager *(m)* passenger
passeport *(m)* passport
passer *to spend; to pass by*
    passer en revue *to review*
passionnant *fascinating*
pause *(f)* break
    pause-café *(f)* coffee break
pauvre *poor*
PDG (président directeur général) *CEO
    (chief executive officer)*
pêche *(m)* peach
pêcher *to fish*
peigner *to comb*
peindre *to paint*
pèlerinage *(m)* pilgrimage
pencher (se) *to lean*
pendant *during; for*
pénombre *(f)* dark
penser *to think*
perché *perched*
père *(m)* father
perfectionner *to improve*
permis de conduire *(m)* driver's license
persil *(m)* parsley
personne *(f)* person
peser *to weigh*
petit déjeuner *(m)* breakfast
petit *small*
petit-fils *(m)* grandson
peu *little*
peur *(f)* fear
peut-être *maybe*
phare *(m)* headlight
pharmacie *(f)* pharmacy
pharmacien *(m)* pharmacist
photo *(f)* picture
piqûre *(f)* injection
pire *(m)* worst
pivoine *(f)* peony
placard *(m)* closet
plaire *to please*
plaisanter *to joke*
plaisir *(m)* pleasure
plan *(m)* map
    plan d'occupation des sols *(m)* zoning
        ordinance

planche (f)   board, plank
planche à voile (f)   windsurfing
plancher (m)   floor
plat (m)   dish
plateau (m)   tray; TV set
plein   full
pleurer   to cry
pleuvoir   to rain
plissé   pleated
plombage (m)   filling
plonger   to dive
plus   more
plusieurs   several
pneu (m)   tire
poêle (f)   frying pan
poêle (m)   stove
poids (m)   weight
poing (m)   fist
pointer   to punch in
poisson (m)   fish
poivre (m)   pepper
politique (f)   politics
poncer   to sand
pont (m)   bridge
portable   wearable; portable (computer, TV, etc.)
portatif (m)   portable (computer, TV, etc.)
porter   to carry; to wear
portière (f)   door (car)
poste (f)   post office
poste (m)   extension
poupée (f)   doll
pouponnière (f)   nursery school
pour   for
pourquoi   why
pourriture (f)   rot
pourtant   however
pourvu que   provided that
pousser   to grow
poutre (f)   beam
pouvoir   can; may
préciser   to specify
préférer   to prefer
premier   first
prendre   to take
   prendre un verre   to have a drink
prénom (m)   first name
préparer   to prepare
près   close; near
présenter   to introduce
préservatif (m)   condom
prêt   ready
   prêt-à-porter (m)   ready-to-wear
prétentieux   pretentious
prévenir   to inform; to preview
prime (f)   bonus
printemps (m)   spring
prise (f)   outlet
privilégier   to favor
prix (m)   price
problème (m)   problem

processus (m)   process, method
   processus de fabrication (m)   manufacturing process
produit (m)   product
professeur (m)   teacher; professor
profiter   to take advantage
programme (m)   program
projet (m)   project
prolonger   to extend
promesse (f)   promise
promouvoir   to promote
proposer   to suggest
protéger   to protect
protéine (f)   protein
province (f)   province
provisions (f.pl.)   supplies
provoquer   to trigger; to cause
prudent   cautious
pub (f)   ad

Q

quand   when
quart (m)   quarter
quartier (m)   neighborhood
quel   what
quelqu'un   someone
quelque chose   something
quincaillerie (f)   hardware store
quoi   what
quotidien (m)   daily; daily paper

R

raccrocher   to hang up
racheter   to buy back
raconter   to tell
radiateur (m)   radiator
radoucir   to soften; to mellow
ramequin (m)   soufflé dish
rang (m)   row
râper   to grate
rapide   fast
rappeller   to call back
rarement   rarely
rarissime   very rare
rattraper   to make up
ravi   delighted
ravissant   delightful
réaffirmer   to reaffirm
recette (f)   recipe
recevoir   to receive; entertain
recherche (f)   research
récif (m)   reef
recommander   to recommend
reconnaissant   grateful
reconnaître   to recognize
reconversion (f)   conversion
recouvrir   to cover, to upholster
reculer   to move back

rédacteur (-trice) *editor*
rédiger *to write*
reflet *gleam*
réforme *(f) reform*
refuser *to refuse*
regarder *to watch*
régime *(m) diet*
région *(f) region*
règlement *(m) regulation*
régler *to settle*
regretter *to regret*
reine *(f) queen*
remède *(m) remedy*
remplir *to fill*
remuer *to stir*
rencontrer *to meet*
rendement *(m) yield, output*
rendez-vous *(m) appointment*
rendre *to return; to render*
  rendre malade *to make sick*
rendre (se) *to go; to surrender*
  rendre compte (se) *to realize*
rênes *(f.pl.) reins*
renommé *famous*
renseignement *(m) information*
renverser *to spill*
répétition *(f) rehearsal*
répondre *to answer*
réponse *(f) answer*
reposer (se) *to rest*
repousser *to postpone*
requis *required*
réservation *(f) reservation*
réserver *to reserve*
respirer *to breathe*
resplendissant *beaming*
restaurant *(m) restaurant*
restauration *(f) restoration*
rester *to stay*
retour *(m) return*
retourner *to go back*
retrouver *to meet, to join*
réunion *(f) appointment, meeting*
réussir *to succeed*
revanche *(f) revenge*
réveiller (se) *to wake up*
revendiquer *to claim*
revenir *to come back*
revenu *(m) income*
rêver *to dream*
revoir *to see again*
rhume *(m) cold*
rideau *(m) curtain*
rien *nothing*
rigoler *to laugh, to joke*
rimer *to rhyme*
robe *(f) dress*
rocher *(m) rock*
roman *(m) novel*
rougeole *(f) measles*
rouillé(e) *rusty*
rouler *to drive*

route *(f) road*
rubéole *(f) rubella*
rustique *rustic*

S

se *oneself, himself, herself, themselves*
  s'appeler *to be called*
  s'apprêter *to get ready*
  s'effondrer *to collapse*
si *if*
  s'il vous plaît *please*
saboter *to sabotage*
sac *(m) bag*
sage-femme *(f) midwife*
saison *(f) season*
salle *room*
  salle à manger *(f) dining room*
salon *(m) living room*
samedi *Saturday*
santé *(f) health*
Saturnisme *(m) lead poisoning*
sauter aux yeux *to stick out, to be obvious*
sauvage *wild, shy*
sauvegarder *to preserve, to save*
savoir *to know*
scène *(f) scene*
sculpteur *(m) sculptor*
se debrouiller *to manage*
se plaindre *to complain*
sécateur *(m) pruning shears*
secret *(m) secret*
secrétaire *(m) secretary; bureau*
sécurité sociale *(f) social security*
séduisant *attractive*
séjour *(m) stay*
semaine *(f) week*
semainier *(m) dresser for a seven-day supply of clothes*
senteur *(f) fragrance*
sentir *to feel*
septembre *September*
sermon *(m) lecture*
serre *(f) greenhouse*
seulement *only*
sévir *to be rampant*
signer *to sign*
sinon *or, otherwise*
sirop *(m) syrup*
sœur *(f) sister*
soie *(f) silk*
soirée *(f) evening; party*
soleil *(m) sun*
sombre *dark*
somnifère *(m) sleeping pill*
somptueux *sumptuous*
son *(m) sound*
sonner *to ring*
sort *(m) fate*
sortir *to go out*
souder *to solder*

369

souffle *(m)*   *breath*
soufflet *(m)*   *bellows*
souffrir   *to suffer*
souhaiter   *to wish*
soulever   *to lift*
soupçon *(m)*   *hint*
sourd   *deaf*
souris *(f)*   *mouse*
sous   *under*
  sous-emploi *(m)*   *underemployment*
souvenir *(m)*   *memory*
souvenir (se)   *to remember*
souvent   *often*
spacieux   *spacious*
spécialité *(f)*   *specialty*
spectacle *(m)*   *performance; show*
spectaculaire   *spectacular*
sport *(m)*   *sport*
stage *(m)*   *internship; training*
stand *(m)*   *booth*
succulent   *delicious*
sucre *(m)*   *sugar*
sud *(m)*   *south*
suffire   *to suffice*
suivant   *following*
suivre   *to follow*
supermarché *(m)*   *supermarket*
supporter   *to bear; to stand*
sur   *on*
surnommer   *to nickname*
surprise *(f)*   *surprise*
surtitres *(m.pl.)*   *supertitles*
susciter   *to generate; to provoke*
suspens *(m)*   *suspense*
syndicat *(m)*   *union*

T

table *(f)*   *table*
  table basse *(f)*   *coffee table*
tableau *(m)*   *painting*
tache *(f)*   *stain*
tâche *(f)*   *task*
taie d'oreiller *(f)*   *pillowcase*
taille *(f)*   *size*
tailleur *(m)*   *tailor, suit*
tant   *so much; so many*
tante *(f)*   *aunt*
taquiner   *to tease*
tard   *late*
tas *(m)*   *pile*
tasse *(f)*   *cup*
taux *(m)*   *rate*
  taux d'intérêt *(m)*   *interest rate*
  taux de change *(m)*   *rate of exchange*
technique *(f)*   *technique*
teindre   *to dye*
teint *(m)*   *complexion*
teinte *(f)*   *shade; color*
télécommande *(f)*   *remote control*
télécopie *(f)*   *fax*

téléphoner   *to call*
télévision *(f)*   *television*
temps *(m)*   *time, weather*
tenir   *to hold, to have*
  tenir à   *to insist; to want*
  tenir au courant   *to keep informed*
  tenir compte   *to take into account*
terrasse *(f)*   *terrace*
terre *(f)*   *earth*
tertiaire *(m)*   *service sector*
tête *(f)*   *head*
thé *(m)*   *tea*
tissu *(m)*   *fabric*
toile *(f)*   *cloth; canvas*
  toile de fond *(f)*   *background*
toit *(m)*   *roof*
toiture *(f)*   *roofing*
tomber   *to fall*
  tomber en panne   *to break down (car)*
tonalité *(f)*   *dial tone*
tôt   *early*
toucher   *to touch*
toujours   *always*
tour *(f)*   *tower*
tour *(m)*   *walk; stroll; trip*
tournage *(m)*   *shooting (film)*
tourner   *to turn*
tout   *all*
  tout de suite   *right away*
  tout droit   *straight ahead*
  tout le monde   *everyone*
toutefois   *however*
trac *(m)*   *stage fright*
traduire   *to translate*
tranche *(f)*   *slice*
travail *(m)*   *work*
travailler   *to work*
travaux *(m.pl.)*   *construction*
traverser   *to cross*
tremblement de terre *(m)*   *earthquake*
très   *very*
trésor *(m)*   *treasure*
trier   *to sort*
trimestre *(m)*   *trimester*
triste   *sad*
tromper   *to deceive; to cheat*
tromper (se)   *to make a mistake*
trop   *too much*
trou *(m)*   *hole*
trouver   *to find*
truc *(m)*   *trick*
tuyau *(m)*   *hose; tip, hint*

U

Union Européenne (UE) *(f)*   *European Union*
  (EU)
université *(f)*   *university*
usine *(f)*   *factory*
usure *(f)*   *wear and tear*
utiliser   *to use*

V

vacances *(f.pl.)* *vacation*
vaccin *(m)* *vaccine*
valise *(f)* *suitcase*
valoir *to be worth*
vedette *(f)* *star*
veine *(f)* *chance*
vendanger *to harvest*
vendanges *(f.pl.)* *harvest*
vendangeur *(m)* *grape picker*
vendeur *(m)* *salesperson*
vendre *to sell*
vendredi *Friday*
venir *to come*
verbe *(m)* *verb*
verdure *(f)* *greenery*
vérifier *to check*
verre *(m)* *glass*
verrière *(f)* *glass roof*
vers *toward*
verser *to pour, to deposit*
vert *(m)* *green*
vestiaire *(m)* *locker room*
viaduc *(m)* *viaduct*
viande *(f)* *meat*
victoire *(f)* *victory*
vieillissement *(m)* *aging*
vierge *virgin, blank*
vieux *old*
vigne *(m)* *vine*
vigneron *(m)* *wine maker*

vignoble *(m)* *vineyard*
ville *(f)* *town, city*
vin *(m)* *wine*
viniculture *(f)* *wine making*
viser *to aim*
visiter *to visit*
vite *fast*
vivre *to live*
voici *here is*
voilà *here is*
voile *(f)* *sail*
voile *(m)* *veil*
voir *to see*
voisin *(m)* *neighbor*
voiture *(f)* *car*
    voiture d'occasion *(f)* *second-hand car*
vol *(m)* *flight*
volonté *(f)* *will, wish*
volontiers *willingly*
voter *to vote*
vouloir *to want*
voyage *(m)* *travel*
voyager *to travel*
vrai *true*
vraiment *truly*

Z

zapper *to change channels (colloquial)*
zut! *shoot! (mild oath)*

ENGLISH–FRENCH

A

a *un, une*
    a lot *beaucoup*
about *environ*
    about twelve *douzaine (f)*
abroad *à l'étranger*
acacia *acacia (m)*
access (to) *accéder*
accuse (to) *accuser*
across *à travers, de l'autre côté*
    across the street *en face*
act *acte (m), action (f)*
    act of God *cas (m) de force majeure (f)*
admit (to) *avouer*
adore (to) *adorer*
advertisement *publicité; pub (f)*
advice *conseil (m)*
advise (to) *conseiller*
after *après*
afternoon *après-midi (f)*
against *contre*
age *âge (m)*
aging *vieillissement (m)*

aim (to) *viser*
aim *but (m)*
air *air (m)*
    air tight *étanche*
all *tout, entier*
    all right *d'accord*
allergic *allergique*
allergy *allergie (f)*
allowance *indemnité (f)*
also *aussi, également*
always *toujours*
amateur *amateur (m)*
amaze (to) *épater*
amber *ambre*
American *américain*
andiron *chenet (m)*
androgynous *androgyne*
announce (to) *annoncer*
answer (to) *répondre*
answer *réponse (f)*
antibodies *anticorps (m.pl.)*
antique *antiquité (f); objet (m) antique*
    antique dealer *antiquaire (m)*
apartment *appartement (m)*

appetizers   *hors-d'œuvre (m.pl.)*
apple   *pomme (f)*
appointment   *rendez-vous (m); réunion (f)*
approach (to)   *aborder*
April   *avril*
architect   *architecte (m)*
architecture   *architecture (f)*
area   *superficie (f); région (f)*
  area code   *indicatif numérique (m)*
armchair   *fauteuil (m)*
armoire   *armoire (f)*
aroma   *arôme (m)*
arrival   *arrivée (f)*
arrive (to)   *arriver*
artichoke   *artichaut (m)*
article   *article (m)*
as   *aussi; comme; tout . . . que*
  as much   *autant*
ask (to)   *demander*
asparagus   *asperge (f)*
at   *à, en*
  at random   *au hasard*
  at your disposal   *à votre disposition*
attain (to)   *atteindre*
attend (to)   *fréquenter; assister*
attractive   *séduisant*
audience   *auditoire (m), public (m)*
August   *août*
aunt   *tante (f)*
autonomy   *autonomie (f)*
availability   *disponibilité (f)*
available   *disponible*

B

back   *dos (m)*
bad   *mauvais*
bag   *sac (m)*
ball   *bal (m)*
bank   *banque (f)*
bankruptcy   *faillite (f)*
bargain (to)   *marchander*
bargain   *bonne affaire (f)*
barrel   *fût (m)*
bathroom   *salle (f) de bain*
be (to)   *être*
  be a big hit (to)   *faire un tabac*
  be anxious (to)   *avoir hâte de*
  be called (to)   *s'appeler*
  be interested (to)   *intéresser à (se)*
  be late (to)   *être en retard*
  be rampant (to)   *sévir*
  be supposed to (to)   *être censé*
  be transferred (to)   *être muté*
  be worth (to)   *valoir*
beam   *poutre (f)*
beaming   *resplendissant*
bean   *haricot (m)*
bear (to)   *supporter*
beat (to)   *battre*
beautiful   *beau (m), belle (f)*

become (to)   *devenir*
bed   *lit (m)*
beef   *bœuf (m)*
beeswax   *cire d'abeille (f)*
before   *avant*
begin (to)   *commencer*
believe (to)   *croire*
bellows   *soufflet (m)*
belong (to)   *appartenir*
bequeath (to)   *léguer*
besides   *en outre; d'ailleurs*
better   *meilleur*
between   *entre*
beverage   *boisson (f)*
bewitch (to)   *envoûter*
bill   *addition (f), facture (f), note (f)*
birth   *naissance (f)*
birthday   *anniversaire (m)*
bitter   *amer*
blackmail   *chantage (m)*
blow   *coup (m)*
blue   *bleu*
blunder   *gaffe (f)*
board (to)   *embarquer*
board   *planche (f)*
boarding   *embarquement (m)*
boil (to)   *bouillir*
boiler   *chaudière (f)*
bonus   *prime (f)*
book   *livre (m)*
booklet   *carnet (m)*
boost   *coup de pouce (m)*
booth   *stand (m)*
border (to)   *longer*
boredom   *ennui (m)*
bother (to)   *déranger; gêner*
bottle   *bouteille (f); flacon (m)*
braid   *tresse (f)*
brass   *laiton (m)*
break (to)   *casser*
  break down (to)   *tomber en panne*
break   *pause (f)*
breakfast   *petit déjeuner (m)*
breath   *souffle (m)*
breathe (to)   *respirer*
  breathe life into (to)   *insuffler*
bridge   *pont (m)*
bring (to)   *apporter*
  bring under control (to)   *maîtriser*
broadcast (to)   *diffuser*
broadcast   *émission (f)*
broom   *balai (m)*
brother   *frère (m), frangin (fam.)*
brother-in-law   *beau-frère (m)*
bubble   *bulle (f)*
  bubble over (to)   *déborder*
build (to)   *construire*
bunch   *bouquet (m); botte (f)*
  bunch of grapes   *grappe (f)*
bureau   *secrétaire (m)*
burn (to)   *brûler*
bus (inter-city)   *autocar (m)*

business *les affaires (f.pl.)*
  business card *carte de visite (f)*
busy *occupé*
but *mais*
butter *beurre (m)*
buy (to) *acheter*
buy back (to) *racheter*
by *par*
  by heart *par cœur*
  by the way *au fait*

C

cabinetmaker *ébéniste (m)*
cake *gâteau (m)*
call (to) *appeler, téléphoner*
  call back (to) *rappeler*
cameraman *cadreur (m)*
can *pouvoir*
canvas *toile (f)*
car *voiture (f)*
card *carte (f)*
career *carrière (f)*
carelessness *insouciance (f)*
Caribbean *antillais (e)*
carry (to) *porter*
carry out (to) *effectuer*
cart *chariot (m)*
cash *argent liquide (m)*
cash register *caisse (f)*
casino *casino (m)*
castle *château (m)*
cat *chat (m)*
cause (to) *provoquer*
cautious *prudent*
cave *cave (f)*
cavity *carie (f)*
cease (to) *cesser*
celebrate (to) *fêter*
cemetery *cimetière (m)*
CEO (chief executive officer) *PDG (président
    directeur général) (m)*
chair *chaise (f)*
chance *chance (f); veine (f)*
change (to) *changer*
change *monnaie (f)*
channel *chaîne*
charity *œuvre de bienfaisance (f)*
charm *cachet (m)*
chat (to) *bavarder*
check (to) *vérifier*
chef *chef (m)*
chestnut *châtaigne (f)*
  chestnut tree *châtaignier (m)*
child *enfant (m., f.)*
chimney *cheminée (f)*
chocolate *chocolat (m)*
choice *choix (m)*
christen (to) *baptiser*
cider *cidre (m)*
cinema *cinéma (m)*

citrus *agrumes (m.pl.)*
claim (to) *revendiquer*
clash (to) *jurer*
class *cours (m)*
clear *limpide*
clear customs (to) *dédouaner*
click (to) *cliquer*
cliff *falaise (f)*
climb (to) *escalader*
close (to) *fermer*
close *près de*
closet *placard (m)*
closing *fermeture (f)*
cloud *nuage (m)*
coast *côte (f)*
coconut tree *cocotier (m)*
coffee *café (m)*
coffee break *pause-café (f)*
coffee table *table basse (f)*
cold *froid*
cold *rhume (m)*
collapse (to) *s'effondrer*
collar *col (m)*
colleague *collègue (m., f.)*
color *couleur (f); teinte (f)*
comb (to) *peigner*
come (to) *venir*
  come back (to) *revenir*
  come close (to) *approcher (se)*
comfortable *confortable*
common *commun*
company *compagnie (f), entreprise (f)*
competition *concurrence (f)*
competitor *concurrent (m)*
complain (to) *se plaindre*
complexion *teint (m)*
compulsory *obligatoire*
computer *ordinateur (m)*
  computer science *informatique (f)*
computerize (to) *informatiser*
conclusion *dénouement (m)*
condom *préservatif (m)*
confide (to) *confier (se)*
congested *encombré*
congratulate (to) *féliciter*
congratulations *félicitations (f.pl.)*
consciously *consciemment*
construction *travaux (m.pl.)*
consumption *consommation (f)*
contemplate (to) *envisager*
continue; to go on (to) *continuer*
conversion *reconversion (f)*
convince (to) *convaincre*
cook (to) *cuire; faire la cuisine*
  cooking time *cuisson (f)*
coral *corail (m)*
corpse *cadavre (m)*
correspondence *correspondance (f)*
cost (to) *coûter*
count (to) *compter*
counterfeiting *contrefaçon (f)*
country(side) *campagne (f)*

couple *couple (m)*
courtyard *cour intérieure (f)*
cousin *cousin(e) (m,f)*
cover (to) *couvrir*
craftsman *artisan (m)*
crazy *fou*
create (to) *créer*
cross (to) *traverser*
crowd *foule (f)*
crowded *bondé*
crown *couronne (f)*
crumb *miette (f)*
cry (to) *pleurer*
cuff *manchette (f)*
cup *tasse (f)*
curator *conservateur (m)*
curtain *rideau (m)*
customs *douane (f)*
cut *coupe (f)*

D

daily paper *quotidien (m)*
dance *danse (f)*
dancer *danseur (m)*
dare (to) *oser*
daring *audacieux*
dark *foncé; sombre*
darkness *pénombre (f)*
darling *chéri*
data *données (f.pl.)*
date *date (f)*
day *jour (m)*
  day off *jour de repos (m)*
daycare *crèche (f)*
deaf *sourd*
dear *cher*
debate *débat (m)*
decade *décennie (f)*
December *décembre*
decide (to) *décider*
decipher (to) *déchiffrer*
decision *décision (f)*
declare (to) *déclarer*
decor *décor (m)*
decorate (to) *décorer*
decorator *décorateur (m)*
degree *diplôme (m)*
delapidated *délabré*
delicious *délicieux*
delighted *enchanté, ravi*
delighted (to be) *être ravi*
delightful *ravissant*
delivery (of a baby) *accouchement (m)*
demanding *astreignant*
demonstrate (to) *manifester*
demonstrator *manifestant (m)*
dentist *dentiste (m)*
department store *grand magasin (m)*

deposit *arrhes (m.pl.)*
desire (to) *désirer*
dessert *dessert (m)*
detect (to) *dépister; détecter*
device *dispositif (m)*
dial (to) *composer*
dial tone *tonalité (f)*
die (to) *mourir*
diet *régime (m)*
different *différent*
dilute (to) *diluer*
dining room *salle à manger (f)*
dinner *dîner (m)*
direction *direction (f)*
director *directeur (m)*
disease *maladie (f)*
dish *plat (m)*
display (to) *arborer*
distribute (to) *distribuer*
dive (to) *plonger*
do (to) *faire*
doctor *médecin (m)*
document *document (m)*
documentary *documentaire (m)*
dog *chien (m)*
doll *poupée (f)*
dolphin *dauphin (m)*
door (car) *portière (f)*
double *double*
  double standard *deux poids, deux mesures*
  double-paned window *double vitrage (m)*
down quilt *couette (f)*
downstairs *en bas*
draft *courant d'air (m)*
drapes *doubles rideaux (m.pl.)*
dream (to) *rêver*
dress *robe (f)*
dress (to) *habiller*
dresser *commode (f)*
dressing room *cabine d'essayage (f)*
dressing table *coiffeuse (f)*
dressmaker *couturière (f)*
drink (to) *boire*
drink to (to) *arroser*
drive (to) *conduire, rouler*
  driver's license *permis de conduire (m)*
drop off (to) *déposer*
dub (to) *doubler*
dubbed *doublé*
during *pendant; lors*
dwelling *demeure (f)*

E

early *tôt*
earn (to) *gagner*
earth *terre (f)*
earthenware *faïence (f)*
earthquake *tremblement de terre (m)*
eat (to) *manger*
editor *rédacteur (trice)*

374

efficient   *efficace*
eggplant   *aubergine (f)*
election   *élection (f)*
elegant   *élégant*
elevator   *ascenseur (m)*
elsewhere   *ailleurs*
embroiderer   *brodeuse (f)*
embroidery   *broderie (f)*
end (to)   *finir*
endow (to)   *doter*
engine   *moteur (m)*
English   *anglais*
enhance (to)   *mettre en valeur*
enough   *assez*
entertain (oneself) (to)   *distraire (se)*
entertain (to)   *recevoir*
entrance   *entrée (f)*
equipped (with)   *muni (de)*
error   *erreur (f); faute (f)*
establish (to)   *établir*
estate   *domaine (m)*
estimate   *devis (m)*
etching   *gravure (f)*
Europe   *Europe (f)*
European Union (EU)   *Union Européenne (UE) (f)*
evening   *soir (m); soirée (f)*
everyone   *tout le monde*
exactly   *exactement*
exaggerate (to)   *exagérer*
exam   *examen (m)*
excellent   *excellent*
exchange (to)   *échanger*
   exchange bureau   *bureau de change (m)*
exercise   *exercice (m)*
exhaust (to)   *crever; épuiser; exténuer*
exhibit   *exposition (f)*
expect (to)   *attendre; compter sur*
   expect a baby (to)   *attendre un enfant*
expense   *dépense (f)*
expensive   *cher*
experiment   *expérience (f)*
explore (to)   *explorer*
expression (facial)   *mine (f)*
exquisite   *exquis*
extend (to)   *prolonger*
extension   *poste (m)*
eye   *œil (m)*

F

fabric   *étoffe (f); tissu (m)*
fairly   *assez*
faithfulness   *fidélité (f)*
fall (to)   *tomber*
fall   *automne (f)*
family   *famille (f)*
famous   *célèbre; renommé*
fantastic   *fantastique*
far   *loin; éloigné*
farewell   *adieu (m)*

fascinating   *passionnant*
fashion   *mode (f)*
   fashion designer   *couturier (m)*
fast   *rapide; vite*
fat   *graisse (f)*
fate   *sort (m)*
father   *père (m)*
father-in-law   *beau-père (m)*
favor (to)   *privilégier*
fax   *télécopie (f)*
fear (to)   *avoir peur; craindre*
fear   *crainte (f); peur (f)*
February   *février*
feel (to)   *sentir*
   feel like (to)   *avoir envie*
festival   *festival (m)*
field   *champ (m)*
figure   *chiffre (m)*
figurehead   *figure de proue (f)*
fill (to)   *remplir*
   fill up (gas) (to)   *faire le plein*
film   *film (m)*
   film director   *metteur en scène*
find (to)   *trouver*
finger   *doigt (m)*
finish (to)   *finir*
fire   *feu (m); incendie (m)*
   fire hazard   *risques d'incendie (m.pl.)*
fireplace   *cheminée (f)*
first   *premier*
   first name   *prénom (m)*
fish (to)   *pêcher*
fish   *poisson (m)*
fist   *poing (m)*
flag   *drapeau (m)*
flaw   *faille (f)*
flea   *puce (f)*
   flea market   *marché aux puces (m)*
flesh   *chair (f)*
flight   *vol (m)*
   flight attendant   *hôtesse de l'air (f); steward (m.)*
float (to)   *flotter*
floor   *plancher; étage (m)*
flower   *fleur (f)*
flowery   *fleuri*
flu   *grippe (f)*
fluently   *couramment*
follow (to)   *suivre*
following   *suivant*
food   *nourriture (f)*
for   *pour*
foreign   *étrange*
   foreign currency   *devises étrangères (f.pl.)*
foreigner   *étranger*
foreman   *contremaître (m)*
forget (to)   *oublier*
formerly   *autrefois*
fragrance   *senteur (f)*
franc   *franc (m)*
frankly   *franchement*
free   *libre*

freedom   *liberté (f)*
French   *français*
  French fry   *frite (f)*
Friday   *vendredi*
friend   *ami(e) (m.,f.)*
fry (to)   *(faire) frire*
  frying pan   *poêle (f)*
full   *plein*
funds   *crédits (m.pl.)*
funny; strange   *drôle*
furious   *furieux*
furniture   *meuble (m)*

green   *vert (m)*
  green bean   *haricot vert (m)*
greenery   *verdure (f)*
greenhouse   *serre (f)*
grind (to)   *affûter*
grocer   *épicier (m)*
grow (to)   *pousser*
growth   *croissance (f)*
guess (to)   *deviner*
guest   *invité (m)*
guru   *gourou (m)*
gutter   *gouttière (f)*

G

gadget   *gadget (m)*
game   *jeu (m); match (m)*
garden   *jardin (m)*
garlic   *ail (m)*
gasoline   *essence (f)*
gastronomy   *gastronomie (f)*
gather (to)   *cueillir*
generate (to)   *susciter*
get (to)   *obtenir, prendre*
  get bored (to)   *ennuyer (se)*
  get married (to)   *marier (se)*
  get off (to)   *descendre*
  get ready (to)   *s'apprêter*
  get up (to)   *lever (se)*
  get used to (to)   *faire à (se)*
  get wet (to)   *se mouiller*
gift   *cadeau (m)*
give (to)   *donner*
glance   *coup d'œil (m)*
glass   *verre (m)*
gleam   *reflet (m)*
global   *global*
glue   *colle (f)*
go (to)   *aller*
  go back (to)   *retourner*
  go down (to)   *descendre*
  go out (to)   *sortir*
  go to bed (to)   *coucher (se)*
  go toward (to)   *diriger*
  go up (to)   *monter*
godfather   *parrain (m)*
godmother   *marraine (f)*
gold   *or (m)*
good   *bon*
  good morning   *bonjour*
  good-bye   *au revoir*
goose liver   *foie gras (m)*
government   *gouvernement (m)*
grandfather   *grand-père (m)*
grandmother   *grand-mère (f)*
grandson   *petit-fils (m)*
grape picker   *vendangeur (m)*
graphology   *graphologie (f)*
grate (to)   *râper*
grateful   *reconnaissant*
gray matter   *matière grise (f)*

H

habit   *habitude (f)*
hair   *cheveux (m.pl.)*
hairstyle   *coiffure (f)*
half   *demi*
halfway   *à mi-chemin*
hamlet   *hameau (m)*
hammer   *marteau (m)*
hand (to)   *tendre*
hand   *main (f)*
handwriting analysis   *graphologie (f)*
hang (to)   *accrocher*
hang up (to)   *raccrocher*
hardly   *à peine; guère*
harvest (grapes)   *vendange (m)*
hat   *chapeau (m)*
hate (to)   *détester*
have (to)   *avoir*
  have a drink (to)   *prendre un verre*
  have dinner (to)   *dîner*
  have fun (to)   *amuser (se)*
  have the opportunity (to)   *avoir l'occasion*
  have to (to)   *être obligé*
  have trouble (to)   *avoir du mal*
head   *tête (f)*
headlight   *phare (m)*
health   *santé (f)*
hear (to)   *entendre; ouïr*
heart   *cœur (m)*
heat   *chaleur (f)*
heated   *enflammé*
heating   *chauffage (m)*
height   *hauteur (f)*
helmet   *casque (m)*
help (to)   *aider*
here   *ici*
  here is   *voici, voilà*
hesitate (to)   *hésiter*
hide (to)   *cacher*
hideous   *hideux*
high   *haut*
high school   *lycée (m)*
highway   *autoroute (f)*
hint   *soupçon (m); tuyau (m)*
hire (to)   *embaucher*
hold (to)   *tenir*
  hold a grudge against (to)   *en vouloir à*

hole   trou (m)
holiday   jour férié (m)
honey   miel (m)
hook   crochet (m)
hope (to)   espérer
horseback riding   faire de l'équitation (f)
hot   chaud
　hot water   eau chaude (f)
hotel   hôtel (m)
house   maison (f)
housing   logement (m)
how   comment
　how are you?   ça va?
　how much   combien
however   pourtant; toutefois
humor   humour (m)
hurt (to)   avoir mal
hydrangea   hortensia (m)

I

idea   idée (f)
ill-fated   infortuné
imply (to)   insinuer
impressive   impressionnant
improve (to)   perfectionner
in   dans, en, à
　in any case   en tout cas
　in depth   à fond
　in front of   devant
　in full expansion   en plein essor
　in quest   en quête
　in spite   en dépit
　in the back   au fond
　in the middle   au milieu
　in-house regulations   règlement intérieur (m)
income   revenu (m)
increase   augmentation (f)
indicate (to)   indiquer
indicator   indice (m)
infant   nourrisson (m)
inform (to)   prévenir
information   renseignement (m)
injection   piqûre (f)
injury   blessure (f)
insist (to)   insister; tenir à
insolent   insolent
instructions   consigne (f)
insulation   isolation (f)
insult   injure (f)
intend (to)   avoir l'intention de
interest   intérêt (m)
　interest rate   taux d'intérêt (m)
interesting   intéressant
internship   stage (m)
interview   entretien (m)
intoxication   ivresse (f)
introduce (to)   présenter
invade (to)   envahir
invest (to)   investir
invite (to)   inviter

island   île (f)
isolation   isolement (m)
it   il, ce, cela
　it is a matter   il s'agit
　it is better   il vaut mieux
Italian   italien
itinerary   itinéraire (m)

J

January   janvier
jet lag   décalage horaire (m)
jewel   bijou (m)
job   boulot (m)
join (to)   retrouver; joindre
joke (to)   blaguer; plaisanter
joke   blague (f)
July   juillet
June   juin

K

keep (to)   tenir; garder
　keep informed (to)   tenir au courant
keyboard   clavier (m)
kilo   kilo (m)
kindergarten   école maternelle (f)
king   roi (m)
kiss (to)   embrasser
kitchen; cooking   cuisine (f)
know (to)   connaître; savoir
knowledge   connaissance (f)

L

label (to)   étiqueter
lady   dame (f)
lake   lac (m)
lamb   agneau (m)
lamp   lampe (f)
　lamp shade   abat-jour (m)
land (to)   atterrir
　land tax   impôt foncier (m)
language   langage (m)
laptop   portatif (m)
large   grand
last   dernier
late   tard
laugh (to)   rire; rigoler
launch (to)   lancer
lawn   gazon (m)
lawyer   avocat; notaire (m)
lazy   paresseux
lead poisoning   Saturnisme (m)
leaf through (to)   feuilleter
lean (to)   se pencher
learn (to)   apprendre
lease   bail (m)
leash   laisse (f)

leather *cuir (m)*
leave (to) *laisser; partir*
lecture *sermon (m), conference (f)*
left *gauche*
leftovers *restes (m.pl.)*
leisure *loisirs (m.pl.)*
lemon *citron (m)*
less *moins*
lie (to) *mentir; être couché; se trouver*
  lie down (to) *allonger (se)*
lift (to) *soulever*
light (in color) *pâle; clair*
light (to) *allumer; éclairer; illuminer*
  light the powder keg (to) *mettre le feu aux*
    poudres
light *lumière (f)*
  lighting engineer *éclairagiste (m)*
lightly *à la légère*
lily-of-the-valley *muguet (m)*
literature *littérature (f)*
little *peu*
live (to) *habiter; vivre*
  living room *salon (m)*
live *en direct*
liver *foie (m)*
load (to) *charger*
locker room *vestiaire (m)*
look (to) *regarder*
  look for (to) *chercher*
love (to) *adorer, aimer*
love *amour (m)*
  love at first sight *coup de foudre (m)*
lower (to) *baisser*
luggage *bagages (m.pl.)*

M

madness *folie (f)*
magical *féerique*
magnificent *magnifique*
mahogany *acajou (m)*
make (to) *faire; fabriquer*
  make a mistake (to) *tromper (se)*
  make an appointment (to) *fixer un rendez-*
    vous
  make fun (to) *moquer (se)*
  make sick (to) *rendre malade*
  make up (to) *rattraper*
man *homme (m)*
manage (to) *débrouiller (se)*
management *gestion (f); direction (f)*
manufacture (to) *fabriquer*
  manufacturing process *processus de*
    fabrication (m)
map *carte routière (f); plan (m)*
maple tree *érable (m)*
March *mars*
market *marché (m)*
masterpiece *chef-d'œuvre (m)*
Master's degree *maîtrise (f)*
maternity leave *congé de maternité (m)*

mature (to) *affiner*
May *mai*
may *pouvoir*
maybe *peut-être*
measles *rougeole (f)*
meat *viande (f)*
mechanic *mécanicien (m)*
medicine *médecine (f) (science or profession);*
  médicament (m) (pills)
meet (to) *rencontrer; retrouver*
meeting *réunion (f)*
memory *mémoire (f); souvenir (m)*
message *message (m)*
Middle Ages *Moyen-Age (m)*
midwife *sage-femme (f)*
mill *moulin (m)*
miracle *miracle (m)*
mirror *miroir (m)*
miss (to) *manquer*
mistake *erreur (f); faute (f)*
mix (to) *mélanger*
model *mannequin (m); modèle (m)*
molding *moulure (m)*
moment *moment (m)*
Monday *lundi*
money *argent (m)*
  money maker *gagne-pain (m)*
month *mois (m)*
mood *humeur (f)*
moody *lunatique*
more *plus*
morning *matin (m)*
moth *mite (f)*
mothball *boule à mite (f)*
mother *mère (f)*
mother-in-law *belle-mère (f)*
mountain *montagne (f)*
mouse *souris (f)*
mouth *bouche (f)*
move (to) *bouger*
move back (to) *reculer*
much *beaucoup*
mumps *oreillons*
murder *meurtre (m)*
murderer *meurtrier (m)*
muscle *muscle (m)*
museum *musée (m)*
mushroom *champignon (m)*
music *musique (f)*
must *devoir*
must *moût (m)*

N

nail *clou (m)*
name *nom (m)*
navy blue *bleu marine*
near *près de*
neck *cou (m)*
need (to) *avoir besoin*
need *besoin (m)*

negotiate (to) *négocier*
neighbor *voisin (m)*
neighborhood *quartier (m)*
never *jamais*
new *nouveau*
news *actualités (f.pl.)*
next to *à côté*
nickname (to) *surnommer*
nicotine *nicotine (f)*
  nicotine addiction *tabagisme (m)*
no *non*
noise *bruit (m)*
nonetheless *néanmoins*
noon *midi*
north *nord (m)*
nose *nez (m)*
nothing *rien*
notice (to) *apercoir*
notion *notion (f)*
novel *roman (m)*
November *novembre*
now *maintenant*
number *nombre (m)*
nurse *infirmier (ère) (m.f.)*
nursery *garderie (f)*

O

oak *chêne (m)*
object *objet (m)*
obviously *évidemment*
October *octobre*
of *de*
  of course *bien sûr*
offer (to) *offrir*
offer *offre (f)*
office *bureau (m)*
  office supplies *fournitures de bureau (f.pl.)*
often *souvent*
oil *huile (f), pétrole (m)*
  oil tank *cuve à mazout (f)*
old *vieux*
on *sur*
  on foot *à pied*
  on sale *en solde*
  on-the-job training *apprentissage sur le tas (m)*
  on the left *à gauche*
  on the right *à droite*
  on the rise (to be) *être à la hausse*
  on the verge (to be) *être sur le point*
one *un(e); on*
  one must *il faut*
  one-way ticket *aller simple*
only *seulement*
open (to) *ouvrir*
opening *ouverture (f)*
opera *opéra (m)*
opinion *avis (m); opinion (f)*
opportunity *occasion (f)*
oppress (to) *opprimer*

optional *facultatif*
or (otherwise) *sinon*
order (to) *commander*
organ *orgue (m)*
organize (to) *organiser*
other *autre*
outfit *tenue (f)*
outlet *prise (f)*
output *rendement (m)*
oven *four (m)*

P

package *paquet (m)*
page *page (f)*
pain *douleur (f)*
paint (to) *peindre*
  paint job *coup de peinture (m)*
painting *tableau (m); toile (f)*
palace *palais (m)*
pale *pâle*
pants *pantalon (m)*
parents *parents (m.pl.)*
park *parc (m)*
parsley *persil (m)*
participate (to) *participer*
partition *cloison (f)*
party; celebration *fête (f)*
party (political) *parti (m)*
pass (a car)(to) *doubler; dépasser*
passenger *passager (m)*
passport *passeport (m)*
peach *pêche (f)*
peel (to) *éplucher*
peony *pivoine (f)*
people *gens (m.pl.)*
pepper *poivre (m)*
perched *perché*
perfect *parfait*
performance *spectacle (m)*
person *personne (f)*
pharmacist *pharmacien (m)*
pharmacy *pharmacie (f)*
pick (to) *cueillir*
pick up (to) *décrocher*
picture *photo (f)*
pile *pile (f); tas (m)*
pilgrimage *pèlerinage (m)*
pill *comprimé (m)*
pillow *coussin (m)*
  pillowcase *taie d'oreiller (f)*
pivot *charnière (f)*
plank *planche (f)*
play (to) *jouer*
player *joueur (m)*
pleasant *agréable*
please (to) *plaire*
please *s'il vous plaît*
pleasure *plaisir (m)*
pleat *pli (m)*
pocketknife *canif (m)*

politician *politique (m)*
politics *politique (f)*
poor *pauvre*
post (to) *afficher*
post office *poste (f)*
poster *affiche (f)*
postpone (to) *repousser*
potato *pomme de terre (f)*
pound *livre (f)*
pour (to) *verser*
prefer (to) *préférer*
pregnancy *grossesse (f)*
prepare (to) *préparer*
prescription *ordonnance (f)*
present *actuel*
presently *actuellement*
preserve (to) *sauvegarder*
pretentious *prétentieux*
prevent (to) *empêcher*
price *prix (m)*
priceless *inestimable*
problem *problème (m)*
product *produit (m)*
professorship *chaire (f)*
program *émission (f); programme
  (m)*
prohibit (to) *interdire*
project *projet (m)*
promise *promesse (f)*
promote (to) *promouvoir*
prospects *débouchés (m.pl.)*
protect (to) *protéger*
protein *protéine (f)*
protest *manifestation (f)*
proud *fier*
provide (to) *fournir, munir*
  provided that *pourvu que*
province *province (f)*
provoke (to) *susciter*
pull (to) *arracher*
punch in (to) *pointer*
put (to) *mettre*
  put on weight (to) *grossir*

Q

quarter *quart (m); trimestre (m)*
queen *reine (f)*
quilt *édredon (m) piqué, couette (f)*
  quilt cover *housse de couette (f)*
quote (to) *citer*

R

racket *raquette (f)*
radiator *radiateur (m)*
rain (to) *pleuvoir*
raise (to) *augmenter*
raise *augmentation (f)*
rarely *rarement*

rate *taux (m)*
  rate of exchange *taux de change (m)*
raw *cru*
read (to) *lire*
ready *prêt*
ready-to-wear *prêt-à-porter*
reaffirm (to) *réaffirmer*
real estate agent *agent immobilier (m)*
realize (to) *apercevoir (se); rendre compte (se)*
receive (to) *recevoir*
receiver (telephone) *appareil (m)*
reception *accueil (m)*
recipe *recette (f)*
recognize (to) *reconnaître*
recommend (to) *recommander*
record (to) *enregistrer*
red *rouge*
reef *récif (m)*
reform *réforme (f)*
refuse (to) *refuser*
region *région (f)*
register (to) *inscrire (se)*
regret (to) *regretter*
rehearsal *répétition (f)*
reins *rênes (m.f.)*
relative *parent (m)*
release (to) *débloquer*
remain (to) *demeurer*
remedy *remède (m)*
remember (to) *se souvenir*
remote control *télécommande (f)*
rent (to) *louer*
rent *loyer (m)*
rental *location (f)*
required *requis*
research *recherches (f.pl.)*
reservation *réservation (f)*
reserve (to) *réserver*
resign (to) *démissionner*
rest (to) *reposer (se)*
restaurant *restaurant (m)*
restoration *restauration (f)*
restroom *toilette (f), w.c.*
résumé *C.V. (m)*
retired *à la retraite*
return *retour (m)*
reveal (to) *dévoiler; divulguer*
revenge *revanche (f)*
review (to) *passer en revue*
rhyme (to) *rimer*
right *droit (m)*
right away *tout de suite*
ring (to) *sonner*
ripen *mûrir*
Riviera *Côte d'Azur (f)*
road *route (f)*
rock *rocher (m)*
roof *toit (m)*
roofing *toiture (f)*
room *chambre (f)*
rot *pourriture (f)*
round-trip (ticket) *aller et retour (m)*

row *rang (m)*
rubella *rubéole (f)*
run (to) *courir*
runner *coureur (m)*
rustic *rustique*
rusty *rouillé*

S

sabotage (to) *saboter*
sad *triste*
sail *voile (f)*
sale *vente (f)*
salesperson *vendeur (m)*
salt *sel (m)*
same *même*
sample *échantillon (m)*
sand (to) *poncer*
Saturday *samedi*
save (to) *sauvegarder*
savings *épargne (f)*
savor (to) *déguster*
say (to) *dire*
scale *gamme (f)*
scary *épouvantable*
scene *scène (f)*
scratch (to) *gratter*
screen *écran (m)*
screwdriver *tournevis (m)*
scribble (to) *gribouiller*
scribbling *gribouillage (m)*
sculptor *sculpteur (m)*
sculpture *sculpture (f)*
seamstress *couturière (f)*
season *saison (f)*
seaweed *algue (f)*
second *second*
second-hand car *voiture d'occasion
    (f)*
secret *secret (m)*
secretary *secrétaire (m., f.)*
see (to) *voir*
  see again (to) *revoir*
  see you soon *à bientôt*
seem (to) *avoir l'air; paraître*
selfish *égoïste*
sell (to) *vendre*
send (to) *envoyer*
September *septembre*
series *feuilleton (m)*
serious *grave*
service (to) *desservir*
  service sector *tertiaire (m)*
setting *toile de fond (f)*
settle (to) *installer (se); régler*
several *plusieurs*
shade *teinte (f)*
shape *forme (f)*
share (to) *partager*
sharpen (to) *affûter*
shelf *étagère (f)*

shellfish *crustacés (m.pl.)*
shirt (man's) *chemise (f)*
shirt (woman's) *chemisier (m)*
shiver (to) *frissonner*
shock (to) *choquer*
shoot! (mild oath) *zut!*
shooting (film) *tournage (m)*
shop (to) *faire les courses*
  shopping cart *caddie (m)*
shop *magasin (m)*
shopkeeper *commerçant (m)*
short *court*
show (to) *montrer*
show *spectacle (m)*
shower *averse (f)*
shudder (to) *frissonner*
sick *malade*
sign (to) *signer*
sign up (to) *inscrire (se)*
silk *soie (f)*
silverware *argenterie (f)*
similar *pareil*
since *depuis*
singer *chanteur (euse) (m., f.)*
sir *Monsieur*
sister *sœur (f), frangine (fam)*
sister-in-law *belle-sœur (f)*
sit down (to) *asseoir (se)*
size *taille (f)*
sketch *croquis (m)*
  sketch out (to) *ébaucher*
skimp (to) *lésiner*
skin *peau (f); épiderme (m)*
skirt *jupe (f)*
sleeping pill *somnifère (m)*
sleeve *manche (f)*
slice *tranche (f)*
slim *mince*
slip (to) *glisser*
small *petit*
  small street *ruelle (f)*
smell *odeur (f)*
smoke (to) *fumer*
smoke *fumée (f)*
smoker *fumeur*
snack *casse-croûte (m)*
snake *serpent (m)*
sniff (to) *humer*
snow *neige (f)*
so *si, tellement; donc; ainsi*
  so much *tant*
soak up (to) *imprégner (se)*
social security *sécurité sociale
    (f)*
sofa *canapé (m)*
soft *moelleux (euse)*
soften (to) *radoucir*
software *logiciel (m)*
solder (to) *souder*
someone *quelqu'un*
something *quelque chose*
soon *bientôt*

sore *endolori*
sorry *désolé*
sort out (to) *trier*
soufflé dish *ramequin (m)*
sound *son (m)*
south *sud (m)*
spacious *spacieux*
speak (to) *parler*
specialty *spécialité (f)*
species *espèce (f)*
specify (to) *préciser*
spectacular *spectaculaire*
spelling *orthographe (f)*
spend (to) *passer*
spider *araignée (f)*
spill (to) *renverser*
sponge *éponge (f)*
sport *sport (m)*
spot *tache (f)*
spring *printemps (m)*
square *carré*
stage *estrade; scène*
  stage fright *trac (m)*
stain *tache (f)*
stalk (to) *égrapper*
stand (to) *supporter*
stand up (to) *dresser (se)*
star *étoile (f); vedette (f)*
start up (to) *démarrer*
starve (to) *mourir de faim*
state *état (m)*
stay (to) *rester*
stay *séjour (m)*
steam *vapeur (f)*
steel *acier (m)*
  stainless steel *acier inoxydable (m)*
steep (to) *macérer*
step *étape (f)*
stick (to) *coller*
stir (to) *remuer*
stop (to) *arrêter (se), cesser*
story; history *histoire (f)*
stove *poêle (m)*
straight ahead *tout droit*
stranger *étranger (m)*
strike *grève (f)*
strike up (to) *entamer*
stroll (to) *flâner*
struggle (to) *lutter*
student *étudiant(e) (m.,f.)*
study (to) *étudier*
study *étude (f)*
stunning *épatant*
sublimation *sublimation (f)*
suburbs *banlieue (f)*
succeed (to) *réussir*
suffer (to) *souffrir*
suffice (to) *suffire*
sugar *sucre (m)*
suggest (to) *proposer*
suit *tailleur (m)*

suitcase *valise (f)*
summer *été (m)*
sumptuous *somptueux*
sun *soleil (m)*
Sunday *dimanche*
superb *superbe*
supermarket *supermarché (m)*
supertitles *surtitres (m.pl.)*
supplies *provisions (f.pl.)*
supply (to) *fournir*
surname *nom de famille (m)*
surprise *surprise (f)*
surrender (to) *capituler; se rendre*
surround (to) *entourer*
survey *cadastre (m)*
suspense *suspens (m)*
swim (to) *nager*
Swiss *suisse*
syrup *sirop (m)*

T

table *table (f)*
tablecloth *nappe (f)*
tactile *tactile*
take (to) *prendre; emmener*
  take advantage (to) *profiter*
  take care (to) *occuper (se)*
  take into account *tenir compte*
  take off (to) *envoler (se)*
  take place (to) *avoir lieu*
task *tâche (f)*
taste (to) *goûter*
taste *goût (m)*
tax *impôt (m)*
tea *thé (m)*
teach (to) *enseigner*
teacher *professeur (m); enseignant (m)*
teaching *enseignement (m)*
team *équipe (f)*
tease (to) *taquiner*
technique *technique (f)*
telephone *téléphone (m)*
  telephone call *coup de fil (m)*
television *télévision (f)*
TV studio set *plateau (m)*
tell (to) *raconter*
tennis ball *balle de tennis (f)*
tennis court *court de tennis (m)*
terrace *terrasse (f)*
thank you *merci*
thanks to *grâce à*
then *alors; ensuite*
there *là; y; là-bas*
  there are *il y a*
therefore *donc*
thigh *cuisse (f)*
thing *chose (f)*
think (to) *penser*
this one *celui*

threaten (to)   *menacer*
throw (to)   *jeter; lancer*
Thursday   *jeudi*
ticket   *billet (m); ticket (m)*
tile   *tuile (f); carreau (m)*
  tile installer   *carreleur (m)*
time   *fois (f); heure (f); temps (m)*
  time clock   *horloge pointeuse (f)*
tip   *pourboire (m); tuyau (m)*
tiptoe (to)   *avancer à tâtons*
tire   *pneu (m)*
toad   *crapaud (m)*
today   *aujourd'hui*
tomorrow   *demain*
too   *trop; aussi*
tool   *outil (m)*
tooth   *dent (f)*
toothpaste   *dentifrice (m)*
touch (to)   *toucher*
tough   *corsé*
tournament   *tournoi (m)*
tow (to)   *remorquer*
toward   *vers*
tower   *tour (f)*
town   *ville (f)*
  town hall   *mairie (f)*
traffic   *circulation (f)*
  traffic jam   *embouteillages (m.pl.)*
  traffic lights   *feux de circulation (m.pl.)*
train (to)   *entraîner (se)*
  train station   *gare (f)*
training   *entraînement (m); stage (m)*
translate (to)   *traduire*
travel (to)   *voyager*
travel   *déplacement (m); voyage (m)*
treasure   *trésor (m)*
trendy   *branché*
trick   *truc (m); tour (m)*
trigger (to)   *provoquer; déclencher*
true   *vrai*
truly   *vraiment*
try (to)   *essayer*
Tuesday   *mardi*
turn (to)   *tourner*
turn   *tournant (m); tour (m)*

U

unbearable   *insupportable*
uncle   *oncle (m)*
undeniable   *indéniable*
under   *sous*
underemployment   *sous-emploi (m)*
understand (to)   *comprendre*
unemployment   *chômage (m)*
unexpectedly   *à l'improviste*
unfortunately   *malheureusement*
union   *syndicat (m)*
United States   *États-Unis (m.pl.)*
until   *jusqu'à*
use (to)   *utiliser*

V

vacation   *vacances (m.pl.)*
vaccine   *vaccin (m)*
valley   *vallon (m)*
varnish (to)   *vitrifier*
vat   *cuve (f)*
veal stew   *blanquette de veau (f)*
veil   *voile (m)*
verb   *verbe (m)*
very   *très*
viaduct   *viaduc (m)*
vial   *fiole (f)*
victory   *victoire (f)*
vine   *vigne (f)*
vineyard   *vignoble (m)*
violence   *violence (f)*
virgin   *vierge*
visit (to)   *visiter*
vote (to)   *voter*

W

wait (to)   *attendre*
wake up (to)   *réveiller (se)*
walk (to)   *marcher*
walk   *tour (m); promenade (f)*
Walkman   *baladeur (m)*
wall   *mur (m)*
wallpaper   *papier peint (m)*
walnut   *noyer (m)*
want (to)   *vouloir*
warehouse   *entrepôt (m)*
watch (to)   *regarder*
water (to)   *arroser*
water   *eau (f)*
weak   *faible*
weakness   *faiblesse (f)*
wear (to)   *porter*
  wear and tear   *usure (f)*
weather   *temps (m)*
Wednesday   *mercredi*
week   *semaine (f)*
weekly   *hebdomadaire*
weigh (to)   *peser*
weight   *poids (m)*
welcome   *accueil (m)*
well   *bien*
what   *quel*
when   *quand*
where   *où*
whip (to)   *fouetter*
whose   *dont*
why   *pourquoi*
wife   *femme (f)*
will   *volonté (f)*
willingly   *volontiers*
win (to)   *gagner*
windsurfing   *planche à voile (f)*
window   *fenêtre (f); guichet (m)*

wine *vin (m)*
  wine maker *vigneron (m)*
winter *hiver (m)*
wish (to) *souhaiter*
wish *volonté (f)*
with *avec*
woman *femme (f)*
wonderfully *à merveille*
woodwork *charpente (f)*
word *parole (f)*
  word of mouth *bouche à oreille (m)*
work (to) *travailler*
work *travail (m); œuvre (f)*
working population *population active (f)*
workshop *atelier (m)*
world *monde (m)*
worry (to) *inquiéter (se), faire (s'en)*

worthy *digne*
write (to) *écrire; rédiger*
wrong (to be) *avoir tort*

Y

year *an (m); année (f)*
yellow *jaune*
yield *rendement (m)*
young *jeune*
youth *enfance (f)*

Z

zoning ordinances *plan d'occupation des sols (m.pl.)*

INDEX